A Guide to Reference Books
for Small and Medium-sized Libraries,
1984–1994

A Guide to Reference Books for Small and Medium-sized Libraries, 1984–1994

G. KIM DORITY

1995
LIBRARIES UNLIMITED, INC.
Englewood, Colorado

LIBRARIES UNLIMITED, INC.
P.O. Box 6633
Englewood, CO 80155-6633
1-800-237-6124

Production Editor: Kevin W. Perizzolo
Copy Editor: Brooke Graves
Indexers: D. Aviva Rothschild and Christine J. Smith
Interior Typesetting and Design: Kay Minnis

Library of Congress Cataloging-in-Publication Data

Dority, G. Kim, 1950–
    A guide to reference books for small and medium-sized libraries,
1984–1994 / G. Kim Dority.
    xviii, 372 p. 17x25 cm.
    Includes bibliographical references and index.
    ISBN 1-56308-103-2
    1. Reference books--Bibliography. 2. Small libraries--United
States--Book lists. I. Title.
Z1035.1.D665   1995
016.0287--dc20   95-22816
                                                    CIP

Contents

Part II
SOCIAL SCIENCES

2—AREA STUDIES

3—ECONOMICS AND BUSINESS

4—EDUCATION

**Part IV
SCIENCE AND TECHNOLOGY**

35—TRANSPORTATION

Introduction

The special constraints of small and medium-sized libraries make reference book selection an extremely difficult, though critical, part of the librarian's job. This book has been compiled with that challenge in mind. It is designed to maximize each library's return on the limited acquisitions dollars, shelf space, and staff time available to invest in the reference collection. For that purpose, it identifies nearly 1,000 main citations and just under 400 secondary citations for the most appropriate and highly recommended reference books in English. Although a small percentage of books identified in the first edition have been retained (the vast majority are now out of print), all annotations have been reviewed and updated to reflect current editions and information.

Most of the titles have been published within the past several years, although some older classics have been included. A few of the works described may no longer be in print. From time to time, a very expensive work or a lengthy multi-volume work has been annotated with the purpose of indicating the existence of an important tool probably available through a larger library. Government publications and children's materials have for the most part been excluded because they are so thoroughly covered in other Libraries Unlimited bibliographies; works dealing with individual authors of literary works have been excluded as well because of the overwhelming amount of reference material in this subject area.

This book generally has been arranged to reflect the organization of Libraries Unlimited's *American Reference Books Annual* (*ARBA*), with an initial chapter devoted to general reference works, followed by 34 subject-oriented chapters divided by topic or form. Subjects covered range from sports and recreation to religion and from genealogy to agriculture to information technology.

Each entry provides the full title of the work; edition number; author, editor, compiler, and so forth; publication data, including name of distributor or reprint publisher and dates; most recent available price (current as of late 1994); ISBN or ISSN numbers; and number of volumes for sets and frequency for serials. The annotations are designed to indicate the coverage, depth, intended audience, special features, and strengths and weaknesses of the books. Whenever possible, similar works or alternative choices (e.g., a less costly work offering less in-depth coverage or a costlier work offering more comprehensive coverage) have been indicated to allow each library to tailor its reference coverage to the needs and priorities of its clientele. In addition, the availability of alternative formats, such as CD-ROM or microfiche, has been noted where appropriate.

The titles included are, for the most part, among those recommended in a broader context by the hundreds of subject specialists at libraries and universities throughout the United States and Canada who review titles for *ARBA*. Titles recommended by reviewers for more specialized *Libraries Unlimited* publications are also included, as are materials recommended by compilers of other standard sources such as Sheehy's *Guide to Reference Books* (10th ed., ALA, 1986) and its supplement (1992). In identifying titles for inclusion, the intent has been to assemble the best reference materials available for small and medium-sized libraries.

It is my hope that this book will be useful to librarians everywhere struggling to meet the challenge of librarianship in the nineties: balancing increasing information resources and decreasing resource budgets. For their assistance in helping me complete this project, I dedicate *A Guide to Reference Books for Small and Medium-sized Libraries, 1984-1994* to Harold Everett and Vera Hedger, who will always light the way; to Lois and Roy Donahue, who not only always believed things were possible but helped to make them so; and to Matt Dority, whose patience, encouragement, faith, and laughter will forever sustain and inspire me.

Part I
GENERAL REFERENCE WORKS

1

General Reference Works

ABBREVIATIONS AND ACRONYMS

1. Mossman, Jennifer, and others, eds. **Acronyms, Initialisms, & Abbreviations Dictionary [yr.]: A Guide to Acronyms, Initialisms, Abbreviations, Contractions, Alphabetic Symbols, and Similar Condensed Appellations.** Detroit, Gale, 1975- . Annual. 3pts. $215.00/set (1994 ed.). ISSN 0270-4404.

Now starting into its third decade, this indispensable tool identifies and defines more than 520,000 acronyms, initialisms, and other forms of abbreviation drawn from all subject areas. (An *acronym* is defined as having the initial letters or parts of a compound term; an *initialism* is essentially the same, but each letter is verbalized; and an *abbreviation* is a shortened form of a word.) Coverage is international, although the focus is on English-language items. Entries generally note meaning of phrase, translation into English, language (if not English), source code, location or country origin, sponsoring organization, and subject category.

A similar title is Ralph De Sola's *Abbreviations Dictionary* (7th ed., Elsevier, 1986, 1240p., $52.75, ISBN 0-444-00807-1). Although there is some duplication between the Elsevier and Gale titles, reviewers generally agree that the works usually supplement rather than duplicate each other. If cost is an issue, a reasonably priced alternative is *The Oxford Dictionary of Abbreviations* (Clarendon Press/Oxford University Press, 1992, 397p., $29.95, ISBN 0-19-869172-6), which covers a wide range of colloquial, popular, slang, general, and subject-related abbreviations, acronyms, initialisms, shortenings, and symbols for everything from popular catchphrases and general terms to sports and economics. For libraries needing strong international coverage, F. A. Buttress's *World Guide to Abbreviations of Organizations* (9th ed., Blackie; distr., Gale, 1991, 875p., $140.00, ISBN 0-8103-5544-2) includes more than 50,000 acronyms and titles of international organizations in the areas of commerce, industry, administration, education, journalism, politics, medicine, science, and technology.

ALMANACS

2. Famighetti, Robert, ed. **The World Almanac and Book of Facts [yr.].** Mahwah, NJ, World Almanac/Funk & Wagnall's, 1868- . Annual. 1v. $19.95; $8.95pa. (1994 ed.). ISSN 0084-1382.

Relied upon for well over a century as the premiere resource for ready-reference questions, *The World Almanac and Book of Facts* presents statistical, directory, and reference information, both current and historical, for a vast range of subjects. In addition to timely feature articles covering the arts and humanities, the physical sciences, and the social sciences, the almanac includes such useful supplementary items as a chronology of the preceding year's events, consumer information, vital statistics, unusual news stories, obituaries, listings of awards, an atlas, and a 16-page color insert of national flags. Two indexes—a general, detailed index that prefaces the almanac and a quick reference one that concludes it—round out this annual.

3. **Information Please Almanac [yr.]: The Ultimate Browser's Reference.** Information Please Staff, eds. Boston, Houghton Mifflin, 1946- . Annual. 1v. maps (col.). index. $21.45; $7.70pa. (1994 ed.). No ISSN available.

This well-known ready-reference tool is by now familiar to all reference librarians. It includes calendars, chronologies of the past year's events, statistics, topical articles, and an abundance of maps, charts, and tables—just the sort of "quick-fix" data many patrons are looking for. Well organized, easy to use, and very affordably priced, this almanac belongs at all ready-reference desks. Its coverage is complemented by that of its primary competitor, *The World Almanac and Book of Facts* (entry 2).

4. Long, Kim. **American Forecaster Almanac [yr.].** Ithaca, NY, American Demographics Books, 1994- . Annual. 1v. illus. index. $29.95 (1994 ed.). No ISSN available.

Kim Long is the forecaster American businesses, nonprofits, and other organizations have been relying on since 1983 to tell them which way the country is heading for the coming 12 months and what trends will be hot along the way. His annual publication, which has been issued by a variety of publishers over the years, synthesizes information drawn from daily newspapers, periodicals, trade journals, newsletters, public information polls and surveys, industry surveys, U.S. government statistical data, personal sources, and private company contacts. As entertaining as it is informative, the *American Forecaster* is a highly recommended purchase for even the smallest library.

5. McLoone-Basta, Margo, and Alice Siegel. **The Kids' World Almanac of Records and Facts.** New York, World Almanac; distr., New York Ballantine/Random House, 1986. 274p. illus. index. $7.95pa. ISBN 0-88687-319-3. **The Second Kids' World Almanac of Records and Facts.** 1987. 274p. illus. index. $7.95pa. ISBN 0-88687-397-5.

As children become increasingly independent information seekers, works like the *Kids' World Almanac of Records and Facts* are gaining in popularity and usefulness. Like other almanacs, the information in these two works (which do not duplicate each other) includes events, facts, and statistics arranged by topical chapter; however, coverage is focused on items likely to be of interest to children. The illustrations are well done and informative, enhancing the education/entertainment mix of the text.

Another excellent almanac for children is *The Information Please Kids' Almanac* (Alice Siegel and Margo McLoone-Basta, eds., Houghton Mifflin, 1992, 363p., $16.95; $7.95pa., ISBN 0-395-64737-1; 0-395-58801-4pa.). Replete with definitions, lists of facts, timelines, tables, maps, and sidebars for such things as modes of transportation, currency equivalents, cloud types, greetings around the world, and star sizes, this work will engage kids of all ages. The almanac is probably more appropriate for browsing than for ready reference, however, because of inconsistencies in indexing.

6. Wallechinsky, David, and Amy Wallace. **The People's Almanac Presents the Book of Lists: The '90s Edition.** Boston, Little, Brown, 1993. 491p. illus. index. $17.95. ISBN 0-316-92079-7.

Although not, strictly speaking, an almanac, this work continues to be a source of bizarre, amusing, and even occasionally enlightening facts and figures. Although its utility as a ready-reference source is questionable because of the highly eclectic mix of information included, *Lists* is a delightful (if addictive) resource for browsing and for serendipitous finds. Its 320 lists are arranged within 16 categories: people, movies and television, the arts, health and food, animals, work, family and relationships, crime, politics and world affairs, America, travel, literature, words, advice, sports, and miscellany. Although certainly not a necessary purchase, this work provides good value for the price and would be a welcome addition to almost all public libraries.

7. Whitaker, Joseph. **An Almanac for the Year of Our Lord [yr.] (Whitaker's Almanack).** London, J. Whitaker; distr., Detroit, Gale, 1868– . Annual. 1v. illus. maps. index. $75.00 (1994 ed.). ISSN 0083-9256.

Whitaker's Almanack remains the standard reference for statistics and facts on all things British. First published in 1868, this annual publication continues to include: obituaries and a list of events from the previous year; statistics on finance, agriculture, shipping, employment, housing, and population; principal British and Irish associations; and information (statistical and otherwise) on Great Britain, the Commonwealth countries, and dependent territories. A detailed and extensive index is located at the front of the almanac.

Another work whose primary focus is Great Britain is *The Annual Register: A Record of World Events, [yr.]* (H. V. Hodson, ed., Gale, 1758– , annual, 1v., $165.00 [1994 ed.], ISSN 0066-4057). Although this is a distinguished annual deservedly respected for its objective and thorough coverage of international events and issues, libraries will have to decide whether there is sufficient patron need to justify its high purchase price.

BIBLIOGRAPHIES

Bibliographic Guides

8. Chalcraft, Anthony, and others, eds. **Walford's Concise Guide to Reference Material.** 2d ed. London, Library Association; distr, Lanham, MD, UNIPUB, 1992. 496p. index. $145.00. ISBN 0-85604-042-9.

An abridgment of the internationally known, three-volume set of *Walford's Guide to Reference Material*, *Walford's Concise Guide to Reference Material* focuses on British reference works, but also includes broader international coverage as well. The annotations are organized under the Universal Decimal Classification system, with each major subdivision further divided into sections within the classification. Annotations do not include prices, but do include references to reviews. Although the majority of entries refer to printed material, the guide also contains online, microform, and CD-ROM sources. Author/title and subject indexes conclude the work.

9. Lang, Jovian P., ed. **Reference Sources for Small and Medium-sized Librar-ies.** 5th ed. Compiled by the ad hoc Subcommittee of the Reference Sources Committee of the Reference and Adult Services Division, American Library Asso-ciation. Chicago, American Library Association, 1992. 317p. index. $38.00pa. ISBN 3406-4-0050.

The fifth edition of this standard bibliographic work is a revision of the earlier editions published as *Reference Books for Small and Medium-sized Libraries* in 1968, 1973, and 1979 and under its current name in 1984. In addition to traditional print sources, the guide also notes microform, online, and CD-ROM materials. References include works for children as well as adults, and the target audience is considered to be public, college, and large secondary school libraries. The 22 chapters are arranged by subject in Dewey Decimal Classification order and are further divided by subtopic and by type of publication. Entries include full biblio-graphic citations and two- to four-sentence annotations. A valuable and reasonably priced purchase for all libraries, regardless of size.

10. March, Andrew L., ed. **Recommended Reference Books in Paperback.** Englewood, CO, Libraries Unlimited, 1992. 263p. index. $37.50. ISBN 0-56308-067-2.

Prepared as a guide to inexpensive reference material suitable for home use, school libraries, and public and college libraries, the second edition of *Recommended Reference Books in Paperback* (providing coverage through 1991) describes some 993 reference books. The titles are organized by section: general reference first, then 36 other sections arranged alphabetically from agriculture to zoology, with further subdivisions by type of material. A highly useful tool for libraries trying to get the most out of their reference book budgets.

11. Nichols, Margaret Irby. **Guide to Reference Books for School Media Centers.** 4th ed. Englewood, CO, Libraries Unlimited, 1992. 463p. index. $38.50. ISBN 0-87287-833-3.

Nichols's goal is to identify in-print, recommended reference works designed specifically for the juvenile and young adult market. Within these parameters, she describes and evaluates more than 2,000 titles grouped within 54 subject categories as to their reference value for schools and the students they serve. Although intended primarily for school media centers, public libraries will also benefit from the author's treatment of information resources for the newest members of the information society.

12. Sader, Marion, ed. **General Reference Books for Adults: Authoritative Evaluations of Encyclopedias, Atlases, and Dictionaries.** New Providence, NJ, R. R. Bowker, 1988. 614p. illus. maps. bibliog. index. $75.00. ISBN 0-8352-2393-0.

According to its editor, this work is intended to provide "authoritative, compre-hensive and objective" reviews of 215 general encyclopedias, atlases, and dictio-naries appropriate for adults. Reviews fall into four categories: encyclopedias, world atlases, dictionaries and word books, and large-print reference sources. Encyclopedias and atlases are arranged alphabetically by title; dictionaries are organized by subject (general, etymological, synonym, antonym). Online and CD-ROM products have been included along with the print resources. Each of the first three sections is introduced by an essay that discusses the type and characteristics of the particular resource being reviewed, as well as the evaluation criteria used in the reviews. Entries range in length from one to eight pages, and occasionally include such supplemental materials as facsimile pages, sample entries, and excerpts from other reviews.

Although occasionally the citations in *General Reference Books* are not as current as one might wish, in general this is a thorough, well-done work.

Libraries may also wish to consider a related work edited by Sader and published by Bowker, *Reference Books for Young Readers: Authoritative Evaluations of Encyclopedias, Atlases, and Dictionaries* (1988, 615p., $52.95, ISBN 0-8352-2366-3). Similar in coverage and format to *General Reference Books*, it covers about 200 reference titles appropriate for children and young adults. Both publications will be useful not only to librarians, but also to interested parents and other adults.

13. Sader, Marion, ed. **Topical Reference Books.** New Providence, NJ, R. R. Bowker, 1991. 892p. illus. index. $109.00. ISBN 0-8352-3087-2.

Topical Reference Books describes the core reference works for 50 subject areas, commencing with "Advertising," "African History," "African Literature," and "Aging," and concluding with "Women's Studies," "World History," "World Literature," and "Zoology." For each topic, there is first a brief introductory essay on salient reference issues, then a checklist of core titles with recommendations for purchase by public, academic, or school libraries. This checklist is followed by annotated lists of core and supplementary titles, then a section of new and noteworthy titles. Although most experienced reference professionals will be familiar with the works described here, others less knowledgeable will benefit from the descriptive and evaluative approach taken in the annotations, the editors' concentration on selecting only the best resources rather than including all possible choices, and the inclusion of newer titles.

14. Sheehy, Eugene, and others, eds. **Guide to Reference Books.** 10th ed. Chicago, American Library Association, 1986. 1560p. index. $50.00. ISBN 0-8389-0390-8. **Guide to Reference Books: Covering Materials from 1985-1990 [Supplement to the Tenth Edition].** 1992. 624p. index. $85.00. ISBN 0-8389-0588-9.

"Sheehy" has long been familiar to librarians, who rely on its international scope, thorough and balanced coverage, detailed bibliographic citations, and brief descriptive (rather than evaluative) annotations. The 10th edition covers approximately 10,000 reference works, the supplement 4,668. As in previous editions, the materials are arranged according to five subject areas: general reference works, humanities, social and behavioral sciences, history and area studies, and science, technology, and medicine.

15. Swidan, Eleanor A. **Reference Sources: A Brief Guide.** 9th ed. Baltimore, MD, Enoch Pratt Free Library, 1988. 175p. index. $7.95pa. ISBN 0-910556-26-1.

Now in its ninth edition, this reference guide from the Enoch Pratt Free Library includes, for the first time, microforms and computer-readable databases. Its purpose remains, however, "to help the reader or library user who is bewildered by the staggering array of reference works that confront him on the shelves of the library." The guide is selective rather than comprehensive, and is organized into three sections: the first section, "References Sources General in Scope," covers encyclopedias, almanacs, indexes, dictionaries, maps, bibliographies, and government publications; the second section, "Reference Sources in Special Subjects," covers humanities, science, and the social sciences; and the third section provides an introduction to database searching. Titles in the areas of medicine, law, and genealogy are excluded. A good basic overview of reference materials for a very reasonable price.

16. Wynar, Bohdan S., ed. **American Reference Books Annual [yr.]**. Englewood, CO, Libraries Unlimited, 1970- . Annual. 1v. index. $85.00 (1994 ed.). ISSN 0065-9959.

A well-known bibliographic tool for all libraries, ARBA is now in its third decade of annually reviewing reference books published on a wide range of subjects. Each year it evaluates approximately 1,800 books, drawn from general reference works, the social sciences, the humanities, and science and technology. Reviews are evaluative and comparative, and range in length from two paragraphs to two pages, depending upon the importance of the work under review. A related publication is the five-year cumulation, *Best Reference Books 1986-1990* (450p., 1991, $58.00, ISBN 0-87287-936-4), also edited by Bohdan Wynar, which provides annotations of the best works covered in five years of ARBA.

Libraries who rely on ARBA's reviews will also want to consider purchasing *Libraries Unlimited's* cumulative indexes, *Index to American Reference Books Annual 1985-1989: A Cumulative Index to Subjects, Authors, and Titles* (1989, 275p., $55.00, ISBN 0-87287-793-0) and *Index to American Reference Books Annual 1990-1994: A Cumulative Index to Subjects, Authors, and Titles* (1994, 288p., $60.00, ISBN 1-56308-272-1). The 1985-1989 edition covers 8,759 books reviewed during this period, and the 1990-1994 edition 9,284 books; both provide access through author, title, and subject.

17. Wynar, Bohdan S., ed. **Recommended Reference Books for Small and Medium-sized Libraries and Media Centers [yr.]**. Englewood, CO, Libraries Unlimited, 1981- . Annual. 1v. index. $42.50 (1994 ed.). ISSN 0277-5948.

This work reprints approximately 500 of the 1,800 citations from the parent publication, *American Reference Books Annual (ARBA)*, considered most appropriate to the special needs of small libraries. Entries are divided into 36 topical chapters under 4 major categories: general reference works, social sciences, humanities, and science and technology. Each source is designated as recommended for college library, public library, or media center collections. Published reviews from other library journals are included for each annotation.

National and Trade Bibliographies

18. **American Book Publishing Record ABPR Cumulative [yr.]: An Annual Cumulation of American Book Production in [yr.]** ... New Providence, NJ, R. R. Bowker, 1960- . Annual. 1v. index. $225.00 (1994 ed.). ISSN 0002-7707.

With the 1991 annual, *ABPR* began cumulating its monthly editions rather than each year's 51 issues of *Weekly Record*, which ceased publication with the December 23, 1991, issue. *ABPR*'s more than 41,000 titles are divided into three sections—Dewey Decimal classification, adult fiction, and juvenile fiction—and include full Library of Congress cataloging information as well as price. Author and title indexes and a subject guide facilitate access to the listings. Bowker also publishes five-year cumulations for *ABPR*.

19. **Books in Print [yr.]**. New Providence, NJ, R. R. Bowker, 1948- . Annual. 10v. $450.00/set (1994 ed.). ISSN 0068-0214.

Books in Print functions as the central clearinghouse for bibliographic and purchasing information on in-print books. Its authority and usefulness are central to the day-to-day operations of libraries (research, cataloging, acquisitions, etc.). Building on that well-deserved reputation, *BIP* has, over the years, created its own cottage industry of spin-off titles: libraries may also purchase *Subject Guide to Books in Print* (annual, 5v., $315.00/set), *Paperbound Books in Print* (annual, 6v., $210.00/set), *Books Out-of-Print 1984–1988* (1988, 3v., $110.00/set), *Children's Books in Print* (annual, 1v., $145.00), *Subject Guide to Children's Books in Print* (annual, 1v., $130.50), and *The Complete Directory of Large Print Books & Serials* (formerly *Large Type Books in Print*; annual, 1v., $134.95pa.), as well as various "Forthcomings" and supplements to the major titles.

Each of the sets in this series is well executed and authoritative; however, most smaller libraries will find that with the other resources they are likely to have on hand, the main 10-volume *Books in Print* set should be sufficient to meet their needs. Many of the titles are also available online, on CD-ROM, on magnetic tape, and on microfiche.

20. Fulton, Len, ed. **Small Press Record of Books in Print [yr.].** Paradise, CA, Dustbooks, 1972- . Annual. 1v. $43.95 (1993–94 ed.). No ISSN available.

Dustbooks has become well known for its work in promoting the works of small independent presses, and this venerable guide is one of its many useful publications in this vein. Part of Dustbook's Small Press Information Library, *Small Press Record of Books in Print* is designed to bring to the attention of booksellers, librarians, and the general public those books (more than 25,000 in this edition) that are not included in Bowker's *Books in Print* because their publishers do not meet *BIP*'s inclusion criteria. Bibliographic citations are thorough and consistent, and often include descriptive notes. Provides full indexing by title, author, subject, and publisher. An important companion to the Books in Print series.

21. **Publishers Trade List Annual [yr.].** New Providence, NJ, R. R. Bowker, 1873- . Annual. 4v. $265.00/set (1994 ed.). ISSN 0079–7855.

This edition of *PTLA* brings together in one source catalogs and booklists from 810 publishers and distributors in the United States and Canada. The majority of the work is taken up by reproductions of catalogs from such publishers as American Library Association, Center for Migration Studies, and University of Harvard Press. Coverage of information technology has expanded to include micropublishing and database publishing. *PTLA* has three indexes: an index to publishers, an index to publishers' series, and a subject index that identifies the specialty areas of various publishers. The set will be particularly useful to libraries that do not have access to the individual publishers' catalogs. Also available online, on CD-ROM, and on microfiche.

22. Wong, Nancy C. and others, eds. **Cumulative Book Index [yr.]: A World List of Books in the English Language.** Bronx, NY, H. W. Wilson, 1898- . Monthly except August. Sold on service basis. ISSN 0011-300X.

An important, established, and well-known part of the national bibliographic "apparatus," *CBI* is an international bibliography of books published in the English language. Cumulated annually, it is arranged dictionary-style by author, title, and subject. The most complete information is provided under author entry: full name, complete title, series, edition, collation, list price, publisher, ISBN, and LC number when available. Title and subject entries are less comprehensive, but are supplemented by numerous cross references. Among the materials excluded are government publications, books with fewer than 50 pages (except for poetry, plays, bibliographies, juvenile literature, and scholarly works), editions of fewer than 500 copies, subsidy press publications, and other fugitive or ephemeral material. A directory of publishers and distributors not only supplies standard ordering information, but

BIOGRAPHIES

International

Dictionaries

23. **The Concise Dictionary of National Biography: From Earliest Times to 1985.** New York, Oxford University Press, 1992. 3v. $195.00/set. ISBN 0-19-865305-0.

This resource contains entries for all of the individuals listed in the 22-volume set and numerous supplements of *The Dictionary of National Biography*. The difference is that the multiple-page profiles of the original have been condensed here to range from a few lines to a few paragraphs. Although the depth of description is somewhat inconsistent in the *Concise DNB*, it can't be beat for breadth. The first source to consult if the person sought is British or Irish and died before 1985.

24. Magnusson, Magnus, and Rosemary Goring, eds. **Cambridge Biographical Dictionary.** New York, Cambridge University Press, 1990. 1658p. index. $44.95. ISBN 0-521-39518-6.

This work was previously known to librarians as the *Chambers Biographical Dictionary*, and as such has long been considered a standard biographical resource for all libraries, regardless of size. The most recent iteration of this work includes information for some 19,000 individuals considered to have been prominent or interesting in any walk of life, although the longest entries appear generally to be for those in the arts, humanities, or politics. The majority of the biographies, ranging in length from one to several hundred lines, treat individuals drawn from Western culture, especially Great Britain and Europe. Although it includes both living and dead notables, its strength lies more with historic ones; coverage of contemporary figures seems a bit spotty.

25. Slocum, Robert B., ed. **Biographical Dictionaries and Related Works: An International Bibliography of More Than 16,000 Collective Biographies, Bio-bibliographies, Collections of Epitaphs ... .** 2d ed. Detroit, Gale, 1986. 2v. index. $160.00/set. ISBN 0-8103-0234-8.

Biographical Dictionaries provides information on some 16,000 sources of biographical material. Coverage is international in scope. Each entry provides basic bibliographic information (author, title, imprint, pagination) plus brief annotations—usually one or two sentences. All entries are arranged under numerous headings within three main categories: "Universal Biography," "National and Area Biography," and "Biography by Vocation." In addition to biographical dictionaries, Slocum includes bio-bibliographies, collections of epitaphs, some genealogical works, dictionaries of antonyms and pseudonyms, historical and subject dictionaries, government and legislative manuals (with biographical material), biographies of individuals and collective biographies, biographical indexes, and selected portrait catalogs among his sources. This work is the most comprehensive publication in its subject area.

also includes imprints, branch offices, agents, and representatives. A reliable work that librarians will turn to well past its hundred-year anniversary. Also available online, on disk, on CD-ROM, and on magnetic tape.

Libraries who need a less extensive (and less expensive) alternative to Gale's bibliography may wish to purchase instead the *ARBA Guide to Biographical Dictionaries* (Bohdan S. Wynar, ed., Libraries Unlimited, 1986, 444p, $47.50, ISBN 0-87287-492-3). This work, based on more than 2,500 biographical sources reviewed by *American Reference Books Annual* during a nearly 20-year period, features the 500 best books covered by *ARBA* plus an additional 200 publications not reviewed in *ARBA* but deemed worthy of inclusion. Each entry provides complete bibliographic and price information as well as a critical evaluation of the work under review. The entries are divided into two major sections. "Universal and National Biographies" first supplies general sources not limited in their coverage to a particular topic, description, nationality, or territory, and then covers those works arranged under national origin. The second section, "Biographies in Professional Fields," incorporates 21 subject-oriented areas. Author/title and subject indexes round out the work.

26. Wasson, Tyler, ed. **Nobel Prize Winners: An H. W. Wilson Biographical Dictionary.** Bronx, NY, H. W. Wilson, 1987. 1165p. illus. $90.00. ISBN 0-8242-0756-4. **Supplement 1987-1991.** 1992. 143p. $35.00. ISBN 0-8242-0834-X.

Geared to the research needs of students, teachers, librarians, and the general public, *Nobel Prize Winners* describes the lives of the 566 Nobel Prize recipients in every category from 1901 through 1986. Entries are arranged alphabetically by name. In addition to standard biographical information and information about the work for which the Nobel Prize was awarded, entries also provide an assessment of the work's impact and significance. The essays range in length from about 1,200 to 1,500 words, and treat not only the laureate's career but also others' contributions to his or her work. Selective bibliographies conclude the entries. The supplement profiles the 49 individuals who have been awarded the Nobel prize since 1987.

The alternative to *Nobel Prize Winners* is the second edition of *The Who's Who of Nobel Prize Winners 1901-1990* (Bernard S. Schlessinger and June H. Schlessinger, eds., Oryx Press, 1991, 234p., $39.50, ISBN 0-89774-599-X). The book is arranged first by subject category of the prize, then chronologically. Although coverage is not quite as extensive in this work, it is a good purchase if budget considerations are primary.

27. **Webster's New Biographical Dictionary.** Springfield, MA, Merriam-Webster, 1988. 1130p. $24.95. ISBN 0-87779-543-6.

A worthy successor to its venerable predecessor, *Webster's Biographical Dictionary*, this *New Biographical Dictionary* provides information for some 30,000 "important, celebrated, or notorious figures" who have walked across the pages of our 5,000 years of recorded history. Citing the impossibility of keeping entries for living figures up to date, the editors have chosen to include only deceased individuals. Entries include pronunciation and end-of-line division information, birth and death dates, nationality, and salient details about the biographee, including his or her influence in history. Scope is not limited to European and North American entrants, ranging instead to include individuals from Africa, Asia, and emerging Third World nations.

28. **Who's Who [yr.]: An Annual Biographical Dictionary.** New York, St. Martin's Press, 1849- . Annual. 1v. $185.00 (1994 ed.). ISSN 0083-937X.

Long considered the premier biographical dictionary for high school, college, and public libraries, *Who's Who* presents more than 28,000 alphabetically arranged biographical profiles. Entries note each individual's occupation, birth, education, clubs, recreational activities, and address. All fields of endeavor and all parts of the world are encompassed, although a British emphasis is detectable. A complete roster of the British royal family and a section on individuals who have died since the preceding edition are included.

Guides, Handbooks, and Yearbooks

29. Andrews, Deborah, ed. **The Annual Obituary [yr.].** Chicago, St. James Press, 1982- . Annual. 1v. index. $92.00 (1994 ed.). No ISSN available.

International in scope, this well-known annual publication describes the lives of approximately 350 recently deceased noteworthies in a vast range of human endeavors. The biographies, which usually range in length from 1,000 to 4,000 words and are unsigned, are delightfully written and informative. Each entry is concluded by a who's-who summary that covers marital information, education, career, publications, honors, and, in the case of artists, individual and group exhibitions. An index by profession is included; photographs are not.

30. Browne, Ray B., ed. **Contemporary Heroes and Heroines.** Detroit, Gale, 1990. 451p. illus. index. $49.95. ISBN 0-8103-4860-8. **Contemporary Heroes and Heroines, Book II.** Deborah Gillan Straub, ed. 1992. 500p. illus. index. $49.95. ISBN 0-8103-8336-5.

International in scope, these valuable books profile individuals who have excelled in many fields of endeavor, including medicine, law, social policy, entertainment, labor, religion, sports, business, journalism, science and technology, the military, education, politics, literature, and others. The sketches are each approximately five pages in length, with sources listed, and discuss the individual's motivations, ambitions, and accomplishments. A half-page photographic portrait and a compelling quotation preface each entry. These works provide a heartening tonic to the daily news headlines.

31. **Current Biography Yearbook [yr.].** Bronx, NY, H. W. Wilson, 1940- . Annual. 1v. illus. index. $60.00 (1994 ed.). ISSN 0084-9499.

Focusing on living individuals, *Current Biography Yearbook* offers well-written biographies of about 300 international leaders per year. An approximately 3,000-word biography is provided for each, accompanied by a photograph, a current address, and a list of sources used to compile the entry. Supplementary materials include an obituary listing for the year, a checklist of sources, and a classified listing of the professions of those featured in the yearbook. Coverage is international and draws from many fields of endeavor, including government, business, literature, religion, education, and entertainment. Not only excellent and reliable for reference work, but great fun for browsing as well. Libraries who rely on *Current Biography Yearbook* will probably also want to have on hand Wilson's *Current Biography Cumulated Index 1940-1990* (1991, 133p., $25.00, ISBN 0-8242-0819-6), which provides access to some 20,000 biographies published between January 1940 and December 1990.

Libraries who wish to supplement the coverage provided by *CBY* should consider Gale's entrant into the field of living biography, *Newsmakers: The People Behind Today's Headlines* (Louise Mooney, ed., $93.00/yr. for the annual cumulation plus three quarterly issues [1994 ed.], ISSN 0899-0417). It treats about one-third fewer people, and covers both living and deceased individuals. There is little duplication between the publications, and many libraries may find they benefit from having both.

32. **The International Who's Who [yr.].** London, Europa Publications; distr., Detroit, Gale, 1936- . Annual. 1v. $260.00 (1994–95 ed.). ISSN 0074-9613.

Europa is known for high-quality, authoritative publications, and this biographical directory regularly upholds that tradition. The work comprises biographical sketches for more than 20,000 persons, including those holding high office throughout the world as well as scientists, artists, writers, religious leaders, business people, entertainers, and others. Entries note the person's date and place of birth, nationality, education, career details, present positions, honors, awards, publications, current address, telephone number, and personal interests. The entries are accurate, detailed, and current; although they follow the standard format for biographical information, they also nevertheless manage to provide a bit of insight into the personal side of the individual described.

33. Snodgrass, Mary Ellen. **Late Achievers: Famous People Who Succeeded Late in Life.** Englewood, CO, Libraries Unlimited, 1992. 286p. index. $28.00. ISBN 0-87287-937-2.

Snodgrass profiles 40 noteworthy individuals, both living and deceased, who "took on new challenges in their thirties, their forties, even their sixties and seventies." Biographees are drawn from the eighteenth through the twentieth centuries and from Europe and the United States. Sketches describe the individuals' early lives, careers, motivations, and successes, with emphasis on how obstacles were overcome and the character traits that helped these diverse individuals find ways to succeed.

34. Stetler, Susan L., ed. **Almanac of Famous People: A Comprehensive Reference Guide to More Than 25,000 Famous and Infamous Newsmakers from Biblical Times to the Present.** 5th ed. Detroit, Gale, 1993. 3v. index. $95.00/set. ISBN 0-8103-6988-5. ISSN 1040-127X.

Formerly titled *Biography Almanac*, this work continues the format of the earlier editions. Its 25,000 profiles provide name (including pseudonym and/or nickname), a one-line description, occupation, birth and death dates and locations, and brief citations to biographical dictionaries containing entries on that individual. The index volume provides access through occupation, chronologically, and geographically. Although no competitor to Gale's monumental *Biography and Genealogy Master Index* (1980- , annual, 1v., $295.00 [1994 ed.]), which indexes more than 450,000 citations to biographical articles appearing in more than 150 editions and volumes of biographical dictionaries and who's-who publications, *Almanac of Famous People* is especially useful for easily locating a small amount of information on a large number of individuals drawn from a vast range of professions and endeavors. Also available online, on disk, and on magnetic tape.

Indexes

35. Breen, Karen. **Index to Collective Biographies for Young Readers.** 4th ed. New Providence, NJ, R. R. Bowker, 1988. 494p. $48.00. ISBN 0-8352-2348-5.

Intended for children's and school libraries, Breen's work indexes the contents of 1,129 collective biographies that include nearly 9,800 people. The main alphabetical section is a listing of individuals with their dates of birth and death, nationality at birth and current country of residence, occupation, and a book code indicating the volume indexed. A second section lists names alphabetically by subject and country of origin and residence. The final section of the book lists each title with master lists of all persons indexed from that source. Also included are the lists of books by their codes and a key to the publishers.

United States

36. **Biography Index: A Cumulative Index to Biographical Material in Books and Magazines.** Bronx, NY, H. W. Wilson, 1946- . Quarterly (August issue is bound annual cumulation); triennial cumulations. $125.00/yr. (1993-94 ed.). ISSN 0006-3053.

This index has been a mainstay of reference work since it was first published in 1946. It indexes biographical material that has been published in more than 2,700 periodicals, over 2,000 books of both individual and collective biographies, incidental biographical material found in nonbiographical sources, and obituaries, collections of letters, diaries, memoirs, and bibliographies. Unless otherwise stated, all biographies indexed are American. Each entry includes author's full name, dates of birth and death (if no longer living), and profession or achievement for which known. A brief bibliographical citation wraps up each entry. "Professions and Occupations," a subject guide to the main index, concludes *Biography Index.* Also available online, on disk, on CD-ROM, and on magnetic tape.

37. **Dictionary of American Biography.** New York, Scribner's, 1957–88. 18v. $1,700.00/set. ISBN 0-684-17323-9. **Comprehensive Index.** 1990. 1v. $85.00. ISBN 0-684-19114-8.

This work was originally 10 volumes; supplemented by 8 updating volumes, coverage of noteworthy Americans now includes nearly 18,000 individuals who died before 1971. Articles are signed and well documented, and range in length from brief entries to lengthy profiles. The comprehensive index provides access through occupation, place of birth, school, contributor, and subject.

Although *DAB* is rightly considered the standard American biographical source, its price may make it a difficult purchase for smaller libraries struggling with budget constraints. An excellent alternative is Scribner's *Concise Dictionary of American Biography* (4th ed., 1990. $150.00. ISBN 0-684-19188-1), which describes the same 18,000 individuals but radically condenses their entries to result in a more affordable single volume.

38. **Who's Who in America [yr.].** Wilmette, IL, Marquis Who's Who, 1898- . Annual. 3v. index. $429.95 (1994 ed.). ISSN 0083-9396.

The purpose of this publication mirrors the goal set forth by A.N. Marquis in 1898 when he first conceived of the "Who's Who" directory: to provide information on the lives of individuals whose achievements and contributions to society make them subjects of widespread reference interest. Reference value is based on either of two factors: "1) the position of responsibility held or 2) the level of significant achievement attained in a career of noteworthy activity." The book includes more than 80,000 biographies of persons in the United States, Canada, and Mexico; entries include name, occupation, vital statistics, parents, marriage, children, education, professional certifications, career, writings, civil and political activities, awards, professional memberships, political affiliations, religion, clubs, and home and business addresses. Also available online, on CD-ROM, and on magnetic tape.

Like Bowker's *Books in Print,* the Marquis Who's Who main editions and spin-off publications have become a virtual cottage industry. Thus we have from Marquis, in varying degrees of regularity: *Who's Who in America: Junior & Senior*

High School Version, Who's Who in the South and Southwest, Who's Who in the East, Who's Who in the Midwest, Who's Who in the West, and Who Was Who in America with World Notables, among others. There is an ongoing concern among reviewers and librarians regarding the appropriateness of the selections, as well as the reference value of the biographies, when all of the entries are based on submissions from the individuals profiled. With those two caveats in mind, libraries should examine the publications in question to determine whether they offer a useful alternative to other works available in these areas or can function as a primary source when there are no alternative works. If libraries do make a substantial investment in the Marquis Who's Who publications, they may also wish to purchase the publisher's annual *Index to Who's Who Books* ($89.95 [1994 ed.]).

CALENDARS, DAYS, AND FESTIVALS

39. **Chase's Annual Events: The Day-by-Day Directory to [yr.].** Chicago, Contemporary Books, 1958- . Annual. illus. index. $42.95pa. (1994 ed.). ISSN 0740-5286.

International in coverage, *Chase's* has been a standard reference in libraries for more than three decades. (It was formerly known as *Chase's Calendar of Annual Events.*) It now includes more than 8,000 entries for special events, anniversaries, birthdays, holidays, and festivals. In addition to its calendar material, it also includes items more usually found in almanacs, such as (in a recent edition) presidential proclamations, national days of countries, data on astronomical phenomena, satellites and their current status, calendar dates projected through coming years, and possible names for upcoming hurricanes. Although this is an excellent resource for ready-reference questions, it is also highly enjoyable to simply browse through.

40. Mossman, Jennifer, ed. **Holidays and Anniversaries of the World: A Comprehensive Catalogue Containing Detailed Information on Every Month and Day of the Year ...** . 2d ed. Detroit, Gale, 1990. 1080p. index. $89.00. ISBN 0-8103-4870-5.

More than 23,000 entries are listed within this comprehensive work's index of names, terms, and events, which gives an idea of how much information is packed into each of the calendar's 366 days. The format is chronological; information noted for each day includes famous birthdays, holidays, historical events, religious observances and events, and saints' days. Coverage is both national and international. Supplementary materials include an essay on the development of the modern calendar, a table of movable holidays, a perpetual calendar, a glossary of time words and abbreviations, and an index that still needs to expand its cross references. An impressive work that nicely complements the other standard in this field, *Chase's Annual Events* (entry 39).

Perhaps the success of this work will encourage Gale to publish a new edition of its now-out-of-print *Festivals Sourcebook: A Reference Guide to Fairs, Festivals and Celebrations* (2d ed., Paul Wasserman, ed., 1984, 721p., ISBN 0-8103-0323-X). Intended to provide "a comprehensive overview of the myriad special occasions celebrated by the people of the United States and Canada in their local communities," the sourcebook did an excellent job of meeting that goal. Although there are many other good publications in this subject area, such as Frances Shemanski's two works, *A Guide to Fairs and Festivals in the United States* (Greenwood Press, 1984, 339p., $42.95, ISBN 0-313-21437-9) and *A Guide to World Fairs and Festivals* (Greenwood Press, 1985, 309p, $42.95, ISBN 0-313-20786-0), and Carol Spivack and

Richard A. Weinstock's *Best Festivals of North America: An Arts Guide ...* (3d ed., Pinwheel Press, 1989, 207p., $10.95pa., ISBN 0-916401-08-1), none offers the breadth or comprehensiveness of *Festivals Sourcebook*. Those libraries fortunate enough to own copies will want to make sure they retain them.

DIRECTORIES

41. Daniels, Peggy Kneffel, and Carol A. Schwartz, eds. **Encyclopedia of Associations** [yr.]. Detroit, Gale, 1965- . Annual. 3v. ISSN 0071-0202. **Volume 1: National Organizations of the U.S.** 3pts. index. $340.00/set (1994 ed.). **Volume 2: Geographic and Executive Indexes.** $275.00 (1994 ed.). **Volume 3: Supplement.** $295.00pa. (1994 ed.).

More than 22,000 trade and professional associations, organizations, and other nonprofit membership groups across a broad range of endeavors are listed in volume 1, the main volume, of *Encyclopedia of Associations*. Included are business, public administration, education, environmental, social welfare, and sports organizations; fraternities; and fan clubs. Entries are arranged alphabetically within 18 broad subject classifications and include contact information as well as information about the organization and its mission; founding date; number of members; paid staff size; purpose and history of the group; related regional, state, and local groups; and affiliations and budgets. The directory also provides information on association publications, conferences, conventions, and commercial exhibits where applicable. Also available online, on disk, on CD-ROM, and on magnetic tape.

Gale publishes two related publications, which essentially follow the same format as that described here. They are *Encyclopedia of Associations: International Organizations* (Jackie Barrett, ed., 2v., 1993, $455.00/set, ISBN 0-8103-8051-X) and *Encyclopedia of Associations: Regional, State, and Local Organizations* (Grant Eldridge, ed., 5v., 1992, $469.00/set, ISBN 0-8103-7696-2). The former publication provides detailed listings for more than 11,000 organizations "of national, international, and global concern," the latter for some 50,000 nonprofit membership groups roughly evenly divided among the Great Lakes, Northeastern, Southern and Middle Atlantic, South Central and Great Plains, and Western states.

42. Downs, Buck J., and others, eds. **National Trade and Professional Associations of the United States** [yr.]. Washington, DC, Columbia Books, 1966- . Annual. 1v. index. $70.00pa. (1994 ed.). ISSN 0734-354X.

Although the Gale directories are considered the standard resources in the area of associations, this annual publication has continued to be a good buy for the money since 1966. It lists about 7,300 national organizations for business, labor, and the professions; included are trade associations, scientific, technical, and learned societies, political action committees, and about 175 national labor unions. The association entries are arranged by subject, and provide contact information plus date of establishment, headquarters staff, number of members, and publications. The directory is indexed by title, keyword, and subject, as well as by geographic location, budget size, acronym, executive officers, and U.S. association management companies.

43. Miles, Steven A., ed. **The National Directory of Addresses and Telephone Numbers: Containing Phone Numbers, Addresses, Fax Numbers and Toll-Free Numbers ...** Detroit, Omnigraphics, 1992- . Annual. 1v. index. $69.96, $59.95pa. (1994 ed.). ISSN 0740-7203.

Published since 1981 by General Information and now by Omnigraphics, this directory is divided into two main sections: an alphabetical listing by company or organization name and a classified listing by subject or standard industrial classification (SIC) code grouping. Some 120,000 of the most useful telephone numbers and addresses are provided within these two sections; in addition, there are profiles of top U.S. cities, an index to area and zip codes, and a subject index. Although any publication of this sort needs regular updating to maintain its usefulness, this directory does a good job of staying current with a rapidly expanding information base.

For coverage of zip codes, libraries will probably want to have *The Instant National Locator Guide* (Creighton-Morgan, 1991, 1v. [various paging], $15.95pa., ISBN 0-9620096-5-2), which enables the user to quickly find zip codes and area codes, and conversely, to learn which areas they represent.

44. Schell, Terri Kessler, ed. **Directories in Print [yr.].** Detroit, Gale, 1990- . Annual. 2v. index. $290.00/set (1994 ed.). ISSN 0275-5580.

This publication is the result of a merger of Gale's *International Directories in Print* with the Directories in Print database (known previously to many of us as *The Directory of Directories*). It describes about 4,000 directories arranged within 26 subject chapters, and includes databases, buyers' guides, membership lists, registers, handbooks, indexes, who's-who books, fact books, yearbooks and annuals, catalogs, and other lists. Entries include name and address of publisher, number of listings, scope of coverage, content and arrangement of entries, and other information as appropriate. Directories available in alternative formats (online, CD-ROM, etc.) are so noted. Three indexes—alternative formats, subject, and title/keyword—make up the second volume. Depending on need and budget priorities, libraries may also wish to purchase each year's mid-edition supplement, which includes about 1,000 new or revised entries, for a cost of about $185.00. *Directories in Print* is also available online, on disk, and on magnetic tape.

45. Siegman, Gita, ed. **Awards, Honors, & Prizes: An International Directory of Awards ... .** 10th ed. Detroit, Gale, 1992. 2v. index. $390.00/set. ISBN 0-8103-7641-5.

This well-known directory lists more than 19,000 awards, honors, and prizes granted by U.S., foreign, and international organizations. Volume 1, covering the United States and Canada, lists entries by sponsoring organization. Volume 2, international and foreign, arranges entries by country and then by sponsoring organization. Entries give a brief description of the purpose and scope of the award, honor, or prize, contact information for the sponsoring organization, and frequency and nature of the award. Both volumes are indexed by organization name, award name, and subject. Scholarship and other academic awards are not included. Also available on disk and on magnetic tape.

A related title in this subject area is the second edition of Gale's *World of Winners: A Current and Historical Perspective on Awards and Their Winners* (Gita Siegman, ed., 1992, 977p., ISBN 0-8103-6981-8). Its focus is on the individuals who have won the awards, honors, and prizes listed in the main volume, and it identifies about 100,000 winners of 2,500 awards presented in the United States, Canada, and worldwide, ranging from Emmys to the Nobel Prizes. They are listed alphabetically by popular name under 12 subject headings, such as arts and letters, business, health and medicine, and so on. Good coverage of a subject area with high patron interest.

ENCYCLOPEDIAS

Selection Guides

46. Kister, Kenneth F. **Kister's Best Encyclopedias: A Guide to General and Specialized Encyclopedias.** 2d ed. Phoenix, AZ, Oryx Press, 1994. 392p. index. $39.95. ISBN 0-89774-744-5.

Kister has long been known for his work in evaluating encyclopedias, and his guides have been a standard resource in every public library. In this, his second edition for Oryx (previous editions were published by Bowker), he reviews 73 general encyclopedias (including the latest electronic packages) plus 800 specialized encyclopedias. His primary focus is on the general encyclopedias, and approximately half of the text is given over to these in-depth reviews. Encyclopedias are listed alphabetically. Each entry provides a comprehensive bibliographic citation followed by authoritative critical comments; comparisons to encyclopedias of similar size, price, and intended usership; sales information; and citations to reviews in other publications. Supplementary materials include comparative charts, an annotated bibliography of sources for further evaluation, and a list of publishers and distributors of encyclopedias in North America. An index that is cross-referenced by title and subject concludes the guide.

47. **Purchasing an Encyclopedia: 12 Points to Consider.** 4th ed. Chicago, American Library Association, 1992. 45p. $7.00pa. ISBN 0-8389-5754-4.

Given the amount libraries invest when purchasing an encyclopedia, this inexpensive publication is an invaluable aid. It suggests 12 points by which to evaluate multi-volume, general encyclopedias, such as ease of locating information, how well subjects relate to the intended audience, and whether racial or gender biases are reflected in the articles. Especially helpful, however, is that the editors then offer practical tips for applying the evaluation criteria; for example, one can verify currency by looking at the year on which statistics are based or if newly formed countries are included. In addition to the evaluation guidelines, the work also reviews nine multi-volume encyclopedias (a reprint of the September 15, 1992, issue of *Booklist/Reference Books Bulletin*). There is also a list of toll-free customer numbers for the four main encyclopedia companies. A "must" purchase for all public and school libraries.

48. Wynar, Bohdan S., ed. **ARBA Guide to Subject Encyclopedias and Dictionaries.** Heather Cameron and G. Kim Dority, asst. eds. Littleton, CO, Libraries Unlimited, 1986. 570p. index. $47.50. ISBN 0-87287-493-1.

Based on reviews from 17 years of *American Reference Books Annual*, this selective guide describes 1,354 subject dictionaries and encyclopedias, serial and nonserial, deemed valuable for all types of libraries. The book's 43 chapters are arranged alphabetically by subject; chapter subdivisions reflect both format and individual disciplines or areas. Entries are descriptive and evaluative, and include title, author or editor, publisher, pagination, price, and ISBN. Author/title and subject indexes round out the work.

Adult Encyclopedias

49. Cummings, Mark, ed. **The Encyclopedia Americana.** International ed. Danbury, CT, Grolier, 1994. 30v. illus. maps. index. $1,400.00/set; $999.00/set (schools and libraries). ISBN 0-7172-0123-6.

The first major encyclopedia to appear in the United States was this one in 1829. The goal was, and is, to serve "as a bridge between the worlds of the specialist and the general reader." Bibliographies accompany all major articles as well as many of the shorter entries. The articles are clear and well-written, and range in length from 600 words to 10 or more pages. Although emphasis has been reduced in the last few years, this encyclopedia is still well known for its coverage of United States and Canadian history, biography, and geography. Bibliographies are reasonably current, illustrations are good, readability is outstanding, and access to the encyclopedia's coverage is facilitated by an extensive analytical index. The *Americana* is revised and republished annually, although reviewers have noted that currency continues to be problematic.

50. Johnston, Bernard, ed. **Collier's Encyclopedia.** New York, Macmillan, 1994. 24v. illus. (part col.). maps. index. $999.00/set; $995.00/set (schools and libraries). ISBN 0-02-942517-4.

Collier's Encyclopedia compares well with its two main competitors—*The Encyclopedia Americana* and *The New Encyclopaedia Britannica*—in terms of breadth and detail of coverage, illustrations, reliability, and ease of use. However, whereas the other two use a more narrowly focused, subject-specific approach to their materials, *Collier's* uses a much broader, conceptual approach. (Consequently, it is essential to use the analytical index of approximately 40,000 entries to find specific information.) The intended audience is students from junior high through college; in fact, curricula formats of colleges and secondary schools have been used as a basis for the encyclopedia's contents. To ensure comprehension, most articles begin with a simple definition followed by basic facts. Although each of the three leading encyclopedias has unique strengths and weaknesses, libraries serving young adults and adults will probably consider *Collier's* as the first choice.

51. McHenry, Robert, ed. **The New Encyclopaedia Britannica.** Chicago, Encyclopaedia Britannica, 1994. 32v. illus. (part col.). maps. index. $1,194.00/set; $1,299.00/set (schools and libraries). ISBN 0-85229-529-4.

Since its first publication in three volumes between 1768 and 1771 in Edinburgh, Scotland, *Britannica* has been considered an authoritative, truly international encyclopedia, providing more depth of coverage on almost all subject areas than any other general encyclopedia in the English language. It can, in fact, be considered the most comprehensive reference source in English. In addition to its outstanding text, *Britannica* offers some 23,000 excellent illustrations. Although its tripartite arrangement (concise articles in the "Micropaedia," more in-depth treatment of subjects in the "Macropaedia," rounded out by the "Propaedia") makes it substantially more difficult to navigate than its competitors, the addition of an extensive index in 1985 (due to public demand) greatly increased usability. Despite its challenges, this monumental set offers an unparalleled wealth of intellectual wonders to those hardy souls patient enough to master its complexities. *Britannica* is also available on CD-ROM as the *Britannica Instant Research System.*

Single-Volume Encyclopedias

52. Chernow, Barbara A., and George A. Vallasi, eds. **The Columbia Encyclopedia.** 5th ed. New York, Columbia University Press; distr., Boston, Houghton-Mifflin, 1993. 3072p. illus. maps. bibliog. $125.00. ISBN 0-395-62438-X.

Despite an increase in international coverage over its predecessors, the fifth edition of this stalwart general encyclopedia remains, in the words of its editors, "an American encyclopedia written for American readers." It offers 50,000 scholarly, authoritative articles, 8,500 bibliographies, 745 illustrations (black-and-white line drawings) and maps, and an astounding 65,000 cross references. Emphases include biography, geographical topics, and scientific and technical subjects, with more-than-adequate coverage of religious and biblical topics as well. Accuracy, currency, and a balanced approach to controversial subjects continue as hallmarks of this outstanding reference, which should be considered a first purchase for all libraries considering a one-volume encyclopedia.

For those unable to afford the full encyclopedia, an alternative to consider is *The Concise Columbia Encyclopedia* (2d ed., Consumers Union and Columbia University Press, 1989, 920p., $39.95, ISBN 0-231-06938-3). Based on the fourth, rather than fifth, edition of *The Columbia Encyclopedia*, this single-volume ency-clopedia has become a standard resource at many ready-reference desks. Librarians have praised its authority, currency, readability, and conciseness, as well as its very reasonable price. The 15,000 articles are written for those of average reading ability; technical terms are defined in language accessible to the general reading public. More than 50,000 cross references guide users to related terms.

53. Crystal, David, ed. **The Cambridge Encyclopedia.** New York, Cambridge University Press, 1992. 1488p. illus. maps. $49.95. ISBN 0-521-39528-3.

The 30,000 entries found in *The Cambridge Encyclopedia* are usually quite brief, averaging only about 50 words each. Thus, the strength of this work is its breadth, rather than depth, of information. The encyclopedia's international scope, biographies, and extensive coverage of the sciences provide a broad base of current information, albeit with a noticeably British emphasis. Although certainly not a first purchase for public libraries, this Cambridge reference could supplement either the Random House (entry 55) or Columbia (entry 52) titles. An exact duplicate of this work is available for $19.98 as the *Barnes & Noble Encyclopedia.*

54. Elliott, Stephen P., Martha Goldstein, and Michael Upshall, eds. **Webster's New World Encyclopedia.** New York, Prentice-Hall General Reference, 1992. 1230p. illus. maps. $75.00. ISBN 0-13-947-482-X.

The 25,000 alphabetically arranged entries found here are short and to the point; they include pronunciation and are current through March 1992. Coverage includes 1990 census data. The work lacks an index or bibliographies, but does include some 3,000 cross references. Although the articles provide little more than essential information about any given topic, the work's strength is its currency; thus, it is an effective supplement to either *The Columbia Encyclopedia* or *The Random House Encyclopedia* (or both).

55. Mitchell, James, ed. **The Random House Encyclopedia.** Rev. 3d ed. New York, Random House, 1990. 2781p. illus. (part col.) maps. bibliog. $129.95. ISBN 0-394-58450-3.

The strengths of this one-volume encyclopedia are its pictorial appeal and the breadth of information presented. Its weaknesses include a somewhat difficult-to-use, two-part format and occasional inconsistency of coverage. The two-part arrangement features a "Colorpedia," comprising 880 two-page articles organized under 7 broad topical headings; and the ready-reference "Alphapedia," made up of 25,000 brief articles that refer back to the more in-depth coverage of the "Colorpedia" as appropriate. Supplementary materials include a chronological time chart, a bibliography, and a world atlas. The work is designed for a popular audience, but could be useful to libraries that already own the *Concise Columbia Encyclopedia* but would like another single-volume encyclopedia. Also available on disk.

Student Encyclopedias

56. Good, Dale, ed. **Compton's Encyclopedia and Fact-Index.** Chicago, Compton's Learning Company, 1993. 26v. illus. maps. index. $499.00/set; $569.00/set (schools and libraries). ISBN 0-85229-572-3.

Now into its eighth decade, *Compton's* comprises about 34,000 articles in the main text plus nearly 29,000 capsule articles in its "Fact-Index." There are more than 16,200 cross references in the main text, plus another 114,000 in the "Fact-Index." Coverage is fairly balanced, although strongest in scientific and geographic topics; the intended audience is secondary school students and young adults. Excellently rendered photographs and illustrations make up about one-third of the volume. As with other encyclopedias, the depth and quality of articles are occasionally inconsistent. Nevertheless, this is an attractive and well-designed encyclopedia that can be considered a useful complement to *Academic American* and *World Book* for school libraries.

57. Jacobs, Dale W., ed. **The World Book Encyclopedia.** Chicago, World Book, 1994. 22v. illus. maps. index. $679.00–$899.00/set; $520.00/set (schools and libraries). ISBN 0-7166-0092-7.

Reviewers have given consistently high marks to *World Book Encyclopedia* for its currency, detailed coverage, attractive design, strong math/science coverage, and general high quality, reliability, and popularity. There are 17,500 entries in this 22-volume set, complemented by some 31,000 illustrations and maps, 24,000 of which are in color. Although two competitors—*Compton's Encyclopedia* (Encyclopaedia Britannica) and *Academic American* (Grolier)—are also highly regarded works in this area, *World Book* is generally considered the first purchase for libraries serving late elementary through senior high school students.

58. Ranson, Anne K., ed. **Academic American Encyclopedia.** Danbury, CT, Grolier, 1994. 21v. illus. maps. index. $1,150.00/set; $719.00/set (schools). ISBN 0-7172-2041-9.

The youngest and most inventive of the leading encyclopedias, *Academic American* is a "short article" encyclopedia most appropriate for high schools and colleges. Topics treated are equally divided among the humanities, the sciences, and the social sciences. The work has been cited for its high degree of accuracy, authority, and currency; its brevity and concentration on essential information rather than on longer articles make it an important addition to every reference collection. In addition, the number and clarity of illustrations, photographs, and maps (most of which are in color) continue to be strong points of this medium-sized encyclopedia. The encyclopedia is also marketed as the *Barnes & Noble New American Encyclopedia*, the *Grolier International Encyclopedia*, the *Lexicon Universal Encyclopedia*, and the *Macmillan Family Encyclopedia*. Also available online and on CD-ROM (as the *New Grolier Multimedia Encyclopedia*).

59. Somerville, James, and others, eds. **Children's Britannica.** Chicago, Encyclopaedia Britannica, 1994. 20v. illus. (part col.). maps. index. $299.00/set. ISBN 0-85229-226-0.

Curriculum-oriented and designed for use by elementary school children, this encyclopedia may be familiar to librarians in its previous iteration, *Britannica Junior Encyclopaedia for Boys and Girls*. The structure, content, and style of the 4,200 main articles and 6,000 brief "reference index" entries reflect the encyclopedia's focus on elementary-level students. The format is attractive, and the cross references and index are adequate. An accurate and reliable school or children's encyclopedia.

There are many multi-volume encyclopedias that, even if not of the caliber of *World Book*, *Academic American*, or *Compton's*, are nevertheless reliable, well-executed, and interesting to their readers. Two of the best of these are *Childcraft: The How and Why Library* (World Book, 1993, 16v., $249.00/set, ISBN 0-7166-0191-5), the premier set for children ages 4 through 10, and *The New Book of Knowledge* (Grolier, 1994, 21v., $995.00/set; $679.00/set [schools and libraries], ISBN 0-7172-0523-1), geared to children from 7 to 14. Two other reliable single-volume alternatives are *Barron's Junior Fact Finder: An Illustrated Encyclopedia for Children* (Barron's Educational Series, 1989, 1v., $19.95, ISBN 0-8120-6072-5), aimed at children in intermediate grade levels, and *Barron's Student's Concise Encyclopedia* (Barron's Educational Series, 1993, 1v, $29.95, ISBN 0-8120-6329-5) for high-school students. Both cover thousands of topics, are well-written, and are good sources for quick, factual information.

GOVERNMENT DOCUMENTS

60. Bailey, William G., comp. **Guide to Popular U.S. Government Publications.** 3d ed. Englewood, CO, Libraries Unlimited, 1993. 289p. index. $39.50. ISBN 0-56308-031-1.

In the third edition of the work originated by LeRoy Schwarzkopf, Bailey has included about 2,500 titles published mostly between mid-1989 and early 1993, with a few citations from earlier years when appropriate. Arrangement is by broad subject heading, subdivided for clarification. Many sections include cross references to related subject bibliographies. Entries include full bibliographic information as well as brief descriptive annotations.

Another tool for accessing government documents is Wiley J. Williams's *Subject Guide to Major United States Government Publications* (2d ed., American Library Association, 1987, 257p., $11.00, ISBN 0-8389-0475-0). It lists significant U.S. government document publications of permanent value under more than 250 broad topics that reflect the wide range of federal government activity. Entries provide full bibliographic information; most also include brief annotations.

61. **Monthly Catalog of United States Government Publications.** Washington, DC, Government Printing Office, 1895- . 1v. Monthly. Price varies. S/N 721-011-00000-3. SuDoc GP 3.8. ISSN 0362-6830.

This well-known government publication identifies between 1,500 and 3,000 new titles in each monthly issue. Arranged by Superintendent of Documents (SUDOC) number, entries include complete purchasing and cataloging information. Access is provided by author, title, subject, and series/report indexes.

MoCat is but one of many government catalogs; for access to the broad array of works available in this area, Steven D. Zink's *United States Government Publications Catalogs* (2d ed., Special Libraries Association, 1988, 292p., $20.00pa., ISBN 0-87111-335-X) is an excellent tool. It contains more than 370 titles of U.S. government agency publications catalogs that cover both print and nonprint works, and includes informative annotations and title and subject indexes.

62. Morehead, Joe, and Mary Fetzer. **Introduction to United States Government Information Sources.** 4th ed. Englewood, CO, Libraries Unlimited, 1992. 474p. index. $38.50; $32.50pa. ISBN 0-87287-909-7; 1-56308-066-4pa.

A comprehensive introduction to the bibliographic structure of federal government information, the fourth edition of Morehead's standard work leads off with a brief overview of public documents. The ensuing chapters treat such topics as government publishing and the Government Printing Office; the depository library system; administrative laws, regulations, and decisions; publications of judiciary and advisory committees and commissions; research and technical report literature; and statistical sources. Each subject is accompanied by illustrative tables, lists, reports, abstracts, and examples. Special attention is given to the proliferation of nonprint sources, such as CD-ROM, that are playing an increasingly important role in disseminating government information.

63. Robinson, Judith Schiek. **Tapping the Government Grapevine: The User-Friendly Guide to U.S. Government Information Sources.** 2d ed. Phoenix, AZ, Oryx Press, 1993. 227p. illus. index. $34.50pa. ISBN 0-89774-712-7.

This is truly a "user-friendly" guide through the byzantine maze of print and nonprint government information resources. In addition to federal materials, it also describes (and explains) selected local, state, foreign, and international sources. Robinson has organized her publication in chapters that reflect the type of information (for example, scientific information or legislative information sources). Each chapter leads off with a "who, what, where, when, and why" summary, then proceeds to offer practical tips on how to use specific materials. There are two very helpful appendixes. One, the "Documents Toolkit," suggests titles for a bare-bones documents reference collection; the other offers a set of learning exercises and solutions. Especially good for introducing patrons to information available through the government.

64. Schwarzkopf, LeRoy D., comp. **Government Reference Books [yr.]: A Biennial Guide to U.S. Government Publications.** Englewood, CO, Libraries Unlimited, 1970- . Biennial. 1v. index. $67.50 (1994 ed.). ISSN 0072-5188.

Issued every two years, this guide to U.S. government titles identifies and describes more than 1,200 books and other resources distributed to depository libraries. Arrangement is by topic within four broad categories (general library reference sources, social sciences, science and technology, and the humanities), with numerous subdivisions in each category. Entries include full bibliographic citation, OCLC and *Monthly Catalog* numbers, LC card number, depository shipping list and item numbers, and LC classification. A descriptive annotation accompanies each entry.

Libraries may also wish to consider Schwarzkopf's companion publication, *Government Reference Serials* (Libraries Unlimited, 1988, 344p., $48.00, ISBN 0-87287-451-6). It describes 583 government publications of reference value issued annually or biennially, as well as quarterly, monthly, or even daily. As with *Government Reference Books*, only items available for distribution through the Government

Printing Office's depository library program are cited. Arrangement and information provided mirror that of its companion work.

GUIDES TO ELECTRONIC
INFORMATION

65. Bjorner, Susanne, comp. and ed. **Newspapers Online: A Guide to Searching Daily Newspapers Whose Articles Are Online in Full Text.** 2d ed. Needham Heights, MA, BiblioData, 1993. 1v. (various paging). index. $120.00 loose-leaf w/binder. ISBN 1-879258-07-2.

Newspapers Online is a loose-leaf directory of more than 150 daily newspapers throughout the world that make their contents available electronically through one of several vendors (e.g., DIALOG, Dow Jones News) or that publish full-text versions on CD-ROM. Coverage encompasses 125 U.S. and Canadian newspapers plus 18 European, Middle Eastern, Asian, and Australian newspapers. Averaging two pages in length, entries generally include name, address, telephone number, and editor; a paragraph-length description of the region covered; a list of the major newsmakers in the area; a description of the paper, its contents, and circulation; electronic availability online and on CD-ROM; and search tips.

66. Desmarais, Norman, comp. **CD-ROMs in Print [yr.].** Westport, CT, Meckler, 1990- . 1v. index. $49.50pa. (1994 ed.). ISSN 0891-8198.

The purpose of this Meckler directory is to provide a comprehensive list of commercially available CD-ROMs, both domestic and international. The bulk of the work is made up of an optical product directory, an alphabetical list of discs by title, and indexes by data provider, publisher, distributor, software provider, and subject. Main entries identify CD title, price, provider, drive, hardware/software requirements, subscription, and product description. Unfortunately, there are no cross references, which would greatly facilitate location of products for which the exact title is unknown. Nevertheless, because the number of CD-ROM titles is expanding exponentially every year, this directory remains an important resource for all libraries, and should be considered a first purchase in this subject area. Also available on CD-ROM.

The major competitor to Meckler's title is Learned Information's biennial, *CD-ROM Finder: The World of CD-ROM Products for Information Seekers* (5th ed., 1993. 592p., $69.50, ISBN 0-938734-70-9) (previously published as the *Optical Publishing Directory*), which describes about 1,400 products, but provides greater detail and depth in its descriptions as well several topical overviews. A third work, *The CD-ROM Directory* (TFPL; Omnigraphics, 1986- , annual. 1v., $139.00pa. [1994 ed.], no ISSN available), provides content similar to that found in *CD-ROMs in Print*, except that it offers much stronger international coverage. Given its cost, however, libraries will have to decide whether they need this added information.

67. Marcaccio, Kathleen Young, ed. **Gale Directory of Databases.** Detroit, Gale, 1993- . Annual, with semiannual updates. 2v. index. $290.00/set (1994 ed.). No ISSN available.

This directory is a melding of three well-known resources—Gale's *Computer Readable Databases*, Cuadra-Gale's *Directory of Online Databases*, and *Directory of Portable Databases*—into a compilation of nearly 8,500 databases available in a variety of electronic formats. The two volumes function (and can be purchased) independently of each other. Volume 1, "Online Databases" ($210.00 [1994 ed.], no

ISSN available), describes 5,000 online databases as to producer name and contact information, summary of content, database language, geographic coverage, year first available, time span, updating, availability, rates, and so forth. Volume 2, "CD-ROM, Diskette, Magnetic Tape, Handheld, and Batch Access Database Products" ($130.00 [1994 ed.], no ISSN available), provides similar information for the 3,525 titles listed. Both volumes include a database producers section, a vendors section, a statistical analysis of the electronic database industry by Martha E. Williams, and master, subject, and geographic indexes. Although this work is expensive relative to other CD-ROM directories, there is simply no more comprehensive resource for libraries interested in acquiring a broad range of electronic titles. Also available online, on disk, on CD-ROM, and on magnetic tape.

68. Motley, Lynn. **Modem USA: Low Cost and Free Online Sources for Information, Databases, and Electronic Bulletin Boards Via Computer and Modem in 50 States.** Takoma Park, MD, Allium Press, 1992. 190p. $16.95pa. ISBN 0-9631233-4-3.

Electronic bulletin boards (EBBs) and online services are becoming increasingly popular among the general population, and thus an inexpensive work like *Modem USA* will be a welcome addition for many libraries supporting a personal-computing clientele. It provides information on a multitude of low-cost or free online reference systems run by federal, state, and local agencies, as well those run by private groups and individuals. Bulletin boards are listed first by subject, then by state within subject. Subjects include medicine, libraries, government, the environment, safety, science, music, jobs, gardening, real estate, genealogy, writing, and computers. Supplementary materials include a brief bibliography on EBBs and telecommunications and a short glossary.

69. Newby, Gregory B. **Directory of Directories on the Internet: A Guide to Information Sources.** Westport, CT, Meckler, 1994. 153p. index. $29.50pa. ISBN 0-88736-768-2.

This concise directory will help both novices and more experienced Internet users find their way through the daunting amount of data, connections, pathways, and information available on the Net. Topics encompassed include resource guides that point to other resources; online public access catalogs (OPACs) worldwide; mailing lists and newsgroups; general-interest resources; FTP directories; resources provided by subject specialists in their areas of expertise; electronic guides to book collections; and various directories to other information, such as dictionaries, bibliographies, electronic texts, and Internet navigation software. Appendixes include a listing of international Internet country codes, a tool for using FTP via e-mail, a list of countries accessible via the X.500 gateway, and a glossary. Indexed by Internet address, by resource type, and by author/maintainer.

70. Nicholls, Paul T. **CD-ROM Buyer's Guide & Handbook: The Definitive Reference for CD-ROM Users.** 3d ed. Wilton, CT, Eight Bit Books, 1993. 699p. illus. index. $44.95pa. ISBN 0-910965-08-0.

Intended to assist anyone involved with CD-ROM, this guide contains three main categories of material: extensive background information on CD-ROM technology and the industry, bibliographical citations for hundreds of articles on all aspects of CD-ROM, and reviews of a core of nearly 200 CD-ROM titles. The CD-ROM reviews are arranged by subject and cover a wide range of products, from children's games to sophisticated periodical indexes. Reviews include ratings for ease of installation and use, quality of data, documentation, and "search power." An

71. Nobari, Nuchine, ed. **Books & Periodicals Online.** New York, Library Alliance, 1992. 1619p. index. $249.00pa. ISBN 0-9630277-1-9.

Expanded by incorporating earlier editions of the *Directory of Periodicals Online,* this catalog lists more than 43,000 publications in 1,800 databases—a total of 84,640 entries. Several nonbibliographical databases, such as reference books and newswires, are included as well. Databases are listed alphabetically and grouped by four categories: bibliographical, full-text, numeric, and referral. Each entry lists the publication's title, country of origin, former or continuing names, publisher, reference numbers, databases where found, vendors for each database, and scope of editorial coverage. Indexed by publication title, publishers' names, vendors' names, databases, and titles available on CD-ROM.

72. Orenstein, Ruth, ed. **Fulltext Sources Online: For Periodicals, Newspapers, Newsletters and Newswires.** Needham Heights, MA, Bibliodata, 1988- . Twice yearly. 1v. $175.00 (1994 ed.). ISSN 1040-8258.

Fulltext Sources Online provides an alphabetical listing (by title) of periodicals, newspapers, newsletters, and newswires that are available in full text through various online services. Entries note the service carrying the text, the file acronym or number, and the date range of coverage. Separate sections list titles according to subject and database vendors, with telephone numbers and addresses.

HANDBOOKS AND YEARBOOKS

73. Berkman, Robert I. **Find It Fast: How to Uncover Expert Information on Any Subject.** Updated ed. New York, Harper & Row, 1990. 333p. $21.95; $9.95pa. ISBN 0-06-055194-1; 0-06-096486-3pa.

An excellent reference for researchers, *Find It Fast* offers practical advice on obtaining information across a broad range of topics, but primarily on business and current affairs. The work is arranged into two primary sections: the first describes libraries, government agencies, organizations, and industries; the second discusses how to find quick information directly from experts in a number of fields. This latter section includes suggestions on how to make contacts, how to interview people, how to evaluate information, and how to organize and write research reports. Two lengthy sample searches that walk the reader through the research process supplement the "how-to" sections.

74. **Guinness Book of World Records, [yr.].** Guinness; distr., New York, Facts on File, 1990- . Annual. 1v. illus. (part col.) index. $23.95 (1994 ed.). ISSN 1057-4557.

A standard ready-reference tool in all libraries, this Guinness handbook continues to offer a selective overview of records considered significant and/or interesting by the editors. The book is divided into 12 major areas: human beings, living world, natural world, universe and space, scientific world, arts and entertainment, world's structures, mechanical world, business world, human world, human achievements, and sports world.

The Guinness Book of Answers: The Complete Reference Handbook (Guinness; distr., New York, Facts on File, 1993, 800p., $21.95, ISBN 0-8160-3007-3) is another useful title in this series. Its 31 major groupings and their subgroupings are placed in random order, but both the table of contents and the index provide quick access to the material. The bulk of the text consists of dates, facts, figures, and other specific data on a wide array of topics. Although a strong British bias is evident, the handbook is nevertheless another useful addition to the Guinness family of publications.

75.   Kane, Joseph Nathan. **Famous First Facts: A Record of First Happenings, Discoveries, and Inventions in American History.** 4th ed. expanded and rev. Bronx, NY, H. W. Wilson, 1981. 1350p. index. $80.00. ISBN 0-8242-0661-4.

More than 9,000 firsts are identified in this ready-reference tool, including both natural events and human achievements. Facts are listed alphabetically under subject, with numerous cross references. The work is indexed by year, by day of the month, by personal name, and by state and city in which an event occurred.

A similar sort of work is Charles Panati's *The Browser's Book of Beginnings: Origins of Everything under (and Including) the Sun* (Houghton Mifflin, 1984, 427p., $9.95pa., ISBN 0-395-36099-4). Panati's book is organized topically, with one main theme for each of its 29 chapters. *Famous First Facts* has long been a key acquisition for the ready-reference desk; *The Browser's Book of Beginnings* should be considered a supplementary purchase.

76.   **Student Contact Book: How to Find Low-Cost, Expert Information on Today's Issues ... .** Detroit, Gale, 1993. 657p. index. $29.95pa. ISBN 0-8103-8876-6.

This handy guide is organized by topical chapters (for example, government and public affairs, social issues, and beliefs, cults, and sects). Each chapter includes a list of ideas for research subjects plus an alphabetically arranged listing of organizations and publications relevant to the topic. Entries note the organization's name, purpose, types of information provided (with brief annotations of books or serials), keywords, contact addresses, and telephone numbers. Access is through the table of contents, a listing of topics covered, and an index that includes organizations, agencies, publications, and subjects.

INDEXES

77.   **Access: The Supplementary Index to Periodicals.** Evanston, IL, John Gordon Burke Publisher, 1975- . 3 issues/yr.; annual cumulation. $157.50 (1994 ed.). ISSN 0095-5898.

The explosive growth in specialized, niche-market magazine publishing over the past decade has made *Access*, published since 1975, even more important in tracking articles in publications not yet indexed in the standard sources. The work focuses primarily on periodicals usually held by libraries; the main subject emphasis is on areas of popular interest such as the arts, entertainment, family life, hobbies, personal finance, sex, sports, and travel. Especially useful for its coverage of regional and city magazines. Also available online.

78.   **Bibliographic Index.** Bronx, NY, H. W. Wilson, 1938- . 3 issues/yr.; annual cumulation. Sold on service basis. ISSN 0006-1255.

Published annually since 1938, *Bibliographic Index* identifies published bibliographies in the Germanic and Romance languages, although most citations are to English-language materials. According to its editors, the index is intended to function as a "subject list of bibliographies published separately or appearing as parts of books, pamphlets, and periodicals." Selection is made from bibliographies that have 50 or more citations.

Although concise, the entries are clear and provide sufficient bibliographic detail to identify them completely. About 2,600 periodicals are scanned to unearth bibliographic material; readers are referred to Wilson's *Cumulative Book Index* for addresses of the publishers of the cited works. Also available online and on disk.

79. **Book Review Digest.** Bronx, NY, H. W. Wilson, 1905- . Monthly (except February and July). Sold on service basis. ISSN 0006-7326.

Book reviews found in about 80 British and American general-interest periodicals are indexed and frequently excerpted in this monthly publication. *Book Review Digest* covers books published or distributed in the United States; works of nonfiction must have received two or more reviews, and fiction four or more reviews, in the selected journals. More than 6,500 books are listed each year, giving for each: author, price, year of publication, publisher, Dewey decimal number, Sears subject headings, ISBN, descriptive note, excerpts reflecting the consensus of critical opinion, and citations for all reviews. Subject and title indexes conclude the digest. Also available online, on disk, on CD-ROM, and on magnetic tape.

80. **Book Review Index.** Detroit, Gale, 1965- . Bimonthly; annual cumulation. $210.00/yr. (1994 ed.). ISSN 0524-0581.

This index identifies book and periodical reviews (150,000 review citations for more than 80,000 titles in 1994) that appear in some 470 publications. The range of reviews indexed varies in length from one sentence to several pages. Entries note author's or editor's name, title under review, an abbreviation of the reviewing source, date and volume number of the source, page number, and a letter code identifying reference works, periodicals, or books for children and young adults. *BRI* is especially useful to the acquisitions librarian researching titles, patrons looking for reviews of specific works, or individuals tracking a book's critical reception. Many libraries who rely on its coverage also subscribe to Gale's related publication, *Children's Book Review Index* (bimonthly, $90.00/yr, ISSN 0147-5681). *Book Review Index* is also available online, on disk, and on magnetic tape.

81. **Essay and General Literature Index.** Bronx, NY, H. W. Wilson, 1934- . Semiannual; bound annual cumulation. $120.00/yr. (1994 ed.). ISSN 0014-083X.

This publication is familiar to scholars, teachers, librarians, and students for its thorough treatment of the humanities and social sciences. It has grown to index nearly 20,000 essays drawn from about 1,600 collections. Strongest in its coverage of "established" and widely recognized disciplines and topics, *Essay and General Literature Index* is also available in five-year cumulations. Authoritative and unique in its comprehensiveness, this work is considered a standard companion to Wilson's *Readers' Guide to Literature*. Also available online, on disk, on CD-ROM, and on magnetic tape.

82. **Facts on File: A Weekly Digest of World Events with Cumulative Index.** New York, Facts on File, 1940- . Weekly loose-leaf. $630.00/yr. (1994 ed.). ISSN 0014-6641.

A digest of and index to recent newsworthy occurrences, *Facts on File* summarizes on a weekly basis current events as reported by the major metropolitan newspapers. Arrangement is chronological (day-by-day) under general subject categories. The weekly digests are exhaustively indexed: semimonthly cumulative indexes, five-year indexes, and an annual yearbook cumulating weekly issues in one volume facilitate use of *Facts on File* as a research tool.

83. **Public Affairs Information Service Bulletin.** New York, Public Affairs Information Service, 1915- . Monthly. Sold on subscription basis. ISSN 0033-3409.

PAIS indexes English-language factual and statistical materials relating to contemporary public issues and the making and evaluation of public policy. It does not attempt to be comprehensive, but instead carefully selects materials (primarily from the extensive documents of the Economics and Public Affairs Division of the New York Public Library) that meet its criteria. International and interdisciplinary in scope, it indexes journals, books, pamphlets, government publications, and private and government reports in the areas of economics, political science, public administration, international relations, sociology and demography, business, finance, law, education, and social work.

84. **Readers' Guide to Periodical Literature.** Bronx, NY, H. W. Wilson, 1900- . Semimonthly, monthly in February, May, July, and August; bound annual cumulation. $190.00/yr. (1994 ed.). ISSN 0034-0464.

Readers' Guide has been commended for "providing quick access to the magazines that best mirror our culture," and it is probably the bibliographic index most familiar to students and the general public. It indexes articles from 240 general-interest, U.S.-published magazines by author, subject, and title. Title entries are provided for criticisms of individual works of drama, opera, ballet, and musical comedy; book reviews, arranged alphabetically by author, are included in a separate section of the index.

Libraries needing less extensive coverage in this area may wish to purchase instead Wilson's *Abridged Readers' Guide to Periodical Literature* ($95.00/yr. [1994 ed.], ISSN 0001-334X), which indexes 82 of the 240 titles included in the main publication, and follows the same format and publishing schedule. Another related publication that many libraries find useful is Wilson's relatively recent launch, *Readers' Guide Abstracts* (1988- , price varies by format, ISSN 0899-1553). This is an electronic-format abstracting service for all of the periodicals covered in the main index, although it is selective in which articles it abstracts. Selection is based on the "substantive nature of the article, its currency and topicality, its reference value, and its relevancy to school and college criteria" (from the preface). *Abstracts* annually covers about 67,000 articles, arranged alphabetically by subject, and includes a brief summary of each article. Available online, on disk, on CD-ROM, and on magnetic tape.

PERIODICALS AND SERIALS

85. Ganly, John V., and Diane M. Sciattara, eds. **Serials for Libraries: An Annotated Guide to Continuations, Annuals, Yearbooks, Almanacs, Transactions, Proceedings, Directories, Services.** 2d ed. New York, Neal-Schuman, 1985. 441p. index. $85.00. ISBN 0-918212-85-5.

Intended as a "reference tool for the selection, acquisition, and control of serials," *Serials for Libraries* has long been considered the complementary title to the Katzs' *Magazines for Libraries*. The 2,000 serials described are English-language titles available in the United States, published on an annual or other continuing basis (but not more often than once a year), and suitable for public, school, academic, and special libraries. The materials are arranged under five broad categories—general works, business, humanities, science, and social sciences—and then further subdivided into areas of special interest, such as banking and finance, chemistry, or sport and recreation. Entries include complete bibliographic information, audience level, where the volume is indexed, and brief descriptive annotations.

86. Katz, Bill, and Linda Sternberg Katz. **Magazines for Libraries.** 7th ed. New Providence, NJ, R. R. Bowker, 1992. 1212p. index. $139.95. ISBN 0-8352-3166-6.

Like previous editions, the seventh edition of this work aims to identify and describe 6,600 of "the best and most useful" magazines for elementary or secondary schools and public, academic, and special libraries. These periodicals cover 145 subject categories and range from scholarly publications to general-interest magazines. Entries are organized by subject and coded according to audience. Each subject section begins with a brief introduction, a list of core periodicals, and a list of basic indexes and abstracts for the subject area. In addition to the basic bibliographic data provided for each entry, the work also notes each title's purpose, scope, and audience.

Another publication on this topic sure to be of interest to librarians is Adeline Mercer Smith and Diane Rovena Jones's *Free Magazines for Libraries* (3d ed., McFarland, 1989, 228p., $19.95pa. ISBN 0-89950-389-6), a work that provides brief informative reviews of 500 free serial publications. Mostly "house magazines" published by corporations, associations, companies, or other sponsoring bodies, the items chosen are based on suitability, availability, and functional utility for libraries. Entries are arranged alphabetically under 62 categories, and include date of establishment, issuing agency or authority, complete bibliographical data, and review. For younger patrons, libraries will want to refer to Selma K. Richardson's American Library Association publication, *Magazines for Children: A Guide for Parents, Teachers, and Librarians* (1991, 139p., $25.00pa. ISBN 0-839-0552-8), and *Magazines for Young People* (Bill Katz and Linda Sternberg Katz, eds., R. R. Bowker, 1991, 361p., $34.95, ISBN 0-8352-3009-0). Both identify and knowledgeably describe a wide range of magazines appropriate to their target age groups.

87. Krol, John, ed. **Newsletters in Print.** 6th ed. Detroit, Gale, 1988- . Annual. 1v. index. $185.00 (1994 ed.). ISSN 0899-0422.

Previously known as the *National Directory of Newsletters and Reporting Services*, Krol's directory lists some 10,000 subscription, membership, and free newsletters, bulletins, digests, updates, and similar serial publications issued in the United States and Canada, and available in print or online. Entries are arranged under 7 broad categories further subdivided into 33 specific subjects. Topics covered include business and industry, family and everyday living, information and communications, community and world affairs, and science and technology, among others. Entries provide standard directory-type information (address, frequency, circulation, distribution, and primary readership) plus a brief description of each publication. Six indexes provide enhanced access: title and keyword, publisher, subject, newsletters available online, newsletters available free, and newsletters that accept advertising.

The main competitor to *Newsletters in Print* is the annual *Oxbridge Directory of Newsletters* (Oxbridge Communications, 1979- , annual, $345.00pa. [1994 ed.], ISSN 0163-7010). Formerly known as the *Standard Directory of Newsletters*, it covers some 20,000 newsletters in 167 subject areas, many of which are highly specialized. Entries provide standard contact information, although with somewhat briefer descriptive capsules than those offered by *Newsletters in Print*. The work is organized by subject; a title index provides rudimentary access. If cost is the primary consideration, the Gale publication is clearly the first choice; however, even if cost is not the primary consideration, most libraries will find that the 10,000 titles covered in *Newsletters in Print* more than meet the needs of their patrons.

88. The Standard Periodical Directory [yr.]. New York, Oxbridge Communications, 1963- . Annual. 1v. index. $495.00 (1994 ed.). ISSN 0085-6630.

The *Standard Periodical Directory (SPD)* has been a standard purchase for libraries since the mid-1960s. Its most recent edition contains information on 75,000 U.S. and Canadian periodicals arranged in 265 subject categories. (To qualify as a *periodical,* a publication must be issued at least once every two years.) Coverage includes magazines and journals of all kinds, as well as newsletters, newspapers, house organs, yearbooks, and transactions and proceedings of scientific societies.

How does this directory compare to its two main competitors, *Ulrich's International Periodicals Directory* and the *Gale Directory of Publications and Broadcast Media?* In addition to standard bibliographic data for each periodical described, *SPD* also provides brief annotations, which *Ulrich's* does not; however, *SPD* focuses only on the United States and Canada, whereas *Ulrich's* is international. *SPD* has a more generalist focus, of use to librarians and their patrons, than the *Gale Directory of Publications and Broadcast Media,* which strives to meet the more specialized needs of advertisers and those in related endeavors.

89. Uhlan, Miriam, and Doris B. Katz, eds. Guide to Special Issues and Indexes of Periodicals. 4th ed. Washington, DC, Special Libraries Association, 1994. 240p. index. $56.00. ISBN 0-87111-400-3.

The fourth edition of the SLA's handy reference tool provides access to the "specials" of more than 1,700 U.S. and Canadian periodicals and journals. Disciplines covered range from business, industry, science, and the arts to technology, specific professions, and consumer interests. Includes regional publications and online sources. A comprehensive index concludes the work.

90. Ulrich's International Periodicals Directory [yr.]: Including Irregular Serials and Annuals. New Providence, NJ, R. R. Bowker, 1932- . Annual. 5v. index. $395.00/set (1993–94 ed.). ISSN 0000-0175.

A standard purchase for all libraries, this five-volume set contains data on nearly 140,000 regularly and irregularly issued serials from 70,000 publishers in 200 countries. All regular, annual, and irregular series are cited except for newspapers of local scope or local interest, administrative publications of major scope or local interest, administrative publications of major government agencies below the state level, membership directories, comic books, and puzzle and game books. Entries include title, frequency of publication, publisher address, country code, and Dewey Decimal Classification number, as well as ISSN, variant titles or translated edition titles, price, and telephone/fax numbers when applicable and available. With the 1993–94 edition, *Ulrich's* began covering more than 2,000 daily, weekly, and specialized U.S. newspapers in its fifth volume. Separate indexes list 3,800 serials available online and 880 serials available on CD-ROM, 2,500 online vendors, title changes, and more than 6,500 refereed serials. Also available online, on CD-ROM, on magnetic tape, and on microfiche.

PROVERBS AND QUOTATIONS

91. Bartlett, John. Familiar Quotations: A Collection of Passages, Phrases and Proverbs Traced to Their Sources in Ancient and Modern Literature. 16th ed. Boston, Little, Brown, 1992. 1405p. index. $40.00. ISBN 0-316-08277-5.

The 17th edition of "Bartlett's," as it is widely known, identifies 20,000 quotations from some 2,550 individuals. As with previous editions, the phrases are

92. **The Oxford Dictionary of Quotations.** 4th ed. New York, Oxford University Press, 1992. 1061p. index. $35.00. ISBN 0-19-866185-1.

The Oxford Dictionary of Quotations and *Bartlett's* are considered by most librarians to be the first choices among quotation books. Unlike *Bartlett's*, which follows a chronological grouping arrangement, the *Dictionary of Quotations* is arranged alphabetically by author; coverage includes classical authors, the Bible, and strong representation of British notables. New to the fourth edition are quotations from hymns and songs. For non-English authors, quotations are given both in the original and in translation. Each author entry includes a brief biography summary that notes nationality, date of birth, and some designation of the person's chief area of importance. A comprehensive, detailed index concludes the work.

Oxford University Press follows a similar format and organization in its related title, *The Oxford Dictionary of Modern Quotations* (Tony Augarde, ed., 1991, 371p., $29.95, ISBN 0-19-866141-X), which encompasses authors active after 1900. Libraries relying on the main work will probably also want to have its more contemporary sibling on hand as well.

Although the works cited are the standard purchases for most libraries, there is a delightful wealth of books that give access to the recorded words and thoughts of humanity. Many are generalized, such as the excellent *Macmillan Dictionary of Quotations* (Macmillan, 1989, 790p., $35.00, ISBN 0-02-511931-1); *The Columbia Dictionary of Quotations* (Robert Andrews, ed., Columbia University Press, 1993, 1092p., $34.95, ISBN 0-231-07194-9), which is now also available online; and *The International Thesaurus of Quotations* (Rhoda Thomas Tripp, comp., Crowell, 1970, 1088p., $19.95, ISBN 0-690-44584-9). Many other wonderful works are quite specialized, though. These include *Respectfully Quoted: A Dictionary of Quotations Requested from the Congressional Research Service* (Congressional Research Service, Library of Congress, 1989, 520p., $29.00, ISBN 0-8444-0538-8); Leonard Safire and William Safire's *Good Advice* (Wings Books, 1992, 400p., $9.99, ISBN 0-517-08473-2) and *Words of Wisdom: More Good Advice* (Simon & Schuster, 1990, 432p., $12.00pa, ISBN 0-671-69587-8); Frank S. Pepper's *The Wit and Wisdom of the 20th Century: A Dictionary of Quotations* (Peter Bedrick, 1987, 406p., $19.95pa, ISBN 0-87226-165-4); Wesley D. Camp's *What a Piece of Work Is Man! Camp's Unfamiliar Quotations from 2000 B.C. to the Present* (Prentice-Hall, 1990, 470p., $12.95pa, ISBN 0-13-952102-X); and the ever-delightful *Portable Curmudgeon* (Jon Winokur, comp., NAL-Dutton, 1992, 320p., $9.00pa, ISBN 0-452-26668-8.). As they say, one can never be too rich nor have too many quotation books.

arranged in chronological groupings, and then alphabetically by individual within groups. Indexed by individual name and keyword, this is perhaps one of the world's most well-known and beloved reference books. A must purchase for all libraries, regardless of size.

Part II
SOCIAL SCIENCES

2

Area Studies

GENERAL WORKS

93. **Countries of the World and Their Leaders Yearbook [yr.]: A Compilation of U.S. Department of State Reports ...** . Detroit, Gale, 1974- . Annual. 2v. illus. maps. $160.00/set (1994 ed.). ISSN 0196-2809.

This standard resource is meant to provide quick information for students, business people, and travelers. Covering 168 countries, its information is based on the U.S. State Department's "Background Notes on the Countries of the World." Reports range from 4 to 20 pages and typically cover such information as government officials and politicians, geography, peoples, defense, agriculture and trade, climate, and so forth. A separate "Travel Notes" section describes customs and immigration requirements, available telephone and telegraphy services, local transportation, and national holidays. A special section of official U.S. advisories to travelers includes information on passport applications, regulations on duties, international health and disease, and instructions on avoiding political dangers. Most—but not all—information is current and reliable. A detailed table of contents facilitates access to this handy two-volume set.

94. **The Europa World Year Book [yr.]**. London, Europa; distr., Detroit, Gale, 1959- . Annual. 2v. $580.00/set (1994 ed.). ISSN 0956-2273.

Formerly titled *Europa Yearbook*, *Europa World Year Book* offers authoritative, comprehensive coverage of the state of more than 200 of the world's nations. The first volume is essentially a contact directory for more than 1,600 international organizations, noting address, purpose, membership, finances, publications, and the like for each. The second volume features individual profiles of the world's nations. For each it provides an introductory survey (location, climate, language, religion, flag, capital, government, defense, economic affairs, social welfare, education, public holidays, weights and measures, recent history); a statistical survey (area and population, agriculture, forestry, fishing, mining, industry, finance, external trade, transport, tourism, communications media, education); and a directory (constitution, government, political organizations, diplomatic representation, judicial system, religion, press, publishers, radio and television, finance, trade and industry, transport, tourism, and atomic energy), as applicable for each country.

Although *The Europa World Year Book* is appropriately considered the primary resource in this subject area, its cost may be prohibitive for some small libraries. In this case, two reasonably priced alternatives to consider are *The Henry Holt International Desk Reference: A Guide to Essential Information Resources of the World's Major Trading Nations* (Gary McClain, ed., Henry Holt, 1992, 606p., $39.95, ISBN 0-8050-1852-2) and *World Economic Data* (Timothy S. O'Donnell, ed., ABC-Clio, 1991, $40.00, ISBN 0-87436-658-5, ISSN 0891-4125). Organized by region and within region by country, the Holt title covers 63 "major trading nations," providing for each about 8 pages of organizations and publications that provide useful information on that nation's business, politics, culture, or education. Types of resources include associations, institutes, societies, newsletters, directories, government publications, and books. *World Economic Data*, in contrast, provides a broad overview of current economic data for 171 countries. It is organized to facilitate economic comparisons between two or more countries, with text divided into data from countries of the world (225 pages) and data concerned with U.S. indicators. A good glossary and a bibliography conclude the guide.

95. Kurian, George Thomas. **Encyclopedia of the First World**. New York, Facts on File, 1990. 2v. illus. maps. index. $145.00/set. ISBN 0-8160-1233-4. **Encyclopedia of the Second World**. 1991. 614p. illus. maps. index. $95.00/set. ISBN 0-8160-1232-6. **Encyclopedia of the Third World**. 4th ed. New York, Facts on File, 1991. 3v. illus. maps. index. $225.00/set. ISBN 0-8160-2261-5.

Now in its fourth iteration, Kurian's *Encyclopedia of the Third World* is the best known of this group of books. A comprehensive treatment of Third World regions and nations, it covers a wealth of detailed information not available in more generalized sources such as *Europa World Year Book*. For purposes of this work, Kurian has defined the *Third World* as "the politically unaligned and economically developing and less industrialized nations of the world." The information provided for each of the 124 countries treated includes a basic fact sheet, location and area, population, ethnic composition, religion, constitution and government, economy, a post-1944 chronology, political parties, and other relevant information. Statistical information is presented in tabular form, making it easy to access and analyze. As in previous editions, a black-and-white map and national emblem are also provided for each country.

The second entry in this group, *Encyclopedia of the First World*, covers the OECD (Organization for Economic Cooperation and Development) countries (except Turkey), Israel, South Africa, and Cyprus—26 countries in all. Abbreviated entries are given for six European mini-states, from Andorra to Vatican City. Major entries range from 18 pages for Luxembourg to 144 for the United States. The most recent publication, *Encyclopedia of the Second World*, describes what were the major socialist countries of the world: the Soviet Union, China, Albania, Mongolia, and the formerly socialist nations of Eastern Europe. (Coverage is current through mid-1990.) Both volumes present information in a format, breadth, and depth similar to that of *Encyclopedia of the Third World*.

96. Sachs, Moshe Y., ed. **Worldmark Encyclopedia of the Nations**. 7th ed. New York, Worldmark Press; distr., New York, John Wiley, 1988. 5v. maps. index. $415.00/set. ISBN 0-471-62406-3.

The goal of this well-known work is to provide factual information and statistical data about the geographical, historical, political, social, and economic statuses of all nations; their international relationships; and the United Nations system. The first volume focuses solely on the UN: its structure and role, programs affecting major issues, and subsidiary organizations and their functions. The remaining four volumes are organized alphabetically by country within continents. Entries range in length from just over 1 to about 32 pages, depending on the importance of the country being discussed. There are many useful illustrations and maps, but no indexes.

97. Showers, Victor. **World Facts and Figures.** 3d ed. New York, John Wiley, 1989. 721p. illus. index. $97.50. ISBN 0-471-85775-0.

This compilation of statistics on world geographic and cultural features provides a good complement to the more generalized world yearbooks. It features comparative rankings of country characteristics in 45 categories, including commerce, transportation, communication, and education. Some 2,644 cities are comparatively ranked as well. Noted for its sensible arrangement, comprehensive detail, and thorough indexing.

UNITED STATES

98. Sachs, Moshe Y., and others, eds. **Worldmark Encyclopedia of the States.** 2d ed. New York, Worldmark Press; distr., New York, John Wiley, 1986. 690p. illus. maps. $120.00. ISBN 0-471-83213-8.

A companion to the same publisher's *Worldmark Encyclopedia of the Nations*, this one-volume encyclopedia provides a useful overview of the demographic, economic, historical, political, and social characteristics of each of the 50 states, Puerto Rico, and the District of Columbia, as well as the U.S. Caribbean and the Pacific dependencies. The material is organized by state; within each state's section, 50 subject headings provide a standard framework that facilitates state-by-state comparisons. Supplementary materials include brief (and often out-of-date) bibliographies that conclude each state's essay, a generous number of black-and-white maps, numerous tables that clarify statistical information, and appendixes that treat topics such as U.S. presidents, abbreviations, and metric conversions.

AFRICA

99. Moroney, Sean, ed. **Africa.** Rev. ed. New York, Facts on File, 1989. 2v. maps. index. $110.00. ISBN 0-8160-1623-2.

Three sections constitute this set. In the first, brief chapters on each African country describe geography, population, political system, history, economy, social welfare, and mass media, and provide biographical sketches and a political map. In the second, there are comparative statistics, based largely on World Bank numbers, on economics, demographics, and social factors. Essays on political, economic, and social affairs written by subject experts make up the third section. A detailed, 70-page index by subject and personal name concludes *Africa*.

There are a number of good resources for information about Africa, and libraries will need to determine which might best suit their needs in terms of patron interest and budget priorities. Two works many libraries are likely to already have on hand—*Europa World Year Book* (entry 94) and *Statesman's Year-Book* (entry 411)—offer reliable, basic coverage of all African nations. Europa Publications' two regional annuals, *Africa South of the Sahara* (1971- , $295.00 [1994 ed.], ISSN 0065-3896) and *The Middle East and North Africa* (1948- , $280.00 [1994 ed.], ISSN 0076-8502) offer excellent, in-depth analyses of each country as well as directory sections with names and addresses of organizations, universities, and publication. (However, with the exception of the topical essays, material presented in these regional spin-offs duplicates that found in *Europa World Year Book*.)

ASIA

General Works

100. **The Far East and Australasia [yr.].** London, Europa Publications; distr., Detroit, Gale, 1969– . Annual. 1v. $320.00 (1994 ed.). ISSN 0071-3791.

An expansion of the coverage provided for this region in the *Europa World Year Book*, *The Far East and Australasia* is divided into three main parts. The first contains several topical overviews of key issues and events, whereas the second provides concise descriptions of regional organizations. The third section, which makes up the bulk of the work, comprises country-specific surveys that include sections on geography, history, and economics, as well as detailed statistical tables, a directory of organizations and addresses, and a selective bibliography. The country surveys, ranging in length from a few pages to more than 60 depending on the relative importance of the country, have been written by respected Asian-affairs scholars. Detailed, accurate, and current, the information provided in this handbook will be welcomed by libraries for which the coverage of this region in the *Europa World Year Book* is not sufficiently extensive.

101. Robinson, Francis, ed. **The Cambridge Encyclopedia of India, Pakistan, Bangladesh, Sri Lanka, Nepal, Bhutan and the Maldives.** New York, Cambridge University Press, 1989. 520p. illus. maps. index. $55.00. ISBN 0-521-33451-9.

This encyclopedic treatment of South Asia covers history, geography, art, architecture, literature, religion, politics, and many other topics relevant to the region. Written by subject specialists, all entries are current, thorough, and readable (words and phrases assumed to be unfamiliar to the general reader are explained throughout). In addition, the work is beautifully illustrated with numerous high-quality maps, photographs, charts, and tables, many of which are in color. A well-executed encyclopedia of value to the lay reader as well as to the scholar.

102. Taylor, Robert H., ed **Asia and the Pacific.** New York, Facts on File, 1991. 2v. maps. index. $125.00/set. ISBN 0-8160-1622-4.

Including coverage of Australia, New Zealand, and the Pacific Island states, *Asia and the Pacific* is a useful compendium of short, country-specific articles that summarize politics and government, social services, educational programs, and mass media; short biographical sketches of country leaders; and longer articles by subject specialists on the special characteristics and issues relative to each country. In addition, there are tables of comparative statistics, as well as authoritative survey articles on regional political, economic, and social affairs. Black-and-white maps that delineate boundaries, resources, precipitation, and vegetation accompany each country's profile. A comprehensive index concludes this excellent publication.

China

103. Blunden, Caroline, and Mark Elvin. **Cultural Atlas of China.** New York, Facts on File, 1983. 237p. illus. (part col.). maps. bibliog. index. $45.00. ISBN 0-87196-132-6.

A highly readable account of China's cultural history from ancient through contemporary times, this work is organized to approach Chinese history from three perspectives: space, time, and symbols and society. The space section provides information on the land and its people. The time section covers the archaic world and its people. The section on symbols and society addresses important aspects of Chinese culture, from language to arts, to medicine, to family life, and to the reciprocal interaction of China and the West. Supplementary materials include well-executed maps and illustrations, a chronological table, a bibliography (annotated and grouped by broad subject), a gazetteer, and an index. Useful to students and scholars as well as to the general reader.

104. Hook, Brian, and Dennis Twitchett, eds. **The Cambridge Encyclopedia of China.** 2d ed. New York, Cambridge University Press, 1991. 502p. illus. (part col.). maps. index. $55.00. ISBN 0-521-355940-X.

Similar to other regional volumes in this series, *The Cambridge Encyclopedia of China* provides an excellent one-volume overview of all aspects of China's geography, natural resources, economy, communications, growth planning, and political structures, as well as of its history and traditional culture. It is strongest in its coverage of modern China. Contents are arranged into seven broad subject areas—land and resources, peoples, society, the continuity of China, mind and senses, art and architecture, and science and technology from a historical perspective—and then further subdivided into short entries on specific aspects of topics. The encyclopedia is generously illustrated with beautifully executed photographs, maps, tables, charts, and drawings; eight appendixes, suggestions for further reading, a brief glossary, and a less-than-terrific index conclude the volume. Despite the weakness of the index, this is an extremely good source for information on modern China.

For more recent coverage of China by the same publisher, libraries may also wish to consider Colin Mackerras and Amanda Yorke's *The Cambridge Handbook of Contemporary China* (1991, 266p., $22.95pa., ISBN 0-521-38755-8), which deals primarily with events of the 1980s in China. Coverage encompasses reference sources, politics, foreign relations, economics, education, population, minorities, culture, and society. A separate section presents a chronology of major events from 1900 to April 1990, biographies of eminent persons (both living and dead), an annotated bibliography, and a gazetteer.

Japan

105. Bowring, Richard, and Peter Kornicki, eds. **The Cambridge Encyclopedia of Japan.** New York, Cambridge University Press, 1993. 400p. illus. maps. index. $55.00. ISBN 0-521-40352-9.

The information presented here is grouped into eight categories: geography, history, language, thought and religion, arts and crafts, society, politics, and the economy. Within these categories, materials are further subdivided into about 10 topical areas that treat, for example, such things as Japan's physical structure, climate, education, family, judicial system, cinema, products, foreign policy, and important historical figures. Supplementary materials include a list of recommended readings by category; full-color and black-and-white photographs, illustrations, and maps; a brief glossary; and a good index.

A reliable alternative for libraries that are unable to afford the Cambridge work is Passport's *Japan Almanac* (Boye De Mente, ed., Passport Books/National Textbook, 1987, 319p., $17.95pa., ISBN 0-8442-8508-0). Arranged in a dictionary-style format, this almanac covers general cultural and historical subjects, including people, places, events, and everyday information (Japan's telephone area codes, the

106. Collcutt, Martin, Marius Jansen, and Isao Kumakura. **Cultural Atlas of Japan.** New York, Facts on File, 1988. 240p. illus. (part col.). maps, bibliog. index. $45.00. ISBN 0-8160-1927-4.

This work covers Japan's geography, archaeology, anthropology, and culture. The culture materials are organized by historical periods and include court and economic life, politics, institutions, religion, art, architecture, gardens, theater, and relations with foreign countries. Prehistoric through contemporary times are covered. Supplementary materials include excellent color photographs, informative and clear maps, a basic bibliography, a list of Japanese rulers, a glossary, a list of illustrations, a gazetteer, and an index. An excellent survey work at a reasonable price.

107. **Japan: An Illustrated Encyclopedia.** Tokyo, Kodansha; distr., New York, Macmillan, 1993. 2v. illus. maps. index. $250.00/set. ISBN 4-06-931098-3.

The stated purpose of this two-volume successor to the nine-volume *Kodansha Encyclopedia of Japan* (1983) is to introduce Japanese history and culture to an international audience. The scope of its brief, well-written articles is broad, covering all aspects of Japanese life, including history, geography, science, technology, folklore, business, and leisure. Some 100 feature articles and pictorial studies dealing with such topics as the place of women in Japan, bonsai trees, and Japanese management techniques, are interspersed with the main entries, as are more than 4,000 color photographs, illustrations, charts, and graphs. Other enhancements include a 16-page atlas (with its own index), a 17-page illustrated chronology of Japanese history, a 13-page subject-arranged bibliography, a bilingual index to entry titles, and a classified guide that groups article titles in a general-to-specific arrangement.

CANADA

108. **Associations Canada: An Encyclopedic Directory.** Toronto, Canadian Almanac & Directory; distr., Detroit, Gale, 1992. 1200p. index. $175.00. ISBN 1-895021-07-3.

Drawn from *Canadian Almanac & Directory* (entry 109), *Associations Canada* provides addresses and descriptions of approximately 20,000 associations (nongovernmental membership organizations; research institutes; chambers of commerce; labor, social planning, arts, and business councils; native friendship and crisis intervention centers; social service agencies; self-help groups; faculty associations; and foundations) as well as information on their conventions and conferences. The second edition also offers essays on nonprofit organizations in Canada, association management, and brief statistics about giving and volunteering in Canada. In addition to its subject index, the directory includes two very helpful access points: a geographic index classified by province and city and a subject-organized index for serial publications.

The primary difference between this publication and its major competitor, *Directory of Associations in Canada* (Micromedia, 1973- , annual, $199.00, ISSN 0316-0734), is that *Associations Canada* provides information on convention planning, a list of association publications by title, and an executive name index.

However, for the most part the two publications complement rather than duplicate each other, so libraries that can afford to do so may want to purchase both.

109. **Canadian Almanac & Directory [yr.].** Toronto, Copp Clark Pitman; distr., Detroit, Gale, 1947- . Annual. 1v. index. $145.00 (1994 ed.). ISSN 0068-8193.

Canadian Almanac offers a less expensive alternative to *Corpus Almanac* (entry 112), as it provides much (though not all) of the same information found in its two-volume competitor. *Canadian Almanac* provides names and addresses of financial institutions, libraries, museums, radio and television stations, boards of education, and universities and colleges, among many others. Information on municipalities, forms of address, flags and badges, and lawyers in private practice is also included. Unfortunately, the index is less thorough and helpful than it might be. Otherwise, this handy and useful work provides a good alternative to the more expensive (and extensive) *Corpus Almanac.*

110. Colombo, John Robert, ed. **The Canadian Global Almanac [yr.]: A Book of Facts.** Toronto, Macmillan Canada, 1991- . Annual. 1v. maps. index. $14.95pa. (1994 ed.). ISSN 1187-4570.

Originally published in 1987 as *Canadian World Almanac and Book of Facts,* this annual's three sections provide information about Canada, international information, and facts about Canadian arts, entertainment, sports, and news events. A quick reference section offers lists and charts for first aid, weights and measures, and travel; the previous year's obituaries and news events are summarized in a concluding section. A thorough index further enhances the usefulness of this information-packed book. Although Canadian coverage is emphasized, the breadth of international coverage included makes this a competitive alternative to such familiar titles as *The World Almanac and Book of Facts* (entry 2) and *Information Please Almanac* (entry 3).

111. Simpson, Kieran, ed. **Canadian Who's Who [yr.].** Toronto and Buffalo, NY, University of Toronto Press, 1910- . Annual. 1v. $165.00 (1994 ed.). ISSN 0068-9963.

This standard biographical reference source profiles more than 11,000 individuals who have made a major contribution to Canadian life. In addition to descriptions of career activities and accomplishments, entries provide an overview of occupational, family, and educational information, as well as noting memberships, interests, and home/office addresses when available. A list of abbreviations in French and English concludes the volume.

112. Sova, Gordon, ed. **Corpus Almanac & Sourcebook, [yr.].** Don Mills, Ontario, Corpus Information Services, 1965- . Annual. 1v. illus. maps. index. $157.50/set (1994 ed.). ISSN 0823-1133.

For American libraries needing current information about their northern neighbor, the well-organized and reliable *Corpus* is probably the first choice, with the *Canadian Almanac & Directory* a close second. *Corpus* provides general information on Canadian life, including current events, business and commerce, public and national affairs, communications, population and demographic trends, and relevant data and statistics, as well as information on the workings, programs, and organization of all levels of Canadian government, including intergovernmental agencies. It also provides coverage of election results. Indexed by subject and by associations.

113. Stamp, Robert M. **The Canadian Obituary Record [yr.]: A Biographical Dictionary of Canadians ... .** Toronto, Dundurn Press, 1988- . Annual. 1v. index. $39.99 (1994 ed.). No ISSN available.

The *Canadian Obituary Record* provides interpretive biographies, ranging in length from 100 to 800 words, of 500 Canadians prominent in all fields of endeavor and all parts of the country who died during the previous year. Each biography concludes with source citations (mostly to newspapers and reference books). A geographical index, arranged by province and then city, includes places of birth and death and major work activity. The identification index uses 19 subcategories, many further subdivided. A three-year, cumulative nominal index concludes the *Record*.

EASTERN EUROPE AND THE COMMONWEALTH OF INDEPENDENT STATES

114. **Eastern Europe and the Commonwealth of Independent States [yr.].** Detroit, Omnigraphics, 1992- . Annual. 1v. maps. $390.00 (1994 ed.). ISSN 0962-1040.

An overview of regional issues (nationalism, international relations, etc.) leads off this annual, which then moves into country-specific chapters treating such topics as geography, history, statistics, government and politics, religion, the media, culture and education, business and finance, and the environment. Coverage for the East European countries is a bit briefer than that afforded the Commonwealth countries. A biographical dictionary profiling some 175 prominent political figures follows the main text. In addition, there are an outline of headings used, a list of full-page maps, a key to abbreviations, and updated information on government figures. Unfortunately, there is no index.

115. Geron, Leonard, and Alex Pravda, eds. **Who's Who in Russia and the New States.** London, I.J. Tauris; distr., New York, St. Martin's Press, 1993. 1v. (unpaged). $185.00. ISBN 1-85043-487-5.

This book is divided into two main parts. In the first, country entries (for Armenia, Azerbaijan, Belarus, Estonia, Georgia, Kazakhstan, Kyrgyzstan, Latvia, Lithuania, Moldova, the Russian Federation, Tajikistan, Turkmenistan, Ukraine, and Uzbekistan) list heads of state, key government officials, and other relevant political information. The second part profiles some 7,000 significant public figures drawn preponderantly from politics, government, and military service, but also including managers, historians, clergy, cosmonauts, engineers, physicists, physicians, ballet dancers, composers, and writers as well. Entries vary in length based on the prominence of the individual, but usually include full name and occupation; family information; education and career history; lists of publications, affiliations, and honors; address; and telephone, telex, and fax numbers. Although expensive, this is a unique and valuable resource for those needing information in this area.

GREAT BRITAIN

116. Gascoigne, Bamber. **Encyclopedia of Britain.** New York, Macmillan, 1993. 720p. illus. maps. $75.00. ISBN 0-02-897142-6.

Intended as a guide to general knowledge about the past and present of Great Britain, Gascoigne's compendium contains 6,000 brief entries ranging in length from perhaps 20 to several hundred words. The well-written, alphabetically arranged entries encompass people, places, events, and institutions from British history, politics, religion, science, and culture, both high- and low-brow. The text is supplemented by numerous color and black-and-white photographs and illustrations, and enhanced through generous use of cross references. Although other references (most notably the *Cambridge Illustrated Dictionary of British Heritage* [1986, 484p., $42.95, ISBN 0-521-30214-5] and the *Dictionary of Britain* [Oxford University Press, 1986, $29.95, $8.95pa., ISBN 0-19211662-2; 0-19-283056-2pa.]) address similar materials, this volume is both more current and broader in its coverage.

LATIN AMERICA

117. Camp, Roderic A. **Who's Who in Mexico Today.** 2d ed. Boulder, CO, Westview Press, 1993. 197p. $65.00. ISBN 0-8133-8452-4.

This helpful biographical source on noteworthy living Mexicans describes the lives of just over 400 entrepreneurial, cultural, military, political, religious, and social leaders. Women, prominent members of the clergy, and opposition political leaders (left and right) are included. Entries are alphabetical by biographees' names, and provide date and place of birth, schooling or educational background, elective political offices (if any), political party offices or candidacies for elective office, appointive government posts, leadership of any national interest group, private sector positions in Mexico or elsewhere, familial ties and important professional and personal friendships, military activities (if any), national awards and prizes, and additional sources of information. A very useful resource for libraries where there is a strong interest in this vital and changing country.

118. Collier, Simon, Harold Blakemore, and Thomas E. Skidmore, eds. **The Cambridge Encyclopedia of Latin America and the Caribbean.** 2d ed. New York, Cambridge University Press, 1992. 479p. illus. (part col.). maps. index. $55.00. ISBN 0-521-41322-2.

Originally published in 1985, this encyclopedia covers Mexico, Central and South America, and the Caribbean area (including the non-Latin Caribbean). Its brief articles are arranged topically under six major headings: "The Physical Environment," "The Economy," "The Peoples," "History," "Politics and Society," and "Culture." For the most part, articles do not focus on particular countries, although emphasis is given to the largest or most newsworthy ones. Very concise (two to eight titles) bibliographies accompany each entry, and the text is supplemented by roughly 50 maps; various tables, charts, and graphs; and numerous photographs of people and places. An excellent introduction to this important geographic region.

119. **South America, Central America, and the Caribbean [yr.].** London, Europa Publications; distr., Detroit, Gale, 1987- . Annual. 1v. $295.00 (1994 ed.). ISSN 0258-1661.

South America follows the format adhered to in the other excellent annuals in this Europa World Year Book series. The first section starts off with a series of eight background essays (for example, economic problems, ecology and land use in Amazonian forests, sovereignty in the Caribbean), followed by a list of major research institutes and Latin American periodicals, and an overview of the important commodities of the region. The largest section comprises a country-by-country survey of the 48 entities that make up the region. A separate section is devoted to coverage of important regional organizations. With the exception of brief introductory surveys for 24 of the countries, the information is essentially what would be found in *Europa World Year Book*. Consequently, libraries that already own the main publication will want to consider whether they have sufficient need (and budget) to justify purchasing this specialized work.

MIDDLE EAST

120. Brawer, Moshe, ed. **Atlas of the Middle East.** New York, Macmillan, 1988. 140p. maps. index. $70.00. ISBN 0-02-905271-8.

The Middle East, for the purposes of this work, comprises Bahrain, Cyprus, Egypt, Iran, Israel, Jordan, Kuwait, Lebanon, Libya, Oman, Qatar, Saudi Arabia, South Yemen, Sudan, Syria, Turkey, United Arab Emirates, and Yemen. (Algeria, Tunisia, and Morocco are excluded.) Both physical and thematic maps are included, with thematic maps covering climate, land use, ethnicity, religion, political conflict, and trade and commerce. Supplementary materials include regional overviews, a list of recommended readings, and an index.

121. **The Middle East and North Africa [yr.].** London, Europa; dist., Detroit, Gale, 1948- . Annual. 1v. maps. $295.00 (1994 ed.). ISSN 0076-8502.

Another of the *Europa World Year Book* spin-off publications, this work reflects the high quality of its parent publication, as it provides clear, concise historical background and current information for the 24 nations that constitute the Middle East and North Africa. It follows the three-part organization of its sister annuals. Part 1 offers a general survey of major themes and issues, and each of its articles includes an overview of the topic at hand, maps, and statistical data where appropriate. Part 2 describes the international and regional organizations pertinent to this region, including for each organization general directory information; member states; and agency organization, purpose, and activities. The final section provides country-by-country overviews of geography, history, economy, and statistics, led off by an introductory essay and wrapped up with a brief, almanac-type listing of such information as diplomatic representation, judicial system, religion, radio and television, and so forth. A highly useful work, although much of it duplicates what is already available (though in less focused form) in *Europa World Year Book*.

122. Mostyn, Trevor, and Albert Hourani, eds. **The Cambridge Encyclopedia of the Middle East and North Africa.** New York, Cambridge University Press, 1988. 504p. illus. (part col.). maps. index. $59.95. ISBN 0-521-32190-5.

This encyclopedia provides a general, comprehensive introduction to the history, society, and culture of a region spreading west to east from Morocco to Afghanistan, and north to south from Turkey to Djibouti and Somalia. Its six parts address lands and peoples; history (from the ancient Near East to the arrival of the modern era, as designated by the commencement of World War II); societies and economies (changes in the areas of agriculture, banking, industry, energy production, society, education, and communications); culture (religion, languages, literature, the arts, music and dance, and Islmaic science and medicine); the countries (current circumstances and recent developments); and interstate relations (for example, the influence of the major world powers in the Middle East, international Islamic movements and institutions, relations among the various Arab nations, and the Iran-Iraq war). A detailed index concludes the encyclopedia.

123. Shimoni, Yaacov. **Biographical Dictionary of the Middle East.** New York, Facts on File, 1991. 255p. illus. maps. $40.00. ISBN 0-8160-2458-8.

Twentieth-century individuals who have played significant roles in countries ranging from Morocco in the west to Iran in the east and from Turkey and Cyprus in the north to Yemen and Oman in the south are profiled in Shimoni's handy biographical resource. The 500 short biographies include rulers, party leaders, government heads, religious figures, and military leaders, as well as (to a lesser degree) writers and artists. Biographies contain standard information such as birthplace, education, and employment, and also place the individuals within the political context in which they lived. Separate sections list the Arab and Israeli delegates to the 1992 Madrid Peace Conference, present seven pages of maps, and provide tables of the Hashemite dynasty and the Egyptian ruling family.

Although the Facts on File title will prove quite sufficient for the needs of most small libraries, if more coverage is needed libraries may want to consider *Who's Who in the Arab World [yr.]* (Gabriel M. Bustros, ed., Publitec; distr., Gale, 1971- , annual, $280.00 [1993–1994 ed.], ISSN 0083-9752), which provides 6,000 biographical sketches of major personalities and political figures from 20 countries in the Arab world.

3

Economics and Business

GENERAL WORKS

Atlases

124. **Rand McNally Commercial Atlas & Marketing Guide.** Skokie, IL, Rand McNally, 1876- . Annual. 1v. (various paging). (col.). maps. index. $325.00 (1994 ed.). ISSN 0361-9723.

The *Commercial Atlas & Marketing Guide* has been a mainstay in the business reference section of public libraries for years, because of its wealth of reliable, well-organized information. Focusing on the United States but also including some Canadian data, the six sections of this large (15 by 21 inches) guide are: metropolitan area maps, transportation and communication data, economic data, population data, state maps, and a U.S. index. Map indexes profile more than 128,000 cities, counties, towns, and villages, noting such key factors as location, railroads, airlines, elevation, population, hospitals, and prisons. A valuable, if costly, resource.

Bibliographies

125. Daniells, Lorna M. **Business Information Sources.** 4th ed. Berkeley, CA, University of California Press, 1993. 744p. index. $35.00. ISBN 0-520-08180-3.

The purpose of Daniells's well-known reference is to serve as a general orientation source for business students, those actively engaged in business, and the librarians who assist them. Twenty chapters describe (rather than evaluate, for the most part) a wealth of business resources in such areas as management, international business, marketing, investments, finance and accounting, and industry statistics and trends. Sources are organized topically (for example, U.S. business and economic trends or management). Within topical chapters, texts, handbooks, periodicals, indexes, online materials, and similar types of resources are presented within subject subdivisions. A recommended purchase for all libraries regardless of size.

126. Geahigan, Priscilla C., and Robert F. Rose, eds. **Business Serials of the U.S. Government.** 2d ed. Chicago, Business Reference and Services Section, American Library Association, 1988. 86p. index. $10.00. ISBN 0-8389-3349-1.

A selective, annotated bibliography of 183 titles, *Business Serials* covers general sources, economic conditions, demographics, international business, agriculture, the environment, labor, small business, patents, government contracts, public finance, taxation, and consumers, as well as 15 specific industries. Handbooks, journals, pamphlets, and loose-leaf services are selectively included. Title and subject indexes round out the work.

127.   Strauss, Diane Wheeler. **Handbook of Business Information: A Guide for Librarians, Students, and Researchers.** Englewood, CO, Libraries Unlimited, 1988. 537p. illus. index. $42.00. ISBN 0-87287-607-1.

According to its author, the purpose of this work is to "give librarians, students, and other researchers a grounding in business basics and to identify, describe, and in many instances illustrate the use of key information sources." The materials are arranged in two parts. Part 1, "Formats of Business Information," comprises chapters devoted to basic business sources, directories, periodicals and newspapers, loose-leaf services, government information and services, statistics, vertical file collections, and electronic business information. Part 2, "Fields of Business Information," is organized into nine specific industry categories, such as credit and banking or stocks. The annotations are supplemented by 150 illustrations; 12 appendixes and an extensive author/title/subject index conclude the work.

128.   Woy, James, ed. **Encyclopedia of Business Information Sources: A Bibliographic Guide to Approximately 20,000 Citations ... .** 10th ed. Detroit, Gale, 1994. 1600p. $245.00. ISSN 0071-0210.

Arranged alphabetically by more than 1,100 subjects, the *Encyclopedia of Business Information Sources* identifies about 21,000 sources deemed useful in tracking down specific types of business and finance information. These include print materials such as bibliographies, dictionaries, encyclopedias, directories, and periodicals, as well as online databases, statistics sources, trade associations, professional societies, and other nonprint sources. Abstracts are provided for some of the entries, but not in any consistent manner. Access to the material is provided by an "Outline of Contents" located at the front of the publication. Recommended for its ability to bring together a substantial amount of valuable information in a single volume. Also available on disk and on magnetic tape.

Biographies

129.   Blaug, Mark. **Great Economists before Keynes: An Introduction to the Lives & Works of One Hundred Great Economists ... .** New York, Cambridge University Press, 1989. 286p. illus. index. $19.95pa. ISBN 0-521-36741-7. **Great Economists since Keynes: An Introduction to the Lives & Works of One Hundred Modern Economists.** New York, Cambridge University Press, 1989. 280p. illus. index. $19.95pa. ISBN 0-521-36742-5.

These works both follow a similar format and adhere to equally high standards of information and presentation. Each of the 200 entries offers a biographical profile, a historical setting of the period in which the economist worked (or works), the economic problems of the day, the contributions of the economist to the solution of these problems, impact on other writers, schools of thought, and the overall development of economics. Most entries also include a portrait of the individual being profiled. Taken together, these two works represent a thorough and accessible overview of the history of economic thought as well as those who have influenced it.

130. Ingham, John N., and Lynne B. Feldman. **Contemporary American Business Leaders: A Biographical Dictionary.** Westport, CT, Greenwood Press, 1990. 788p. index. $105.50. ISBN 0-313-25743-4.

The 150 American business leaders profiled in this highly selective biographical dictionary were chosen because of their "historically significant" involvement in key business developments and trends occurring in the United States since World War II. Usually several pages long, entries are organized alphabetically and conclude with a bibliography of materials by and about the individual profiled. Complementing the biographical profiles are appendixes that list individuals by industry, company, place of business, and place of birth; a brief list of contemporary black and female business leaders; and an index that includes personal, company, and product names.

Where there is strong patron interest (and an accommodating budget), libraries may also wish to purchase Ingham's earlier work, the four-volume *Biographical Dictionary of American Business Leaders* (Greenwood Press, 1983, $395.00, ISBN 0-313-21362-3), which profiles 1,100 "significant figures in American industry and commerce." Most individuals included are deceased, although several, such as Lee Iacocca, are still very active. Entries range in length from a paragraph to several pages in length, depending on the importance of the individual in question, and end with a selective bibliography. In addition, there are appendixes that group the biographees by industry, company, birthplace, place of business, religion, ethnicity, year of birth, and sex, as well as an excellent index that covers company, industry, person, place, topic, and (occasionally) key phrase or slogan.

Chronologies

131. Robinson, Richard, comp. **United States Business History, 1602-1988: A Chronology.** Westport, CT, Greenwood Press, 1990. 643p. index. $69.50. ISBN 0-313-26095-8.

Robinson's year-by-year calendar of events in U.S. business development is arranged in two sections: "general events" and "business events." The general events section comprises those events that caused or influenced changes in living conditions and lifestyle; the business events section is extraordinarily detailed and often includes company-specific items. Although the index includes names of individuals and organizations, it unfortunately does not include general concepts. This work is a handy, if fairly expensive, resource for business reference, as well as a delight for trivia buffs and information browsers.

Dictionaries and Encyclopedias

132. Cole, Don, ed. **The Encyclopedic Dictionary of Economics.** 4th ed. Guilford, CT, Dushkin, 1991. 270p. illus. $13.95pa. ISBN 0-87967-884-4.

There are 1,400 entries and articles to be found in this introductory survey of economics. Most are brief and concise, but major concepts, products, and processes (e.g., market operation, business cycles) are treated in lengthier signed articles. Of the 1,400 entries, 69 are biographies. Definitions frequently note current statistics that further clarify the concept under review. Supplementary materials include 33 topic guides (boxed text that accompanies the regular definition and recommends related topics and subject maps); 21 subject maps; and numerous other maps, diagrams, organization charts, and photographs. A user-friendly, well-executed work at a very reasonable price.

133.   Greenwald, Douglas, ed. **McGraw-Hill Encyclopedia of Economics.** 2d ed. New York, McGraw-Hill, 1994. 1093p. index. $99.50. ISBN 0-07-024410-3.

Familiar to librarians in its earlier iteration, *Encyclopedia of Economics* (1982), this reference comprises more than 300 alphabetically arranged articles written by subject specialists well known in the field of economics. Topics encompass concepts, institutions, historical periods, processes, markets, and myriad other areas of importance to those involved in the study of economics, and a successful effort has been made to update the material by deleting less current articles and replacing them with contemporary entries such as contestable markets, debt and deficits, and real business cycles. The encyclopedia's clear writing makes it especially useful for educated lay readers unfamiliar with economics jargon.

134.   Terry, John V. **Dictionary for Business & Finance.** 2d ed. Fayetteville, AR, University of Arkansas Press, 1990. 399p. maps. $12.95pa. ISBN 1-55728-170X.

Banking and finance, investments, insurance, real estate planning, economics, management, communications, and employee benefits are among the business specialties covered by the 5,865 terms defined in *Dictionary for Business & Finance.* Legal aspects of each of these disciplines have been touched on as well.

Terry's dictionary is but one of several good, reasonably current works that often supplement, rather than duplicate, each other's coverage. Probably the best known of these alternatives is the *Dictionary of Business and Management* (Jerry M. Rosenberg, 3d ed., John Wiley, 1993, 384p., $39.95; $14.95pa., ISBN 0-471-57812-6; 0-471-54536-8pa.), which defines some 7,500 terms from more than 40 different fields of business. As with the previous editions, this third edition remains an excellent resource for the lay reader, because of its clarity and the nontechnical nature of the definitions. Another recommended work is Christine Ammer and Dean S. Ammer's *Dictionary of Business and Economics* (rev. and exp. ed., Free Press; distr., Macmillan, 1984, 507p., $40.00, ISBN 0-02-900790-9). Although it includes fewer terms than Rosenberg, the Ammers's book provides longer definitions, occasionally supplemented with charts, graphs, and formulas. The most important characteristic of *Dictionary of Business and Economics*, however, is its interdisciplinary focus, which encompasses economic theory, biographical profiles of influential economists, and legislative issues as well as basic business and finance concepts.

Directories

135.   Boyden, Donald P., and Robert Wilson, eds. **Business Organizations, Agencies, and Publications Directory.** 7th ed. Detroit, Gale, 1993. 2v. index. $330.00/set. ISSN 0888-1413.

Although expensive, this regularly revised Gale publication provides such a broad range of business-related information that it is useful in many different reference situations. Materials are arranged according to five primary categories: national and international organizations, government agencies and programs, facilities and services, research and education, and publication and information services. The more than 25,000 entries provide name, address, contact person, and telephone number, and also often include a brief description of the organization. Although most of the information found in *Business Organizations, Agencies, and Publications Directory* can, with some searching, be found in the same publisher's *Encyclopedia of Associations*, the fact that it has been gathered together for the business researcher makes this a useful reference to have on hand.

136. **Directory of Corporate Affiliations.** Wilmette, IL, National Register; distr., New Providence, NJ, R. R. Bowker, 1967- . Annual. 2v. $687.00 (1994 ed.). ISSN 0070-5365.

Approximately 6,000 companies (those with $10 million or more in annual sales), along with their 50,000 subsidiaries, divisions, and affiliates, are listed here. For each company, the directory lists name, address, officers, divisions, subsidiaries, and the locations of corporate plants. Volume 1 comprises an alphabetically arranged master index and the primary company descriptions, arranged by parent company. Volume 2 provides a geographic (city and state) index, an SIC index, and an executives' personal name index. Also available online and on CD-ROM.

Similar information is provided by *America's Corporate Families: The Billion Dollar Directory* (Dun's Marketing Services, 1982- , annual, 3v., $795.00 [1994 ed.], ISSN 0740-4018), which lists about 9,000 companies and their 45,000 divisions and subsidiaries. Although there is considerable overlap between the two works, they tend more to complement rather than duplicate each other, so libraries that can afford to do so may wish to purchase both.

137. Gifford, Courtney D. **Directory of U.S. Labor Organizations.** Washington, DC, BNA Books, 1982- . Biennial. 1v. index. $45.00 (1994 ed.). ISSN 0734-6786.

About 300 labor unions (representing approximately 17 million employees) are identified in this familiar resource. Its three sections cover the structure of the AFL-CIO and the role of its 35-member executive council, along with union reporting requirements and membership data; a list of the AFL-CIO headquarters and central bodies; and a list of all other major AFL-CIO and independent unions in the United States. Indexes access the material by abbreviation of labor union, by common name, and by officers.

If libraries need more extensive coverage of organized labor, Gale's mammoth *American Directory of Organized Labor: Unions, Locals, Agreements, and Employers* (Cynthia Russell Spomer, ed., 1992, 1638p., $275.00, ISBN 0-8103-8360-8) will probably fill the bill. Divided into four sections, the first profiles about 230 national or parent labor organizations; the second provides contact information for nearly 40,000 regional, state, and local labor organizations; and the last two present general information on 1,500 current bargaining agreements (listed first by union and then by employer). Indexes by industry, by state and city, by AFL-CIO affiliate, and by keyword provide access.

138. O'Meara, Meghan, ed. **Brands and Their Companies [yr].** Detroit, Gale, 1991- . Annual. 2v. $390.00/set (1994 ed.). ISSN 1047-6407.

This directory was published from 1976 to 1989 as Gale's *Trade Names Dictionary*. In its new iteration, it still identifies consumer-oriented trade names and the companies associated with them. Given for each of the approximately 267,000 consumer products listed in the 12th edition are the trade name, a short description of the product, the company name, and a code identifying the source consulted. In addition, there is a "company yellow pages" directory section that lists the name, address, telephone number, and source code for each of the 40,000 manufacturers and importers cited in the entries. Gale publishes two other works in conjunction with this directory: *Brands and Their Companies Supplement* (1976- , 1v., irregular, $260.00 [1994 ed.], no ISSN available) and *Companies and Their Brands* (1976- , 2v., $390.00/set [1994 ed.], ISSN 0277-0369). The latter lists the companies and then their products' trade names. Because all of the works in this family of titles are expensive, small libraries may want to purchase only the main publication.

139. Popovich, Charles J., and M. Rita Costello, eds. **Directory of Business and Financial Services.** 9th ed. New York, Special Libraries Association, 1994. 488p. $75.00. ISBN 0-87111-420-8.

First published in 1924, this SLA directory describes nearly 4,000 services (in both print and nonprint formats), many of which have an investment focus. Coverage includes 1,250 abstracted sources from more than 370 business specialty publishers, full-text sources, numeric data, and association newsletters. Entries are arranged by the title of the service, and include the publisher's name and address, a brief description, and notation as to format, size, and frequency. A master title index, a subject index, and a publisher index conclude the directory.

140. **Standard & Poor's Register of Corporations, Directors and Executives.** New York, Standard & Poor's, 1929- . Annual, with supplements. 3v. $525.00 (1994 ed.). ISSN 0361-3623.

Volume 1 of this well-known set lists 55,000 businesses (mostly U.S.) alphabetically by company name. Each entry provides company name, address, and telephone number; principal officers; names of the company's accounting, bank, and law firms; descriptions (including SIC codes) of the company's major products and services; and annual sales and number of employees, when known. For publicly held companies, the directory also notes the exchanges on which the company's stock is traded. Divisions and subsidiaries are listed with the parent company unless large enough to merit their own profile. Volume 2 comprises biographical information on some 70,000 company officers, directors, and trustees. Volume 3 is made up of a broad range of specialized materials: indexes listing SIC classifications and the companies categorized thereunder; a geographic index; a list of additions to the directory; an obituaries section; and a corporate "family tree" index that traces the interrelationships among parent companies, divisions, subsidiaries, and affiliates. Also available online and on CD-ROM.

Other directories of this type that libraries may want to have on hand, depending on budget and patron interest, are the *Million Dollar Directory* (Dun's Marketing Services, 1959- , 5v., annual, $1,185/yr. [1994 ed.], ISSN 1051-3442), which provides basic directory-type information for 160,000 U.S. companies whose net worth exceeds $500,000, and the *Thomas Register of American Manufacturers and Thomas Register Catalog File* (Thomas, 1905- , 21v., annual, $240.00 [1994 ed.], ISSN 0362-7721), which profiles about 135,000 American manufacturers, distributors, and suppliers. *Thomas* also includes the catalogs of 1,200 companies in its "Thomcat" Catalog File.

141. **Ward's Business Directory of U.S. Private and Public Companies [yr.].** Detroit, Gale, 1961- . Annual. 5v. $1,210.00/set (1994 ed.). ISSN 1048-8707.

Ward's provides reliable information on more than 133,000 companies in its first three volumes. Provided for each company are: name, address, telephone and fax numbers, financial information, fiscal year end date, number of employees, public or private status, ticker symbol, stock exchange, year founded, import/export designation, SIC codes, description of business, and top officers. Volume 4 offers geographically organized listings plus several top-1,000 lists. Volume 5 presents companies ranked by sales within four-digit SIC codes. The publisher offers the option of purchasing only the first three volumes.

Handbooks and Yearbooks

142. Freed, Melvyn N., and Virgil P. Diodato. **Business Information Desk Reference: Where to Find Answers to Business Questions.** New York, Macmillan, 1991. 513p. index. $85.00. ISBN 0-02-910651-6.

Intended as a research handbook for business people new to business research, this work is organized to reflect a problem-solving approach. The first section discusses how to select and evaluate sources, the second section links the type of information needed to the type of source that delivers it, and the third section identifies specific sources appropriate to actual business information questions. The material is divided into 24 broad categories, such as personnel management or taxation, further subdivided into narrower topics such as forecasting or forms and records. The fourth and fifth sections comprise an annotated bibliography of 500 print and 400 online resources. Appendixes list major trade associations and relevant U.S. government agencies. Although expensive, this comprehensive guide to business information resources is well worth its cost.

143. Godin, Seth, ed. **The Information Please Business Almanac and Desk Reference, [yr.].** Boston, Houghton Mifflin, 1993- . Annual. 1v. maps. index. $29.95 (1994 ed.). ISSN 1070-4639.

The more than 750 topics engagingly and knowledgeably addressed in the *Business Almanac and Desk Reference* include such items as business law and government, communications, finance, human resources, marketing, manufacturing, corporate planning and administration, office management, and personal computing. Within these topics one finds facts, directory information, rankings, contacts, addresses, fax and telephone numbers, online services, travel maps, and such esoteric (but useful) information as a listing of highly rated restaurants of larger U.S. cities. Additional materials include a glossary of common business terms and concepts, a list of public library reference contacts, and a list of industry newsletters. A densely packed business information resource at a very reasonable cost.

144. Hoover, Gary, and others, eds. **Hoover's Handbook of American Business [yr.].** Austin, TX, Reference Press, 1990- . Annual. 1v. $34.95 (1994 ed.). ISSN 1055-7202.

Hoover's Handbook provides alphabetically arranged, one-page profiles of 500 enterprises, including approximately 20 governmental and nonprofit ones. Firms included have been selected on the basis of size, growth, visibility, and breadth of coverage. Each profile includes an overview of the history, development, and focus of the company, plus coverage of its key people, products, and services, and financial performance. This information is presented in a standard eight-section format: overview, when, how much, who, where, what, rankings, and competition. In addition to the company profiles, the handbook offers a wide range of supplementary materials, including 40 separate listings of top, largest, leading, and other noteworthy rankings, generally grouped according to industry. Related titles are *Hoover's Handbook of World Business* (1993- , 1v., annual, $32.95 [1993-1994 ed.], ISSN 1055-7199), which describes close to 200 of the largest companies based outside the United States, and *Hoover's Handbook of Emerging Companies* (1993- , 1v., annual, $32.95 [1993-1994 ed.], ISSN 1069-7519), which profiles 250 high-growth American companies. All three of these handbooks do a good job of presenting practical, well-organized information at a very reasonable price. *Hoover's Handbook of American Business* is also available on CD-ROM as *Multimedia Business 500.*

145. Lavin, Michael R. **Business Information: How to Find It, How to Use It.** 2d ed. Phoenix, AZ, Oryx Press, 1992. 499p. index. $49.95; $38.50pa. ISBN 0-89774-556-6; 0-89774-643-0pa.

A valuable source of information for novice business researchers, Lavin's handbook is organized into five sections. The first two provide an overview of types of business information and a survey of the directories, indexes, bibliographies, and catalogs that lead the researcher to other business sources. The third section covers the resources available to investigate both public and private companies; the fourth focuses on statistical data. The concluding section covers local area information, business and labor law, marketing, and taxation and accounting. Each chapter leads off with a brief outline of topics covered and identification of the major sources described, followed by a lengthy explanation of the concepts addressed by the sources under review. Supplementary materials include subject and title indexes and an appendix that recommends titles for ongoing reading. Where patron interest warrants, librarians may also wish to consider a related Oryx title, *International Business Information: How to Find It, How to Use It* (Ruth A. Pagell and Michael Halperin, 1994, 371p., $74.95, ISBN 0-89774-736-4), which contains a selective list of English-language print and electronic resources on international companies, industries, markets, and finance.

146. Levy, Richard C. **Inventing and Patenting Sourcebook: How to Sell and Protect Your Ideas.** 2d ed. Detroit, Gale, 1992. 1022p. index. $85.00. ISBN 0-8103-7616-4.

Levy leads off his sourcebook with a useful overview of how to protect and license an invention, then provides a 13-part directory of such things as national and regional inventor associations, invention consultants and research firms, and invention and trade shows. Two appendixes—one covering U.S. Patent Classifications and the other a Patent and Trademark Office telephone directory— account for well over 200 pages. The work is very well organized, so the information sought can be quickly located (no small feat in a resource packed with this much material). A glossary and a comprehensive, well-thought-out index round out the sourcebook.

147. Monty, Vivienne. **The Canadian Small Business Handbook.** 2d ed. Don Mills, Ontario, CCH Canadian, 1991. 201p. index. $24.95pa. No ISBN available.

Monty's helpful handbook is arranged into four sections: how to start and run a successful small business; a bibliography; sources of information; and a library/ information center for small business. Although much of the "how to" guidance needs to be supplemented by more thorough, detailed coverage, such as is found in other small-business start-up manuals, the annotations of information resources are clear and precise and will be especially helpful both for new Canadian firms and for foreign firms considering setting up a Canadian branch. Topics are indexed, titles are not.

148. O'Hara, Frederick M., Jr., and Robert Sicignano. **Handbook of United States Economic and Financial Indicators.** Westport, CT, Greenwood Press, 1985. 224p. index. $42.95. ISBN 0-313-23954-1.

For patrons requiring information on economic time series data, the *Handbook of United States Economic and Financial Indicators* encompasses more than 200 standard measures of U.S. economic and financial activity: where they have been, where they are currently (or were in 1985, when this handbook was published), and where they are (were) heading. Entries are arranged alphabetically by name of the indicator, and provide a brief description of the indicator, how it is produced and used, who compiles it, where it first appears, and the frequency with which new statistics are issued. In addition, there are a list of national publications that regularly update the statistics given, and a short bibliography of materials for further information. An index that lists indicators by subject covered concludes the work. Although now nearly 10 years old, this is still a valuable resource for the broad overview it provides of U.S. economic and financial data.

149. Stevens, Mark. **The Macmillan Small Business Handbook.** New York, Macmillan, 1988. 408p. index. $35.00. ISBN 0-02-614490-5.

There are a number of good guides and handbooks for would-be entrepreneurs; not surprisingly, as more and more individuals choose to start their own businesses, more and more publishers respond to this growing market. The Stevens handbook is an excellent representative of these small-business start-up guides: it is clearly written, reassuring to the aspiring entrepreneur, and well organized. In addition, the work is supplemented by a very thorough subject index that facilitates quick access to the material or information sought without needless "wandering" through extraneous text.

William A. Cohen's *The Entrepreneur and Small Business Problem Solver: An Encyclopedic Reference and Guide* (2d ed., John Wiley, 1990, 565p. $70.00; $27.95pa. ISBN 0-471-50124-7; 0-471-50123-9pa.) is another outstanding resource in this subject area. Its mission is to identify, explain, evaluate, and provide how-to information on a wide variety of topics (and problems) relevant to small businesses, especially in the areas of finance, marketing, and managing. The text is enhanced by charts, step-by-step guidelines, examples of business forms, and other illustrative materials. Bibliographies for additional information are included for all topics covered, and an appendix lists government organizations and associations, investment companies, and additional examples of business forms. A detailed subject index completes the guide.

Indexes

150. **Business Periodicals Index.** Bronx, NY, H. W. Wilson, 1958- . Monthly (except July); annual cumulations. Sold on service basis. ISSN 0007-6961.

BPI got its start in life as part of Wilson's *Industrial Arts Index*; in 1958, the *Industrial Arts Index* was split into two separate publications, the *Business Periodicals Index* and the *Applied Science and Technology Index*. For the past 25 years, *BPI* has served as a subject index to periodical articles across a wide array of business topics. Currently the work indexes 345 periodicals as well as a select number of government documents. Topics include accounting, acquisitions and mergers, advertising, banking, building and construction, communications, computers, economics, electronics, engineering, finance and investments, government regulations, industrial relations, insurance, international business, management, marketing, occupational health and safety, oil and gas, personnel, publishing, real estate, small business, and taxation. A standard resource for all but the smallest libraries. Also available on disk, online, on CD-ROM, and on magnetic tape.

BUSINESS SERVICES AND INVESTMENT GUIDES

151. Bernhard, Arnold. **Value Line Investment Survey.** New York, Value Line, Inc., 1931- . Weekly. 1v. $525.00/yr. (1994 ed.). ISSN 0042-2401.

This loose-leaf advisory service evaluates about 1,700 of the most widely traded stocks drawn from 95 industries. The work is arranged in three parts: "summary and index," "selection and opinion" (essentially a newsletter that provides business/financial and stock market outlook, plus the Value Line averages), and "ratings and reports" (the stock profiles). The work numerically ranks each stock as to investment safety, probable price performance and yield in the coming year, and estimated appreciation potential for the next three to five years. It also includes tables of the best and worst performing stocks and lists of the companies whose stocks are most highly rated for safety and performance. A must purchase for all libraries.

152. Dutile, Patty, ed. **Morningstar Mutual Fund Sourcebook [yr.].** Chicago, Morningstar, 1984- . Annual. 2v. index. $225.00/set (1994 ed.). ISSN 8755-4151.

The Morningstar evaluation services are well known to mutual fund investors for their reliability and comprehensiveness. This sourcebook upholds those standards in its evaluations of several thousand U.S.-based equity and fixed-income funds. Each review contains a broad assortment of data (for example, performance summary, manager profile, basic operational information, investment criteria); in addition, a readers' guide for novice investors explains topics addressed in the reviews. Funds are indexed alphabetically, by family (management), by objective (growth, growth and income, etc.), and by fund manager.

If the cost of the two-volume sourcebook is prohibitive, libraries may want to consider its less expensive sibling, *Morningstar Mutual Fund 500, [yr.]: An In-Depth Look at 500 Select Mutual Funds ...* (distr., Business One Irwin, 1993- , annual, 1v., $35.00pa. [1994 ed.], ISSN 1067-6228), which surveys 500 funds considered to be "of exceptional merit."

153. Esposito, John J., ed. **Moody's Handbook of Common Stocks.** New York, Moody's Investors Service, 1955- . Quarterly. 1v. (various paging). $65.00pa. (1994 ed.). ISSN 0027-0830.

An authoritative reference in the field of investments, this handbook profiles more than 900 commonly held stocks and gives summary charts for other New York Stock Exchange (NYSE) companies. Included in the profiles are capitalization, P/E ratios, dividends, dividends per share, price ranges, profit margins, average yield, and return on equity. Sections on background, recent developments, and prospects provide information on markets, internal changes, product developments, analysis of sales, and possible future movement of the stock in question. Most data are reported over a 10-year period, facilitating comparison among stocks. Stocks are evaluated and ranked as to "high grade," "investment grade," "medium grade," or "speculative."

Moody's Investors Service publishes a large number of excellent (and expensive) investment guides, which libraries may want to consider for purchase if there is sufficient patron interest. However, because subscription costs often range between $1,000.00 and $1,500.00 each for the specialized Moody's reporting services, most smaller libraries will probably choose to stick with just the basics.

154. Lesko, Matthew. **The Investor's Information Sourcebook.** New York, Perennial Library/Harper & Row, 1988. 433p. index. $19.95; $9.95pa. ISBN 0-06-055110-0; 0-06-096237-2pa.

Matthew Lesko has been dubbed the information guru of an information-anxious age. *The Investor's Information Sourcebook* is demonstrative of the kind of publication he has become known for: a user-friendly sourcebook that identifies a mind-boggling number of print, nonprint, and personal-contact sources of information, supplemented by a wealth of guidelines, tips, and useful appendix materials. The work is divided into four sections: "Starting Points" (information for the beginner), "Economic Resources" (economic indicators and their role in investing), "Investment Vehicles" (an exploration of the myriad investment options available to individuals), and "Investing for Lifelong Security" (retirement and heirs). Appendixes identify teaching aids, programs, comics that teach investment basics to children, and information on what recourse is available if an investor feels cheated by a securities dealer.

155. Levine, Sumner N., and Caroline Levine, eds. **The Business One Irwin Business and Investment Almanac. [yr.]** Homewood, IL, Business One Irwin, 1977- . Annual. 1v. index. $75.00 (1994 ed.). ISSN 1057-5014.

Formerly known as *Dow Jones-Irwin Business and Investment Almanac* and *Dow Jones-Irwin Business Almanac*, this annual has long been a standard among consumer investment publications. Perhaps the best one-volume business and investment reference available, the almanac covers business, real estate, finance, and commodities; within these areas, it presents statistics, charts, comparisons, definitions, and easy-to-understand explanations. It leads off with a brief review of the previous year's business activities, then provides surveys of between 10 and 20 industries. Following these sections are overviews of business and economic indicators, performance of leading economic indicators, U.S. demographics, government budget data, stock market performance, taxes, and the European Community. A detailed business information directory is appended.

Depending on patron interest, libraries may also wish to purchase a related annual by the same publisher, *The Business One Investor's Handbook* (Phyllis S. Pierce, ed., 1982- , annual, 1v., $25.00pa. [1994 ed.], ISSN 1062-0028). Formerly known as the *Dow Jones Investor's Handbook*, this familiar compendium reviews the previous year's stock, bond, and mutual fund trading as well as the Dow Jones and several other market averages. Numerical tables on such items as the earnings and daily and yearly closings on the averages; the previous year's trading information for the New York Stock Exchange and the American Stock Exchange stocks and bonds; basic information on foreign markets and their monthly highs, lows, and closes for a three-year period—these are but a sample of the many types of data presented annually in the handbook. Its organization and logical approach will help beginning investors understand the averages and what they represent.

156. Perritt, Gerald W. **The Mutual Fund Encyclopedia.** Chicago, Dearborn Financial, 1993. 567p. index. $35.95pa. ISBN 0-7931-0617-6.

Mutual funds are becoming the investment of choice for more and more individuals, and thus libraries will do well to purchase this authoritative, well-written, and well-organized guide. The work leads off with a brief definition and history of mutual funds, then discusses gains, losses, and taxation. Next it describes criteria for selecting funds, identifies risk exposure, and reviews the investment strategy of asset allocation. After this introductory material, Perritt then profiles more than 1,300 load, no-load, and low-load mutual funds. Organized by type of fund (money market, aggressive growth, growth, growth and income, international, precious metals, convertible bond, taxable bond, and tax-exempt bond), the profiles note the fund's name, address, and toll-free number; investment objectives and strategies; portfolio description; minimum investment amount; charges (if any); five-year average returns; and bear and bull market performance.

The Handbook for No-Load Fund Investors (1v., $40.00pa. [1994 ed.], ISSN 0736-6264), published annually by Dow Jones-Irwin, is another excellent reference for both novice and more experienced investors. It provides comprehensive listings for no-load mutual funds of all types, as well as updates of their annual and multi-year performance records. It includes numerical charts and graphic presentations of information, which facilitate easy comparison among funds.

157. Rosenberg, Jerry M. **Dictionary of Investing.** New York, John Wiley, 1993. 368p. $39.95; $14.95pa. ISBN 0-471-57433-3; 0-471-57434-1pa.

Rosenberg's helpful dictionary provides precise definitions for more than 7,000 terms related to various financial markets. The primary focus is on stocks, bonds, and mutual funds, but other areas of investment, such as real estate and commodities, are covered as well. (Relevant symbols, acronyms, and abbreviations are also defined.) Definitions provide a basic context for each term and frequently refer to related terms. This reasonably priced dictionary will be useful for both the novice investor and the experienced investor considering new markets.

The other standard reference in this subject area is John Downes and Jordan Elliot Goodman's *Dictionary of Finance and Investment Terms* (3d ed., Barron's Educational Series, 1991, 437p., $10.95pa., ISBN 0-8120-4631-5), which defines about 3,000 terms drawn from the world of stocks, bonds, and other securities. Its coverage is obviously not nearly as broad as that of the Rosenberg title, but it is a good second choice.

158. Shook, R. J., and Robert L. Shook. **The Wall Street Dictionary.** Englewood Cliffs, NJ, Prentice-Hall, 1990. 470p. $14.95pa. ISBN 0-13-950189-4.

Providing more than 5,000 brief definitions of investment terms, this work has the advantage of currency and breadth over several similar titles, most notably *Wall Street Words* (David Scott, Houghton Mifflin, 1988, 404p., $8.70, ISBN 0-395-64777-2) with 3,600 terms, and *A to Z of Wall Street* (Sandra Hildreth, Dearborn Financial, 1988, 299p., $16.95pa, ISBN 0-88462-711-X) with 2,500 terms. The Shooks' definitions are usually two to three lines each; although reliable, they lack the more expansive explanations found in the other two works noted here. Thus, libraries that can afford to do so will want to have all three on hand for a balance of currency, clarity, and completeness.

CAREER

159. Arden, Lynie. **The Work-at-Home Sourcebook.** 4th ed. Boulder, CO, Live Oak, distr., Emeryville, CA, Publishers Group West, 1992. 279p. illus. index. $14.95pa. ISBN 0-911781-09-9.

Home-based work is an increasingly popular option for a broad spectrum of Americans, and this sourcebook offers them a lot of the information they need to get started. Arden examines factors that affect the work force, such as technology, work styles, and the employment process. A section on how to get started is followed by a job bank with listings in six topical areas (arts, crafts, computers, etc.). The sourcebook covers more than 1,000 work-at-home opportunities in art, crafts, telecommuting, computer-based home work, office support positions, work with people, industrial home work, and sales. The entries on specific opportunities, listed alphabetically by company, provide the name and address of the company offering at-home work, type of work available, requirements, and provisions. Supplementary information includes a "resource guide" that notes additional periodicals, books, and organizations appropriate to the topic under consideration; a geographic index; and an index to opportunities for the disabled. Especially noteworthy in the fourth edition is the section on telecommuting, which examines converting a present position into a work-at-home one through technology.

160. **Dictionary of Occupational Titles.** 4th ed. By the U.S. Department of Labor Employment and Training Administration. Lanham, MD, Bernan Press, 1991. 2v. index. $49.95/set. ISBN 0-89059-0001.

First published in 1939 by the U.S. Department of Labor to provide standardized occupational information, this work arranges its job descriptions by numeric code, ranging from a broad-category, single-digit code to a very specific, nine-digit code. Concluding each definition is an indication of when the information was last updated, the time required to learn the job, and the education needed. The second volume provides a glossary of technical terms and appendixes that explain the meaning of various designations, as well as an alphabetical index of occupational titles and an index of the titles categorized by industry. Although the *DOT* is available for less money through the Department of Labor, the hardback binding and useful arrangement of the Bernan Press edition recommend it to all libraries.

161. **The Directory of Jobs & Careers Abroad.** 8th ed. Oxford, England, Vacation Work; distr., Princeton, NJ, Peterson's Guides, 1993. 408p. index. $16.95pa. ISBN 1-85458-025-6; ISSN 0143-3482.

This directory is arranged in two main sections. The first discusses how to proceed when looking for work abroad (who to contact, language training, legal requisites, etc.), and then provides information on 11 sectors (for example, journalism, teaching, the United Nations) plus addresses of relevant associations, companies, and government agencies. The second section provides information on work in Europe, the Americas, Australasia, Asia, Africa, and the Middle East. Not surprisingly, materials are strongest and most detailed for the most developed countries; other than the Baltic states, the former Soviet Union is not covered.

162. **Directory of Special Programs for Minority Group Members: Career Information Services, Employment Skills Banks, Financial Aid Sources.** 5th ed. Garrett Park, MD, Garrett Park Press, 1990. 1v. (unpaged). illus. index. $30.00pa. ISBN 0-912048-89-1.

America's minorities encompassed here include Blacks, Hispanics, Asians, and Native Americans. The directory describes scholarships, fellowships, loans, grants, assistantships, internships, academic enrichment, educational counseling, summer study, occupational information, employment assistance, counseling, job placement, prizes or honors, career guidance, summer employment, and other programs. Each entry provides a brief description of the opportunity along with the address of the offering organization. Although somewhat ungainly in organization, this work nevertheless is an important and valuable resource for all libraries.

163. **Internships. [yr.]: 50,000 On-the-Job Training Opportunities for Today's Job Market.** Princeton, NJ, Peterson's Guides, 1981- . Annual. 1v. bibliog. index. $29.95pa. (1994 ed.). ISSN 0272-5460.

Internships describes about 30,000 internships (approximately half of which provide some sort of payment) offered by roughly 1,700 sponsoring organizations. There are about 25 career areas grouped within broad categories; in addition to the descriptive listings, the directory offers professional advice, other interns' "insider information" and tips, and a brief bibliography. A useful addition for most public libraries.

164. LeCompte, Michelle, ed. **Job Hunter's Sourcebook: Where to Find Employment Leads and Other Job Search Resources.** 2d ed. Detroit, Gale, 1993. 1131p. index. $57.00. ISBN 0-8103-8201-6.

LeCompte's sourcebook is divided into two sections. The first comprises a bibliography and directory of job opportunity information for 165 high-interest professional and vocational occupations, with publications, organizations, audiovisual and electronic resources that give job seekers employment leads, and other useful information provided for each. The second section is a clearinghouse of topically arranged information relevant to job searching, covering such areas as opportunities for older workers and negotiation of compensation packages. Most entries are annotated.

Reflecting the upheaval in the workplace of the 1990s, there is a rapidly increasing number of publications aimed at helping displaced or dissatisfied workers find new jobs or pursue new careers. Another good general title is *The Encyclopedia of Career Choices for the 1990s: A Guide to Entry Level Jobs* (Career Associates, Walker, 1991, 862p., $75.00, ISBN 0-8027-1142-1). *Career Choices* profiles 42 career fields (for example, broadcasting, data processing, and real estate), providing for each a broad, concise overview and the field's areas of specialization, the job outlook, a geographic profile, qualifications, salaries and working conditions, and resources. Among special-topic titles, there is *The Hidden Job Market: A Job Seeker's Guide to America's 2,000 Little-Known, Fastest-Growing High-Tech Companies* (CorpTech, Peterson's Guides, 1991, 268p., $16.95pa., ISBN 1-56079-110-1), drawing from a wide range of industries, including biotechnology, computers, environment, medical, telecommunications, and transportation; Carol Kleiman's *The 100 Best Job$ for the 1990s and Beyond* (Dearborn Trade, 1992, 362p., $19.95pa., ISBN 0-79310-420-3), which focuses on education, skills, employment outlook, career paths, and salaries with projections to the year 2000; and *Working for Your Uncle: The Complete Guide to Finding a Job with the Federal Government* (Breakthrough, 1993, 824p. $19.95pa., ISBN 0-914327-27-5), which provides strategies, explanations, and examples to demystify the federal hiring process plus more specific information such as pay schedules, job descriptions, statistics, and contact information.

165. **Occupational Outlook Handbook [yr.].** Compiled by the United States Department of Labor. Indianapolis, IN, JIST Works, 1992- . Annual. 1v. illus. index. $21.95; $16.95pa. (1994 ed.). ISSN 0082-9072.

Originally published by the Government Printing Office beginning in 1949, *Occupational Outlook Handbook* is a standard career reference, based on information drawn primarily from the U.S. Department of Labor. It describes about 250 occupations in detail plus others in summary. Occupations are arranged in broad groupings that allow readers to explore related career paths and job functions. The one- to two-page descriptions give a broad overview of the nature of the work, working conditions, required education and training, overall job outlook, advancement, earnings, and related occupations, and include additional sources of information such as trade and professional publications and organizations. Prefatory material explains the organization of the handbook, where to go for additional information (organizations and publications), and a survey of forces likely to affect employment opportunities to 2005. Because the GPO versions of *Occupational Outlook Handbook* are not copyrighted, libraries considering purchase of this important resource will want to compare the prices and binding quality of the six versions (GPO hardcover/paperback, National Textbook hardcover/paperback, and JIST Works hardcover/paperback) available to see which best suits their needs.

Two works that handily complement the *Occupational Outlook Handbook* are *The Encyclopedia of Careers and Vocational Guidance* (9th ed., William E. Hopke, ed., J. G. Ferguson, 1993, 4v., $129.95/set, ISBN 0-89434-149-9) and *Professional Careers Sourcebook: An Information Guide for Career Planning* (3d ed., Kathleen M. Savage and Joseph M. Palmisano, eds., Gale, 1994, 1500p., $85.00, ISBN 0-8103-5470-5). The four-volume *Encyclopedia of Careers* covers much the same information as *OOH*, but does so much more comprehensively and in greater depth. Volume 1 profiles approximately 70 industries grouped within 16 functional categories; volumes 2, 3, and 4 describe specific jobs with professional and educational requirements, potential earnings, work conditions, and social and psychological factors. *Professional Careers Sourcebook* arranges its material to correspond to the information organization of *OOH*, in effect supplementing and extending the data found therein. In addition to basic career-specific information, the sourcebook also identifies professional associations, educational directories and programs, and basic reference guides and handbooks.

166. Reddy, Marlita A. **American Salaries and Wages Survey: Statistical Data Derived from More Than 300 Government, Business & News Sources.** 2d ed. Detroit, Gale, 1993. 897p. $95.00pa. ISBN 0-8103-8591-0.

Compiled from salary information cited in various state and federal publications and from trade associations and journals, this resource answers salary questions for more than 4,500 occupational classifications at different experience levels. The data are arranged alphabetically by job title, with geographical breakdowns under each title. Appendixes provide sources, wage conversions, metropolitan cost-of-living data, a list of abbreviations, and major occupations 1986–2000. Although there are gaps in the data due to the inconsistent nature of what salaries are tracked and reported (as well as to the publisher's inability to obtain permission to reprint certain data), this is nevertheless a good starting point for tracking down current wage and salary information.

167. Smith, Devon Cottrell, and James LaVeck, eds. **Great Careers: The Fourth of July Guide to Careers, Internships, and Volunteer Opportunities in the Nonprofit Sector.** 2d ed. Garrett Park, MD, Garrett Park Press, 1990. 605p. index. $35.00. ISBN 0-912048-74-3.

Dubbed "the fourth sector" by business guru Peter Drucker, the nonprofit sector is generating substantial interest for its challenging career opportunities and increasing commitment to professionalism and innovation. As a directory of resources, internships, and volunteer opportunities, this work will be especially useful to individuals wishing to work in any of the hundreds of nonprofit organizations in existence primarily in the United States, although one chapter does cover international groups. There are 28 subject-specific chapters; each leads off with a brief introduction, then provides an annotated listing of books and directories, professional organizations, nonprofit organizations, periodicals, and job listings. Indexed by title, as well as title within individual chapters.

168.   Williams, Marcia P., and Sue A. Cubbage. **The National Job Hotline Directory.** New York, McGraw-Hill, 1994. 306p. $12.95pa. ISBN 0-07-07593-3.

The job hotlines included herein are organized alphabetically by state, with a few national, international, and mail joblines identified separately. Within states, the roughly 3,500 entries are further categorized according to employer, such as city, country, state, federal, bank, education, hotel, medical/hospital, and miscellaneous. Almost all of the joblines are accessible 24 hours a day. Given the unpredictable nature of today's workplace, *The National Job Hotline Directory* will be a useful addition to almost all reference desks.

CONSUMER

169.   Brennan, Shawn, ed. **Consumer Sourcebook.** 8th ed. Detroit, Gale, 1993. 627p. index. $205.00. ISBN 0-8103-5407-1.

Billed as "a comprehensive digest of accessible resources and advisory information for the American consumer," this familiar resource does a good job of helping consumers identify and protect their rights. The sourcebook, divided into 26 topical chapters, describes about 8,000 no- or low-cost programs and services available through the auspices of federal, state, county, and local governments and their agencies, as well as through organizations and associations. In addition, Brennan lists corporate consumer affairs and customer service departments. Also available on disk and on magnetic tape.

For a less exhaustive—but also much less expensive—consumer title, consider *The Smart Consumer's Directory* (Thomas Nelson, 1992, 401p. $9.99pa. ISBN 0-8407-4503-6), a compendium of practical information such as tips on airline travel, dangerous diets, home shopping, mail fraud, and buying used cars. Separate sections are devoted to directory-type information for obtaining consumer assistance (corporate customer service numbers, Better Business Bureaus, etc.); recreation, travel, and leisure consumer information (tourist bureaus, toll-free numbers for major airlines, etc.); and personal finance (consumer credit, student loans, etc.). Practical, handy, and inexpensive—just what a savvy consumer needs.

170.   **Consumer Reports [yr.] Buying Guide Issue.** Yonkers, NY, Consumer Reports Books, 1936- . Annual. 1v. index. $8.95pa. (1994 ed.). ISSN 0010-7174.

This guide summarizes (and, when appropriate, updates) major product reports from the previous several years of *Consumer Reports*. The products covered in the *Buying Guide* vary from year to year and may range from insurance to household cleaning products to peanut butter to personal computers. Each year's guide does, however, include frequency-of-repair records for used cars for the previous five model years. This is a useful work to have available for all public libraries; back issues of the *Guide* should be kept on hand as well because coverage is rarely duplicated year-to-year. A five-year index is included.

171.   **Consumers Index to Product Evaluations and Information Sources.** Ann Arbor, MI, Pierian Press, 1974- . Quarterly, with annual cumulation. $129.00/yr.; $225.00/yr. with cumulation (1994 ed.). ISSN 0094-0534.

Although coverage varies from year to year, this index usually covers about 100 periodicals that regularly review and evaluate products of interest to consumers. The annotated entries are arranged under 17 broad subject categories, further divided by topical headings. In addition to the indexed periodical articles and reviews, there is also a separate section that annotates books, pamphlets, and other print materials of assistance to consumers. Five indexes aid the user in finding specific information by product name, subject, alerts/warnings, recalls, and company name.

172. Gillis, Jack, and Mary Ellen R. Fise. **The Childwise Catalog: A Consumer Guide to Buying the Safest and Best Products for Your Children.** 3d ed. New York, HarperCollins, 1993. 448p. illus. index. $14.00pa. ISBN 0-06-273182-3.

Reviewing specific products and services as well as general issues related to young children, *The Childwise Catalog* is arranged in three sections. The first section, on products, covers materials for three age groups: newborn to six months, six months to two years, and two to five years. Items are listed alphabetically by product category under age group. The second section, services, covers child care, preschools, babysitting, health, and travel with children. The third section presents general information on child safety and protection, both in and out of the home. Supplementary materials include checklists, charts and other lists, product recalls, and a directory of key resources for parents and children.

There are a number of good buying guides for parents, each with a different focus. *Guide to Baby Products*, by Sandy Jones, Werner Freitag, and the editors of Consumer Reports Books (3d ed., Consumer Reports Books, 1991, 368p., $12.95pa., ISBN 0-89043-360-7), follows the format, approach, and strong safety focus of other Consumer Reports publications, giving buying advice on the entire range of baby products (baby food, bassinets, cribs, diapers, high chairs, strollers, etc.). For bargain hunters, there is the annual *Free Stuff for Kids* (Meadowbrook Press, 1987- , 1v., $5.00pa. [1994 ed.], no ISSN available), which describes how and where to obtain more than 250 items such as ballpoint pens shaped like tennis racquets, baseball bat keychains, tool kits, miniature pianos, stickers, stamps, wildlife coloring books, and world coins.

173. McCullough, Prudence, ed. **The Wholesale-By-Mail Catalog [yr.].** By the Print Project. New York, HarperPerennial/HarperCollins, 1979- . Annual. 1v. index. $15.00pa. (1994 ed.). ISSN 1049-0116.

This directory of more than 500 discount mail- and telephone-order shopping opportunities is arranged alphabetically by 25 subject categories. Entries give name of the company/store, mailing address, telephone and fax numbers, availability and price of catalog or brochure, estimated percentage of savings, methods of payment, list of products sold, and presence of a store. Each firm and its products are briefly described and evaluated. Each category has cross references to firms listed throughout the catalog that carry similar or related merchandise. The wealth of detailed and comprehensive information in *Wholesale-By-Mail* plus its very reasonable price make it a good purchase for all libraries regardless of size.

ENTREPRENEURSHIP

174. Blum, Laurie. **Free Money for Small Businesses and Entrepreneurs.** 3d ed. New York, John Wiley, 1992. 227p. $29.95; $14.95pa. ISBN 0-471-58108-9; 0-471-58122-4pa.

The leading cause of small-business failure is undercapitalization. Blum's book, which focuses on nonprofit and for-profit grant opportunities, can help entrepreneurs avoid this problem. The work is divided into three main sections: program-related investments, flow-through funding, and federal money. A definition of the type of funding in question leads off each section; in each of the first two sections, a list of foundations by state and by business category follows the introductory definition.

The third section, identifying available federal monies, is organized by business category only. Entries note each program's address, contact person, restrictions and limitations, focus, total dollar amount available, average amount of each grant, application deadlines, board meeting dates, and number of proposal copies required.

175. Friedlander, Mark P., Jr., and Gene Gurney. **Handbook of Successful Franchising.** 3d ed. Blue Ridge Summit, PA, Liberty Hall Press/TAB Books, 1990. 520p. index. $34.95. ISBN 0-8306-4090-8.

Drawing on the U.S. Commerce Department's *Franchise Opportunities Handbook* (1972- , annual), this introductory work first surveys trends in franchising, lists key points to consider when reviewing a franchise opportunity, and addresses critical points in franchising law, legal contracts, and agreements. The next section, arranged alphabetically by broad subject area, lists hundreds of franchise opportunities, providing for each the address, a description of the operation, number of franchises, date of business establishment, equity capital required, financial and managerial assistance available, and training offered. A nine-page bibliography and an index by franchise name round out the work.

There is an increasing number of publications being churned out to meet the public's growing interest in franchising, and libraries may wish to purchase several of these, depending on patron request. Among the more useful and reliable titles are Robert E. Bond's *The Source Book of Franchise Opportunities* (Dow Jones-Irwin, 1988- , annual, 1v., $35.00 [1994 ed.], no ISSN available), which authoritatively profiles about 1,000 franchises, and Dennis Foster's two works, *The Rating Guide to Franchises* (Facts on File, 1991, 298p., $40.00, ISBN 0-8160-2517-7), which stresses each franchise's "financial and legal status and relative position in the marketplace," and *The Encyclopedia of Franchises and Franchising* (Facts on File, 1989, 465p., $65.00, ISBN 0-8160-2081-7), which presents a much broader overview not only of specific franchises but also of the entire industry, as well as the franchising process.

176. Maki, Kathleen E., ed. **Small Business Sourcebook: The Entrepreneur's Resource.** 7th ed. Detroit, Gale, 1994. 2v. index. $235.00/set. ISBN 0-8103-8904-5.

Volume 1 of this popular reference profiles more than 200 different small businesses (accountants, computer stores, fur farms, tattoo parlors, yogurt shops, etc.); volume 2 presents information on topics of interest to small business entrepreneurs, such as taxation, unions and labor relations, credit, and collection. In addition, there are state listings of small business organizations and programs, Canadian listings, and federal government assistance organizations and programs. A glossary of business terms and a combined index to both volumes conclude the set.

For libraries unable to afford *Small Business Sourcebook*, a good alternative purchase would be Daniel Starer's *Who Knows What: The Essential Business Resource Book* (Henry Holt, 1992, 1239p., ISBN 0-8050-1853-0). Its thousands of entries for information resources are arranged by subject, and include 10 to 20 entries per topic or industry. Each entry includes address, telephone number, and a brief description of the subject scope or services offered. Although some of its information is duplicated in the Gale sourcebook, there is enough unique information that libraries that can afford to do so will want to purchase both.

TAXATION

177. Edwards, Chris, ed. **Facts & Figures on Government Finance.** Washington, DC, Tax Foundation, Inc., 1941- . Annual. 1v. index. $55.00 (1994 ed.). ISSN 0071-3678.

Facts & Figures is a review of taxing and spending practices at the federal, state, and local levels of government. It contains hundreds of tables of statistics that include thousands of entries among them. Tables are self-explanatory and most are retrospective, facilitating cross-year comparisons. Each section begins with summary data, then moves on to more specialized information, such as tobacco taxes or death-and-gift tax collections. A glossary concludes the work. Although the information it contains may not be the most heartening to browse through, this is an authoritative and useful work that belongs at every reference desk.

178. **Lasser's Your Income Tax [yr].** By the J. K. Lasser Institute. New York, Prentice-Hall, 1937- . Annual. 1v. $14.00pa. (1994 ed.). ISSN 0084-4314.

Lasser provides detailed explanations that are as understandable as possible when dealing with the byzantine U.S. Tax Code. Written for individuals who want to prepare their own income tax returns, the guide discusses income tax fundamentals, personal and family status, deductions, sources of income other than wages, losses, capital gains, tax-saving ideas, and tax planning, as well as many other key topics. Red type is used to flag potential problems of deductions, changes in the tax laws, and other court decisions. In addition to detailed examples and numerous cross references, a tax organizer, a glossary, and an index are also provided. Given the chaotic nature of tax legislation, libraries will want to purchase a new volume each year.

Libraries will probably also want to purchase the other popular "user-friendly" tax guide, Consumer Reports Books' *Guide to Income Tax Preparation* (Warren H. Esanu and others, 1986- , annual, 1v., $14.99 [1994 ed.], no ISSN available). Reflecting the pro-consumer stance of all Consumer Reports publications, this handy guide will benefit taxpayers whether they prepare their own returns or hire professionals to do it for them. An introductory chapter outlining the previous year's tax law changes is followed by sections on filing and dependents, income, alimony, business, depreciation, sale or exchange of property, and myriad other tax issues. In addition, the guide provides sample tax forms, a glossary, a list of IRS publications, where to file, IRS toll-free numbers, an annual tax table, and an index.

179. **Master Tax Guide, [yr].** By CCH Tax Law Editors. Chicago, Commerce Clearing House, 1913- . Annual. 1v. index. $25.00pa. (1994 ed.). ISSN 0083-1700.

Geared to the needs of tax professionals rather than the general public, this is an annual survey of U.S. taxation laws. Detailed coverage is provided for topics such as corporate taxes, exempt organizations, and foreign income and taxpayers. The language is not simplified, as the editors have clearly assumed an audience made up of sophisticated—if not professional—tax preparers. Supplementary materials include a summary of the previous year's legislative and nonlegislative tax law changes, a directory of where to file, tax due dates, tax rates for all types of returns, checklists, flowcharts, and special tax tables.

Education

GENERAL WORKS

Bibliographies

180. Buttlar, Lois J. **Education: A Guide to Reference and Information Sources.** Englewood, CO, Libraries Unlimited. 1989. 258p. index. $35.00. ISBN 0-87287-619-5.

This guide provides descriptions of more than 900 titles that represent important sources of information in education and related fields. Entries include major guides, bibliographies, indexes, abstracts, and other reference sources. In addition, online databases, research centers and organizations, and 50 major periodicals are described. Sources are predominantly English-language American works. The entries, which include brief annotations and complete bibliographic citations, are arranged in 20 subject chapters that range from the most general reference sources to specific topics such as art curriculum, bilingual and multicultural education, women's studies, special education, and higher education. With its citations to newer titles, this work is a good complement to Woodbury's *A Guide to Sources of Educational Information* (entry 182).

181. O'Brien, Nancy Patricia, and Emily Fabiano. **Core List of Books and Journals in Education.** Phoenix, AZ, Oryx Press, 1991. 125p. index. $39.95. ISBN 0-89774-559-0.

Intended to help librarians and researchers identify resources critical to "locating information relevant to education," O'Brien and Fabiano's guide describes 979 current reference works, monographs, and journal titles. The titles are arranged by 18 subject chapters under two format categories, books and journals. Subjects covered include educational psychology, multicultural education, and educational technology and media. The books identified are accompanied by brief (25- to 75-word) annotations; journals are listed but not annotated. Author, title, and subject indexes conclude the bibliography.

182. Woodbury, Marda. **A Guide to Sources of Educational Information.** 2d ed. Arlington, VA, Information Resources Press, 1982. 430p. index. $39.95. ISBN 0-87815-041-2.

The second edition of this standard resource in education describes about 700 print, nonprint, and organizational sources for educational research. An introductory chapter explains the steps involved in the research process and the usefulness of the various types of sources. Each chapter begins helpfully with an overview of the types of sources described and their most effective use. Although some of the citations in this work have become obsolete, it nevertheless will continue to be an important acquisition for libraries because its outstanding (and still timely) discussions of the research process.

Dictionaries, Encyclopedias, and Thesauri

183. Houston, James E. **Thesaurus of ERIC Descriptors.** 12th ed. Phoenix, AZ, Oryx Press, 1990. 650p. $69.50. ISBN 0-89774-561-2.

This thesaurus is a mandatory purchase for any library that supports research in the ERIC (Educational Resources Information Center) print materials (*Resources in Education, Current Index to Journals in Education*) or the ERIC computerized database. It identifies nearly 10,000 index terms, or *descriptors*, used as a controlled vocabulary to access the wealth of documents and information indexed through the ERIC system. The thesaurus also provides an alphabetical display, rotated descriptor display, hierarchical display, and descriptor group display, which is essentially a table of contents for the descriptors.

184. Kurian, George Thomas, ed. **World Education Encyclopedia.** New York, Facts on File, 1988. 3v. bibliog. index. $195.00/set. ISBN 0-87196-748-0.

More a handbook than an encyclopedia, this work provides a concise yet comprehensive overview of the history and structure of formal educational systems in 179 countries. The arrangement is alphabetical by country within three broad categories: "Major Countries," "Middle Countries," and "Minor Countries" (one wonders at the choice of adjectives here). The following areas are addressed for the countries identified as "major": basic data (statistical); history and background; overview of the system (grading system, textbooks, etc.); primary and secondary education; higher education; administration, finance, and educational research; non-formal education; and teaching profession. A summary or general assessment of the system and projections for the future, a glossary of terms, and a bibliography round out the country overviews, many of which also feature tables that depict the national system in graph format. Some—but not all—of this information is also included for the "middle" and "minor" countries.

185. Reynolds, Cecil R., and Lester Mann, eds. **Encyclopedia of Special Education: A Reference for the Education of the Handicapped and Other Exceptional Children and Adults.** New York, John Wiley, 1987. 3v. $325.00/set. ISBN 0-471-82858-0.

The more than 2,000 authoritative, succinct, alphabetically arranged entries that make up Wiley's *Encyclopedia of Special Education* address such special education issues as educational and psychological tests, techniques of intervention, various disabling conditions, major legal cases and legislation, and the services supporting special education. Supplementary materials include end-of-entry bibliographies, generous cross referencing, and cumulative name and subject indexes.

For libraries unable to afford the three-volume set, a good alternative is Wiley's *Concise Encyclopedia of Special Education* (Cecil R. Reynolds and Elaine Fletcher-Janzen, eds., 1990, 1215p., $115.00, ISBN 0-471-51527-2). For this work, almost all biographical entries found in the original encyclopedia have been eliminated, technical and medical entries have been recast to briefer definitions, entry length in general has been cut approximately 60 percent, and technical articles have been rewritten for lay readers. Although some entries have been updated, many others have not. Nevertheless, this work does a good job of surveying a complex discipline.

186.   Shafritz, Jay M., Richard P. Koeppe, and Elizabeth W. Soper. **The Facts on File Dictionary of Education.** New York, Facts on File, 1988. 503p. $40.00. ISBN 0-8160-1636-4.

Although for many years Carter V. Good's *Dictionary of Education* (3d ed., McGraw-Hill, 1973) was deservedly considered the standard work in this field, education has been undergoing a vast upheaval in the past decade that is reflected in its vocabulary as well as everywhere else. This Facts on File publication steps in to update our knowledge of the terminology of U.S. education, kindergarten through 12th grade. Its more than 5,000 entries (averaging a paragraph in length) include terms, individuals, legislation, court cases, periodicals, government agencies and organizations, and tests. Cross references are numerous and appropriate and recommendations for further reading accompany many of the entries. Supplementary materials include descriptive charts that indicate states in which lotteries benefit education; IQ classifications; and average state expenditures for students and teachers.

Directories

187.   **The Directory for Exceptional Children [yr.]: A Listing of Educational and Training Facilities.** 12th ed. Boston, Porter Sargent, 1950- . Biennial. 1v. illus. index. $50.00 (1994 ed.). ISSN 0070-5012.

About 2,600 facilities and organizations that address the learning needs of children with developmental, organic, and/or emotional disabilities are described in this Porter Sargent publication. Each organization's profile provides information about the facility, disabilities treated, educational and therapy programs, enrollment, staff, and costs. A list of associations, foundations, societies, and government agencies that provide services for exceptional children is also included.

Another helpful resource in this area is Midge Lipkin's *The School Search Guide to Private Schools for Students with Learning Disabilities* (Schoolsearch Press, 1989, 334p., $29.95pa., ISBN 0-9620326-1-1), which profiles just over 300 U.S. private schools that offer programs for special-needs students. Organized in three parts, the work addresses (1) schools that specialize in students with severe learning disabilities; (2) schools that offer a supplementary program for children with moderate, specific learning disabilities in addition to their normal curriculum; and (3) regular private schools that offer appropriate tutorial services.

188.   Mackenzie, Leslie, ed. **The Complete Directory for People with Learning Disabilities, [yr.]: A One-Stop Sourcebook for Individuals and Professionals.** Lakeville, CT, Grey House, 1992- . Annual. 1v. index. $125.00 (1994 ed.). ISSN 1063-0023.

This new annual reference provides (for most entries) brief narrative descriptions of associations, magazines, newsletters, support groups, vocational and educational programs, rehabilitation facilities, sports opportunities, media (for example, computer programs, toys, classroom materials), and government agencies of use to professionals and other individuals working with learning-disabled people. Its broad scope makes this work extremely useful; it is to be hoped that in future editions, descriptions will accompany all entries. Also available on disk and on magnetic tape.

189. **Patterson's American Education.** Mt. Prospect, IL, Educational Directories, 1904- . Annual. 1v. $79.00 (1994 ed.). ISSN 0079-0230.

American Education comprises directory listings for more than 34,000 public, private, and church-affiliated secondary schools; 11,400 school districts; and about 6,000 post-secondary institutions such as colleges, universities, junior and community colleges, and vocational, technical, and trade schools throughout the United States. The work is organized by state, then by community within state; information on statewide organizations and agencies leads off each state's listings. A similar format is followed in *Patterson's Elementary Education* (Educational Directories, 1989- , annual, $65.00 [1994 ed.], ISSN 1044-1417), which lists 13,000 public school districts, 59,000 public elementary schools, and 10,000 private and church-affiliated elementary schools, giving for each a code for population, district name, a code for total system enrollment, superintendent's name and address, and a listing of schools, their addresses, and principals.

190. **The World of Learning [yr.].** London, Europa; distr., Detroit, Gale, 1950- . Annual. 1v. index. $370.00 (1994 ed.). ISSN 0084-2117.

This international directory encompasses 26,000 academic institutions of all types, including universities, major libraries, museums, art galleries, research centers, and other institutions focused on facilitating the learning process. The first section describes more than 400 international organizations; thereafter, entries are arranged alphabetically by country. All entries include the organization's address, telephone and telex numbers, date of founding, officials and other staff members, number of faculty and students, membership, calendar, and publications. An index by institution concludes this directory, which is widely regarded as the most comprehensive and authoritative source available for information of this nature.

Handbooks

191. Deckard, Steve. **Home Schooling Laws in All Fifty States.** 4th ed. St. Louis, MO, Steve Deckard, 1989- . Annual. 1v. $22.00. spiralbound. ISSN 1051-5771.

Home schooling is a topic of increasing interest to parents, educators, and legislators struggling to deliver the best education possible to America's children. This self-published annual directory offers information about the legal aspects of home schooling on a state-by-state basis. Information is presented alphabetically by state as well as in summary chart form. For each state, Deckard identifies the name and address of that state's contact person; a description of the application process; teacher certification requirements; a list of records that must be maintained (attendance, immunization, assessment, etc.); testing, evaluation, and curricular issues; and health and safety provisions. Although the home schooling legal information is surrounded by other less useful material (such as eight pages of paid advertisements for creation science instructional materials), this work will nevertheless be helpful for libraries that have patrons considering home schooling as an education alternative.

192. **The Handbook of Private Schools.** Boston, Porter Sargent, 1919- . Annual. 1v. illus. index. $75.00 (1994 ed.). ISSN 0072-9884.

Some 1,700 leading private schools located in the United States are described and compared in this work. Schools are listed geographically by state and alphabetically by city within state. In addition to the standard name and address data, each school's profile notes name of admissions officer, grades offered, academic orientation, number of yearly admissions in each grade, total student enrollment, and number of faculty. A graduate record category is also provided for each school, giving the total number of students in the previous year's graduating class, the number of students continuing on to college, and the six colleges chosen by the most graduating class members. All data are arranged to facilitate comparison between schools.

If libraries wish to add another resource in this subject area, a good second choice would be either *Peterson's Guide to Independent Secondary Schools* (Peterson's Guides, 1980- , annual, 1v., $22.95 [1994 ed.], ISSN 0894-9409), which covers about 1,350 secondary schools (no elementary), or *The College Board Guide to High Schools* (2d ed., College Board, 1994, 2024p., $125.00pa., ISBN 0-87447-466-3), which describes more than 25,000 public and private secondary schools.

193. Harrison, Charles. **Public Schools USA: A Comparative Guide to School Districts.** 2d ed. Charlotte, VT, Williamson, 1991. 496p. index. $44.95pa. ISBN 1-56079-081-4.

This helpful guide profiles approximately 400 school districts with enrollments of 2,500 or more students; all are located within 25 miles of a large city. Among the 27 categories of statistics compared are enrollment, current expenses per student, average combined score on the SAT or ACT, percentage of graduates enrolling in two- or four-year colleges, subjects in which advanced-placement courses are offered, teacher-student ratios in elementary and secondary grades, teacher salaries, and number of students per music and art specialist (elementary grades). Additionally, an "Effective Schools Index," rating the school districts in each category against the national average, has been computed for each district that returned its statistical profile. This information will be especially helpful for relocating parents who are trying to make informed choices regarding their children's education.

194. **Peterson's Summer Opportunities for Kids and Teenagers [yr.].** Princeton, NJ, Peterson's, 1983- . Annual. 1v. illus. index. $19.95pa. (1994 ed.). ISSN 0894-9417.

Summer Opportunities lists 1,200 state, national, and international summer programs embracing a wide range of alternatives and emphases. Program profiles are arranged alphabetically, and provide cost, length of program, location, emphases, year established, and the name, address, and telephone number of a contact person. In addition to the profiles, there is a quick reference chart that facilitates comparison between programs on the basis of gender, age and grade level, lodging availability, and activities emphasized, as well as two-page overviews provided by camp directors of selected programs. Programs with religious affiliations, those offering financial assistance, and programs designed for emotionally disturbed, handicapped, or disabled children are also noted. Highly useful for identifying camp opportunities as well as potential employment opportunities for those seeking work as camp counselors.

There are two other choices in this subject area that libraries may also wish to consider, depending on patron interest. The first is Porter Sargent's *The Guide to Summer Camps and Summer Schools* (1936- , biennial, $26.00; $21.00pa. [1994 ed.], ISSN 0072-8705), published approximately every two years and similar in scope to the Peterson's directory. The other is Shirley Levin's *Summer on Campus: College Experiences for High School Students* (College Board, 1989, 392p., $9.95pa., ISBN 0-87447-322-5). *Summer on Campus* describes 258 summer programs on 150 college and university campuses from Maine to Alaska. Programs, listed alphabetically, provide program name, calendar, address, telephone number, contact person, course requirements, content, focus, cost, financial aid availability, housing, admission requirements, and credit options. An appendix cross-references the materials according to college and university name, program name, state-by-state location, financial aid and scholarships, credit programs, and course programs.

Indexes

195.   **Current Index to Journals in Education: CIJE.** Phoenix, AZ, Oryx Press, 1969- . Monthly; semiannual cumulation. 1v. $235.00/yr. (1994 ed.). ISSN 0011-3565.

CIJE, one of the Educational Resources Information Center (ERIC) publications sponsored by the National Institute of Education, is a monthly guide to current periodical literature in education covering articles published in approximately 800 major educational and education-related journals. Each main entry provides the article's complete bibliographic data, a list of descriptors and identifiers, and a brief annotation. Entries are identified by both accession and clearinghouse numbers, and are arranged sequentially by these numbers. Items available in reprint through University Microfilms International (about two-thirds of the titles indexed) are so noted. Indexed by subject (using each main descriptor and major identifier), author, source journal, and journal contents. *CIJE* is also available on disk and on CD-ROM.

196.   **Education Index: An Author and Subject Index to Educational Publications in the English Language.** Bronx, NY, H. W. Wilson, 1929- . Monthly (except July and August); annual bound cumulation. Sold on service basis. ISSN 0013-1385.

This indispensable reference tool indexes more than 400 English-language periodicals, yearbooks, and monographs in series, arranged alphabetically in its integrated, single-alphabet author and subject listing, with a separate section devoted to book review citations. All aspects of education are addressed, including new technologies, counseling and guidance, teacher evaluation, adult education, curriculum development, special education, and classroom management. Although it indexes fewer items than *CIJE* and does not include annotations, its coverage is often stronger in certain areas; thus, the two titles should be considered complementary rather than competitive. Libraries will benefit from both their strengths. Also available on disk, online, on CD-ROM, and on magnetic tape.

COLLEGE GUIDES

197.   Bear, John. **Bear's Guide to Earning College Degrees Non-Traditionally.** 11th ed. Benecia, CA, C & B, 1994. 304p. illus. index. $23.95. ISBN 0-962-9312-0-9.

John Bear's guides to alternative education opportunities are well known to independent learners as sources of information and inspiration. In addition to this work, he is also known for *College Degrees by Mail: 100 Good Schools That Offer Bachelor's, Master's, Doctorates, and Law Degrees by Home Study* (Ten Speed Press, 1993, 211p., $12.95pa., ISBN 0-89815-589-4). *Earning College Degrees Non-Traditionally* leads off with useful information on evaluation and accreditation of colleges, scholarships, and alternative methods of earning credit. Next comes a lengthy section that lists and describes accredited and nonaccredited schools offering bachelor's, master's, and doctoral programs, as well as weekend colleges. Information provided for each includes cost; degrees offered and in what areas;

whether the programs are residency, short residency, or nonresidency; and short descriptive notes.

There are an increasing number of useful resources in the area of alternative education that libraries may also wish to have on hand. One of the best of these is the familiar *Macmillan Guide to Correspondence Study* (5th ed., Macmillan, 1993, 799p., $100.00, ISBN 0-02-87139-1), which describes correspondence programs available through approximately 260 colleges and universities, proprietary schools, and private, nonprofit, and governmental institutions, as well as computer-based programs. Listings are arranged alphabetically by school name, then by subject. Each entry gives course title and a full course description. The guide also notes course prerequisites, names of institution faculty members, tuition, materials required, library facilities, and accreditation. If less thorough or extensive coverage is acceptable, then *The Independent Study Catalog: NUCEA's Guide to Independent Study through Correspondence Instruction* (National University Continuing Education Association, Peterson's Guides, 1964– , triennial, 1v., $16.95pa. [1994 ed.], ISSN 0733-6020) will cover much of the same territory for substantially less money. And of course, *The Independent Learners' Sourcebook* (Robert M. Smith and Phyllis M. Cunningham, American Library Association, 1987, 306p., $20.00, ISBN 0-8389-0459-9) is highly recommended as a guide to information resources for both independent learners and the librarians who work with them. The sourcebook identifies 34 subject areas determined to be those most typically studied by independent learners; for these subjects, the sourcebook provides evaluative annotations for key documents, magazines and journals, online databases, indexes, useful books, government documents, references and introductory publications, and agencies and organizations.

There are three other titles that libraries may also want to have on hand, depending on patron interest. First is Marcie Kisner Thorson's *Campus-Free College Degrees* (5th ed., Thorson Guides, 1992, 158p., $16.95pa., ISBN 0-916277-32-1), which focuses on nontraditional degree programs that accept credit for prior learning, both formal and informal, with the remainder of study for the degree completed through off-campus directed study with little or no residency required. Another is *The Electronic University: A Guide to Distance Learning* (Peterson's Guides, 1993, 193p., $15.98pa., ISBN 1-56079-139-X), a directory that lists degree programs and individual courses offered electronically, organizing them alphabetically by institution name. Finally, Eugene Sullivan's *The Adult Learner's Guide to Alternative and External Degree Programs* (Oryx Press, 1993, 227p., $39.95pa., ISBN 0-89774-815-8), describes 192 alternative degree programs and 91 external degree programs.

198. **Chronicle Vocational School Manual: For [yr.] School Year.** Moravia, NY, Chronicle Guidance, 1979– . Biennial. 1v. $24.95pa. (1994 ed.). ISSN 0276-0371.

This resource profiles about 750 programs offered by some 4,300 post-secondary occupational education institutions. Programs are listed by subject specialty, giving state and name of school in the first section. The second section comprises charts that detail admissions requirements, tuition and fee costs, current enrollment, financial assistance, and student services. Rounding out the program listings and charts are an index to the various programs, additional specialized information about specific programs, and a list of accrediting associations.

Another useful (if somewhat outdated) work on vocational education is the *Technician Education Directory* (Lawrence W. Prakken, ed., Prakken Publications, 1986, 329p., $20.00, ISBN 0-911168-61-3), formerly known as *Technician Education Yearbook*. It profiles more than 2,000 institutions that offer career training, noting for each enrollment figures, admission policies, accreditation information, names of relevant personnel, and a list of programs offered. Entries are organized

199. Estell, Doug, Michele L. Satchwell, and Patricia S. Wright, eds. **Reading Lists for College-Bound.** New York, Arco/Prentice-Hall, 1990. 255p. $8.95pa. ISBN 0-13-635251-0.

This work is simply a compilation of nearly 100 lists (of highly varied usefulness) of recommended books for college-bound individuals, as suggested by 103 colleges. A composite "100 Most-Often-Recommended Works" list is included for those not planning to attend one of the 103 colleges featured. Although the Arco work can be useful for high-school seniors and those advising them, it cannot help but cause teachers, parents, and librarians to hope that the American Library Association will soon consider publishing a new edition of its now out-of-print *Outstanding Books for the College Bound* (1984).

200. Mangrum, Charles T. II, and Stephen S. Strichart, eds. **Peterson's Guide to Colleges with Programs for Students with Learning Disabilities.** Princeton, NJ, Peterson's Guides, 1994. 398p. index. $31.95pa. ISBN 1-56079-400-3.

Mangrum and Strichart, both recognized learning-disabilities specialists, describe 1,600 two- and four-year schools responding to special-needs students, including more than 700 schools having services available to, but not specially designed for, learning-disabled students. All schools listed are either accredited or have candidate status. In addition to the school profiles, the authors also discuss choosing and getting admitted to the right college, describe sources of additional information, and provide a geographic index.

Depending on patron interest, libraries may also wish to consider the *Directory of College Facilities and Services for People with Disabilities* (3d ed., Carol H. Thomas and James L. Thomas, eds., Oryx Press, 1991, 376p., $115.00, ISBN 0-89774-604-X). Although considerably more expensive than the Peterson guide, this Oryx publication encompasses a much larger concept of disability, and therefore is useful across a broader spectrum of patron needs.

201. **Peterson's Guide to Four-Year Colleges.** Princeton, NJ, Peterson's Guides, 1970- . Annual. 1v. index. $18.95pa. (1994 ed.). ISSN 0894-9336.

This annual guide and its companion—*Peterson's Guide to Two-Year Colleges* (1969- , annual, 1v., $16.95pa. [1994 ed.], ISSN 0894-9328)—are well known to public and school librarians. *Four-Year Colleges* is divided into two sections; the first comprises profiles of nearly 2,000 U.S. and Canadian schools arranged alphabetically by college name; the second is made up of in-depth descriptions of approximately 800 colleges. Entries in the first section provide basic information such as enrollment, tuition, room and board costs, undergraduate profile, graduation requirements, financial aid, special programs, housing, campus life/student services, and, often, an SAT/ACT profile of incoming freshmen. Supplementary materials include indexes to majors and entrance difficulty, a geographical table of vital statistics, and introductory essays on admissions, financial aid, and the like. Similar works by the same publisher include *Peterson's Guide to Certificate Programs at American Colleges and Universities* (George J. Lopos and others, eds., 1988, 343p., $35.95pa. ISBN 0-87866-741-5); *Peterson's Competitive Colleges* (1981- , annual, 1v., $15.95pa. [1994 ed.], ISSN 0887-0152); and the Peterson's Graduate Education series. *Peterson's Guide to Four Year Colleges* is also available online.

geographically and are indexed by 170 areas of specialization. Although four-year and extension courses from selected colleges and universities are included, by far the bulk of the programs described are offered by community and junior colleges, technical institutions, and trade schools.

The Peterson guides are highly recommended; however, the alternatives among college directories seem almost as numerous as colleges themselves. Although there are too many guides to describe in detail here, the following publications all offer reliable and somewhat distinctive information: *The College Blue Book* (Macmillan, 1923- , biennial, 5v., $225.00/set [1994 ed.], ISSN 0069-5572), which lists 3,000 U.S. and Canadian colleges; *American Universities and Colleges* (Walter de Gruyter, 1928- , quadrennial, 1v., $149.95 [1994 ed.]; ISSN 0066-0922), which identifies 1,900 institutions that offer the baccalaureate or higher degrees; the College Board's *College Handbook* (1962- , annual, 1v., $20.00pa. [1994 ed.], no ISSN available), with its 3,150 institutions, and its companions, *The College Handbook for Transfer Students [yr.]* (1989- , annual, 1v., $17.00pa. [1994 ed.], no ISSN available) and *Index of Majors and Graduate Degrees [yr.]* (1988- , annual, 1v., $17.00pa. [1994 ed.], no ISSN available); and *Lovejoy's College Guide: A Complete Reference Book to Some 2,500 American Colleges and Universities* (Lovejoy's College Guide, Inc., 1940- , semiannual, 1v., $24.95, $14.95pa. [1994 ed.], ISSN 0076-132X).

202. Steen, Sarah J., ed. **Academic Year Abroad.** New York, Institute of International Education, 1964- . Annual. 1v. index. $39.95pa. (1994 ed.). No ISSN available.

Steen's guide describes more than 2,000 post-secondary study-abroad programs that are open to U.S. citizens and that take place during the academic year. Entries are organized by country, then by city within country. Descriptions include location, host institution, dates, subjects, eligibility, credits, language and format of instruction, costs, housing, deadlines, contacts, and other practical information (such as the availability of financial aid). Indexed by sponsoring institution or consortia, field of study, special options, and cost ranges. Libraries may also wish to purchase this guide's companion work, *Vacation Study Abroad* (1947- , annual, 1v., $31.95pa. [1994 ed.], ISSN 1046-2104), which provides similar information for vacation learning opportunities.

FINANCIAL AID

203. **Chronicle Financial Aid Guide for [yr.] School Year.** Moravia, NY, Chronicle Guidance, 1961- . Annual. 1v. index. $24.95pa. (1994 ed.). ISSN 0190-339X.

More than 2,000 financial aid programs offered by private and government organizations for undergraduate, graduate, and postgraduate studies are described in the *Chronicle Financial Aid Guide* (more familiar to many librarians in its earlier guise, *The Chronicle Student Aid Annual*). Scholarships, grants, loans, work/study programs, and awards are among the types of financial assistance identified; entries for each note institutions and application addresses, eligibility requirements, amounts of awards, and criteria for selection. States' aid programs for their own residents are covered in a separate section. Indexed by subject, name of sponsoring organization, and name of specific program. A good complement to *The College Costs and Financial Aid Handbook* (entry 204).

There are a variety of inexpensive publications that attempt to help students and their parents figure out how to cope with the rising costs of college attendance. *Peterson's College Money Handbook* (Peterson's Guides, 1983- , annual, 1v., $19.95pa. [1994 ed.], ISSN 0894-9395) focuses on financial aid offered by the schools themselves. For these four- and five-year colleges and universities, *Peterson's* gives data on typical expenses, types of financial aid offered, a profile of which students receive aid and how much is received, and a contact name in the school's financial aid office. Daphne A. Philos's *The A's and B's of Academic Scholarships* (Octameron, 1993, 144p., $7.00pa., ISBN 0-945981-74-0) profiles 1,200 colleges and the 100,000 awards they make available to outstanding students. Prentice-Hall publishes *The Scholarship Book: The Complete Guide to Private Scholarships, Grants, and Loans for Undergraduates* (3d ed., 1990, 400p, $29.95; $19.95pa., ISBN 0-13-792052-0; 0-13-792060-1pa.), which describes 1,753 scholarships from a vast range of unusual—and frequently unheard-of—sources. *The Student Loan Handbook* (Lana J. Chandler and Michael D. Boggs, Betterway Publications, 1987, 159p., $7.95pa, ISBN 0-932620-82-5) is especially useful for its focus on federally supported loans and grants available to post-secondary students who are seeking financial aid for college, trade school, or technical training. Finally, Marguerite J. Dennis's *Complete College Financing Guide* (2d ed., Barron's Education Series, 1992, 251p., $13.95pa., ISBN 0-8120-4950-0), a revised edition of her 1989 *Dollars for Scholars*, is essentially a how-to manual written primarily for students and their parents who are looking for undergraduate college financing. Each of these works has a slightly different spin on college financing, and as such complement rather than compete with each other.

204. **The College Costs and Financial Aid Handbook [yr.].** New York, College Board, 1980– . Annual. 1v. illus. $16.00pa. (1994 ed.). ISSN 0270-8493.

Based on the College Board's annual survey of American colleges and universities, this standard guide (previously titled *College Cost Book*) describes the costs of attending about 3,000 two- and four-year institutions. The profiles, arranged alphabetically by state, present their information in chart form to facilitate easy comparison; thus, the reader is able to see how expenses (tuition, books, housing, etc.) and financial assistance (loans, grants, scholarships, etc.) stack up among various colleges. In addition to the essential cost information, *The College Costs and Financial Aid Handbook* provides a very useful overview (including worksheets) of the financial planning process, a glossary of collegiate finance terms, a list of colleges offering tuition and fee waivers, and an alphabetically arranged list of schools included.

205. Kirby, Debra M., and Eric G. Carlson, eds. **Scholarships, Fellowships and Loans, [yr.]: A Guide to Education-Related Financial Aid Programs for Students and Professionals.** Detroit, Gale, 1974– . Biennial. 1v. index. $110.00 (1994 ed.). ISSN 1058-5699.

Recently brought on board as a Gale publication, this well-known resource describes some 2,600 grants, awards, contests, and loans available from private corporations and foundations, religious groups, professional associations, and a handful of government sources. Descriptive entries note qualifications, selection criteria, award amount, addresses, and telephone and fax numbers. Most helpfully, this wealth of data is indexed by vocational goals (with extensive classification), field of study, legal residence, place of study, special recipients, and sponsoring organization.

206. Schlachter, Gail Ann, with Sandra E. Goldstein. **Directory of Financial Aids for Minorities [yr.]: A List of Scholarships, Fellowships, Loans, Grants, Awards, and Internships ... .** San Carlos, CA, Reference Service Press, 1984– . Biennial. 1v. index. $47.50 (1994 ed.). ISSN 0738-4122.

More than 2,250 sources of financial aid and educational benefits for minorities are described in Schlachter's valuable directory. The sources include private foundations, government and other public agencies, professional associations, honor societies, special institutes, and universities and higher education boards. Each entry notes program title, address and telephone number of sponsoring agency, purpose, eligibility, dollar amount of award, duration of the awards and number given per year, limitations, and application deadline. Two related titles from the same publisher are *Financial Aid for Disabled Students and Their Families [yr.]: A List of Scholarships, Fellowships, Loans, Grants, Awards, and Internships* (1988- , biennial. 1v., $38.50 [1994 ed.], ISSN 0898-9222) and *The Directory of Financial Aids for Women [yr.]: A List of Scholarships, Fellowships, Loans, Grants, Awards, and Internships* (1978- , biennial, $45.00 [1994 ed.], ISSN 0732-5215).

INSTRUCTIONAL TECHNOLOGY

207.   **AV Market Place [yr.]: The Complete Business Directory ...** New Providence, NJ, R. R. Bowker, 1969- . Biennial. $132.00pa. (1994 ed.). ISSN 1044-0445.

AV Market Place lists more than 5,900 companies as well as 1,300 audiovisual products and services, including such state-of-the-art items as digital audiotapes and computer graphics packages. For companies, the directory lists name, address, telephone number, contact person, and availability of catalogs. Separate sections list associations, film and television commissions, awards and festivals, a calendar of meetings and conventions, periodicals and reference books, and an industry yellow pages. *AV Market Place* is an excellent resource for keeping up with changes in this burgeoning and increasingly important field.

Another resource in this area, less expensive and more narrow in scope than *AV Market Place*, is *The Equipment Directory of Audio-Visual, Computer and Video Products* (Kim Williams, ed., International Communications Industries Association, 1953- , annual, 1v., $60.00 [1994 ed.], ISSN 0884-2124), which covers more than 2,000 items of equipment in the fields of audiovisual, video, computers, computer graphics, and photographics. The directory furnishes information on manufacturers, producers, and dealers, and all items listed include specifications, photographs, and prices. In addition, there is a wealth of supplementary material of use to prospective purchasers of equipment, such as a directory of media producers; lists of names, addresses, and products of ICIA members; consultants; film and video distributors; and a 1,000-term glossary.

208.   Diffor, John C., and Elaine N. Diffor, comps. and eds. **Educators' Guide to Free Films.** Randolph, WI, Educators Progress Service, 1953- . Annual. 1v. index. $27.95pa. (1994 ed.). ISSN 0070-9395.

Published annually since 1953, this work is familiar to librarians and educators wishing to avail themselves of free films across a wide range of topics (the work lists just under 1,900 films organized within roughly 20 subject headings such as accident prevention and music). Sponsors range from the National Gallery of Art to the National Rifle Association, and include U.S. government agencies, foreign consulates and tourist bureaus, industries, religious groups, educational organizations, and professional associations. For each film, the guide notes date of production (if known), format (with few exceptions, 16mm with sound), running time, descriptive (rather than evaluative) annotation, and source agency or organization. Supplementing the core listings are a title index, a subject index, and a source and availability index that provides names and addresses of groups from which the films can be borrowed. A useful resource for most libraries.

209. Ely, Donald P., and Barbara B. Minor, eds. **Educational Media and Technology Yearbook [yr.].** Englewood, CO, Libraries Unlimited, 1973- . Annual. 1v. illus. index. $60.00 (1994 ed.) ISSN 8755-2094.

Published in cooperation with the Association for Educational Communications & Technology (AECT), this yearbook aims to provide scholars and practitioners an overview of new technological applications in education, current trends, issues, and research related to educational media and technology. It includes directories of graduate programs in instructional technology and educational computing, professional foundations, and associations. Separate articles address major trends and the status of research in the field. An annotated mediagraphy describes key resources for media specialists, instructional designers, and other media/technology/communications professionals.

210. **The Latest and Best of T.E.S.S.: The Educational Software Selector.** Hampton Bays, NY, Educational Products Information Exchange, 1984- . Annual. 1v. index. $39.95pa. (1994 ed.) ISSN 8755-5107.

Since it was first published in 1984, T.E.S.S. has evolved into a mammoth undertaking: the most recent edition lists more than 7,000 software titles available from some 500 producers and distributors. Programs are arranged alphabetically by subject (more than 100 are listed), then by grade level, then by supplier. Provided for each are program title, supplier's catalog number, release date, program type (tutorial, skills practice, etc.), grade level, author, ISBN, uses, scope, group, brief descriptive annotation, copy protection status, availability of network version, components, required hardware, price, supplier, review citations, and names and addresses of individuals who have used the program. Access points to the programs listed include subject, specific topic, grade level, program title, and hardware type.

211. Rosenberg, Kenyon C., and John J. Elsbree. **Dictionary of Library and Educational Technology.** 3d ed. Englewood, CO, Libraries Unlimited, 1989. 196p. $32.50. ISBN 0-87287-623-3.

This work is divided into two sections. The first comprises five essays, which are detailed descriptions of the various components of such electronic items as projectors, sound systems, videotape systems, reproduction equipment, and computers. The second provides an alphabetical listing of approximately 1,000 terms, organization names, and specifications used in the essays in the first part. Includes numerous cross references for abbreviations and related terms.

212. Sorrow, Barbara Head, and Betty S. Lumpkin. **CD-ROM for Librarians and Educators: A Resource Guide to Over 300 Instructional Programs.** Jefferson, NC, McFarland, 1993. 155p. index. $24.95pa. ISBN 0-89950-800-6.

Intended as "a dependable and useful annotated collection of CD-ROM resources" for teachers and librarians, this work presents instructional CD-ROM titles appropriate for kindergarten through college. Entries are arranged alphabetically under 27 subjects and categories, including reference, art, AIDS, science, music, English, foreign languages, consumer information, travel, and current affairs. The standard format followed for each CD-ROM entry includes title, producer, format, subject, grade level, hardware, special software needed, distributor, and a descriptive review of the program. Separate sections include a concise discussion of CD-ROM basics, including CD-ROM networks; a sample lesson plan; search strategies and tips; and examples of common menu commands.

READING

213. Books for Adult New Readers: A Bibliography Developed by Project: LEARN. 4th ed. revised by Frances Josephson Pursell. Cleveland, OH, Project: LEARN; distr., Syracuse, NY, New Readers Press, 1989. 210p. index. $15.95. ISBN 0-88336-599-5.

Project LEARN is a literacy project sponsored by the Greater Cleveland Interchurch Council and affiliated with Laubach Literacy Action. The fourth edition of this well-known bibliography identifies 675 titles deemed appropriate for the reading needs of English-speaking adults who read at the seventh-grade level or below. They have been chosen for their broad appeal to new readers, and include both fiction (general fiction, mystery and horror, science fiction, and classics and folklore) and nonfiction (arranged by Dewey classification). Appendixes include a recommendation for a core collection, series comments and index, books at the library for adult new readers, a section on computer learning, suggested readings for librarians, suggested readings for tutors, and general readings on literacy. Indexed by title and subject.

Two other valuable resources in adult literacy are *High/Low Handbook: Encouraging Literacy in the 1990s* (3d ed., Ellen V. Libretto, comp. and ed., R. R. Bowker, 1990, 290p, $43.00, ISBN 0-8352-2804-5) and *Easy Reading: Book Series and Periodicals for Less Able Readers* (2d ed., Randall J. Ryder and others, International Reading Association, 1989; facsimile ed., Books on Demand, 90p., $26.00pa., ISBN 0-7837-4586-9). The *High/Low Handbook* is a standard reference for those (including librarians) who work with disabled or reluctant readers, and focuses on the identification, criticism, and employment of high-interest/low-reading-level print and nonprint materials for adolescents. *Easy Reading* exhaustively describes and critically reviews 44 book series and 15 periodicals that will engage the interest of "new literates." In addition to the main series and periodical descriptions, the work includes an introductory overview of the reading process; a bibliographic essay; a content index that places each series within a specific literary genre; an ethnicity and literacy form index; an index categorizing each series by reading and grade interest level; and a list of publishers and addresses. Another excellent adult literacy resource is Vickie L. Collins's *Reader Development Bibliography: Books Recommended for Adult New Readers* (4th ed., Free Library of Philadelphia; distr., New Readers Press, 1990, 194p, $14.95, ISBN 0-88336-559-6). It comprises brief, evaluative annotations for close to 400 carefully selected titles. Special features include skill level charts for English as a Second Language (ESL) and Adult Basic Education (ABE) readers; literacy materials for the deaf; materials for tutors and teachers; an explanation of the Gunning Fog Readability Index; and a list of publishers and distributors.

214. Trelease, Jim. **The New Read-Aloud Handbook.** New York, Viking Penguin, 1989. 290p. illus. index. $10.95pa. ISBN 0-14-046881-1.

Trelease's well-known and popular guide addresses the why, wherefore, and how-to of reading aloud to children, and then annotates some 300 recommended titles with an indication of age/grade level and suggested related works.

The New Read-Aloud Handbook is an excellent work that should be available to parents in all libraries. There are a number of other works that can provide a good complement to Trelease should libraries wish to offer more resources in this very important subject area. These include Judy Freeman's *Books Kids Will Sit Still For* (2d ed., R. R. Bowker, 1990, $39.00, ISBN 0-8352-3010-4), and *For Reading Out Loud* (Margaret Mary Kimmel and Elizabeth Segel, Dell, 1991, 352p., $8.95pa., ISBN 0-440-50400-7). Both of these works offer excellent guidance for parents who are striving to create a love of reading in their youngsters.

5

Ethnic Studies and Anthropology

GENERAL WORKS

Atlases

215. Allen, James Paul, and Eugene James Turner. **We the People: An Atlas of America's Ethnic Diversity.** New York, Macmillan. 1988. 315p. (part col.). maps. index. $160.00. ISBN 0-02-901420-4.

This publication has won wide acclaim for its excellent graphic rendering of the U.S. distribution of 67 ethnic and racial groups, as well as its overview of their historical background and current situation as of the 1980 census. In addition to the 67 major groups, subgroups (Serbians, Catholic and Protestant Irish, French Canadians, Hmong from Laos, Basques, Sephardic Jews, and others) are also covered in the text. The primary focus of the work is its 115 maps (all but 4 in color); in fact, the first three chapters of *We the People* discuss the preparation and interpretation of the maps and cartograms. The following nine chapters present the maps, organized by broad area of geographic ancestry origin and then by country. These chapters are "Early North American" (Indian and Eskimo); "Western," "Northern," "Eastern," and "Southern European"; "Middle Eastern"; "African"; "Middle and South American"; and "Asian and Pacific Island." A chapter discussing general patterns of ethnic identity follows the regional chapters. The final third of the atlas comprises appendixes of county-by-county ethnic census data.

Bibliographies and Videographies

216. Kibbee, Josephine Z. **Cultural Anthropology: A Guide to Reference and Information Sources.** Englewood, CO, Libraries Unlimited, 1991. 205p. index. $47.50. ISBN 0-87287-739-6.

A comprehensive guide to all aspects of anthropology, this annotated bibliography organizes its 668 entries within nine sections: general and social science reference materials, general anthropology, bibliography, subfields of anthropology, anthropology and humanities (art, ethnomusicology, folklore, and religion), special topics (visual anthropology, history, research methods, ethnohistory, museums, and topical bibliographies), area studies, periodicals, and appendixes of professional organizations and of archives, libraries, and publishers. Coverage includes archaeology, physical/biological anthropology, and linguistics, as well as such subdisciplines as applied, medical, and psychological anthropology. Kibbee has emphasized works published between 1970 and 1991, although noteworthy retrospective works are described as well.

217. Stevens, Gregory I., with Sarah Parker Scotchmer, eds. **Videos for Understanding Diversity: A Core Selection and Evaluation Guide.** Chicago, American Library Association, 1993. 217p. $40.00pa. ISBN 0-839-0612-5.

The 126 videos described and evaluated in this ALA review deal with one or more themes central to diversity issues—race, ethnicity, gender, religion, culture, life stages, stereotypes—in a sensitizing, humanizing, or uplifting manner. The videos are intended for an audience of teenagers and college students, but many would be effective in a family setting as well. The authors' introductory material is well written and instructive, and the entries provide complete purchase and rental information, a summary of contents, and critical comments. A valuable work for all school and public libraries.

Dictionaries and Encyclopedias

218. Auerbach, Susan, ed. **Encyclopedia of Multiculturalism.** North Bellmore, NY, Marshall Cavendish, 1994. 6v. illus. maps. index. $449.00/set. ISBN 1-85435-670-4.

A marvelous celebration of this country's cultural mosaic, *Encyclopedia of Multiculturalism* comprises some 1,400 alphabetically arranged entries geared toward the interests and educational level of the general reader. The articles range from brief, 100-word sketches to 5,000-word overview essays, and cover the people, places, concepts, events, laws, and organizations that have influenced the multicultural experience in the United States. The work encompasses all eras of U.S. history and all ethnic groups, such as those of Afghan, Brazilian, or New Zealand origin. The engagingly written text is augmented by bibliographies of suggested readings for articles of more than 500 words, and is generously cross-referenced within both the text and the index. A two-part subject list that arranges all encyclopedia entries by both population group and broad subject concludes the work.

219. Gonen, Amiram, ed. **The Encyclopedia of the Peoples of the World.** New York, Henry Holt, 1993. 703p. illus. maps. index. $125.00. ISBN 0-8050-2256-2.

Encompassing more than 4,200 of the world's ethno-linguistic groups among its 2,000 entries, Gonen's encyclopedia provides a thorough introduction to the peoples of the world. Entries are arranged alphabetically, and range from a brief descriptive phrase to a multiple-page overview. Demographic information, primary location, language, religion, political history, socio-economic climate, and related groups are noted for each group as available, and entries are supplemented by 250 black-and-white illustrations and 48 pages of color photographs.

220. Hoggart, Richard, ed. **Oxford Illustrated Encyclopedia of Peoples and Cultures.** New York, Oxford University Press, 1992. 391p. illus. maps. $49.95. ISBN 0-19-869139-4.

The 2,200 alphabetically arranged entries found here present concise information on such topics as religion, education, social structures, environmental issues, popular culture, and leisure among the peoples and cultures of the world. There is a separate section devoted to countries of the world, including the independent states of the former Soviet Union. Color photographs, maps, and many graphs supplement and enhance the text.

221. Thernstrom, Stephan, and others, eds. **Harvard Encyclopedia of American Ethnic Groups.** Cambridge, MA, Harvard University Press, 1980. 1076p. $100.00. ISBN 0-674-37512-2.

Thernstrom's one-volume encyclopedia encompasses 106 American ethnic groups, complemented by 29 thematic essays ("Concept of Ethnicity," "Naturalization and Citizenship," etc.), 87 black-and-white maps, and numerous cross references. The length of the ethnic-group entries ranges from one to more than sixty pages; a typical entry includes information on historical background, migration, settlement, culture and language, organizations, and group maintenance, and concludes with a brief bibliography. Although the work is in need of both subject and name indexes, it is nevertheless an excellent and important resource in the area of ethnic studies.

Directories

222. **Minority Organizations: A National Directory.** Garrett Park, MD, Garrett Park Press, 1978- . Annual. 1v. illus. index. $50.00pa. (1994 ed.). ISSN 0162-9034.

First published in 1978, this directory lists about 7,700 organizations related to the interests of Alaskan natives, Native Americans, Blacks, Hispanics, and Asian-Americans. Organizations listed include cultural, historical, service, trade, and professional groups. Organized alphabetically by title rather than by ethnicity, entries give each organization's name, address, telephone number, and a brief profile of its goals and purpose. Access to the listings is facilitated by five indexes: minority group, organization type, program focus, professional or academic area, and geographic location.

223. **World Directory of Minorities.** Edited by the Minorities Rights Group. Chicago, St. James Press, 1989. 427p. maps. index. $85.00. ISBN 0-55862-016-8.

Covering 11 geographic regions of the world, more than 160 minority groups—defined here as units within a dominant culture that have different ethnic, religious, or linguistic characteristics—are described in this unusual directory. Entries provide a historical overview as well as specific information on population, religion, and languages spoken. An appendix of primary source documents, a number of detailed maps, and a subject index that includes generous cross references supplement the text. This is a recommended complement to the coverage provided by the *Harvard Encyclopedia of American Ethnic Groups* (entry 221).

Handbooks

224. Moss, Joyce, and George Wilson. **Peoples of the World: North Americans: The Culture, Geographical Setting, and Historical Background of 37 North American Peoples.** Detroit, Gale, 1991. 441p. illus. maps. index. $42.00. ISBN 0-8103-7768-3.

Moss and Wilson's fascinating study explores the background of 37 North American native and immigrant groups, including African-Americans, British

Canadians, the Sioux, and religious groups such as the Quakers. Entries focus on the human dimension in historical and current events, including reasons for immigration and the group's circumstances today. Geographical setting and culture are examined in detail. Supplementary materials include a glossary of unusual or foreign terms; a bibliography; about 120 maps, photographs, and illustrations; and a general subject index.

Where patron interest merits, libraries may also wish to consider the six other titles in Gale's Peoples of the World series, all priced at $42.00: *Asians and Pacific Islanders* (1993, 385p., ISBN 0-8103-8866-9); *Africans South of the Sahara* (1991, 443p., ISBN 0-8103-7942-2); *Eastern Europe and the Post-Soviet Republics* (1993, 415p., ISBN 0-8103-8867-7); *Latin Americans* (1989, 323p., ISBN 0-8103-7445-5); *The Middle East and North Africa* (1992, 437p., ISBN 0-8103-7941-4); and *Western Europeans* (1993, 438p., ISBN 0-8103-8868-5). All follow a format similar to *North Americans* and treat about 30 to 40 groups per volume.

ASIAN-AMERICANS

225. Gall, Susan B., and Timothy L. Gall, eds. **Statistical Record of Asian Americans.** Detroit, Gale, 1993. 796p. index. $89.50. ISBN 0-8103-8918-5.

Statistical Record of Asian Americans comprises statistics for 19 Asian nationality groups living in the United States or Canada, including Cambodian, Chinese, Hmong, Indonesian, Japanese, Korean, and Laotian peoples. The work's 850 charts, graphs, and tables are organized within 11 chapters covering such topics as population, immigration, business and economy, domestic life, and employment. Data are based on the 1990 census and on information provided by private research organizations. Supplementary materials include a subject and nationality index that covers geographic locations and a bibliography that lists both general works and nationality-specific sources.

226. Montney, Charles B., ed. **Asian Americans Information Directory.** 2d ed. Detroit, Gale, 1994. 480p. index. $75.00. ISBN 0-8103-8501-5.

This sourcebook identifies more than 5,200 organizations, agencies, institutions, programs, services, and publications related to Asian-American life and culture. Separate sections treat 19 Asian-American groups that can be traced back to East Asia, Southeast Asia, the Indian subcontinent, or the Pacific Islands. Within nationality section, entries are arranged by type of resource; they include brief descriptive and contact information. A name and subject index conclude the directory.

227. Unterburger, Amy, ed. **Who's Who among Asian Americans.** Detroit, Gale, 1994. 550p. index. $75.00. ISBN 0-8103-9433-2.

The more than 5,000 individuals profiled here include Americans who trace their lineage to China, Japan, Korea, the Philippines, the Pacific Islands, and the countries of Southeast Asia and the Indian subcontinent. Entries provide biographical data, career information, and address; indexes include occupation, geographic information, and ethnic/cultural heritage. A separate section provides obituaries.

BLACKS

228. Estell, Kenneth, ed. **African-American Almanac**. 6th ed. Detroit, Gale, 1994. 1622p. illus. index. $150.00. ISBN 0-8103-5409-8.

The most complete single-volume reference work currently available about Black Americans, this work encompasses historical overviews, biographical sketches, a history of Africa, conditions in Africa today, and a synopsis of the Black experience throughout the Western hemisphere. The greatest amount of coverage, however, is devoted to the situation of Blacks in American society today, including the Black role in politics, law, business, labor, the economy, education, the family, religion, the arts, sports, and science. Illustrations, photographs, charts, and graphs clarify the text, and an extensive index facilitates easy access to the material covered. Formerly titled *The Negro Almanac*.

229. Hornsby, Alton, Jr. **Chronology of African-American History: Significant Events and People from 1619 to the Present.** Detroit, Gale, 1991. 526p. $60.00. ISBN 0-8103-7093-X.

Although its coverage of the past 375 years is thorough, this work is especially strong in its recounting of contemporary events. Entries, including events, awards, births and deaths of noteworthy individuals, and biographical sketches, are arranged chronologically by year, month, and day. Supplementary materials include an appendix that presents excerpts from selected documents, an extensive classified bibliography, and a 19-page index.

230. Horton, Carell Peterson, and Jessie Carney Smith, comps. and eds. **Statistical Record of Black America.** Detroit, Gale, 1990- . Biennial. 1v. index. $95.00 (1994 ed.). ISSN 1051-8002.

Nearly 1,000 tables and figures in this statistical guide are arranged by 19 broad topical chapters, such as education, religion, the arts, health, employment, and military affairs. For the most part, they have been reproduced exactly as first rendered in the original source. Although the work suffers from a failure to note the statistics' sample size, location, or methodology, it is nevertheless an important reference that will answer many patron questions.

Horton and Smith's work is complemented by another statistical overview, Alfred N. Garwood's *Black Americans: A Statistical Sourcebook* (Numbers & Concepts, 1990- , annual, 1v., $49.95; $39.95pa. [1994 ed.], ISSN 1048-6992), which presents 183 statistical tables drawn mostly from the *Statistical Abstract of the United States*. The material is arranged under eight broad subject categories (e.g., vital statistics and health) and includes comparative national statistics for Black, Caucasian, and total populations.

231. Johnson, R. Benjamin, and Jacqueline L. Johnson, comps. **The Black Resource Guide.** 10th ed. Washington, DC, Black Resource Guide, 1992. 390p. illus. $69.95. ISBN 0-9608374-8-5.

The Black Resource Guide identifies roughly 4,000 African-American individuals and organizations, arranged according to about 50 categories. The work is divided into two main parts: the first provides topical lists of businesses and organizations (profit and nonprofit) directly involved with or developed by Blacks, and the second lists statistical information of interest to or about Blacks. Entries for the organizations listed in the first part include the group's name, address, telephone number, and contact person. Statistical information includes overviews of Black population distribution, revenue and expenditures of major businesses, and health and mortality figures. New to this edition is information on African-American sports agents, union officials, and scholarship sources for college financial aid.

232. Phelps, Shirelle, ed. **Who's Who among Black Americans.** Detroit, Gale, 1976- . Biennial. 1v. index. $140.00 (1994 ed.). ISSN 0362-5753.

The more than 20,000 individuals listed in this *Who's Who* draw from a wide geographic range: the 50 states, the Caribbean, Canada, Europe, and Zimbabwe. They have been selected based on their accomplishments and contributions to their chosen profession; those who are not American citizens have been included because they live and work in the United States. Biographical profiles include name, occupation, family background, education, career development, organizational affiliations, and military affiliations (where applicable). Because the information given may have been provided by either the individual profiled or by professional associates (a fact noted by the editors with an asterisk), the profiles vary somewhat in both thoroughness and reliability of coverage. Nevertheless, this is an important and useful work that in general reflects the usual high standards of its publisher. Also available online, on disk, and on magnetic tape.

233. Smith, Darren L., ed. **Black Americans Information Directory [yr.]: A Guide to Approximately 4,800 Organizations, Agencies, Institutions, Programs, and Publications ... .** Detroit, Gale, 1990- . Biennial. 1v. index. $75.00 (1994 ed.). ISSN 1045-8050.

Drawing on material found in other Gale directories as well as from the *United States Government Manual* and the *Catalog of Federal Domestic Assistance*, Smith's mammoth compilation of information and resources about and for Black Americans comprises more than 5,200 entries. Coverage includes associations, religious groups, libraries, research centers, awards, publications, videos, federal agencies, state and local agencies, domestic assistance programs, museums and cultural agencies, colleges and Black studies programs, leading Black-owned businesses, television and radio stations serving the Black community, and a host of other resources. A single keyword/name index provides access. A highly informative, well-organized reference. Also available in customized versions on disk and magnetic tape.

Another Gale title in this subject area that also merits consideration is *Contemporary Black Biography* (1992- , twice yearly, 1v., $45.00/vol. [1994 ed.], ISSN 1058-1316), which presents about 70 well-written biographies (of both living and dead individuals) per volume.

234. Williams, Michael W., ed. **The African American Encyclopedia.** North Bellmore, NY, Marshall Cavendish, 1993. 6v. illus. maps. index. $449.95/set. ISBN 1-85435-545-7.

The *African American Encyclopedia* successfully attempts to bring together the accomplishments of both well-known and lesser known individuals and groups in a well-written, concise, easy-to-read collection. Its broad scope encompasses the dynamic history of past generations and incorporates the many achievements (as well as failures) that have shaped the present for African-Americans. This work is especially useful for exploring the lives of individuals not so well known as Frederick Douglass, Martin Luther King, George Washington Carver, and others whose contributions have been widely chronicled.

HISPANICS

235. Furtaw, Julia C., ed. **Hispanic Americans Information Directory [yr.]: A Guide to Approximately 4,800 Organizations, Agencies, Institutions, Programs, and Publications ...** Detroit, Gale, 1990- . Biennial. 1v. index. $75.00 (1993-94 ed.). ISSN 1046-3933.

Like the *Black Americans Information Directory*, this publication draws its material from a number of other Gale directories, including *Awards, Honors, and Prizes, Encyclopedia of Associations, Directory of Special Libraries and Information Centers,* and *Publishers Directory*. Its 16 topical chapters cover roughly 5,400 associations, organizations, federal agencies and programs, awards, research centers, library collections, museums, businesses, publishers, television and radio stations, and videos. Entries include name, address, and telephone number, as well as a brief description of the subject. The strength of this work is in the volume and range of materials included; however, the information varies in thoroughness and consistency of organization, and access would be greatly enhanced by adding a personal name component to the master name/keyword index. Despite these drawbacks, the directory remains a valuable resource for all libraries, and especially for those serving Hispanic constituencies.

For libraries that would like a less expensive alternative to the Gale directory, however, a good choice is Alan Edward Shorr's *Hispanic Resource Directory [yr.]: A Comprehensive Guide to Over 6,000 National, Regional and Local Organizations, Associations, Agencies, Programs and Media ...* (Denali Press, 1992, 380p., $47.50pa. ISBN 0-938737-26-0). It lists 6,167 national, state, and local Hispanic organizations and associations; included among these are research centers, libraries and museums, state and local Hispanic commissions, Hispanic studies programs, educational institutions with significant Hispanic enrollment, migrant and bilingual education, migrant health, human rights agencies, Hispanic chambers of commerce, minority business programs, Hispanic employment programs, print and electronic media, and Latin American diplomatic offices in the United States. Although information provided for each listing is minimal, the directory does do a good job of identifying the broad range of resources in existence.

236. Kanellos, Nicolas, ed. **The Hispanic-American Almanac.** Detroit, Gale, 1993. 780p. $99.50. ISBN 0-8103-7944-9.

Modeled after Gale's *The African-American Almanac,* this sourcebook of information on Hispanic-American culture and civilization comprises 26 topical chapters covering such areas as Spanish explorers and colonizers, significant documents, racial diversity, law and politics, labor and employment, the family, media, education, and art and theater. Photographs, maps, and charts augment the text; bibliographies for further research conclude each of the chapters. In addition, there are a glossary, an appendix that lists table and charts located throughout the text, and a keyword index.

237. Schick, Frank L., and Renee Schick, comps. and eds. **Statistical Handbook on U.S. Hispanics.** Phoenix, AZ, Oryx Press, 1991. 255p. index. $49.50. ISBN 0-89774-554-X.

This is a compilation of 298 tables and charts gathered from the Hispanic Statistics Branch of the Population Division of the Bureau of the Census. Reflecting the format and layout of the originals, some of the materials are well organized and very readable—others are less so. The tables and charts are organized within eight broad categories: demographics, immigration and naturalization, social characteristics, education, health, politics, labor force, and economic conditions. Each of the major category sections leads off with a brief overview that notes important trends and provides an introduction to the topic at hand. A short glossary of statistical terms and abbreviations and a cross-referenced subject/name index accompany the materials.

Not surprisingly, Gale also offers a statistical work on U.S. Hispanics, entitled *Statistical Record of Hispanic Americans* (Marlita A. Reddy, ed., 1993, 1173p., $89.50, ISBN 0-8103-8962-2), which describes the current circumstances of U.S. Hispanics through some 900 charts, tables, and graphs drawn from a wide variety of published information. A third publisher, Numbers & Concepts, puts out *Hispanic Americans: A Statistical Sourcebook* (1991– , annual, 1v., $44.00pa. [1994 ed.], ISSN 1056-7992), a statistical summary of information on America's Hispanic community issued by the U.S. government. Because each of these titles differs in both cost and coverage, libraries will have to determine how much coverage they need and/or can afford in this subject area, and purchase accordingly.

238. Unterburger, Amy L., ed. **Who's Who among Hispanic Americans [yr.].** Detroit, Gale, 1991– . Biennial. 1v. $96.00 (1993–94 ed.). ISSN 1052-7354.

More than 5,000 Hispanic-Americans—individuals whose lineage traces to Mexico, Puerto Rico, Cuba, Spain, or the Spanish-speaking countries of Central and South America—who have achieved prominence in professional occupations or civic contribution are profiled in this valuable new "Who's Who." The individuals profiled hail from the fields of medicine, social issues, labor, sports, entertainment, religion, business, law, journalism, science and technology, education, politics, and literature, among others. The listings, which are arranged alphabetically by name, note each individual's education, career development, organizational affiliation, special honors and achievements, and business address. Occupation, geographic location, and ethnic/cultural heritage indexes conclude the directory. Also available on disk, online, and on magnetic tape.

If libraries can afford a second biographical resource on Hispanics, a good choice would be Susan Sinnott's *Extraordinary Hispanic Americans* (Children's Press, 1991, 277p., $31.90, ISBN 0-516-00582-0). Organized chronologically, from the European arrival in America to the modern era, Sinnott's work comprises individual biographical entries enhanced by brief, well-written essays on significant events or periods and articles on groups such as the first Angeleños (Los Angeles's first settlers). Although some sports figures and entertainers are profiled, the preponderance of biographees are drawn from a broader range of pursuits, including the military, business, politics, and science. Brief bibliographies, photographs, and illustrations supplement the text, which is appropriate for young through adult readers.

JEWS

239. Alpher, Joseph, ed. **Encyclopedia of Jewish History: Events and Eras of the Jewish People.** New York, Facts on File, 1986. 287p. illus. (part col.). maps. index. $40.00. ISBN 0-8160-1220-2.

This well-received, one-volume work provides concise information "about events, eras and key figures in the annals of the Jewish people, from the dawn of its history until modern times" (from the preface). Its 100 chronologically arranged historical entries comprise a main article accompanied by captioned illustrations, photographs, maps, and diagrams. Two unusual features of this work are its use of a diagrammatic "key" that provides a visual summary of each of the articles, and its "connections," references found on each pair of pages that direct the reader to related chapters throughout the book. In addition, the encyclopedia offers 12 appendixes on Jewish culture and ethnography, a 26-page chronology, a glossary, and an index to both text and illustrations.

For historical treatment of America's Jewish community, libraries should consider Jack Fischel and Sanford Pinsker's *Jewish-American History and Culture: An Encyclopedia* (Garland, 1992, 710p., $95.00, ISBN 0-8240-6622-7). Chronicling Jewish life in America from colonial to contemporary times, the entries in this excellent encyclopedia range from what are essentially topical mini-monographs to well-written extended essays to brief overviews, all written by highly regarded subject specialists. The writing style is appropriate for lay readers; clear and engaging. Coverage includes biographical, geographical, institutional, and historical arenas, touching on such subjects as academe, movie moguls, television, and Zionism. Supplementary materials include an introductory list of entries and a concluding index.

240. **American Jewish Year Book.** By the American Jewish Committee. New York, American Jewish Committee, 1899- . Annual. 1v. index. $30.00 (1994 ed.). ISSN 0065-8987.

International in its coverage, this well-known reference surveys Jewish developments and issues of concern in the United States and throughout the world. In addition to timely topical essays and coverage of population statistics, the yearbook provides a directory of national Jewish organizations, federations, welfare funds, and community councils; a listing of obituaries for notable Jewish Americans who died the previous year; condensed monthly religious calendars; and a selection of articles of interest published during the preceding year.

241. Barnavi, Eli, ed. **A Historical Atlas of the Jewish People from the Time of the Patriarchs to the Present.** New York, Alfred A. Knopf/Random House, 1992. 299p., illus. maps. index. $50.00. ISBN 0-679-40332-9.

The nearly constant travels of the Jews over some 3,000 years are graphically rendered here in a blend of scholarly text, evocative maps, and abundant illustrations. The atlas is arranged chronologically, beginning with the Old Testament world of Abraham, and moves through the possible routes of the Exodus; the conquest of Canaan; the destruction of the Kingdom of Israel and the fall of its capital, Samaria; and the many ensuing diasporas. Thematic chapters detail the effect of gentile events upon the Jews; the attitudes toward Jews wherever they went; the internal struggles, tragedies, and accomplishments; and the ways in which the Jews' nation-within-a-nation status shaped them. An excellent resource at a reasonable price, appropriate for all public libraries.

Where interest merits, libraries may also wish to consider two other atlases that complement the coverage provided by Barnavi. These are *Atlas of the Jewish World* (Nicholas de Lange, Facts on File, 1984, 240p. $45.00. ISBN 0-87196-043-5) and Evyatar Friesel's *Atlas of Modern Jewish History* (Oxford University Press, 1990, 159p., $55.00, ISBN 0-19-505393-1). de Lange's excellent atlas features maps of the world that depict various aspects of the history and life of the Jewish people. Population distribution and migration, languages, houses of worship and scholarship, the history of Jewish religious freedom, the locations of archeological discoveries, and numerous other topics are displayed. The text is arranged in three sections: a historical overview, topical articles, and geographical surveys. There are also a detailed bibliography, a glossary, a gazetteer, and a thorough index. Friesel's atlas traces modern Jewish history, here defined as two distinct periods: from the 17th century to 1939, and from 1948 through the present. (The two periods are separated by World War II.) Within these time frames, Friesel presents about 500 maps, charts, graphs, and illustrations that portray geographic centers, economic trends, religious and cultural institutions, and the rise of anti-Semitism. In addition, there are a multitude of diagrams, illustrations, sketch portraits, and photographs, as well as a bibliography. Indexed by subject and by geographical region.

242. Holtz, Barry W. **The Schocken Guide to Jewish Books: Where to Start Reading about History, Literature, Culture, and Religion.** New York, Schocken Books; distr, New York, Random House, 1992. 357p. illus. index. $17.00pa. ISBN 0-8052-1005-9.

This collection of 15 bibliographical essays recommends books on Jewish history, philosophy, literature, and religion appropriate to the serious lay reader (rather than to students, scholars, or researchers). The bibliographical references include title, author, publisher, and date. The guide is well organized and clearly written, and enhanced by mostly black-and-white illustrations. A useful selection and reader's advisory tool for librarians and their patrons.

243. Wigoder, Geoffrey, ed. **Dictionary of Jewish Biography.** New York, Simon & Schuster Academic Reference Division, 1991. 567p. illus. $55.00. ISBN 0-13-210105-X.

Approximately 1,000 distinguished Jewish figures from the past are profiled in Wigoder's biographical dictionary. Individuals hail from the arts, literary pursuits, biblical times, the political arena, and various other areas of achievement. Entries range in length from one-and-a-half to two-and-a-half columns, and provide background and biographical information. Brief bibliographic references conclude the entries; extensive illustrations and a sprinkling of quotations from writers and politicians complement the text.

NATIVE AMERICANS

244. Champagne, Duane, ed. **Native North American Almanac.** Detroit, Gale, 1994. 1300p. illus. index. $75.00. ISBN 0-8103-8865-0.

Like similar titles in Gale's ethnic almanac series, this work provides broad coverage of all major aspects of the circumstances (both historic and contemporary) and culture of its subject group, the indigenous peoples of the United States and Canada. Materials include signed essays, annotated directory information, documentary excerpts, and biographies. Subject-specific bibliographies for each chapter, plus some 400 charts, maps, and photographs, add to the information presented in the text; in addition, there are alphabetical and geographical lists of tribes, a multimedia bibliography, a glossary, an appendix listing tables and charts in the text, and occupational and keyword indexes. An abridged version of this work, *Native America: Portrait of the Peoples* (1994, 786p., $18.95pa., ISBN 0-8103-9452-9) is also available from the publisher.

245. Furtaw, Julia C., and Kimberly Burton Faulkner, eds. **Native Americans Information Directory: A Guide to Organizations, Agencies, Institutions, Programs, Publications, Services, and Other Resources ...**. Detroit, Gale, 1992. 371p. index. $79.00. ISBN 0-8103-8854-5.

Native Americans Information Directory identifies nearly 4,500 organizations, agencies, institutions, programs, services, and publications concerned with Native American life and culture. Materials fall under five broad sections: American Indians, Alaskan natives, native Hawaiians, aboriginal Canadians, and general resources on Native Americans. Fifteen subheadings and listings for schools, libraries, museums, research centers, print and broadcast media, publishers, videos (except for Hawaiians), and educational financial assistance further subdivide each of the five major sections. Entries are brief but usually include complete contact information (name, address, telephone number, etc.) and often a descriptive annotation. An extensive master name and keyword index concludes the directory.

246. Hirschfelder, Arlene B., and others, eds. **Guide to Research on North American Indians.** Chicago, American Library Association, 1983. 330p. $30.00. ISBN 0-8389-035303.

This ALA bibliography annotates about 1,100 English-language books, articles, and government documents. The materials are organized into topical chapters that cover 27 areas related to study of North American Indians, with author-title and subject indexes facilitating access. Although in need of updating, this work is nevertheless an excellent starting place from which to initiate research in this subject area.

247. Reddy, Marlita A., ed. **Statistical Record of Native North Americans.** Detroit, Gale, 1993. 1661p. index. $89.50. ISBN 0-8103-8963-0.

The "current" statistical data on native North Americans (United States and Canada, including Eskimo/Inuit) provided here are drawn primarily from the 1980 U.S. Census (with some 1990 data), as well as from the 1986 Canadian Census. U.S. and Canadian data appear separately, with the U.S. material organized into 11 topical chapters covering history, demographics, family, education, culture and tradition, health and health care, social and economic conditions, business and industry, water and land management, government relations, and law and law enforcement. A 200-page index to tribes, subjects, and places provides access to the wealth of information contained in this useful publication.

248. Waldman, Carl. **Encyclopedia of Native American Tribes.** New York, Facts on File, 1988. 293p. illus. maps. index. $45.00. ISBN 0-8160-1421-3.

Waldman's excellent reference provides encyclopedic coverage of 140 individual tribes, while also presenting general entries for regional groupings such as the Southeast Indians and the Subarctic Indians. Organized alphabetically by tribe/region, entries provide an overview of tribal culture and history from earliest through contemporary times. Main entries vary in length according to the current or historical importance of the group in question, and are supplemented by more than 300 color illustrations. The index is detailed and thorough. Although there are a number of very scholarly publications on Native Americans, *Encyclopedia of Native American Tribes*—written for the layperson—stands out for its combination of thoroughness, authority, and accessibility.

Libraries may also wish to consider another excellent work by Waldman, the *Atlas of the North American Indian* (Facts on File, 1985, 276p, $17.95pa, ISBN 0-8160-2136-8). The atlas combines more than 100 two-tone maps, line drawings, and narrative to explore 7 broad topics: "Ancient Indians," "Ancient Civilizations," "Indian Lifeways," "Indians and Explorers," "Indian Wars," "Indian Land Cessions," and "Contemporary Indians." Written for the interested student or layperson rather than for the scholar, this is a good complement to Waldman's encyclopedia.

6

Genealogy

DICTIONARIES

249.   Harris, Maurine, and Glen Harris. **Ancestry's Concise Genealogical Dictionary.** Salt Lake City, UT, Ancestry, 1989. 259p. $10.95pa. ISBN 0-916489-06-X.

The Harrises' dictionary is designed to help the beginning researcher understand the terms likely to be encountered when pursuing genealogical information. The alphabetically arranged definitions are concise (occasionally trading brevity for clarity) and include terms drawn from legal, medical, and governmental disciplines. Although a list of abbreviations follows (but is not included with) the text, the definitions that accompany the abbreviations are not sufficiently detailed to be useful. Although this dictionary has much room for improvement in its next edition, it is currently the only genealogical dictionary available and as such is recommended to libraries whose patrons are active in genealogical research.

DIRECTORIES

250.   Bentley, Elizabeth Petty. **Directory of Family Associations.** Baltimore, MD, Genealogical, 1993. 336p. $29.95pa. ISBN 0-8063-1383-8.

The hundreds of groups identified in this directory include family associations, reunion committees, and single-name societies. Although most of the data have been gathered from questionnaire responses, information has also been derived from notices appearing in standard family history journals and newsletters. Entries are arranged alphabetically by family surname, and list contact address and publication title (if any). Cross references identify name variations or interrelated families. It is not yet clear how often this publication will be updated.

251.   Bentley, Elizabeth Petty. **The Genealogist's Address Book.** Baltimore, MD, Genealogical, 1991. 391p. $29.95pa. ISBN 0-8063-1292-0.

Bentley's "address book" comprises the names and addresses of those organizations and institutions deemed to be most important or useful to genealogists. The work's several sections include national and state organizations, ethnic and religious organizations, special resources, and periodicals and newsletters. Archives, libraries, and historical and genealogical societies are listed in the state section; the "special resources" section includes information for hereditary societies, adoption registries, immigration research centers, and publishers, among others.

252. Burgess, Michael, Mary A. Burgess, and Daryl F. Mallett. **The State and Province Vital Records Guide.** San Bernardino, CA, Borgo Press, 1993. 96p. $20.00; $10.00pa. ISBN 0-89370-815-1; 0-89370-915-8pa.

Genealogical researchers will rely on this directory to find out where to order birth, death, marriage, and divorce certificates in the United States, U.S. insular areas and territories, and Canada. The information was current as of early 1993. Entries for each state, insular area, territory, and province provide addresses, telephone numbers, fees, years of coverage, and restrictions, all in a clear, concise manner.

253. Eichholz, Alice, ed. **Ancestry's Red Book: American State, County & Town Sources.** Rev. ed. Salt Lake City, UT, Ancestry, 1992. 858p. maps. index. $39.95. ISBN 0-916489-47-7.

Intended as a guide for beginners in family research, this Ancestry publication describes various categories of genealogical resources (types of records, serial and book publications, local history, maps, archives, libraries, and societies), first in broad (national) terms, then in separate, alphabetically arranged state chapters. Maps identify counties within each state and bordering counties in neighboring states. Charts for county and town records note date of establishment, parent county, first year for which primary sources are available, and local address for correspondence. Although the index is less thorough than might be hoped, this is nevertheless a standard, and very useful, purchase for libraries that field genealogical questions.

HANDBOOKS

254. Greenwood, Val D. **The Researcher's Guide to American Genealogy.** 2d ed. Baltimore, MD, Genealogical, 1992. 609p. illus. index. $24.95. ISBN 0-8063-1267-X.

This work is an outstanding introductory guide for beginners on the techniques of locating and analyzing genealogical records. Chapter topics include, among others, using U.S. court records, using cemetery records, searching census documents, evaluating evidence, and using the personal computer to organize and maintain family group sheets and pedigree charts (although the coverage of available genealogy software programs and of the CD-ROM-based *International Genealogical Index* need improvement). Includes examples of search strategies.

For librarians needing direction on how to help patrons with genealogical research, *Genealogical Research and Resources: A Guide for Library Use* (American Library Association, 1988, 70p., $18.00pa., ISBN 0-8389-0482-3) by Lois Gilmer offers advice on how to direct researchers to sources of possible answers, how to help patrons in defining clearer questions, how to advise patrons of available sources, and how and when to refer patrons to other repositories. Chapters cover genealogical reference service, genealogical research and organization of data, primary and secondary sources, and conclusion of the search. Selective bibliographies accompany each chapter; an appendix lists major genealogical organizations and societies.

255. Jarboe, Betty M. **Obituaries: A Guide to Sources.** 2d ed. Boston, G. K. Hall, 1989. 362p. index. $80.00. ISBN 0-8161-0483-2.

Noted for its coverage of obscure titles, Jarboe's guide identifies 3,547 books, articles, pamphlets, and serials that provide or lead to obituary information. One section treats international sources; another covers the United Kingdom, France, Germany, and other foreign countries. The work, which is arranged by state, is indexed by names of counties or towns as well as by titles of serials.

256. Kemp, Thomas J. **International Vital Records Handbook.** Baltimore, MD, Genealogical, 1994. 447p. illus. $29.95pa. ISBN 0-8063-1424-9.

Vital Records Handbook is designed to assist readers in obtaining copies of birth, marriage, and death certificates, whether for personal use (such as driver's license or passport) or for purposes of genealogical research. Enlarged by a third since its previous edition, the work is divided into three parts: the United States, United States Trust territories, and selected foreign countries. Application forms issued by the records departments of the appropriate offices and the procedures for obtaining birth, marriage, and death certificates are given for each state, province, territory, or country. The forms included in *International Vital Records Handbook* may be photocopied and used to apply for the needed document.

257. Neagles, James C. **The Library of Congress: A Guide to Genealogical and Historical Research.** Salt Lake City, UT, Ancestry, 1990. 381p. index. $35.95. ISBN 0-916489-48-5.

The Library of Congress boasts an impressive array of materials useful for genealogical research, but identifying what and where those materials are has always been somewhat problematic. Neagles's handbook provides valuable guidance that will enable genealogical researchers to make the most of these valuable resources. The volume is organized into three sections: "The Library: Its History, Divisions, and Catalog Systems," "Categories of Research," and "Key Source Material: Regional and State." Text, maps, photographs, and suggested research procedures guide readers through the Library of Congress buildings, then through various divisions and reading rooms and their catalogs, indexes, bibliographies, and numerous other resources. More than 2,700 titles—most of which are finding aids for state, geographical, immigration, and ethnic records—are noted; call numbers for books listed and suggested LC subject headings for various types of genealogical research help readers design a research strategy. Although the index could use improvement in detail, comprehensiveness, and subject access, this is nevertheless a useful tool for those wishing to explore the genealogical resources of the Library of Congress.

Another guide to our national genealogical materials that libraries may want to have on hand is the *Guide to Genealogical Research in the National Archives* (National Archives and Records Service, 1982, 304p., $35.00, $25.00pa., ISBN 0-911333-00-2; 0-911333-01-0pa.). Arranged in four sections, the guide covers population and immigration, military records, records relating to particular groups (American Indians, civilian government employees, etc.), and a variety of other useful records, such as claims records, court records, and cartographic records. Because NARS has kept only government records (and few from the colonial period), those are the only materials included here.

257A. Sinko, Peggy Tuck. **Guide to Local and Family History at the Newberry Library.** Salt Lake City, UT, Ancestry, 1987. 202p. index. $16.95. ISBN 0-916489-24-8.

Although written for the serious genealogist, Sinko's well-organized and readable work will be valuable for the novice as well. The Newberry Library's Local and Family History Section is one of the country's preeminent resources for genealogical research; this work describes its holdings by type of material (published sources, census records, church records, ethnic sources, military records, heraldic societies, passenger lists, special Newberry sources, and miscellaneous collections) and also describes its state-specific sources. Bibliographies, guides, periodicals, and serial publications are noted in each chapter.

CHAPTER

7

Geography

ATLASES

World Atlases

258. **Geography on File.** New York, Facts on File, 1992. 1v. (various paging). maps. index. $165.00. Loose-leaf with binder. ISBN 0-8160-2803-6.

A table of contents, a half-page foreword, a page of sources, and an index accompany this compendium of 250 maps, tables, and graphs. The work is intended to offer "the student, teacher and researcher a wide variety of images on both human and physical geography." The work is divided into two sections: the first covers general skills, climate and weather, the Earth, people, economy, and resources; the second treats the regional geography of such major areas as the United States and Canada, Southeast Asia, and North Africa. All of the material in *Geography on File* is copyright-free and designed to be reproduced on standard photocopiers. Annual updates are available for $40.00 each.

Libraries may also wish to purchase *Geography on File*'s companion title, *Maps on File* (1992, $175.00, loose-leaf with binder, ISBN 0-8160-2802-8), which consists of approximately 400 maps plus a comprehensive 5,000-entry index. The maps cover every country, every U.S. state and Canadian province, and all oceans and continents, as well as major economic and political issues in the news. Annual updates are also available at $40.00 each.

259. **Hammond Atlas of the World.** Maplewood, NJ, Hammond, 1992. 303p. illus. maps. index. $65.00. ISBN 0-8437-1175-2.

The Hammond atlases are well known for quality and authority, and this mid-sized atlas, based on a computerized geographic database, is no exception. The main body of the atlas consists of 160 pages of maps (more than 60 of which are double-page spreads), including those of the continents and their most important regions at increasing scales. Introductory material includes brief sections on the history of cartography, map projections, and use of this atlas. A thematic section of eight pages is devoted to global relationships regarding environment, population, language and religions, living standards, energy and resources, agriculture and manufacturing, climate, and vegetation. A map index on the inside front cover, the table of contents, and an alphabetical quick-reference guide simplify the location of maps of specific areas.

92

For libraries that favor the Hammond approach but need a less expensive alternative, the *Hammond Atlas of the World, Concise Edition* (1993, 231p., $39.95; $24.95pa., ISBN 0-8437-1180-9; 0-8347-1181-7pa.) is a good choice. Its 120 maps are preceded by several helpful sections, including "Interpreting Maps," "Quick Reference Guide," "Global Relationships," "The Physical World," and "Geographical Comparisons."

260. **National Geographic Atlas of the World.** 6th ed. Washington, DC, National Geographic Society, 1990. 1v. (various paging). illus. maps. index. $74.95; $59.95pa. ISBN 0-87044-399-2; 0-87044-398-4pa.

National Geographic Society maps have a richly deserved reputation for quality and attention to detail; this general-reference atlas reflects those characteristics as well. It consists of 133 double-page plates that include thematic maps of the habitable Earth (biosphere, climate, population, food, minerals, energy, physical world, and political world). Stunning satellite mosaic images are reproduced for each continent. Although the large physical and political maps are the focus of this excellent compendium, there are also smaller maps that represent topical data such as population, land use cover, resources and industry, transportation, and environmental stress. Supplementing the maps are short text profiles for 176 countries and for individual U.S. and Canadian states and provinces, and a 150,000-name gazetteer.

261. **The New International Atlas.** Chicago, Rand McNally, 1994. 1v. (various paging). illus. (col.). maps. index. $150.00. ISBN 0-528-83693-5.

Considered a world standard, this annually revised, multilingual (English, German, Spanish, French, and Portuguese) atlas comprises about 40 pages of global distribution maps; 288 continental, regional, and local plates; 31 pages of glossary, urban population figures, and abbreviations; and a 200-page place-name index. Although expensive, *The New International Atlas* is worth its price for libraries that can afford it.

262. **Rand McNally Goode's World Atlas.** 18th ed. Edward B. Espenshade, Jr., ed. Skokie, IL, Rand McNally, 1990. 367p. illus. (col.). maps. index. $28.95. ISBN 0-528-83128-3.

Goode's continues to provide reliable information, competently produced, in a convenient size and format, for an exceptional price. Standard items, such as the index of pronunciation and introductions to maps and imaging, have been retained in this edition, while maps have been revised to reflect (to the extent possible) current geopolitical changes. Data on nuclear and geothermal energy, military and economic alliances, iron ore, ferroalloys, and precious metals have been incorporated into new and revised maps; data on health care, cancer and heart disease, hazardous waste sites, poverty and unemployment, and educational expenditures have been incorporated into the U.S. maps. For libraries that can only afford one atlas and need the best buy for the money, *Goode's* would probably be the first choice.

In the crowded and highly competitive market for world atlases, Rand McNally has numerous offerings, of which *Goode's* is the standard-bearer. The main competitor to the Rand McNally publications, however, is Hammond, which has an equally daunting number of quality atlases among which hapless librarians must attempt to differentiate. In general, the Hammond atlases contain maps that are clear and easy to use, their information is up-to-date and reliable, and the publications are reasonably priced. Therefore, it will often be simply a matter of personal preference or familiarity when choosing between competing Hammond and Rand McNally atlases.

Both of these publishers produce excellent works that have served reference librarians and the public well for many years.

263. **Reader's Digest Atlas of the World.** Pleasantville, NY, Reader's Digest; distr., Rand McNally, 1987. 240p. illus. (part col.). maps. index. $34.95. ISBN 0-89577-264-7.

Reader's Digest's reasonably priced atlas comprises a 128-page "core atlas" of world and regional maps; 63 pages of maps that describe physical and cultural phenomena (geology, hydrology, climatology, anthropology, history, and finance); an information table of several pages; and a 42-page index. The maps, created by Rand McNally, are graphically clean and well reproduced. This is a good atlas for the price, and a nice complement to the standard *Goode's* (entry 262).

264. **Times Atlas of the World.** 8th comprehensive ed. New York, Times Books, 1990. 225p. $159.95. ISBN 0-8129-1874-6.

The eighth edition of the *Times Atlas of the World* continues the high standards of its predecessors. It offers very detailed maps of most geographic and urban locations, preceded by nearly 50 pages of introductory text. In addition, there are graphic size comparisons for continents, oceans, river basins, islands, and inland water bodies, and a 210,000-item place-name index that includes latitude and longitude coordinates. This is a standard purchase for libraries that can afford it.

United States

265. Bacon, Josephine. **The Doubleday Atlas of the United States of America.** New York, Doubleday, 1990. 125p. illus. maps. index. $17.95. ISBN 0-385-26395-3.

This is a reasonably priced, visually stimulating atlas of the United States that, unlike the Rand McNally publications, does not include Canada. Arrangement is by three broad geographic groupings. Within groupings, each state is accorded a two-page treatment that includes state name; popular name; state bird, flower, and tree; a relief map that notes major geological features; capital; scale; several photographs of representative scenery; cash crops; and demographics.

266. Glassborow, Jilly, and Gillian Freeman, eds. **Atlas of the United States.** New York, Macmillan, 1986. 127p. illus. maps. index. $50.00. ISBN 0-02-922830-1.

Using a thematic and comparative approach to describing the United States within the context of the rest of the world's nations, Glassborow and Freeman's atlas comprises 35 state-unit maps and 25 world maps based on country units. The U.S. maps cover natural resources, population, the economy, transportation, and social conditions; the maps of the world treat population, gross national product, food, foreign aid, minerals and energy, manufacturing, international trade, foreign investments, transport and communications, literacy and learning, health, alliances, and military expenditures. Concise narratives and useful graphics accompany the maps, and data sources are fully documented.

Another more recent work by Macmillan is Catherine M. Mattson and Mark T. Mattson's *Contemporary Atlas of the United States* (1990, 118p., $90.00, ISBN 0-02-897281-3), a thematically based atlas that covers a broad range of "contemporary" issues, such as toxic waste sites, AIDS occurrence, and the AMTRAK rail network. It is arranged in seven sections—"The Land," "The Past," "The People," "The Economy," "Transportation and Communication," "The Government," and "The Environment"—and includes a concise index and bibliography.

267. **Rand McNally Road Atlas: United States, Canada, Mexico.** Skokie, IL, Rand McNally, 1994. 1v. (various paging). maps. index. $7.95pa. ISBN 0-528-81084-7.

A standard, inexpensive purchase for all libraries, the annually updated *Rand McNally Road Atlas* is an indispensable guide to traveling by car through North America. It includes free and toll limited-access highways, four-lane divided highways, principal highways, other through highways, unpaved roads, and scenic routes, as well as rest areas, campgrounds, airports, dams, national parks and forests, points of interest, mountain peaks, major colleges and universities, and ferries.

Two other useful road atlases are *USAtlas: Richard Saul Wurman's Road Atlas* (Richard Saul Wurman, New York, ACCESS Press; distr., Prentice-Hall, $9.95pa., ISBN 0-13-057027-3), written to identify the smartest way to get to a given location by the author best noted for his Access Travel Guidebook series, and the *United States, Canada, [and] Mexico Road Atlas* (H. M. Gousha; distr., Prentice-Hall, 1990, $3.95pa., ISBN 0-13-622390-7), an inexpensive and handy (8-1/2 by 11-inch) ready-reference tool that provides quick answers but not too much detail.

268. **State Maps on File.** New York, Facts on File, 1993. 7v. maps. index. $425.00 loose-leaf with binders/set. ISBN 0-8160-0116-2. (Volumes may be purchased separately.)

The maps included in this multi-volume, loose-leaf set are meant to help students, educators, and other nonprofit groups that need to make photocopies of state maps. The black-and-white maps, printed on heavy paper, are fairly general (and occasionally simplistic) in presentation, and include topical coverage of such areas as historical, physical, legal, and administrative data. An average of 20 maps are included for each state; all maps are updated to reflect the legislative changes since the 1990 census.

Canada

269. **National Atlas of Canada.** 5th ed. Ottowa, Energy, Mines, and Resources, Canada; distr., Canada Publications Center, 1985- . Individual sheets. $152.00/set; $5.00 Canadian/sheet. No ISBN or ISSN available.

Produced by the Canadian government, this is a regularly updated thematic atlas that describes the physical features and resources of Canada. As noted in the preface, the fifth edition of the *National Atlas of Canada* is a serial publication of separate maps that will be published over a period of years. Materials are organized into 44 separately titled and numbered "realms of information" that together do a good job of surveying the diverse geographic elements of coast-to-coast Canada. The atlas, also available in French, is a standard purchase for those needing geographic information on Canada.

BIBLIOGRAPHIES

270. Harris, Chauncy D., and others, eds. **A Geographical Bibliography for American Libraries.** Washington, DC, Association of American Geographers and National Geographical Society, 1985. 437p. index. $25.00. ISBN 0-89291-193-X.

The stated purpose of this volume is to assist libraries in their efforts to identify, select, and acquire important geographical books and serials. Within these parameters, the bibliography describes 2,903 entries, arranged by 4 major form or subject categories: general geographical aids and sources; history; theory and methodology of geography; and specific fields (e.g., human geography, applied geography, regional geography). A separate section notes publications especially suited to the needs of school libraries.

271. Kister, Kenneth F. **Kister's Atlas Buying Guide: General English-Language World Atlases Available in North America.** Phoenix, AZ, Oryx Press, 1984. 236p. index. $10.95. ISBN 0-912700-62-9.

Best known for his dictionaries and encyclopedia buying guides, Kister here presents information on 105 English-language general world atlases published between the 1970s and early 1980s. The work contains concise evaluative reviews arranged alphabetically by atlas title; each review includes full bibliographic and purchasing information, a history of the work, a brief evaluation that often compares the work to similar publications, and review citations. The reviews are supplemented by numerous cross references; a brief bibliography of articles on maps and atlases; a comparison chart of atlases by size, price, and other features; a 26-page section describing how to evaluate an atlas; and a comprehensive index that includes former and variant titles, of which there are many.

BIOGRAPHIES

272. Bohlander, Richard E., ed. **World Explorers and Discoverers.** New York, Macmillan, 1992. 531p. illus. maps. index. $85.00. ISBN 0-02-897445-X.

The 313 individuals profiled in *World Explorers and Discoverers* encompass significant explorers from all times and all places, including persons whose work as geographers, inventors, and historians (for example, Herodotus) has helped advance exploration. Entries range from 400 to 4,000 words, and provide nationality, vital dates, and major accomplishments. Brief bibliographies conclude longer entries. Supplementary materials include a glossary, lists of explorers by nationality and by area of exploration, an extended general bibliography, and an index of personal names, places, and subjects.

Libraries looking for a less expensive but still reliable reference in this subject area may want to consider Carl Waldman and Alan Wexler's *Who Was Who in World Exploration* (Facts on File, 1992, 712p., $65.00, ISBN 0-8160-2172-4). With more than 800 entries and 120 illustrations, this biographical dictionary ranges in scope from ancient through contemporary times, although the primary focus is on the "Age of Exploration," roughly the 15th through 19th centuries. Each entry provides standard biographical data, a brief chronology highlighting the biographee's contributions to world exploration, plus several paragraphs of historical narrative about the person. Although the book lacks an index, it does offer two appendixes (one listing explorers by region of exploration and the other presenting 15 maps of the world that show important countries and locations in the history of exploration); many black-and-white prints of old maps scattered throughout the text; and a 14-page bibliography.

273. Burton, Rosemary, Richard Cavendish, and Bernard Stonehouse. **Journeys of the Great Explorers.** New York, Facts on File, 1992. 224p. illus. maps. index. $34.95. ISBN 0-8160-2840-0.

The stories of 30 famous travelers, from the time of Alexander the Great to the Space Age, are chronicled here in engaging biographical essays. Among those featured are Christopher Columbus, James Cook, and Thor Heyerdahl, plus lesser-knowns such as explorer/scholar Alexander von Humbolt and travel writer Freya Stark. The biographical essays are complemented by nine topical essays addressing topics such as the exploration of Australasia and the Pacific, naturalists and plant hunters, and pioneer women travelers. Black-and-white and color photographs and pictures, detailed and well-executed maps of exploration routes, numerous sidebars, and a short index of people, places, and subjects further enhance the text.

DICTIONARIES AND ENCYCLOPEDIAS

274. Garrett, Wilbur E., ed. **National Geographic Index 1888-1988.** Washington, DC, National Geographic, 1989. 1215p. illus. maps. $26.95. ISBN 0-87044-764-5.

National Geographic magazine has been a standard purchase for most public libraries for more than a century. For those libraries, this index is a must. It provides 1,148 entries encompassing 7,000 magazine articles, as well as videos, map supplements, books, and other National Geographic materials. Preceding the entries are 100 pages of front matter that describe the history of the journal, its stories, illustrations, writers, and photographers. The index is arranged by subject category; within category, by reverse chronological order.

275. Reynolds, Jean E., ed. in chief. **Lands and Peoples.** Danbury, CT, Grolier, 1993. 6v. illus. maps. index. $166.00/set. ISBN 0-7172-8016-0.

Geared to the intellectual abilities of fifth-graders and above, the multi-volume *Lands and Peoples* has been a standard reference for school and public libraries for years. Its stated purpose is to provide accurate, interesting, and readable information about all countries, their peoples, and their ways of life, and it consistently meets this goal. Countries of the world are listed alphabetically within continent; the final volume includes an index to the set and a section with information on Earth extremes (wettest, driest, etc.); continental extremes; and information on significant mountain peaks, deserts, oceans, seas, islands, rivers, and cities. Among a wealth of other supplementary materials are checklists of emperors, tsar, shoguns, and other rulers; lists of dynasties, presidents, and prime ministers; a four-page overview of important dates in world history; a four-page glossary of geographical terms; and selected conversion tables.

276. Small, John, and Michael Witherick. **A Modern Dictionary of Geography.** 2d ed. New York, Edward Arnold; distr., Routledge, Chapman & Hall, 1989. 247p. maps. $45.00; $17.95pa. ISBN 0-340-49317-8; 0-340-49318-6pa.

This highly regarded dictionary integrates terms from both physical and cultural geography to produce an accessible overview of the language of geography. Generous cross references and about 125 illustrations complement the entries. Although there is no index and no bibliographic citations have been included, *A Modern Dictionary of Geography* is nevertheless a good basic introductory work for those undertaking geography studies.

If there is strong patron interest (and expertise) in this area, libraries may also wish to consider two other works. The first is the *Dictionary of Human Geography* (3d ed., R. J. Johnston and others, eds., Basil Blackwell, 1993, 576p., $89.95; $22.95pa., ISBN 0-631-18141-5; 0-631-18142-3pa.), a standard work geared toward anthropology students and practicing anthropologists, which provides more technical definitions of terms related to the study of human beings in their social and cultural environments. The second is Andrew Goudie's *The Encyclopedic Dictionary of Physical Geography* (Basil Blackwell, 1988, 528p., $85.00; $22.50pa., ISBN 0-631-13292-9, 0-631-15581-3), which includes brief definitions as well as longer, scholarly, signed articles accompanied by brief bibliographies.

277. **Webster's New Geographical Dictionary.** Springfield, MA, Merriam-Webster, 1988. 1376p. maps. $24.95. ISBN 0-87779-446-4.

Published on an ongoing basis since the mid-1950s, this standard resource includes more than 47,000 entries, 200-plus maps, and about 15,000 cross references. This wealth of material covers individual countries, dependencies, major administrative subdivisions, largest cities, and significant natural features. Entries include spelling, pronunciation, and—for geographic areas—information on location, population, size, economy, and history. Although international in scope, entries for the United States, Canada, and English-speaking countries predominate, based on the assumption that these countries are the primary audience for the dictionary.

The Cambridge World Gazetteer: An A–Z of Geographical Information (5th ed., David Munro, ed., Cambridge University Press, 1990, 1v. [various paging], $44.95, ISBN 0-521-39438-4), a pronouncing geographical dictionary, is the work most frequently mentioned as the complement to *Webster's*. Although it includes only about half as many entries as its competitor, and focuses more strongly on Great Britain, for the areas it does cover the *Cambridge World Gazetteer* offers more detailed information than *Webster's*.

GEOGRAPHY AND TRAVEL GUIDES

278. Frome, Michael. **National Park Guide [yr.].** New York, Prentice-Hall General Reference, 1966- . Annual. 1v. $16.00pa. (1994 ed.). ISSN 0734-7960.

All 49 U.S. national parks are described in Frome's handy guide. Each park's entry leads off with a photograph and a brief essay touching on the area's historical and geological facts, followed by a "practical guide" that notes weather, facilities, and programs; hiking trails and roads; tours offered; and opportunities for activities like fishing, bird-watching, and photography. Additional chapters address U.S. archaeological, historical, natural, and recreational areas. Recent editions of this annual have included suggestions for disabled travelers and information on children's activities.

279. Hecker, Helen. **Travel for the Disabled: A Handbook of Travel Resources and 500 Worldwide Access Guides.** Portland, OR, Twin Peaks Press, 1985. 185p. index. $19.95pa. ISBN 0-933261-00-4.

Hecker's valuable guide is intended to take a lot of the frustration out of travel for the disabled and those traveling with them. Printed in large type on heavy stock, it describes 500 access guides and accessible locales in the United States, Canada, and internationally. Guides to hotels, motels, parks, and campgrounds are described; separate chapters describe travel options by automobile, bus, train, aircraft, and ship.

Another recommended publication in this area is Wendy Roth and Michael Tompane's *Easy Access to National Parks: The Sierra Club Guide for People with Disabilities* (Sierra Club Books; distr., Random House, 1992, 404p., $16.00pa., ISBN 0-87156-620-6). Based on the personal experiences of one of the authors as a wheelchair-bound traveler, this work's strength is the first-hand knowledge and practical advice contained in the detailed, descriptive entries for each park.

280. Heise, Jon O., and Julia R. Rinehart. **The Travel Book: Guide to the Travel Guides.** 2d ed. Metuchen, NJ, Scarecrow, 1993. 397p. index. $42.50. ISBN 0-8108-2697-6.

This annotated bibliography arranges its 385 English-language travel guides by continent and then by individual country; for North America and selected European countries, separate treatment is extended to states, regions, and individual cities. Walking guides, automobile-club guides, outlet shopping directories, and guides to ghost towns in Texas are but a few of the types of resources listed. Entries typically provide standard bibliographical information plus an annotation that is both descriptive and evaluative. Indexing is by geographical location or series title; no individual titles are given.

281. Hyman, Mildred. **Elderhostels: The Students' Choice.** 2d ed. Santa Fe, NM, John Muir, 1991. 304p. illus. $15.95pa. ISBN 0-945465-98-X.

The Elderhostel program has been wildly successful over the past 15 years, but unfortunately the enterprise's official catalog leaves much to be desired in terms of comprehensiveness of information. Hyman's guide steps in to fill the void, using information about courses and campuses/facilities provided by the students themselves. Grouped in chapters by state or country, individual programs from throughout the world are described and evaluated as to courses of study, quality of instructors, environment, housing, food, unique attributes, shortcomings, getting in, and getting there.

282. Simony, Maggie, ed. **The Traveler's Reading Guide: Ready-Made Reading Lists for the Armchair Traveler.** Rev. and updated ed. New York, Facts on File, 1993. 510p. index. $50.00. ISBN 0-8160-2648-3.

In her third iteration of a much-loved work, Simony describes about 5,150 monographs that will delight armchair travelers everywhere. The reading guide is organized by format within geographic categories, with a range of travel books and guides that reflect the writing of such notables as Robert Louis Stevenson, Paul Theroux, and John McPhee. Half of the items cover North America and about one-quarter focus on Europe, with the remaining works devoted to destinations in the rest of the world. In addition to the standard travel books and guides, roughly one-third of the entries are fiction; an appendix lists novels with English settings. An excellent resource for all public libraries, regardless of size.

In addition to the titles noted here, most libraries will also want to have on hand the standard works such as *Baedecker's*, *Birnbaum's*, *Fielding's*, *Fodor's*, *Michelin*, the Mobil guides, and the Insight guides. Depending on patron interest, however, libraries may also wish to have in their collections some of the more specialized works that deal with topics such as vacationing with the kids, bed-and-breakfast guides, adventure travel, and cruise guides.

8

History

ARCHAEOLOGY

283. Coe, Michael, Dean Snow, and Elizabeth Benson. **Atlas of Ancient America.** New York, Facts on File, 1986. 240p. illus. (part col.) maps. bibliog. index. $45.00. ISBN 0-8160-1199-0.

The six parts of this work are "The New World" (an overview of cultures and the environment, European discovery, native peoples, and New World archaeology), "The First Americans" (a survey of the movement of peoples into the New World), "North America," "Mesoamerica," "South America," and "The Living Heritage" (a brief summary of present-day cultures). The North America, Mesoamerica, and South America sections comprise the bulk of the atlas. Although the approach of this work is scholarly, it is written in a manner easily accessible to the lay reader, and is especially noteworthy for its balanced presentation of conflicting theories and interpretations. Outstanding illustrations, excellent color maps and photographs, a selective bibliography, a detailed gazetteer, and a thorough subject index further enhance the reference value of the atlas.

Where there is strong patron interest in archaeology, libraries may also wish to have on hand Franklin Folsom and Mary Elting Folsom's publication, *America's Ancient Treasures: A Guide to Archeological Sites and Museums in the United States and Canada* (4th ed., University of New Mexico Press, 1993, 459p. $37.50; $19.95pa., ISBN 0-8263-1424-4; 0-8263-1450-3pa.). A guide to archaeology sites in the United States and Canada that can be visited by the general public, the work is arranged by region (and by state within region), and includes a glossary, a list of suggested readings, a guide to national, state, and local archaeological societies, and an index.

284. Whitehouse, Ruth D., ed. **The Facts on File Dictionary of Archaeology.** Rev. ed. New York, Facts on File, 1984. 597p. illus. bibliog. index. $35.00. ISBN 0-87196-048-6.

The definitions that make up this overview of archaeological terminology range in length from several hundred words to one or two pages. Although the definitions are somewhat technical, they are for the most part accessible to the educated lay reader or beginning archaeology student. Charts, illustrations, and a very detailed topical subject index supplement the entries.

WORLD HISTORY

General Works

Atlases

285. Barraclough, Geoffrey, and Geoffrey Parker, eds. **The Times Atlas of World History.** 4th ed. Maplewood, NJ, Hammond, 1993. 360p. illus. maps. index. $95.00. ISBN 0-7230-0534-6.

Since it was first published in 1978, *The Times Atlas of World History* has been a standard purchase for most libraries, regardless of size, and this beautifully produced and authoritative edition continues the tradition. It contains more than 600 maps and illustrations interwoven with about 300,000 words of text contributed by more than 100 historians. The atlas also provides a glossary that further describes people, groups, events, and treaties identified in the text, and an index of historical place names that notes both where a significant event took place and where it is mentioned in the book. Although expensive, this historical atlas is well worth its purchase price.

286. Vidal-Naquet, Pierre, ed. **The Harper Atlas of World History.** Rev. ed. New York, HarperCollins, 1992. 355p. illus. (part col.). maps. index. $40.00. ISBN 0-06-270067-7.

Essentially an atlas of human history, *The Harper Atlas of World History* is replete with diagrams, maps, illustrations, and photographs, all accompanied by extensive texts explaining everything from human evolution and the origins of humans in Africa to the Gulf War of 1990–1991. After a brief overview of cartography, the basic organization of materials is chronological. In addition to the stunning maps, detailed textual commentary describes the art, society, economy, demography, history, politics, and science and technology of a given age, civilization, or culture. The atlas is current through the reunification of Germany, the dissolution of the Soviet Union, and the birth of the Commonwealth of Independent States.

In addition to these sweeping overviews of the history of humanity, libraries will also want to have on hand a number of more specialized historical atlases. Examples of these include *Atlas of Ancient Egypt* (1980, $45.00, ISBN 0-87196-334-5); *Atlas of the Islamic World since 1500* (1982, $45.00, ISBN 0-87196-629-8); *Atlas of the Roman World* (1982, $17.95, ISBN 0-87196-652-2); *Atlas of the Greek World* (1981, $45.00, ISBN 0-87196-448-1); *Atlas of Medieval Europe* (1983, $45.00, ISBN 0-87196-133-4); and *The Middle Ages* (1990, $17.95, ISBN 0-8160-1973-8), all published by Facts on File.

Biographies

287. Deford, Miriam, and Joan Jackson. **Who Was When.** 3d ed. Bronx, NY, H. W. Wilson, 1976. 184p. $50.00. ISBN 0-8242-0532-4.

Arranged chronologically, this compendium lists the birth and death dates of 10,000 influential figures who passed this way between 500 B.C. and 1974 A.D. An index to individuals by birth and death dates is included. The main list also categorizes individuals by one of ten broad fields of activity.

288. Magill, Frank N., ed. **Great Lives from History: Twentieth Century Series.** Pasadena, CA, Salem Press, 1990. 5v. index. $365.00/set. ISBN 0-89356-565-2.

This multi-volume Magill publication is one of a series of similar works that describe influential individuals from the United States, Great Britain and the Commonwealth, and the rest of the world to 1900. This work excludes American and British figures, and its 475 profiles focus primarily on individuals (both living and dead) whose career trajectories or personal influence have taken place since 1900. Biographees include state leaders, artists, scientists, philosophers, religious leaders and thinkers, filmmakers, and musicians. The format follows the standard Magill approach: a brief headnote with vital information and a concise description of the biographee, his or her early life, life's work, summary, and a selected English-language bibliography of six to eight items.

For a single-volume biographical work focusing on the 20th century, *The International Dictionary of 20th Century Biography* (Edward Vernoff and Rima Shore, New American Library, 1989, 736p., $12.95pa. ISBN 0-452-00952-9), offers more than 5,600 entries. Although it does not include bibliographies, it is relatively inexpensive and provides handy ready-reference information.

Chronologies

289. Grun, Bernard. **The Timetables of History.** 3d ed. New York, Simon & Schuster, 1991. 724p. index. $35.00pa. ISBN 0-671-74271-X.

As with previous editions, this familiar resource continues to arrange its material in seven parallel chronologies of events: history and politics; literature and theater; religion, philosophy, and learning; visual arts; music; science, technology, and growth; and daily life. History "starts" at 5,000 B.C. and runs through the end of 1991. There are so many reference uses for this chronology, and its price is so reasonable, that it is strongly recommended for all libraries, regardless of size.

290. Scarre, Chris. **Smithsonian Timelines of the Ancient World.** New York, Dorling Kindersley, 1993. 256p. illus. maps. index. $49.95. ISBN 1-56458-305-8.

For the purposes of this engaging chronology, Scarre's definition of the ancient world ranges from the origins of life to the European Renaissance. Within these parameters, some 2,000 illustrations, drawings, and maps detail the movement of history both regionally and globally. The accompanying text is well written and accessible to both children and adults. An excellent reference for homes as well as libraries.

291. Tapsell, R. F. **Monarchs, Rulers, Dynasties, and Kingdoms of the World.** New York, Facts on File, 1983; facsimile ed., Ann Arbor, MI, Books on Demand, 1988. 511p. $138.00pa. ISBN 0-7837-2668-6.

Tapsell's chronology provides uniquely comprehensive coverage of history's various rulers and ruling groups, including kings and queens, maharajas and amirs, sultans and czars. The work falls into two broad areas: the first is an encyclopedic, alphabetically arranged guide to dynasties and states; the second a listing of dynasties, grouped geographically. The listing of dynasties is enhanced by a coding system that enables the reader to keep track of what would otherwise be highly confusing family relationships.

292. Trager, James. **The People's Chronology: A Year-by-Year Record of Human Events from Pre-history to the Present.** Rev. ed. New York, Henry Holt, 1992. 1237p. illus. index. $45.00. ISBN 0-8050-1786-0.

Less scholarly than either *Timetables of History* or *Smithsonian Timelines of the Ancient World*, Trager's chronology goes beyond the standard categories of politics, economics, religion, arts, education, communications, technology, and sports, to include such "contemporary" areas as nutrition, consumer protection, and the environment. Although ostensibly international in its scope, the chronology nevertheless contains information of most interest to a U.S. readership. A 110-page cross index concludes this entertaining and informative resource.

Dictionaries and Encyclopedias

293. Drexel, John. **The Facts on File Encyclopedia of the 20th Century.** New York, Facts on File, 1991. 1046p. illus. maps. index. $79.95. ISBN 0-8160-2461-8.

The aim of *Encyclopedia of the 20th Century* is to be a guide to the important people, places, events, and ideas that have shaped the contemporary world. The categories covered among its 10,000 entries include world leaders and politicians; writers, artists, and musicians; intellectual movements, ideas, and "isms"; popular culture; war, international crises, and terrorism; diplomacy and law; and science and aviation. Coverage is current through mid-1990. About 1,000 photographs and maps and a thorough index round out the encyclopedia.

294. **Great Events: The Twentieth Century.** Pasadena, CA, Salem Press, 1992. 10v. illus. maps. index. $250.00/set. ISBN 0-89356-796-5.

Although not specifically designated an encyclopedia, this multi-volume set is truly encyclopedic in its coverage of the 472 events the editors believe have shaped the destiny of the 20th century. Written by experts, the chronologically arranged entries all begin with a descriptive title followed by a sidebar listing basic information of what, when, where, and who. Both the background of the event and its subsequent consequences are discussed in clearly written prose that is accompanied by a contemporary photograph or print. Five indexes—chronology, key words, categories, geography, and people—facilitate access to this excellent historical resource.

295. Langer, William L. **Encyclopedia of World History: Ancient, Medieval and Modern, Chronologically Arranged.** 5th ed., rev. and enl. Boston, Houghton Mifflin, 1972. 1569p. illus. maps. genealogical tables. index. $44.00. ISBN 0-395-13592-3.

Langer's well-known historical encyclopedia is arranged in broad chronological periods, then geographically within periods and then again chronologically within geographic region. Focusing for the most part on political, military, and diplomatic history up through 1970, the descriptions of events are concise but authoritative and are enhanced by numerous cross references. Supplementary materials include genealogical tables; lists of emperors, popes, and rulers; chronological outlines and outline maps; and a detailed, comprehensive index.

296. **Larousse Dictionary of World History.** New York, Larousse Kingfisher Chambers, 1994. 996p. $40.00. ISBN 0-7523-5001-3.

Although an effort has been made to achieve geographic balance (Asian, African, Latin American, and East European) in this Larousse dictionary, the focus of the roughly 7,500 single-paragraph entries it offers is political and military biography; in fact, artists, writers, religious figures, philosophers, and even scientists have been excluded unless their contributions had political or military significance. In addition, the work is somewhat inconsistent in its organization and presentation.

However, its dictionary-style treatment of the entire span of recorded history and its currency relative to other offerings make it a recommended purchase for concise, up-to-date coverage of world history.

United States

Atlases

297. **Historical Atlas of the United States.** Rev. ed. Washington, DC, National Geographic Society, 1993. 289p. illus. maps. index. $71.45. ISBN 0-87044-970-2.

Written by subject specialists, the revised edition of this highly regarded atlas reflects the usual exacting standards librarians have come to expect from Society publications. The first part of the work is arranged into six thematic sections: land, people, boundaries, economy, networks of transportation, and communities. These groupings are followed by chronological chapters that reflect major events in American history and development. A thorough, detailed bibliography (including map and illustration notes, selected sources, and names of consultants), an extensive index, and an accompanying folder that contains large historical maps of 17 U.S. regions complete this outstanding atlas.

Libraries looking for a less expensive, if also considerably less ambitious, historical atlas may wish to consider the *Atlas of American History* by Robert H. Ferrell and Richard Natkiel (Facts on File, 1993, 192p, $27.95; $19.95pa, ISBN 0-8160-2883-4; 0-8160-2884-2pa.). The bulk of its 250 two- and four-color maps, 150 color and black-and-white illustrations, and substantial narrative are presented in six chronologically arranged chapters; statistical information, territorial expansion and population maps, and presidential election maps follow. Libraries that own the Scribner's American History group of reference works may also wish to purchase the *Atlas of American History* (2d rev. ed, Macmillan, 1984, 306p, $70.00, ISBN 0-684-18411-7), an authoritative, scholarly work that is also accessible to the lay reader.

Bibliographies and Source Documents

298. Adams, James Truslow, ed. **Album of American History.** New York, Scribner's, 1982. 3v. illus. index. **Supplement I.** 1984. 350p. ISBN 0-684-16848-0/set.

Editor of the well-known *Dictionary of American History* and *The Atlas of American History*, Adams and his editors searched museums, libraries, private collections, and public institutions throughout the United States to obtain the pictorial material used in these volumes. The items are arranged chronologically: volume 1 treats the colonial period and the years 1783 to 1853 (roughly the period of westward expansion); volume 2 addresses 1853 through 1917; and volume 3 treats 1917 through 1968. In addition, volume 3 provides a comprehensive index to the set's 6,300 pictures. The supplement covers the years 1968-1983, and adds about 900 illustrations to the set.

299. Adler, Mortimer J., and others, eds. **The Annals of America.** Chicago, Encyclopaedia Britannica, 1987. 21v. $449.00/set. ISBN 0-87927-199-6.

Some 2,300 source materials (laws, speeches, stories, diaries, journals, books, articles, reminiscences, and other primary sources) reflective of American life, culture, events, and thought comprise this highly regarded, chronologically arranged historical reference. The documents, covering the years from 1492 to 1986, were selected for their historical importance and contemporary relevance. Prefatory and introductory essays, numerous lengthy chronologies, many color maps, some 100 pages of illustrations, and a biographical index of authors are included in each volume. A two-volume conspectus and a one-volume index complete the set.

If *The Annals of America* is deemed too costly either in terms of budget or shelf space, *Documents of American History* (10th ed., Henry Steele Commager and Milton Cator, eds., Prentice-Hall, 1988, 2v., $41.00/v., ISBN 0-13-217274-7 [v. 1], 0-13-217282-8 [v. 2]) is a good alternative. Designed to illustrate the course of American history from the Age of Discovery to the present, this basic reference work is a chronologically organized compendium of official and quasi-official documents relating to American history and life. The 727 items include treaties, letters, speeches, Supreme Court decisions, historic acts, proclamations, and other documents of historical significance. The materials are arranged chronologically, beginning with the privileges and prerogatives granted Columbus, dated April 30, 1492, and ending with 1987 documents. A topic and personal name index keyed to document rather than page number facilitates access.

300. Blazek, Ron, and Anna H. Perrault. **United States History: A Selective Guide to Information Sources.** Englewood, CO, Libraries Unlimited, 1994. 411p. index. $55.00. ISBN 0-87287-984-4.

A comprehensive, annotated bibliography of U.S. social history, this work is arranged into general sources by format, topics (e.g., military history, regional history), and issues (e.g., law and crime, the gay experience, sports, and games). Nearly 950 titles and electronic reference sources are described and evaluated as to strong and weak points, with coverage current through mid-1993. Access to the entries is facilitated by separate author/title and subject indexes.

301. Cohen, Norman S. **The American Presidents: An Annotated Bibliography.** Pasadena, CA, Salem Press, 1989. 202p. index. $40.00. ISBN 0-89356-658-6.

Aimed at students and general readers, *American Presidents* annotates some 750 easily accessible books that address either the presidency or those who have held that office. It is divided into three sections: bibliographies on the presidency and presidents in general, general studies of the presidency, and works that focus on specific presidents (the bulk of the titles listed). Each entry includes a bibliographic citation and a 25- to 250-word evaluative annotation. This work provides an excellent starting place for undergraduate and interested laypersons seeking to learn more about previous White House occupants.

302. VanMeter, Vandelia. **American History for Children and Young Adults: An Annotated Bibliographic Index.** Englewood, CO, Libraries Unlimited, 1990. 324p. index. $32.50. ISBN 0-87287-731-0.

This bibliographic index of American history books published primarily between 1980 and 1988 is designed to serve the needs and interests of school and public librarians and secondary level students. Each of the 2,901 entries contains title, author/editor, series, publisher/distributor, publication date, cost, physical description, grade level, and a brief annotation. Arrangement is by Sears subject heading within chronological division and subdivision; author, title, subject, series, and grade level indexes are included. The bibliography is published with a corresponding computer disk compatible with IBM, Macintosh, or Apple II computers.

Biographies

303. Kane, Joseph Nathan. **Facts about the Presidents: A Compilation of Biographical and Historical Information.** 6th ed. Bronx, NY, H. W. Wilson, 1993. 432p. illus. index. $55.00. ISBN 0-8242-0845-5.

Facts about the Presidents, a standard reference source in almost all libraries, arranges its information in two sections. The first describes (in a chapter for each) the lives of America's presidents, including family background, political career and significant events, election, administration, and cabinet appointments. The second section presents comparative information for the presidents, such as number of children, number and titles of books written, and so on. In addition, information regarding the presidency in general, such as presidential and vice-presidential salaries, cabinet officers, and perquisites of the office, is included. *Facts about the Presidents* is current through Bill Clinton.

Another excellent reference in this subject area is William DeGregorio's *The Complete Book of U.S. Presidents* (4th ed., Barricade Books, 1994, 740p., $21.00, ISBN 0-942637-92-5). Each president is accorded his own chapter, within which there may be as many as 38 different subheadings, an arrangement that facilitates quick access to sought-after information. For an inexpensive but handy reference, libraries may also wish to consider Charles A. Beard's familiar *The Presidents in American History: George Washington to George Bush* (2d ed., Simon & Schuster, 1989, 227p., $14.95; $6.95pa., ISBN 0-671-68574-0; 0-671-68575-9pa.). Especially appropriate for the needs of school-age children, the work consists of individual profiles (including a picture and a brief biographical essay) for each president, accompanied by a biographical section that notes each president's birth, death, marriages, public career, and terms of offices, as well as cabinet members and popular and electoral vote tallies.

304. Klapthor, Margaret Brown. **The First Ladies.** 6th ed. Washington, DC, White House Historical Association; distr., Sewall, 1989. 90p. illus. $9.95pa. ISBN 0-912308-39-7.

Jointly undertaken by the White House Historical Association and the National Geographic Society, *The First Ladies* comprises double-page entries for each woman: a full-page portrait (most in color) accompanied by a page of narrative. The text provides a warm, personal account of the first ladies' private and political lives.

America's first ladies are chronicled in a number of worthwhile publications, each of which has its own special approach and strengths. Diana D. Healy's *America's First Ladies* (Atheneum, 1991, 314p., $25.00, ISBN 1-56956-182-6) offers thematically arranged, three- to nine-page biographies that concentrate on each woman's role, attitudes, and behavior. Carole Waldrup's *Presidents' Wives: The Lives of 43 Women of Strength* (McFarland, 1989, 381p., $24.95, ISBN 0-89950-393-4) focuses more on the personal than the public/political side of each of the lives described. *Presidential Wives* (Paul F. Boller, Oxford University Press, 1988, 544p., $24.95, $10.95pa., ISBN 0-19-503763-4; 0-19-505976-Xpa.) offers essays of a more anecdotal nature, and Peter Hay's *All the Presidents' Ladies* (Viking, 1988, 368p., $9.95, ISBN 0-14-009755-4) brings humor, lively gossip, and intriguing detail to the subject at hand. Also, lest we forget the importance of the second-in-command, libraries may also wish to consider for acquisition *Our Vice-Presidents and Second Ladies* (Leslie W. Dunlap, Scarecrow, 1988, 397p., $35.00, ISBN 0-8108-2114-1), an entertaining and informative book that profiles 43 vice-presidents (John Adams to George Bush) and their relationships with their wives.

305. Purcell, L. Edward. **Who Was Who in the American Revolution.** New York, Facts on File, 1993. 548p. illus. index. $60.00. ISBN 0-8160-2107-4.

Purcell's book profiles more than 1,500 men and women who played major and supporting roles in the American Revolution, whether as patriots, Loyalists, French allies, or British foes. The alphabetically arranged entries range in length from one paragraph to several pages, and include birth and death dates as well as standard biographical background. Additionally, bibliographies are appended to many of the profiles.

306. Sifakis, Stewart. **Who Was Who in the Civil War.** New York, Facts on File, 1988. 766p. illus. bibliog. index. $35.00pa. ISBN 0-8160-1055-2.

Some 2,500 Civil War participants—generals and lesser officers, federal and state officials, members of Congress, political activists, journalists, diplomats, foreign leaders, engineers, and others—are profiled in Sifakis's biographical dictionary. The brief entries focus on the individual's participation in the war effort, and include birth and death dates, ranks and positions, major contributions, and a historical perspective of the individual's influence. Supplementary materials include roughly 250 primary-source illustrations and photographs, a monthly chronology of the war's major events, a list of officers who received the thanks of the U.S. Congress for their wartime contributions, a selected bibliography, and indexes of people, places, and topics.

For specific coverage of Confederate individuals, there is Jon L. Wakelyn's *Biographical Dictionary of the Confederacy* (Greenwood Press, 1977, 601p., $85.00, ISBN 0-8371-6124-X), which covers leaders who made outstanding political, business, intellectual, and/or military contributions to the South's war efforts. In addition to helpful bibliographical citations, the work includes appendixes that classify the profiled individuals by geographical movements pre- and post-Civil War, occupation, religious affiliation, education, and party affiliation.

Chronologies

307. Carruth, Gordon. **The Encyclopedia of American Facts & Dates.** 9th ed. New York, HarperCollins, 1993. 1039p. index. $40.00. ISBN 0-06-270045-6.

The ninth edition of this highly regarded reference brings its coverage current through Bill Clinton's election as president in November 1992, thus covering more than 1,000 years of American history. Arranged chronologically and concurrently according to four general (and somewhat eclectic) categories, the encyclopedia presents roughly 15,000 facts and dates laid out on two-page spreads. Although the format occasionally makes it difficult to follow text from one page to another, this is nevertheless a handy resource whose wealth of details (accessed by an extensive index) make it a good complement to *Timetables of American History* (entry 310).

308. Gross, Ernie. **This Day in American History.** New York, Neal-Schuman, 1990. 477p. index. $49.95. ISBN 1-55570-046-2.

Some 11,000 events and individuals drawn from America's past are noted in a handy month-by-month, day-by-day format. A detailed 70-page index facilitates easy access to the items included, which range from 1492 through 1989 and include events and people from such diverse fields of endeavor as entertainment, government and politics, sports, literature, and religion.

309. Kirshon, John W., and Daniel Clifton, eds. **Chronicle of America.** Liberty, MS, J. L. International, 1993. 984p. illus. maps. index. $54.95. ISBN 1-872031-50-1.

Chronicle of America is the perfect reference for those who prefer their facts in "news-bite" form rather than placed in a broader context or on a historical continuum. Ranging from pre-history through 1988, the materials are organized by era, with each section introduced in a single-page overview. At least two pages are devoted to each year; these two-page spreads lead off with a list of important events, then segue into a newspaper-like narrative supplemented by more than 3,000 color and black-and-white photographs, illustrations, and reproductions of works by major American artists. Although this work is heavier in poundage than in intellect, it is nevertheless a useful reference for patrons who are content and comfortable with a *USA Today*-style approach to history.

310. Urdang, Laurence, ed. **The Timetables of American History.** New York, Simon & Schuster, 1983. 470p. index. $20.00pa. ISBN 0-671-25246-1.

Inspired by Bernard Grun's *Timetables of History* (entry 289), Urdang's chronologically arranged work presents in columnar fashion concurrent events in America and "elsewhere" (i.e., the rest of the countries of the world). Entries are subsumed under "History and Politics," "The Arts," "Science and Technology," and "Miscellaneous." Coverage starts with A.D. 1000 ("Norsemen under Leif Ericson land on the coast of North America") and goes through 1980. An index provides access to the events listed.

Dictionaries and Encyclopedias

311. **Dictionary of American History.** Rev. ed. New York, Scribner's, 1976. 8v. index. $695.00/set. ISBN 0-684-13856-5.

Some 7,200 articles written by 800 subject specialists describe America's political, economic, social, and cultural history in this standard, authoritative work. Entries vary in length from a short paragraph to several pages, and are signed by their contributors; the longer articles are subdivided chronologically and, if necessary, by specific aspects of the subject. Brief bibliographies (whose citations unfortunately do not include publisher or date of publication) accompany many of the entries, and there is a thorough, generously cross-referenced index. First published in 1940, the *Dictionary of American History* does not include biographical profiles, to avoid overlap with its companion publication, the *Dictionary of American Biography* (entry 37).

For libraries facing severe budget constraints, a good alternative to the multi-volume set is its single-volume abridgment, *Concise Dictionary of American History* (David William Voorhees, ed., Macmillan, 1983, 1140p. $95.00, ISBN 0-684-17321-2). Its 6,000 unsigned entries are well written and informative, and provide a quick overview rather than the more in-depth coverage found in the parent publication.

312. Faragher, John Mack, ed. **The Encyclopedia of Colonial and Revolutionary America.** New York, Facts on File, 1990. 484p. illus. index. $50.00. ISBN 0-8160-1744-1.

About 1,500 alphabetically arranged entries, from "Abortion" to "Peter Zenger," cover the military, political, social, cultural, economic, religious, and ethnicity-related issues and events that transpired during this dynamic period of American history. Coverage begins with the earliest explorations and discoveries and concludes with the Treaty of Paris in 1783. Entries, many of which are signed, range in length from 50 to several thousand words and often include bibliographies for further reading. Supplementary materials include 150 black-and-white illustrations and maps, 18 topic guides, and a reliable index.

Handbooks and Guides

313. Johnson, Thomas H. **The Oxford Companion to American History.** New York, Oxford University Press, 1966. 906p. $49.95. ISBN 0-19-500597-X.

This reasonably priced but highly regarded work is a biographical and historical guide to the lives, events, and places that figured prominently in America's history and development. In just over 4,700 entries (most about 2,000 words in length), the work manages to cover the social, political, and economic bases, as well as art, science, commerce, literature, education, and law. Its approach is informational rather than scholarly; although clearly not a resource for recent history, the *Companion* nevertheless is an excellent resource for the eras that it does cover.

314. Prucha, Francis Paul. **Handbook for Research in American History: A Guide to Bibliographies and Other Reference Works.** 2d ed. Lincoln, NB, University of Nebraska Press, 1994. 256p. index. $25.00; $9.95pa. ISBN 0-8032-3701-4; 0-8032-8731-3pa.

Intended to introduce beginning historians (and mystified students) to the resources (both print and electronic) available to them in the library, rather than to serve as a comprehensive listing of all such resources, Prucha's handbook identifies and frequently describes more than 1,500 titles in American history. The work is divided into two parts. The first consists of 17 sections covering traditional library reference sources (bibliographies, library catalogs, periodical indexes, archival guides, etc.), with separate chapters on oral history materials, government sources, guides to legal resources, geographical sources, and databases. Part 2 is devoted to individual historical disciplines, and covers in 15 sections such topics as political, military, social, economic, and technological histories. A comprehensive author/title/subject index completes the handbook.

Australia

315. **The Oxford Illustrated Dictionary of Australian History.** New York, Oxford University Press, 1993. 316p. $49.95. ISBN 0-19-553243-0.

This book is an alphabetically arranged dictionary of significant events, people, and places found throughout Australia's history, from its earliest days through the mid-1980s. It comprises about 550 brief, readable entries (ranging from "Aboriginal flag" to "Zeehan") supplemented by numerous cross references. Coverage includes Australia's political, military, economic, social, cultural, and scientific disciplines, and the institutions, ideas, movements, events, and documents drawn from them. Many black-and-white illustrations are judiciously interwoven with the text, enhancing its value as an excellent and easily used ready-reference source for historical questions about the land down under.

Canada

316. Bercuson, David J., and J. L. Granatstein. **The Collins Dictionary of Canadian History: 1867 to the Present.** Don Mills, Ontario, Collins, 1988. 270p. illus. maps. $24.95. ISBN 0-00-217758-7.

Surveying Canadian history from Confederation through the mid-1980s, this dictionary offers about 1,600 alphabetically arranged entries, ranging in length from a couple of paragraphs to a couple of pages. Coverage is especially strong for politics and labor, less so for sports and the arts. The work is generously cross-referenced, and includes a sprinkling of black-and-white illustrations, a timeline, and appendixes listing governors general, prime ministers, provincial premiers, election results, immigration statistics, and other useful information.

For a reasonably priced and reasonably current chronology of Canadian history, libraries may wish to consider Jay Myers's *The Fitzhenry & Whiteside Book of Canadian Facts and Dates* (Fitzhenry & Whiteside, 1986, 354p., $24.95pa, ISBN 0-88902-584-3). Coverage runs from *Leif the Lucky* (first European in North America) through the early 1980s; arrangement of its nearly 6,000 facts is by month within year. Name and subject indexes conclude this handy work.

317. **Historical Atlas of Canada.** Toronto and Cheektowaga, NY, University of Toronto Press, 1987- . 3v. illus. maps. $95.00/v. ISBN 0-8020-2495-5 (v. I); 0-8020-34447-0 (v. II); 0-8020-3448-9 (v. III).

It is likely that in the coming decades Canada will play an increasingly important role in the economic, trade, and political fortunes of countries throughout the world, and especially the United States. Consequently, this multi-volume set will be an important, if expensive, purchase for libraries whose patrons want to learn more about Canada, whether for understanding or opportunity. The three volumes are: "From the Beginning to 1800" (v.1, 1987), "The Land Transformed, 1800-1891" (v.2, 1993), and "Addressing the Twentieth Century, 1891-1961 (v.3, 1990). Beautifully illustrated in full color, the volumes graphically render a broad range of physical and social aspects of Canadian history and prehistory. Coverage is truly multidisciplinary, encompassing national, geographic, ethnic, regional, provincial, and thematic data. Artists' renderings, paintings, maps, charts, tables, and text are interwoven with the maps throughout. Although a scholarly undertaking, the *Historical Atlas of Canada* is presented at an intellectual level appropriate and quite useful to lay readers.

China

318. O'Neill, Hugh B. **Companion to Chinese History.** New York, Facts on File, 1987. 397p. maps. $27.50. ISBN 0-87196-841-X; 0-8160-1825-1pa.

Encyclopedic in nature, O'Neill's work provides basic information on Chinese history from pre-history to the mid-1980s. The approximately 1,000 entries range from "abacus" to "Zhejiang" and encompass facts, figures, biographies, and descriptions of events, people, places, movements, and institutions central to the development of China. In addition to the core entries, which are generously cross-referenced and occasionally include suggestions for further reading, there are a chronology and several historical maps.

Eastern Europe

319. Magosci, Paul Robert. **Historical Atlas of East Central Europe.** Seattle, WA, University of Washington Press, 1993. 218p. maps. index. $75.00. ISBN 0-295-97248-3.

The 90 maps found in this valuable atlas chronicle the rich history of East Central Europe from the early fifth century through 1992. Coverage includes Poland, the Czech Republic, Slovakia, Hungary, Romania, Slovenia, Croatia, Bosnia-Herzegovina, Yugoslavia, Macedonia, Albania, Bulgaria, and Greece, as well as the eastern parts of Germany, Bavaria, Austria, northeastern Italy, historical Poland-Lithuania, Belarus, Moldavia, western Turkey, and parts of the Ukraine. Arranged chronologically, the maps are accompanied by text that describes the history of a particular region; in addition, many of the maps show key historical events and items, including military actions, ecclesiastical structures, culture and education, demography, ethnicity, and economic factors. An excellent index concludes the work.

Europe

320. Cook, Chris, and John Stevenson. **The Longman Handbook of Modern European History 1763–1985.** White Plains, NY, Longman, 1987. 435p. maps. bibliog. index. $25.95pa. ISBN 0-582-48584-3.

This handbook encompasses the political, diplomatic, social, and economic history of France, Germany, Austria-Hungary, Italy, and Spain from the latter half of the 18th century through the mid-1980s. It is divided into eight sections, which contain a list of principal rulers and ministers; an overview of major events relating to single or several countries; a brief description of principal wars, campaigns, and treaties; statistical and demographic information; 180 brief, alphabetically arranged biographies; a glossary; a topical bibliography (35 topics are briefly described, then readings and essay topics are recommended); and 11 maps. A detailed index rounds out the work. Although by no means a comprehensive or definitive work in this subject area, this Longman handbook works well for ready-reference questions.

321. Gutman, Israel, ed. **Encyclopedia of the Holocaust.** New York, Macmillan, 1990. 4v. illus. maps. index. $440.00. ISBN 0-02-896090-4.

As defined by the editors of this important encyclopedia, the Holocaust was "the physically destroy the Jews of Europe." This attempt, including its antecedents and subsequent effects, is exhaustively chronicled in articles that include biographies (Nazis, resistance fighters, Jews both inside and outside of occupied Europe, world leaders such as Churchill and Pius XII, collaborators, and relief workers); treatments of the "machinery" of the Holocaust (gas chambers, gas vans, death marches, deportation, forced labor, medical experimentation, etc.); descriptions of individual extermination camps; surveys of the broad range of anti-Semitic activities, programs, and symbols promoted by the Nazi state; and examinations of the effect of Nazism and the Holocaust on the Jewish and non-Jewish populations of countries spread throughout the world. Articles are signed and include recommendations for further reading; cross references are numerous. Photographs, maps, and appendixes (a chronology; a glossary; lists of Jewish organizations, Einsatzgruppen, and war crimes defendants; and a country-by-country estimate of Jewish losses during the Holocaust), along with a well-constructed index, round out the encyclopedia. Although libraries that already own *The Encyclopaedia Judaica* (entry 776) will have a substantial amount of

Holocaust information provided by that work, *The Encyclopedia of the Holocaust* is highly recommended for libraries where there is strong patron interest in this devastating period of history.

For libraries that would like to offer a broader range of works to support Holocaust studies, Harry James Cargas's *The Holocaust: An Annotated Bibliography* (2d ed., American Library Association, 1985, 196p., $15.00, ISBN 0-8389-0433-5) is highly recommended. Arranged in 15 topical chapters, the work describes and often evaluates about 500 English-language titles appropriate for high schools, colleges, and public libraries.

Great Britain

322. Isaacs, Alan, and Jennifer Monk, eds. **The Cambridge Illustrated Dictionary of British Heritage.** New York, Cambridge University Press, 1986. 484p. illus. maps. bibliog. $42.95. ISBN 0-521-30214-5.

An informative, authoritative, and engaging overview of British life and British history, *The Cambridge Illustrated Dictionary of British Heritage* comprises 1,500 unsigned entries plus a generous number of cross references, maps, genealogies, charts, and 150 black-and-white photographs. The editors have been delightfully broad in their approach, so that the range of topics addressed includes not only the basics (battles, folklore, schooling, religious denominations, royalty) but also many of the unusual and interesting aspects of British life and history that, taken together, define the "British heritage." A valuable and reasonably priced resource for all libraries.

Latin America

323. Lombardi, Cathryn L., and John V. Lombardi, with K. Lynn Stoner. **Latin American History: A Teaching Atlas.** Madison, WI, published for the Conference on Latin American History by the University of Wisconsin Press, 1983. 1v. (various paging). maps. index. $22.50. ISBN 0-299-09710-2.

This reliable, inexpensive historical atlas includes maps on the Latin American environment; the Iberian background; the pre-Columbian period; the period of discovery and conquest; the colonial governments; trade, resources, and competition; the campaigns for independence; Latin American boundaries from independence to modern times; and Latin American international relations in the 20th century. A 40-page index both provides access to the information in the text and serves as a gazetteer to Latin American place names.

Russia

324. Paxton, John. **Encyclopedia of Russian History: From the Christianization of Kiev to the Breakup of the USSR.** Santa Barbara, CA, ABC-Clio, 1993. 484p. maps. $65.00. ISBN 0-87436-690-9.

This work contains some 2,500 entries ranging from 30 to 300 words. Coverage is very broad, including not only history but also literature, the arts, political science, geography, education, and other disciplines of the social sciences. Although reviewers have noted that coverage is occasionally spotty or misleading, overall the work stands as a good source of information on more than a thousand years of Russian history. A glossary and a well-thought-out bibliography supplement the text.

325. **The Soviet Union.** 3d ed. Daniel C. Diller, ed. Washington, DC, Congressional Quarterly, 1990. 352p. illus. maps. index. $22.95pa. ISBN 0-87187-574-8.

Comprising brief, reasonably current, and accurate articles, *The Soviet Union* offers essays on Imperial Russia and the Stalin, Khrushchev, and Brezhnev eras. Other lengthy entries address the challenges inherent in structural, economic, and political reform; ethnicity; foreign policy; the military; and U.S.-Soviet relations. Emphasis throughout is on the Russian people and Moscow, rather than on the outlying regions. In addition to the excellent articles, there are numerous useful appendixes, documentary inserts, and illustrations.

9

Law

GENERAL WORKS

Bibliographies

326. Baker, Brian L., and Patrick J. Petit, eds. **An Encyclopedia of Legal Information Sources: A Bibliographic Guide to Approximately 29,000 Citations for Publications, Organizations, and Other Sources of Information ... .** 2d ed. Detroit, Gale, 1993. 1083p. $165.00. ISBN 0-8103-7439-0.

Although intended for "lawyers and law-related professionals," this compendium of 29,000 citations to books, journals, online databases, organizations, and audiovisual materials will be useful to any researcher (in any field) needing to find bibliographical or directory information on legal resources. Emphasis is on titles published from 1980 forward, although some older classic works have been included. Materials are organized under 480 topical headings, further subdivided by type of source (textbooks, directories, handbooks, etc.). Entries include full publication information, frequency (if appropriate), and publisher/producer address; prices are not included. An extensive outline of contents plus a generous number of *see* and *see also* references help users not familiar with legal terminology navigate the vast amount of information found here.

327. Eis, Arlene L., comp. and ed. **Legal Looseleafs in Print.** Teaneck, NJ, Infosources, 1981- . Annual. 1v. index. $90.00/yr. (1994 ed.). ISSN 0275-4088.

Stern's indispensable work identifies roughly 4,000 law-related loose-leaf services, published by hundreds of publishers as well as an occasional government agency. Each entry includes title, author/editor, publisher, year of initial publication, number of volumes, frequency of supplementation, and annual cost. The publisher list provides full directory information. A subject index, based on Library of Congress subject headings, gives title and publisher and then refers the user back to the title list for more complete information. Especially helpful for the librarian needing to verify ordering, bibliographic, cost, and frequency information. The same publisher also offers a companion annual, *Legal Newsletters in Print* (1v., $90.00/yr. [1994 ed.], ISSN 8755-416X), which offers information similar to that found in *Looseleafs* for legal newsletters.

328. Houdek, Frank G. **Law for the Layman: An Annotated Bibliography of Self-Help Law Books.** Littleton, CO, Fred B. Rothman, 1991. 1v. (various paging). index. $42.50/loose-leaf with binder. ISBN 0-8377-0685-8.

Houdek's annotated bibliography of self-help law titles offers a good starting point for laypersons trying to track down books appropriate to their legal needs. The text comprises two parts, the first a very short section on general and comprehensive works and the second a lengthy section on specific subjects such as adoption, bankruptcy, and immigration. Each entry provides standard bibliographical data plus a brief descriptive annotation. The work also includes author, title, and jurisdiction indexes, as well as a publisher list with addresses and telephone numbers.

Biographies

329. Cushman, Clare, ed. **The Supreme Court Justices: Illustrated Biographies, 1789–1993.** Washington, DC, Congressional Quarterly, 1993. 576p. illus. index. $39.95. ISBN 0-87187-723-6.

Cushman's compendium presents chronologically arranged biographies for the 106 current (as of 1993) and past U.S. Supreme Court Justices who have helped interpret and mold the laws of the land. The book succeeds in its goal of introducing the general reader to all of the Justices—those fallen into obscurity as well as those better known—and to give less well-known biographical information about the most famous. Bibliographies of general and in-depth sources for further reading and research accompany each profile. Although its biographical profiles are certainly no substitute for individual works devoted to the Justices themselves, the strengths of the biographies found here are the added historical sources, views of contemporaries, and lively anecdotes.

330. **Martindale-Hubbell Law Directory.** Martindale-Hubbell, 1931- . Annual. 24v. $605.00/yr. (1994 ed.). ISSN 0191-0221.

Martindale-Hubbell lists all attorneys who have been admitted to the U.S. bars, plus leading attorneys and law firms from more than 130 other countries. Arrangement is alphabetical by state, city within state, and attorneys and law firms within city. Biographical information includes birth date, colleges and law schools attended, date of bar admission, and area of legal expertise. A rating based on other attorneys' assessments of an individual's professional abilities is included for many of the attorneys listed. Also available online and on CD-ROM.

331. **Who's Who in American Law.** Chicago, Marquis Who's Who, 1977/78- . Biennial. 1v. index. $249.95 (1994 ed.). ISSN 0162-7880.

Who's Who in American Law provides biographical sketches of leading lawyers and judges, as well as legal educators, law librarians, legal historians, social scientists, and others in law-related fields. The individuals profiled, all of whom provide their own biographical information, are selected based on position of responsibility or noteworthy achievement. Each profile includes vital statistics, education, career history, awards, publications, memberships, and areas of professional interest. The cumulative index lists individuals by legal specialty as well as by geographic area. Also available on CD-ROM and on magnetic tape.

Libraries may also wish to consider a more specialized guide to American law specialists, Steven W. Naifeh and Gregory White Smith's biennial, *The Best Lawyers in America* (Woodward/White, 1v., $110.00/yr. [1994 ed.], ISSN 1067-4756). Issued every two years, it includes an alphabetical listing of attorneys within each state and the District of Columbia by category, city (small as well as large), and name. Entries include name, firm association, address, and telephone number, and occasionally area of specialization. Inclusion is based on telephone interviews with attorneys familiar with those selected.

Dictionaries and Encyclopedias

332. Black, Henry Campbell, and others. **Black's Law Dictionary.** 6th ed. St. Paul, MN, West, 1990. 1657p. $29.00. ISBN 0-314-76271-X.

A standard ready-reference tool in most public libraries, the approximately 30,000 entries found in *Black's* cover all areas of the law, including taxes, accounting, commercial transactions, civil procedure, criminal procedure, federal court rules, evidence, finance, insurance, labor relations, estate planning, federal agencies, Restatements of the Law, and uniform model laws. Definitions are detailed, include case citations, and frequently provide cross references to related terms. Appendixes include a table of abbreviations, the U.S. Constitution, an organizational chart of the U.S. government, and several other useful tables and charts.

Similar coverage is provided for about 30,000 terms by *Ballentine's Law Dictionary* (3d ed., James Arthur Ballentine, Lawyers' Cooperative, 1969, 1429p., $25.00, ISBN 0-686-14540-2), so most small libraries will find their needs met adequately by either one. If a less expensive work is desired, however, either West Gilmer's *The Law Dictionary: A Dictionary of Legal Words and Phrases with Latin and French Maxims of the Law Translated and Explained* (6th ed., Scribner's, 1986, 426p., $14.95; $9.95pa, ISBN 0-684-18385-4; 0-684-18429-Xpa.), which contains concise but understandable definitions of legal terms and law-related definitions of common words, or *Ballentine's Law Dictionary: Legal Assistant Edition* (Jack Handler, Delmar/Lawyers Cooperative, 1994, 614pp, $16.95pa, ISBN 0-8273-4874-6), which defines about 10,000 terms of use to paralegals, law students, and legal assistants.

333. Leonard, Robin D., and Stephen R. Elias. **Family Law Dictionary: Marriage, Divorce, Children & Living Together.** Berkeley, CA, Nolo Press, 1990. 193p. illus. $13.95pa. ISBN 0-87337-129-1.

Family Law Dictionary includes a diverse range of alphabetically arranged terms related to family relations, including marriage, divorce, adoption, support, custody, guardianship, cohabitation (living together), paternity, and abortion. Both legal and nonlegal terms are covered. The definitions do a good job of avoiding "legalese," and all entries indicate the context in which the terms are used. The text is supplemented by generous use of cross references, charts, state-by-state comparisons, and several light-hearted illustrations.

334. Mellinkoff, David. **Mellinkoff's Dictionary of American Legal Usage.** St. Paul, MN, West, 1992. 703p. $39.95. ISBN 0-314-00068-2.

An easy-to-use source for clear definitions of often complex legal concepts in U.S. common law, *Mellinkoff's Dictionary* uses nonlegal terminology to precisely define (or translate) words while using cross references to identify relationships. The alphabetically arranged entries vary in length from brief paragraphs to several pages, and include origin, translation (if the term is non-English), and cross references from slang terms to standard phrases or other alternate usages. An index of entries that repeats all terms, variant spellings, and cross references found in the main section appears at the end of the dictionary; however, because it lacks page references, its usefulness is questionable.

Directories

335. Bosoni, Anthony J. **Legal Resource Directory: A Guide to Free or Inexpensive Assistance for Low Income Families, with Special Sections for Prisoners.** Jefferson, NC, McFarland, 1992. 148p. index. $28.95. ISBN 0-89950-737-9.

Nearly 1,800 agencies that offer free or inexpensive help for low-income individuals are described in the *Legal Resource Directory.* Services range from information and referral to hands-on representation in court. Listings are organized by state, then subdivided by civil law offices, criminal law offices, and special programs for prisoners. A second section lists organizations that fight death penalty sentences. A third section lists state chapters of an organization that seeks to improve prison conditions and the correctional processes.

Libraries will want to supplement this title with the National Legal Aid & Defender Association's *Directory of Legal Aid and Defender Offices in the United States and Territories* (1989- , biennial, $30.00 [1993–1994 ed.], no ISSN available), which lists hundreds of legal aid/defender offices at the city as well as state level and also identifies agencies by specialized type of assistance needed.

336. Wasserman, Steven R., and Jacqueline Wasserman O'Brien, eds. **Law and Legal Information Directory: A Guide to More Than 30,500 National and International Organizations ...** 7th ed. Detroit, Gale, 1993. 2v. index. $320.00/set. ISBN 0-8103-7624-5.

Wasserman and O'Brien's massive, two-volume directory identifies national and international organizations, bar associations, bar examination and admission requirements, the federal court system, highest state courts, federal regulatory agencies, law schools, research centers, legal periodicals, legal aid and public defender offices, and a multitude of other legal institutions, services, and facilities. Many sections have their own title/keyword indexes and include descriptive information that goes well beyond the basics. The scope and magnitude of this directory's coverage make it an excellent resource for libraries that regularly field patron questions about the law, its systems, and its practitioners.

Documents and Primary Sources

337. **Code of Federal Regulations.** Office of the Federal Register, National Archives and Records Administration. 1949. Annual updates. 4v. indexes. $620.00/set (1994 ed.). S/N 869-013-00000-5.

CFR brings together all the myriad regulations adopted by federal agencies and executive departments and reported daily in the *Federal Register.* The work is arranged according to broad subject area, and contains information on legally binding rules and regulations that affect the day-to-day affairs of businesses and municipal governments and agencies. Because of the interdependent nature of *CFR* and the *Federal Register,* libraries will wish also to subscribe to the daily publication. Also available on CD-ROM, on magnetic tape, and on microfiche and microform.

338. **United States Code, Containing the General and Permanent Laws of the United States in Force on January 3, 1989.** 1988 ed. Office of the Law Revision Counsel of the House of Representatives; distr., Washington, DC, Government Printing Office, 1989. 27v. plus annual supplements. indexes. Price varies by volume. Y1.2/5:988/[v.].

As a basic source document of the codified laws of the United States, the *U.S. Code* should be in every public library, regardless of size. It includes all general and permanent (as distinct from temporary or emergency) statutory laws currently in force, arranging them into 50 subject groupings called *titles*. The multi-volume set is updated annually with supplements; new editions of the entire work are produced approximately every six years.

Handbooks and Sourcebooks

339. Eisaguirre, Lynne. **Sexual Harassment: A Reference Handbook.** Santa Barbara, CA, ABC-Clio, 1993. 217p. index. $39.50. ISBN 0-87436-723-9.

Eisaguirre's handbook leads off with an overview of the issues and the feminist, legal, management, and male perspectives, followed by a chronology and a biographical section profiling 29 individuals who have influenced the sexual harassment debate. A key chapter reviews laws and cases on sexual harassment, statistics and surveys on the incidence of sexual harassment, the incidence of sexual harassment among particular groups and professions, characteristics of the harasser, how victims respond, and the impact of the Anita Hill/Clarence Thomas affair, among other topics. Other chapters provide a directory of pertinent organizations, an overview of selected print resources, and a list of films and videocassettes. A helpful glossary and thorough index complete the handbook.

340. Jacobstein, J. Myron, and Roy Mersky. **Fundamentals of Legal Research.** 5th ed. Westbury, NY, Foundation Press, 1990. 734p. index. $30.75. ISBN 0-88277-794-7.

As in previous editions of this standard legal reference, American law is the primary focus of the discussion and bibliography. The authors lead off with a description of how the law works through legislation, administrative regulations, and court decisions. They then describe the publications that provide access to the law and how to use them. Additional materials include a glossary of terms, a 118-page table of legal abbreviations, a bibliography of state guides to legal research, a brief discussion of legal research in U.S. territories, an explanation of the national reporter system, a list of specialized report services by subject, and an index.

341. Millman, Linda Josephson. **Legal Issues and Older Ad···** Santa Barbara, CA, ABC-Clio, 1992. 273p. index. $45.00. ISBN 0-87436-594-5.

The aim of Millman's helpful guide is "to identify some common legal issues and provide some basic background to seniors and their advocates." It is organized into two sections. Part 1 provides a narrative description of key legal issues (living wills, income security, health care, housing, consumerism, family law, and estate planning) and describes what legal services and providers are available. Part 2 offers a directory of organizations, primarily those related to issues discussed in part 1. Both sections contain lengthy bibliographies of current literature and reference works. A glossary of terms and a detailed index complete this work, which will be a welcome addition to all public libraries.

342. Mitchell, Ralph. **CQ's Guide to the U.S. Constitution: History, Text, Index, Glossary.** Washington, DC, Congressional Quarterly, 1986. 108p. index. $14.95pa. ISBN 0-87187-392-3.

CQ's Guide to the U.S. Constitution is a very useful resource for tracking down all manner of constitution-related materials. It provides a brief but informative history of the conceptual development (and political negotiating and compromise) that culminated in the writing of the Constitution; the text itself; a subject index that provides references to the exact article or amendment, section, and paragraph in question; and a glossary of terms. This remains a handy, very reasonably priced quick-reference resource on the Constitution.

343. **The State-by-State Guide to Women's Legal Rights.** N.O.W. Legal Defense and Education Fund and Renee Cherow-O'Leary. New York, McGraw-Hill, 1987. 523p. $19.95; $12.95pa. ISBN 0-07-047779-5; 0-07-047778-7pa.

States differ radically in their laws regarding women's rights. Consequently, there is a strong need for a publication such as this guide, which for a very reasonable price covers a great amount of territory. It is arranged in two parts. The first begins with a clearly written summary of the legal process itself, and then offers an overview of four areas as they relate to women: home and family (marriage, divorce, reproductive freedom); education (including athletic scholarships); employment (wages, comparable worth, sexual harassment, Social Security and pension law); and the community (including rape, women in the military, pornography). The second part provides a state-by-state guide to law in each of these areas, with statutory citations. Rounding out the guide are a directory of regional offices for civil rights, chapter notes that frequently include case citations, and a bibliography (current through the mid-1980s) of selected readings.

344. Whalen, Lucille. **Human Rights: A Reference Handbook.** Santa Barbara, CA, ABC-Clio, 1989. 218p. index. $39.50. ISBN 0-87436-093-5.

Whalen's handbook offers both sources of information and documents that will be useful to anyone researching human rights "without regard for political or any other perspective." It includes a chronology of major human rights events spanning 1941 through 1988, a section of biographical sketches of human rights leaders, an annotated listing of organizations and print/nonprint sources of information on human rights, and the actual text of major human rights documents. Access to authors, titles, organizations, documents, and topics is provided through indexing.

If libraries wish a less expensive but adequate introductory information sourcebook, they may want to consider *Human Rights: A Resource Directory* (Thomas P. Fenton and Mary J. Heffron, comps. and eds., Orbis Books, 1989, 156p., $12.95pa., ISBN 0-88344-534-4), which briefly describes organizations, books, periodicals, pamphlets and articles, and audiovisuals related to human rights issues.

345. Witt, Elder. **Guide to the U.S. Supreme Court.** 2d ed. Washington, DC, Congressional Quarterly, 1990. 1060p. index. $189.95. ISBN 0-87187-502-0.

The first edition of this CQ guide was published in 1979, and since that time librarians have come to rely on *Guide to the U.S. Supreme Court* for both current and retrospective information about the Court. Coverage includes the history, organization, operation, and traditions of the Court and the individuals who are a part of it; an overview of the pressures and external parties (from the president and Congress to the media and public opinion) that seek to influence Court decisions; and an examination of the impact of those decisions on government and private citizens. In addition, there are brief biographies of the 105 Justices and extensive bibliographies for five of the seven major sections, as well as appendixes that provide significant Court-related documents and texts, a nominations chart, a glossary, and a list of congressional acts that the Court has ruled unconstitutional. The work is indexed by subject and case. Updated biennially by *The Supreme Court Yearbook* (Congressional Quarterly, 1990– , 1v., $29.95 [1994 ed.], ISSN 1054-2701).

Although the CQ title is usually considered the standard reference in this area, two other publications might also be considered as complementary purchases. These are *The Oxford Companion to the Supreme Court of the United States* (Kermit L. Hall and others, Oxford University Press, 1992, 1032p., $49.95, ISBN 0-19-505835-6) and Elder Witt's *The Supreme Court A to Z: A Ready Reference Encyclopedia* (Congressional Quarterly, 1993, 528p., $110.00, ISBN 0-87187-777-5). The Oxford title has been widely hailed as a scholarly, encyclopedic treatment of almost every imaginable aspect of the Supreme Court (e.g., cases, trivia, procedure, policies, biographies), with the added benefit of crisp, engaging writing. Witt's book successfully attempts to cover all legal terminology, ideas, issues, politics, and people connected with the Court, while also touching on sociology, political science, cultural mores, literature, and similar broad topics. In addition, *A to Z* offers tables on Supreme Court nominees, seating charts of the Justices, the Constitution, and an index that includes all works cited.

CRIMINOLOGY

346. Becker, Harold K., and Donna Lee Becker. **Handbook of the World's Police.** Metuchen, NJ, Scarecrow, 1986. 340p. maps. $32.50. ISBN 0-8108-1863-9.

Handbook of the World's Police surveys the police systems of 160 countries, arranged according to the seven major geographic areas of Africa, the Caribbean, Europe, the Far East, the Middle East, North America, and South America. For each country or territory studied, there is an outline map and then information under the headings "National Name," "Demography" (population, ethnic characteristics, language, religion, literacy, geographic area, capital, and boundaries), "History," "Government," and "Police" (which includes paramilitary forces). Unfortunately, there is no index.

347. DeSola, Ralph. **Crime Dictionary.** Rev. ed. New York, Facts on File, 1988. 222p. bibliog. $27.95. ISBN 0-8160-1872-3.

Although the revised edition of this work has been criticized for inconsistencies in coverage and occasional errors of fact, it nevertheless remains the standard choice for definitions of terms, phrases, institutions and associations, and acronyms related to crime. Thousands of items are defined in brief entries that serve as introductions to, rather than in-depth explanations of, the phrases in question.

348. Fay, John J. **The Police Dictionary and Encyclopedia.** Springfield, IL, Charles C. Thomas, 1988. 370p. $36.25. ISBN 0-398-05494-0.

This dictionary defines nearly 5,000 terms, phrases, and concepts in law enforcement. Entries generally range in length from one to ten sentences, and include slang terms ("sandwiching," "dropping the leather," etc.) likely to be encountered on the street. In addition to the basic definitions, there are clear and informative summaries of Supreme Court rulings that have directly affected the conduct of law enforcement officers. Definitions of felonies, felony sentences, capital offenses, methods of execution, and a Social Security number index are all treated in appendixes; a six-page bibliography concludes the work.

349. Knappman, Edward W., ed. **Great American Trials.** Detroit, Gale (Visible Ink Press [pa.]), 1994. 872p. illus. index. $44.95; 17.95pa. ISBN 0-8103-8875-8; 0-8103-9134-1pa.

Ranging from the Salem witch trials to Rodney King, the 200 cases profiled by Knappman in *Great American Trials* were selected based on historical or legal significance, political controversy, public attention, legal ingenuity, and literary fame. Entries range from several pages to 15 or more, in a writing style that is engaging and understandable to the lay reader. Supplementary materials include 3 separate tables of contents, a 6-page glossary, and a 37-page index.

350. Kohn, George C. **Dictionary of Culprits and Criminals.** Metuchen, NJ, Scarecrow, 1986. 447p. index. $39.50. ISBN 0-8108-1877-9.

It seems there is no limit to our fascination with "bad guys" (male or female), and George Kohn's delightful work is the perfect resource for just such inquiries. Drawing his 1,160 criminals from the past five centuries (but primarily from the last two), Kohn describes basic "career" facts, personality quirks, legal names and nicknames, and birth and death dates. The entries are arranged alphabetically by name, and include those who specialized in burglary, arson, gunfighting, racketeering, murder, piracy, prostitution, rape, smuggling, or megalomania, to name but a few of the preferred professional paths. There are numerous cross references, including *see also* notes to partners in crime. Perhaps of greatest interest to librarians, however, is Kohn's citation of literary references for criminals who have been immortalized in prose.

351. Sifakis, Carl. **The Encyclopedia of American Crime.** New York, Facts on File, 1982. 802p. illus. index. $49.95. ISBN 0-87196-620-4.

More than 1,700 individuals (starting with the Vikings and ending up in the 1980s) are profiled in this popular record of criminals and those who have fought them. The entries are arranged alphabetically by name, and are supplemented by black-and-white photographs, charts, and drawings. Sifakis has made generous use of cross references, and provided subject and geographic access through indexing.

Where there is sufficient patron interest, libraries may also wish to purchase another excellent book by Sifakis, *The Mafia Encyclopedia* (Facts on File, 1987, 367p., $40.00, ISBN 0-8160-1172-9), which describes in approximately 400 entries the players, their special terminology, activities, locations, organizations, and events. Also, for "most wanted" buffs, consider Michael Newton and Judy Ann Newton's *The FBI Most Wanted: An Encyclopedia* (Dell, 1993, 342p., ISBN 0-440-214370-8). It describes the individuals who have shown up on the FBI's most-wanted list from March 14, 1950, when the program was first instituted, through the summer of 1992. For each, it provides background, offenses, prison time, cohorts, and life in crime; many entries include mug shots.

Libraries and Publishing

LIBRARIES

General Works

Bibliographies

352. Hoffmann, Frank. **Intellectual Freedom and Censorship: An Annotated Bibliography.** Metuchen, NJ, Scarecrow, 1989. 244p. index. $27.50. ISBN 0-8108-2145-1.

Intended to serve as a general introduction to the fields of intellectual freedom and censorship, the titles described in this valuable bibliography are predominantly books, periodical articles, and legal materials selected for their research value. They are organized into five broad subject areas: the theoretical foundations of censorship and intellectual freedom; key court cases; professions concerned with intellectual freedom; pro-censorship/anti-censorship representative individuals and groups; and cases of censorship in the mass media. Subheadings further categorize the broad groupings. An excellent index, wherein all materials relevant to a specific subject are identified by means of a code number, rounds out the bibliography.

Dictionaries and Encyclopedias

353. Green, Jonathon. **The Encyclopedia of Censorship.** New York, Facts on File, 1990. 388p. index. $45.00. ISBN 0-8160-1594-5.

A brief overview of the history of book banning leads off Green's work; the balance is devoted to brief, clearly written, and informative articles about banned books, court cases, organizations, and major figures who have either engaged in or been the target of censorship. Although Third World and Eastern countries are included, the emphasis is on Western society. The index is extensive and provides many cross references of names to geographical areas, trials, acts, and broad categories such as art, broadcast media, films, libraries, and literature. The list of books frequently banned (current and retrospective) is both fascinating and depressing.

354. Prytherch, Ray, comp. **Harrod's Librarians' Glossary ... and Reference Book.** 7th ed. Brookfield, VT, Gower, 1990. 673p. $89.95. ISBN 0-566-03620-7.

The 2,800 terms in *Harrod's* reflect the changing role of librarians, as computers and electronic systems become as commonplace as books. The alphabetically arranged entries include acronyms and abbreviations, especially useful in the acronym-ridden field of modern librarianship. Although the definitions are brief, they are well written and understandable. However, some of the abbreviations used within the definitions, as well as some of the cross references, are confusing and should be clarified in future editions.

Directories

355. **American Library Directory [yr.].** New Providence, NJ, R. R. Bowker, 1923- . Annual. 1v. $225.00 (1993–1994 ed.). ISSN 0065-910X.

With information on more than 38,000 U.S. and Canadian public, academic, special, and government libraries and library-related organizations, *ALD* is a familiar resource in all but the smallest libraries. Libraries are listed alphabetically by state and city; entries provide information on personnel, statistical data, subject interests, and special collections. Includes registries of library schools and library consortia as well as a separate section on library services and supplies. Also available on online and on CD-ROM.

356. Coffman, Steve, ed. **The FISCAL Directory of Fee-Based Research and Document Supply Services.** 4th ed. Chicago, American Library Association, 1993. 445p. index. $70.00pa. ISBN 0-8389-2161-2.

The 445 fee-based services identified here include document supply, online database searching, and subcontracted research services offered by all types of libraries. To be included, the service must be "enhanced" over routine library services and must be available to outside clientele. Entries are arranged alphabetically by parent organization name, and provide details about contacts, types of services, online vendors available, research specialties, general price ranges, turn-around time, and basic service policies. Several indexes provide extensive access to the entries by service name, services offered, OCLC codes, online services, research specialties, and geographic location.

357. Kessler, Jack. **Directory of Fulltext Online Resources.** Westport, CT, Meckler, 1992. 138p. index. $30.00pa. ISBN 0-88736-833-6.

A "user-friendly" guide to the chaotic world of the global Internet, Kessler's work offers chapters on the nature of full text in the network environment, commercial full text, CD-ROM, OPACs, bulletin board systems, interest groups, electronic conferences, electronic journals, electronic libraries, and universally available local resources. Each chapter includes lists or examples of possibilities, along with suggestions on how to access them. The book concludes with references, a bibliography, and a less-than-adequate index (an unfortunate circumstance given the wealth of valuable material to be found within the directory's pages).

The *Burwell Directory of Information Brokers* (Helen P. Burwell and Carolyn H. Hill, eds., Burwell Enterprises, 1978- , annual, $59.50 [1994 ed.], ISSN 0147-1678) is another useful resource in this subject area. Previously titled *Directory of Fee-Based Information Services*, the directory contains 1,300 entries for information brokers, freelance librarians, independent information specialists, information packagers, public and academic libraries, and other information retailers in the United States and 44 other countries.

Handbooks and Yearbooks

358. Hillard, James M. **Where to Find What: A Handbook to Reference Service.** 3d ed. Metuchen, NJ, Scarecrow, 1991. 333p. $35.00. ISBN 0-8108-2404-3.

Intended to help librarians help patrons, Hillard's handbook provides a good starting point from which to launch an information search. Hillard has arranged, under 607 subject headings, some 2,000 titles that provide help with patrons' most commonly asked questions. Entries for each title include a bibliographic citation and a brief annotation; although some resources cited have been replaced by more recent editions than those noted, librarians will nevertheless appreciate the directions given. As with previous editions, an essential tool for the ready-reference desk.

359. Kuhlthau, Carol Collier, M. Elspeth Goodin, and Mary Jane McNally, eds. **School Library Media Annual [yr.].** Englewood, CO, Libraries Unlimited, 1982- . Annual. 1v. index. $42.50 (1994 ed.). ISSN 0739-7712.

The aim of *SLMA* is to help professionals in the school library media field to gain new information and stay abreast of the news of the year. To these ends, it explores professional concerns of importance to school library media specialists; describes events and influences that have had a major impact on the school media field in the preceding year; evaluates materials, equipment, and collection development practices; reviews and appraises important current issues and future trends; and analyzes program elements that contribute to improved media services.

360. Olson, Stan, and Ruth Kovacs, eds. **National Guide to Funding for Libraries and Information Services.** 2d ed. New York, Foundation Center, 1993. 190p. index. $85.00pa. ISBN 0-87954-497-X.

Olson and Kovacs list 574 grantmaking foundations and 28 direct corporate giving programs that have shown a substantial interest in libraries, either in their stated purpose or through grants of $10,000 or more in the latest year of record. The five categories of agencies are independent foundations, company-sponsored foundations, direct corporate giving, operating foundations, or community foundations. Entries note address and telephone number, date of establishment, donors, foundation type, financial data, purpose and activities, fields of interest, types of support, limitations, publications, application information, officers and trustees, number of staff, Employer Identification Number, and recent library and information services grants. Additional materials include a glossary, a bibliography of funding guides, a list of Foundation Center publications, and a list of free funding information centers.

361. Simora, Filomena, comp. and ed. **The Bowker Annual Library and Book Trade Almanac [yr.].** New Providence, NJ, R. R. Bowker, 1955- . Annual. 1v. index. $149.95 (1994 ed.). ISSN 0068-0540.

Comprehensive, well-organized, and easy to navigate, *The Bowker Annual* is an indispensable tool not only for the book trade, but also for libraries. It arranges its wealth of facts, figures, tables, directories, news, and trends in five sections. Part 1, "Reports from the Field," summarizes the news of the year, including information contributed by national, international, and federal associations. Part 2, "Legislation, Funding, and Grants," covers the legislative and financial issues affecting libraries and publishing. The third part, "Library/Information Science Education, Placement, and Salaries," reports on trends in these areas and lists accredited library schools (a rapidly diminishing number) and scholarship sources. Part 4, "Research and Statistics," presents separate statistical overviews for libraries and the publishing industry. Part 5, "Reference Information," comprises bibliographies, ready-reference information, and a list of the year's award-winning books. A directory of organizations (including library and school media associations, networks, consortia, and book trade associations), a two-year calendar of events, and an index complete the almanac. Also available on CD-ROM.

Indexes

362. Library Literature [yr.]: An Index to Library and Information Science. Bronx, NY, H. W. Wilson, 1921- . 6/yr. with annual cumulations. 1v. Sold on service basis. ISSN 0024-2373.

Library Literature remains the outstanding index for the library and information science fields. It indexes materials derived from periodicals, articles, books, pamphlets, and library school theses from more than 200 journals and 600 monographs, with subject coverage encompassing automation, cataloging, government funding, CD-ROM and online searching, and publishing, among others. Citations to individual book reviews follow the main body of the annual cumulation. Also available on online, on disk, on CD-ROM, and on magnetic tape.

363. Vertical File Index: Guide to Pamphlets and References to Current Topics. Bronx, NY, H. W. Wilson, 1932- . 11/yr. $50.00 (1994 ed.). ISSN 0042-4439.

Librarians have relied on the *Vertical File Index* to locate free and inexpensive pamphlets and other paperbound items of current interest for more than 60 years. Charts, posters, and maps for classroom use are included, as well as a section of references to current topics that lists citations to periodical articles on subjects of current interest. Entries are listed alphabetically under subject headings, and contain complete bibliographic information, ordering instructions, and (usually) brief annotations. Although monthly issues feature a title index only, the quarterly and semi-annual issues include subject indexes.

Collection Development

364. Children's Catalog. 16th ed. Bronx, NY, H. W. Wilson, 1991. 1346p. index. $90.00. ISBN 0-8242-0805-6.

The 16th edition of *Children's Catalog* identifies more than 6,000 titles considered to constitute a basic print collection for children's libraries. Audiovisual and other nonprint materials have not been included. Classified by subject, the entries contain full bibliographic information, Dewey Decimal Classification number, Sears subject headings, reading level ability, and brief annotations apparently taken mostly from reviews. An extremely helpful combined author/title/subject/analytical index complements the text.

Similar coverage is provided by two other Wilson publications in this series, *Junior High School Library Catalog* (6th ed., 1990, 802p., $105.00, ISBN 0-8242-0799-8) and *Senior High School Library Catalog* (14th ed., 1992, 1464p., $115.00, ISBN 0-8242-0831-5). The junior high edition identifies and briefly annotates 3,219 titles appropriate for grades seven through nine, the senior high edition approximately 6,000 titles for grades ten through twelve. As with the *Children's Catalog*, no audiovisual or other nonprint materials are noted.

365.   Entin, Paula B., and Juliette Yaakov, eds. **Public Library Catalog.** 9th ed. Bronx, NY, H. W. Wilson, 1989. 1338p. index. $180.00. ISBN 0-8242-0778-5.

Long considered an important selection tool for librarians in public libraries of all sizes, Wilson's *Public Library Catalog* presents a mixture of older titles, new editions, and new titles that reflect the best materials in a wide range of hardbound titles published through 1988 and still in print. It includes journals, reference titles, and nonfiction titles that reflect both long-term concerns and contemporary issues such as AIDS, alternative practices in medicine, and problems of the elderly. The more than 7,000 titles and 8,000 analytical entries are classified by subject and include complete bibliographic citations, as well as descriptive annotations. The *Catalog* concludes with a directory of publishers and distributors and an author/title/subject index.

A similar, though more recent, title is Bowker's *Best Books for Public Libraries: The 10,000 Top Fiction and Nonfiction Titles* (Steven Arozena, ed., 1992, 840p., $75.00, ISBN 0-8352-3073-2). This reference consists of some 6,000 nonfiction and 4,000 fiction titles deemed "suitable for general readers (patrons who possess a layperson's knowledge of a wide variety of subjects)." Arrangement is by Dewey Decimal Classification for nonfiction, by genre, and then alphabetically by author for fiction. Brief annotations, citations to reviews, and a listing of major awards accompany each entry. Exclusions include scholarly books, reference titles, works for children, and most titles published prior to 1985. Consequently, *Best Books for Public Libraries* should be considered a complement to, rather than a substitute for, *Public Library Catalog*.

366.   Gallant, Jennifer Jung. **Best Videos for Children and Young Adults: A Core Collection for Libraries.** Santa Barbara, CA, ABC-Clio, 1990. 185p. index. $45.00. ISBN 0-87436-561-9.

Designed as a collection development tool for librarians and educators and as a rental/purchase guide for parents, Gallant's guide provides a selective, annotated list of approximately 350 VHS video titles deemed to be "the best" available for children and young adults. Videos are listed alphabetically by title rather than subject; entries include title, director, producer, distributor, release date, running time, color or black-and-white, sound or silent, price, suggested audience, use (e.g., classroom, discussion group), and a short—but very informative—annotation. Although the index needs to be strengthened in the next edition, this is nevertheless an excellent resource for developing an increasingly popular area of the library's collection.

367.   Gillespie, John T., and Corinne J. Naden, eds. **Best Books for Children: Preschool through Grade 6.** 4th ed. New Providence, NJ, R. R. Bowker, 1990. 1002p. index. $48.00. ISBN 0-8352-2668-9.

The more than 11,000 titles described in this familiar resource are organized by broad subject and curricular area, and then further subdivided into more manageable topical headings. Annotations are very brief (frequently a phrase or short sentence) and indicate subject and grade level; entries include review citations and ISBNs. Indexed by author, illustrator, title, and subject/grade level.

The two other publications in this Bowker series are *Best Books for Junior High Readers* (John T. Gillespie, 1991, 600p., $43.00, ISBN 0-8352-3020-1) and *Best Books for Senior High Readers* (John T. Gillespie, 1000p., 1991, $48.00, ISBN 0-8352-3021-X). Following the standard format described for *Preschool, Junior High Readers* annotates more than 6,000 books for young teens (ages 12 to 15), noting an additional 750 titles appropriate for more advanced readers. *Senior High Readers* annotates more than 10,000 titles to engage the interest (and help with the studies) of teens aged 15 to 18. All three guides are important resources for all libraries, regardless of size.

368. Jensen, Julie M., and Nancy L. Roser, eds. **Adventuring with Books: A Booklist for Pre-K–Grade 6.** 10th ed. National Council of Teachers of English, Committee on the Elementary School Booklist. Urbana, IL, National Council of Teachers of English, 1993. 395p. index. $19.95pa. ISBN 0-8141-0079-1.

This familiar NCTE booklist annotates roughly 1,800 children's books recommended for preschoolers through sixth-graders. Selected on the basis of literary and artistic quality as well as fair and appropriate treatment of minorities, the titles included were published between 1988 and 1992; thus, libraries that hold earlier editions of *Adventuring with Books* tend to retain them and use more recent editions as supplements. Newbery and Caldecott winners are noted. Author, title, and subject indexes provide access to the text.

Another excellent and important NCTE reading list is *Books for You: A Booklist for Senior High Students* (11th ed., Shirley Wurth, ed., 257p, 1992, $16.95pa., ISBN 0-8141-0365-0). Only those books deemed enjoyable for teenagers to read are included. The works are categorized by subject and genre, and are presented in a single, alphabetically arranged, annotated list. A directory of publishers and author, title, and subject indexes are included.

369. Lee, Lauren K., and Gary D. Hoyle, eds. **The Elementary School Library Collection: A Guide to Books and Other Media.** 18th ed. Williamsport, PA, Brodart, 1992. 1254p. index. $99.95. ISBN 0-87272-095-0.

The *Elementary School Library Collection* has become a standard selection tool for school and public libraries for its recommendations of books, audiovisual materials, and computer software programs for preschoolers through sixth-graders. Entries for the nearly 14,000 recommended titles include cataloging and ordering information, a descriptive annotation, interest and reading level estimates, acquisition priority, availability of audiovisual formats, and foreign-language editions. Titles available from the National Library for the Blind and Physically Handicapped, as well as those available in large print, are also noted. Arrangement is by Dewey Decimal classification, followed by author, title, and subject indexes. Appendixes include an author's series list of titles by an author who has written three or more books about a particular character, and a publisher's series list of recommended titles. Although the coverage is similar to that provided by the *Children's Catalog* (entry 364), the two titles complement rather than duplicate each other. When only one can be purchased, it should be *ESLC*, because of its coverage of audiovisual and CD-ROM products as well as print.

370. O'Brien, Geoffrey, ed. **The Reader's Catalog: An Annotated Selection of More Than 40,000 of the Best Books in Print ... .** New York, Reader's Catalog; distr., Random House, 1989. 1382p. illus. index. $24.95pa. ISBN 0-924322-00-4.

A dream come true for bibliophiles, *The Reader's Catalog* provides author, title, and broad subject access to more than 40,000 English-language titles spanning more than 200 different subject categories. Although the somewhat casual approach to selection criteria and inconsistent nature of the annotations detract from the catalog's value as a collection development tool, reviewers have lauded its coverage of subjects frequently marginalized or ignored in mainstream publications and its explicit acknowledgment of the diversity of human experience as brought to life in the world's greatest books.

371. Smallwood, Carol, comp. **Free Resource Builder for Librarians and Teachers.** 2d ed. Jefferson, NC, McFarland, 1992. 313p. index. $24.95pa. ISBN 0-89950-685-2.

Smallwood describes 5,435 items available for free from government agencies and nonprofit organizations. The materials are grouped within 14 topics, including alcohol, disabilities, drug abuse, education, and women; there is a separate section on vertical file headings, resources, and management. Entries have been selected based on usefulness to educators and librarians as well as authority of the source. Access is provided by a detailed list of subgroups in the table of contents as well as by a full index.

PUBLISHING and BOOKSELLING

372. **American Book Trade Directory [yr.].** New Providence, NJ, R. R. Bowker, 1915- . Annual. 1v. index. $215.00 (1994 ed.). ISSN 0065-759X.

This Bowker annual lists well over 27,000 booksellers, wholesalers, and publishers in the United States, Canada, the United Kingdom, and Ireland. Bookstores are arranged alphabetically by city within state; information provided for each includes size of stock, telephone number, areas of specialization, names of owners and buyers, chain affiliation (if applicable), and SAN (Standard Address Number). In addition, one can find information on bookstore chain and franchise headquarters, wholesalers of books and magazines, auctioneers and appraisers of literary property, foreign-language specialists, and exporters and importers. Fortunately, the work also includes an extensive, comprehensive, topically divided index that offers a multitude of access points to this information-packed resource. Also available on CD-ROM.

373. Fulton, Len, and Ellen Furber, eds. **International Directory of Little Magazines and Small Presses.** Paradise, CA, Dustbooks, 1965- . Annual. 1v. $42.95; $26.95pa. (1994 ed.). ISSN 0037-7228.

Dustbooks is well known for its coverage of small and independent presses and magazines, and this work is its flagship publication. It provides alphabetically arranged listings for some 5,200 independent presses, many of which never quite make it into the mainstream publishing directories. Entries include standard information (i.e., name, address, telephone number, areas of specialization, etc.). Supplementing the listings are subject and regional indexes; a list of distributors, jobbers, and agents; and a list of acronyms for industry organizations.

Other works by the Dustbooks folks that most libraries will want to have on hand are *The Directory of Small Press & Magazine Editors & Publishers* (1970- , 1v., $22.95pa. [1994 ed.], ISSN 0095-6414), and the *Small Press Record of Books in Print* (1971- , 1v., $42.95pa. [1994 ed., no ISSN available]). With these three titles, libraries will have the best possible coverage of small and independent presses.

374. **Literary Market Place [yr.]: The Directory of the American Book Publishing Industry with Industry Yellow Pages.** New Providence, NJ, R. R. Bowker, 1940- . Annual. 1v. index. $158.00pa. (1994 ed.). ISSN 0075-9899.

This standard reference work provides directory information for more than 15,800 companies, organizations, associations, and individuals related to the publishing industry in the United States and Canada. The information is presented in 85 chapters, ranging from major publishing companies to small, independent presses to literary agents to magazine subscription agencies, with many subdivisions within each chapter. Chapter indexes and running heads, an index to the book trade and allied associations, and indexes by subject and type of publication all help to orient the reader within this wealth of data. For similar information on an international level, libraries may also want to have Bowker's *International Literary Market Place [yr.]* (1965- , annual, $174.00pa. [1994 ed.], ISSN 0074-6827). *LMP* and *ILMP* are also available on CD-ROM.

375.   **Publishers, Distributors, & Wholesalers of the United States [yr.].** New Providence, NJ, R. R. Bowker, 1978- . Annual. 1v. $165.00pa. (1994 ed.). ISSN 0000-0671.

In addition to its standard directory-type information of mainstream publishers, distributors, and wholesalers, this work also provides unique coverage of small independent and alternative presses; professional, trade, and volunteer organizations; museums; and myriad other groups that publish print materials, audiovisual materials, and software. A total of 70,000 groups are identified. Coverage includes publishing companies not included in other sources such as *Books in Print* or the *American Book Trade Directory*, so it is complementary to those works. Also available on CD-ROM.

376.   Shiflett, Lee. **Bookman's Guide to Americana.** 10th ed. Metuchen, NJ, Scarecrow, 1991. 514p. $49.50. ISBN 0-8108-2464-7.

The tenth edition of *Bookman's Guide to Americana* provides the current prices for some 9,500 predominantly 20th-century American, first-edition novels and nonfiction books on American history and culture that are of sufficient significance to be sought by collectors and librarians. As in previous editions, information is derived from price quotations gathered from out-of-print booksellers' catalogs. Entries are listed alphabetically by author. In addition to title, they provide place and date of publication, publisher, and estimate of current market value. Because newer editions do not necessarily duplicate the coverage of previous editions, it is recommended that libraries keep earlier copies of *Bookman's Guide* for a convenient source of book prices.

GENERAL WORKS

Biographies

377. Dupuy, Trevor N., Curt Johnson, and David L. Bongard. **The Harper Encyclopedia of Military Biography.** New York, HarperCollins, 1992. 834p. $65.00. ISBN 0-06-270015-5.

Renowned military historian Dupuy and his co-authors have produced the standard reference in the field of military biography in this widely hailed work. It profiles more than 3,000 world military leaders and thinkers, from Sun Tzu and Julius Caesar to Colin Powell and Norman Schwarzkopf. Entries range between 200 and 1,000 words and conclude with brief bibliographies of sources. Although many Asian leaders are included, emphasis is on those familiar to students of Western civilization.

A good complement to the coverage and depth of *The Harper Encyclopedia of Military Biography* is Martin Windrow and Francis K. Mason's *A Concise Dictionary of Military Biography: The Careers and Campaigns of 200 of the Most Important Military Leaders* (John Wiley, 1991, 337p., $29.95, ISBN 0-471-53441-2). Although certainly less exhaustive than the Dupuy title, the *Concise Dictionary of Military Biography* is cross-cultural in its study of careers and campaigns, and includes great leaders of non-Western culture.

378. Hawkins, Walter L. **African American Generals and Flag Officers: Biographies of Over 120 Blacks in the United States Military.** Jefferson, NC, McFarland, 1993. 264p. illus. index. $25.95. ISBN 0-89950-774-3.

The one- to two-page career biographical summaries in this volume chronicle the 120 African-Americans who have risen to the rank of general officer or its Navy equivalent. In addition to the biographical profiles, the book includes a chronology of significant dates and actions in the history of Blacks and the U.S. military, a list of significant firsts by Blacks in the military, identification of general officers by service and number of stars, and listings by the states where they were born and the colleges and universities they attended. A thorough index concludes the volume.

Dictionaries and Encyclopedias

379. Ali, Sheikh R. **The Peace and Nuclear War Dictionary.** Santa Barbara, CA, ABC-Clio, 1989. 294p. index. $49.50. ISBN 0-87436-531-7.

The language of nuclear war changes as rapidly as its technology; thus, staying current on the most recent weaponry, systems, acronyms, and buzzwords is difficult. *The Peace and Nuclear War Dictionary* is one of the best of a substantial number of dictionaries that treat this topic. It defines about 300 words, phrases, and acronyms in language appropriate for nonspecialists, and each entry is followed by an informative section on the significance of the term or phrase. An index rounds out the dictionary. This is a recommended purchase for all libraries; however, small libraries that already own similar works—for example, *The ABCs of Armageddon* (Donald J. Colen, World Almanac/Random House, 1988, 208p., $16.95, ISBN 0-345-35224-6) or *The Language of Nuclear War* (Eric Sember and others, Perennial Library/Harper & Row, 1987, 325p., $22.50; $9.95pa., ISBN 0-06-055051-1; 0-06-096123-6pa.)—may find they have coverage sufficient to meet their patrons' needs through those publications.

380. Dupuy, R. Ernest, and Trevor N. Dupuy. **The Encyclopedia of Military History: From 3500 B.C. to the Present.** 4th ed. New York, HarperCollins, 1993. 1654p. maps. index. $65.00. ISBN 0-06-270056-1.

Ernest and Trevor Dupuy's massive volume surveys military history from 3500 B.C. through 1983. It is presented as a series of 21 chronologically and geographically organized narratives of wars, warfare, and military affairs, divided into 22 time-period chapters. Introductory essays at the beginning of each chapter examine major military trends. Chronological surveys of the main wars of the period follow the introduction, and presentations of military events and developments by geographical region conclude each of the chapters. The text is generously interwoven with maps and illustrations. A large, extensively cross-referenced, general index, as well as separate battle and war indexes, facilitate access to the materials.

Trevor Dupuy has also co-authored (with Curt Johnson and Grace P. Hayes) the highly regarded *Dictionary of Military Terms: A Guide to the Language of Warfare and Military Institutions* (H. W. Wilson, 1986, 237p., $42.00, ISBN 0-8242-0717-3). Arranged alphabetically, it defines about 2,500 military terms from ancient times through the nuclear ages, including strategy, tactics, weapons, fortifications, ranks, and administration. It is an excellent companion to the *Encyclopedia of Military History*.

381. Eggenberger, David. **An Encyclopedia of Battles: Accounts of Over 1560 Battles from 1479 B.C. to the Present.** Rev. ed. New York, Dover Publications, 1985. 533p. maps. bibliog. index. $14.95pa. ISBN 0-486-24913-1.

An Encyclopedia of Battles provides the essential details of well over 1,500 major armed encounters from the battle of Megiddo in 1479 B.C. to the American invasion of Grenada in 1983. The entries are listed alphabetically and identified by war, revolution, or political movement. Each entry describes the strategic situation, date of battle, military commanders, quantity of opposing forces employed, tactics used, casualties suffered, and the battle's outcome. Nearly 100 battle maps (8 from the Civil War) complement the text. Appendixes treat the Yom Kippur War, Vietnam, Afghanistan, Grenada, Lebanon, and the Falkland Islands.

For quick reference, libraries may wish to purchase John Laffin's *Brassey's Battles: 3,500 Years of Conflict, Campaigns, and Wars from A–Z* (Brassey's/ Pergamon Press, 1986, 484p., $44.00, ISBN 0-08-031185-7), which offers more

382. Jessup, John E., ed. **Encyclopedia of the American Military: Studies of the History, Traditions, Policies, Institutions, and Roles ...** . New York, Scribner's, 1994. 3v. maps. index. $320.00/set. ISBN 0-684-19255-1.

Jessup's encyclopedia comprises 70 original, lengthy, signed essays by leading military historians and political scientists. The work is arranged into thematic sections that address "War in the American Experience," "Formulation of American Military Policy," "The Roles of the Armed Forces," "The American Military in War and Peace," "Military Arts and Sciences," and "Military Practices." Bibliographies follow each essay, and maps and charts further clarify the text. In addition, there is a valuable 80-page chronology divided into columns of presidents and key leaders, general American history, and American military history. An excellent resource for all libraries.

383. Luttwak, Edward, and Stuart Koehl. **The Dictionary of Modern War.** New York, HarperCollins, 1991. 680p. $45.00. ISBN 0-06-270021-9.

This work not only describes weapons, institutions, ideas, and treaties, but also explains them in the context of modern military parlance. The authors make little pretense to objectivity in their entries, choosing instead to infuse their definitions with their own opinions on the subject at hand. This makes for a slightly different approach to lexicography than most librarians are comfortable with, but the dictionary nevertheless does a good job of translating modern warfare terminology into language that is accessible to the average reader.

384. Tarassuk, Leonid, and Claude Blair, eds. **The Complete Encyclopedia of Arms & Weapons: The Most Comprehensive Reference Work Ever Published on Arms and Armor from Prehistoric Times to the Present.** New York, Simon & Schuster, 1982. 544p. illus. (part col.) bibliog. $41.50. ISBN 0-671-42257-X.

Obviously, a work that is now more than 10 years out of date will miss a substantial amount of information on weapons that have been developed and deployed over the past decade. Nevertheless, *The Complete Encyclopedia of Arms and Weapons* does a good job of comprehensively surveying the arms and armor of the periods it does encompass. Arranged alphabetically, the work concentrates on individual weapons and styles of armor. It contains more than 1,250 illustrations (250 in color), photographs, reproductions of artworks, and charts. Entries vary in length (from one line to four pages) based on the importance of the term being addressed, and span both time and geographic location. Selective bibliographies accompany the text.

Guides, Handbooks, and Yearbooks

385. **America's Top Military Careers: The Official Guide to Occupations in the Armed Forces.** Indianapolis, IN, JIST Works, [1993]. 473p. illus. index. $19.95pa. ISBN 1-56370-124-3.

America's Top Military Careers, an unabridged commercial version of the Government Printing Office's 1992 *Military Careers* at half its price, provides vocational information on nearly 200 military careers. The primary division of the volume is by enlisted occupations and officers' careers. Each career or assignment's description includes job attributes, work environment, training, physical demands, and career opportunities. Similar civilian jobs are listed, as is an interpretive chart relating the enlisted careers to the Armed Service Vocational Aptitude Battery (ASVAB). A separate section identifies typical career paths for 38 different assignments, indicating military career expectations for actual service people. Indexed by job title and by *Dictionary of Occupational Titles* terms.

386. **The Military Balance [yr.].** International Institute for Strategic Studies. London, Brassey's, 1959- . Annual. 1v. $58.00 (1994 ed.). ISSN 0459-7222.

Arranged by geographic region, this annual compiles independent and authoritative statistics on military power and defense expenditures for countries ranging from Afghanistan to Zimbabwe. For each country, the first part of the volume provides key economic and demographic information; an overview of defense expenditures; and statistical descriptions of each country's army, navy, and air force strengths. A second section reviews ongoing military negotiations and other timely topics. For a current and reliable guide to contemporary military affairs throughout the world, *The Military Balance* should be considered a primary purchase.

REVOLUTIONARY WAR

387. Symonds, Craig L. **A Battlefield Atlas of the American Revolution.** Baltimore, MD, Nautical and Aviation, 1986. 110p. illus. maps. bibliog. $22.95. ISBN 0-933852-53-3.

This small (7 inches by 10 inches) atlas provides a clear picture of the major campaigns and battles of the Revolutionary War. Arranged chronologically, the maps are accompanied by one-page texts that explain the specific events portrayed. The maps are clearly drawn and rendered with simplicity and the reader's ease of use in mind; thus, movements of forces are readily traced and symbols quickly understood. Although an index would have proved helpful, the work does include a brief bibliography of suggested readings for the topics surveyed in each map.

CIVIL WAR

388. Bowman, John S., ed. **The Civil War Almanac.** New York, Facts on File, 1982; repr. World Almanac, 1987. 400p. illus. index. $14.95pa. ISBN 0-88687-401-7.

The bulk of *The Civil War Almanac* is a chronology that begins with the purchase of Blacks in Jamestown, Virginia, in 1619 and continues through the salient events in American history that in retrospect have been understood as contributing to the start of the Civil War. Separate sections describe the weapons used, survey the naval warfare of the era, and provide biographic profiles of key Civil War figures. The text is complemented by outstanding illustrations (including a 16-page color section), maps, reproductions of posters and paintings, and old photographs.

A related title by Facts on File is Philip Katcher's *The Civil War Source Book* (1992, 320p, $35.00, ISBN 0-8160-2823-0). This compendium of Civil War facts includes a brief chronological history of the war, a description of tactics and weaponry, the organizations within the services, soldiers' first-person accounts of fighting in the battles, and brief biographies of the war's major figures. Other materials include a listing of sources used in Civil War studies; key statistics, calendars, and measurements; and a 700-item glossary of Civil War terms.

389. **Great Battles of the Civil War.** Woodstock, NY, Beekman House; distr., Publications International, 1981. 96p. illus. maps. index. $24.99. ISBN 0-517-68765-8.

Thirty-six major Civil War battles are described in this handbook, which has been cited for its full-color reproductions of the 1880s and 1890s chromolithographs of Louis Kurz and Alexander Allison. The work provides a brief introduction to the background of the war with a year-by-year account of the major developments; sidebars describe major figures and events. Additional diagrams and photographs further enhance the descriptive narrative provided for each of the battles.

For a different approach to Civil War battles, libraries may also want to have Frances H. Kennedy's *The Civil War Battlefield Guide* (Houghton Mifflin, 1990, 317p. $29.95; $16.95pa. ISBN 0-395-52282-X; 0-395-52283-8pa.) on hand for patrons. The work describes 65 battlefields in the National Park System as well as others lesser known. Photographs and a map illustrating the topology and movements of the armies accompany each essay. Battlefield maps illustrate the contemporary landmarks and those of the period, enabling readers to visualize battles as they progressed. Strategy, significant military leaders, casualties, and current status of land ownership and preservation are noted for each campaign and battlefield.

390. Stephenson, Richard W., comp. **Civil War Maps: An Annotated List of Maps and Atlases in the Library of Congress.** 2d ed. Washington, DC, Geography and Map Division, Library of Congress, 1989. 410p. $46.00. ISBN 0-8444-0598-1.

This cartobibliography describes 2,240 maps and charts and 76 atlases and sketchbooks held by the Geography and Map Division of the Library of Congress. An additional 162 maps in the Library's Manuscript Division and several atlases in its general book collections are also annotated. Subject and title indexes and a state-by-state arrangement of the materials enhance its ease of use.

391. Symonds, Craig L. **A Battlefield Atlas of the Civil War.** 3d ed. Annapolis, MD, Nautical and Aviation, 1993. 115p. illus. maps. bibliog. $22.95. ISBN 1-877853-25-9.

The Civil War has long been considered one of the pivotal events in American history; its hold on us continues unabated a century later. This slim volume will answer many patron questions regarding Civil War engagements from Fort Sumter to Appomattox. Its materials are arranged in four chronological sections: "Opening 'Amateur Armies' Period," "Organized War Follow-on," "Confederate High Tide," and "Total War Finale." The 50 two-color battle maps and map insets are clean, easy to read, accompanied by a brief explanatory essay, and enhanced by photos of leading Southern and Northern general officers. Although this atlas presents a fairly elementary overview of the major Civil War battles, it does the job well.

WORLD WAR I

392. Livesay, Anthony O. **Great Battles of World War I.** New York, Macmillan, 1989. 200p. illus. maps. index. $39.95. ISBN 0-02-583131-3.

This work drew attention when it was first published for its unusual battle maps, which are three-dimensional, computer-generated graphic reconstructions of the battle sites. The striking maps contribute to the overall excellence of this work, which comprehensively chronicles the history of World War I from the 1914 guns of August to the 1918 collapse of Germany and the November 11 armistice. The informative, well-written text is complemented by interesting sidebars (weapons, commanders, ships, airplanes, newspapers of the day, etc.), as well as by the generous deployment of photographs, maps, drawings, and reproductions of paintings. Perhaps one of the greatest strengths of this work is that it does a remarkably good job of portraying the horror and slaughter of a war that resulted in the deaths of 8 million people.

WORLD WAR II

393. Keegan, John, ed. **The Times Atlas of the Second World War.** New York, HarperCollins, 1989. 254p. $50.00. ISBN 0-06-016178-7.

The core of this oversized, authoritative atlas is 450 beautifully reproduced, full-color maps that are arranged chronologically and regionally. In addition to the maps, there are 150 photographs and illustrations; a month-by-month, regionally arranged chronology of the major events both preceding and during World War II; and an extensive, well-written narrative that surveys the course of the war, its major and minor theaters, and the outcomes and long-term effects of the war's most significant battles. Although the military undertakings that drove the war machine are the focus of Keegan's excellent atlas, he has also examined and described the political, economic, and social impacts of this devastating global conflict.

394. Young, Peter, ed. **The World Almanac Book of World War II.** Mahwah, NJ, World Almanac, 1992. 624p. illus. index. $18.95pa. ISBN 0-88687-712-1.

Appropriate for the needs of both the lay reader and the specialist, Young's almanac is divided into three main sections. The largest is a detailed, day-by-day chronology of the military campaigns in all theaters of the war, as well as significant political and diplomatic developments, which portrays the events that took place from August 1939 to September 1945. Occasionally, crucial pre- and post-war events that fall outside the parameters of the main chronology (e.g., the June 1919 Treaty of Versailles) are noted also. The second section describes and analyzes the weaponry and equipment (land, sea, and air) used throughout the war by the major combatants. A biographical dictionary that provides profiles of World War II notables—military and political leaders, diplomats and journalists, spies and war aces, and other participants—makes up the third and last section. The astute, well-written text is complemented by an intelligent selection of area and world maps, drawings, and more than 100 photographs, a handful of which are in color.

KOREAN WAR

395. Summers, Harry G., Jr. **Korean War Almanac.** New York, Facts on File, 1990. 330p. illus. index. $24.95. ISBN 0-8160-1737-9.

The first of this work's three sections outlines the setting of the Korean War, discussing geographical and historical realities and the two Koreas. Next, a chronological section outlines events in the war from June 25, 1950, to September 6, 1953. The following section comprises the bulk of the almanac, consisting of 375 alphabetically arranged entries on people, battles, weaponry, strategy and tactics, political factors, and effects on countries involved. Entries range in length from one paragraph to one or more pages, and are interwoven with cross references, maps, and black-and-white photographs. A good selective bibliography and index round out this handy reference.

If patron interest warrants more Korean War coverage, a good second purchase is James I. Matray's *Historical Dictionary of the Korean War* (Greenwood Press,

VIETNAM WAR

396. Pimlott, John. **Vietnam: The Decisive Battles.** New York, Macmillan. 1990. 200p. illus. maps. index. $39.95. ISBN 0-02-580171-6.

In *Vietnam: The Decisive Battles*, Pimlot chronicles and analyzes 17 key battles of the war, from the French defeat at Dien Bien Phu in 1954 to the fall of Saigon in 1975. The presentation is based on computer-generated, three-dimensional maps generated from standard two-dimensional maps of each battle. From these three-dimensional maps, artists have developed two-page, full-color paintings that illustrate all the details (including weapons deployment, troop movement, and weather conditions) of each battle at critical moments. In addition, each major battle is analyzed by military experts. Although the excellent commentary on the many military, political, and historical aspects of the war are a major strength of Pimlot's handbook, its innovative and creative use of graphics is what sets it apart from all other works of this nature.

397. Summers, Harry G. Jr. **Vietnam War Almanac.** New York, Facts on File, 1985. 414p. $27.95; $14.95pa. ISBN 0-8160-1017-X; 0-8160-1813-8pa.

The *Vietnam War Almanac* provides two types of information. The first two chapters survey the physical and historical conditions in Vietnam, providing a context for the events that took place there. The rest of the almanac is made up of some 500 entries that describe (from an American viewpoint) the individuals, events, equipment, and social factors of the Vietnam War. A substantial number of the entries include recommendations for further reading, although obviously these citations do not include recent scholarship or publications. About 120 photographs and 20 maps supplement the narrative.

1991, 626p., $85.00, ISBN 0-313-25924-0), comprising 500 signed entries on the war's people, events, weapons, and battles. Twenty detailed maps; a list of acronyms; and appendixes of relevant statistics, personnel changes in the high command, a chronology, and a selected bibliography all contribute to the value of this scholarly work. Although there is some overlap between the two titles, there are enough differences in coverage and treatment to merit purchase of both books if possible.

Political Science

GENERAL WORKS

Atlases

398.   Chaliand, Gerard, and Jean-Pierre Rageau. **A Strategic Atlas: Comparative Geopolitics of the World's Powers.** 3d ed. New York, HarperCollins, 1993. 224p. maps. $40.00; $18.00pa. ISBN 0-06-271554-2; 0-06-273153-Xpa.

The intent of this atlas is to present "the geopolitics of the relations of force" from post-World War I through 1992. The work uses a variety of maps to depict the world's geopolitical realities and relationships as seen by those outside the traditional European/North American viewpoint—for example, from the Chinese, South American, or African perspective. A world statistical survey brings together in one table diverse information on countries, such as the percentage of urban population and adult literacy rates in each country. Although much of the data found in *A Strategic Atlas* is available from other familiar reference sources, its arrangement here in a single location facilitates easy comparison among countries. An important work for libraries to have on hand as our global village becomes increasingly interconnected.

Bibliographies

399.   Holler, Frederick L. **Information Sources of Political Science.** 4th ed. Santa Barbara, CA, ABC-Clio, 1986. 417p. index. $89.50. ISBN 0-87436-375-6.

Holler's well-known guide has been relied upon by librarians since the first edition debuted in 1982. The work leads off with an essay entitled "Political Reference Theory," an overview of the author's conceptual framework for the retrieval of political information. The bulk of the work, however, is the 2,423 descriptive annotations found in the bibliography's seven sections: "General Reference Sources," "Social Sciences," "American Government, Politics, and Public Law," "International Relations and Organizations," "Comparative and Area Studies of Politics and Government," "Political Theory," and "Public Administration." Coverage includes books, periodicals, radio and television broadcasts, newspapers, translations, micropublications, electronic sources, and government documents; most materials are copyrighted 1983 or earlier. Entries note author, title, publisher, frequency of publication (for serials), and date and place of publication. Author, title, subject, and typology indexes facilitate access.

400. York, Henry E. **Political Science: A Guide to Reference and Information Sources.** Englewood, CO, Libraries Unlimited, 1990. 249p. index. $38.00. ISBN 0-87287-794-9.

This guide provides descriptive (and occasionally critical) annotations for more than 800 sources of information in political science and related fields. Materials cited include books, periodicals, databases, organizations, and publishers; most print materials identified were published between 1980 and 1988. Six chapters cover general social sciences, specific related social science disciplines, political science in general, and specific subfields of political science. Separate author/title and subject indexes complete the volume. This work is especially useful for updating Frederick L. Holler's standard bibliography, *Information Sources of Political Science* (entry 399).

Biographies

401. **The Columbia Dictionary of Political Biography.** New York, Columbia University Press, 1991. 335p. index. $40.00. ISBN 0-231-07586-3.

The more than 2,000 current world political leaders profiled here represent more than 165 countries and include among them heads of state, top ministers, party leaders, influential legislators, state and local officials, union leaders, prominent dissidents, and similar important figures. Profiles include the individual's country of origin, birth place and date, and career highlights and contributions. Emphasis is on public activities rather than personal background; the narrative approach is popular rather than scholarly. A brief glossary, a list of abbreviations used, and an index of individuals by country round out the work.

Dictionaries and Encyclopedias

402. Krieger, Joel, and others, eds. **The Oxford Companion to Politics of the World.** New York, Oxford University Press, 1993. 1056p. maps. index. $49.95. ISBN 0-19-505934-4.

Written by nearly 500 experts from more than 40 countries, the 650 alphabetically arranged articles that constitute *The Oxford Companion to Politics of the World* range from abortion to (Gamal) Abdel Nasser to Zionism. In between, they touch on nations, individuals, political and diplomatic concepts, international affairs, international law, environmentalism, the welfare state, gender, and myriad other topics central to world politics. Articles are signed and range in length from several paragraphs to several pages; many include brief bibliographies and *see* references to related entries. Typical of the Oxford "companions," this is an authoritative resource that can field a broad spectrum of inquiries.

403. O'Toole, G. J. A. **The Encyclopedia of American Intelligence and Espionage: From the Revolutionary War to the Present.** New York, Facts on File, 1988. 539p. illus. bibliog. index. $50.00. ISBN 0-8160-1011-0.

O'Toole, a former CIA employee, has compiled an extensive, knowledgeable survey of the American intelligence and espionage effort from the Revolutionary War through the 1980s. Entries range from several sentences to 16 pages, and cover organizations, the role of intelligence efforts in America's major wars, important topics (such as cryptology) in America's espionage history, key events, and noteworthy individuals. Generous use of cross references, an extensive bibliography, and a solid index complement the text.

Although the O'Toole book covers the basics well, patrons may wish for even more information on this popular subject. A good second purchase that will fill the bill is *The Dictionary of Espionage: Spookspeak into English* (Henry S. A. Becket, Dell, 1987, 203p, $3.95pa., ISBN 0-440-11955-3). Armchair Cold Warriors should find that both of these works help ease a bad case of George Smiley withdrawal.

404. Plano, Jack C., and Roy Olton. **The International Relations Dictionary.** 4th ed. Santa Barbara, CA, ABC-Clio, 1988. 446p. index. $42.95; $18.00pa. ISBN 0-87436-477-9; 0-87436-478-7pa.

First published in 1969, this well-known reference attempts to explain basic concepts of international relations rather than simply to define individual words or phrases. The dictionary is arranged in 12 topical chapters that facilitate tracing of interrelationships between terms; an index enables readers to rapidly find the term sought. The 570 entries are well written and easy to read; each has a "significance" paragraph that places the term within the broader context of international relations. A fifth edition is due out in summer 1995.

405. Shafritz, Jay M. **The Facts on File Dictionary of Public Administration.** New York, Facts on File, 1985. 610p. $40.00. ISBN 0-8160-1266-0.

Shafritz's dictionary is intended for students, teachers, public officials, researchers, practitioners, and interested laypeople. His stated goal is to define all the words, names, phrases, laws, and processes encountered in the study or practice of public administration and related disciplines. In addition, the work describes several hundred court cases related to public management and labor relations. The organizational entries include all major federal government agencies and many private organizations and professional societies, with statement of purpose, addresses, and telephone numbers. Generous cross references and bibliographic references enhance the dictionary's already extensive coverage.

406. Shafritz, Jay M.. Phil Williams, and Ronald S. Calinger. **The Dictionary of 20th-Century World Politics.** New York, Henry Holt, 1993. 756p. illus. $60.00. ISBN 0-8050-1976-6.

The Dictionary of 20th-Century World Politics defines more than 4,000 names, terms, and phrases that have affected international politics during the 20th century. Entries on foreign words, core concepts, theories, practices, institutions, and major international organizations are interspersed with those on biographical and historical references; boxed-in comments located throughout the text provide insight and occasionally humorous comments on a number of definitions. In addition to the definitions, the dictionary provides numerous cross references and an appendix of key concepts.

407. Wilczynski, J. **An Encyclopedic Dictionary of Marxism, Socialism, and Communism.** Hawthorne, NY, De Gruyter, 1981. 660p. $97.00. ISBN 3-11-008588-7.

The world's political systems seem to be in such a state of flux that it is sometimes difficult to determine just what ideological threads still weave through many of the world's governments. The *Encyclopedic Dictionary of Marxism, Socialism, and Communism* furnishes a starting point for understanding global political issues by providing an objective means of exploring the economic, conceptual, political, sociological, and institutional underpinnings of these three key ideologies.

The definitions (for terms both classical and contemporary) are clear and easily understood, and are complemented by numerous cross references.

Directories

408. Schiavone, Giuseppe. **International Organizations: A Dictionary and Directory.** 3d ed. New York, St. Martin's Press, 1992. 337p. index. $75.00. ISBN 0-312-09143-5.

The main body of *International Organizations* contains alphabetically arranged entries for approximately 100 international organizations, including the United Nations, its specialized agencies, and regional or subregional groups. Entries generally range in length from one-half to several pages, and include information about the organization's objectives, powers, and activities as well as address, principal officers, primary publications, and (occasionally) a brief list of other information sources. In addition to the main directory entries, there are an introductory essay, separate indexes by acronyms and full organization names, detailed membership charts, a list by year of organizations' founding dates, and a classified index by type of organization.

The primary competitor to Schiavone's directory is *The International Organizations and World Order Dictionary* (Sheikh R. Ali, ABC-Clio, 1992. 283p. $55.00. ISBN 0-87436-572-4). This work emphasizes the United Nations and its related agencies in nearly 300 entries dealing with the various aspects of international organizations and world order. However, although it identifies about 70 of the same groups covered by its competitor, Ali's work functions most effectively as a dictionary of salient terms or as a ready-reference source rather than as a detailed directory of organization information, as provided by Schiavone.

Handbooks and Yearbooks

409. Banks, Arthur S., ed. **Political Handbook of the World: [yr.].** State University of New York at Binghamton, Center for Social Analysis. New York, McGraw-Hill, 1927- . Annual. 1v. maps. index. $49.95 (1994 ed.). ISSN 0193-175X.

Political Handbook of the World has a strong record as a dependable handbook for current political and governmental data. Arranged alphabetically, the handbook's main section contains encyclopedic articles on the countries of the world. Entries include information on population, urban centers, languages, and monetary units, followed by narrative sections on the government and political parties. This section also lists government officials and summarizes foreign affairs, international disputes, and domestic political issues. The second part of the handbook identifies and describes intergovernmental organizations, noting for each its purpose, history, function, activities, and leadership. An appendix provides a chronology of the major international events of the past four decades. Access to the text is provided by geographical, organizational, and personal name indexes.

Although other political handbooks, such as the *Statesman's Year-Book* (entry 411), provide more directory information on government, business, and political leaders, as well as more extensive economic and social statistics, the *Political Handbook of the World* excels in its presentation of background information and commentary. (Although the *Europa World Year Book* [entry 94] is rightly considered to be the most exhaustive treatment of world circumstances, its price and broader focus put it in a different league than the works considered here.)

For libraries needing a less expensive alternative and that do not mind sacrificing the currency of a yearbook, the *Facts on File World Political Almanac* (2d ed., Chris Cook, comp., Facts on File, 1992, 496p., $45.00, ISBN 0-8160-2603-3) is a good choice. Cook's international handbook covers factual information about national and world politics since World War II, with much of the data presented in tabular or statistical form. Although none of the wealth of topics included is treated comprehensively, *World Political Almanac* does provide frequently required facts and figures in a handy and authoritative manner.

410. Robert, Henry M. **The Scott, Foresman Robert's Rules of Order.** 9th ed. New York, Scott, Foresman/HarperCollins, 1990. 706p. index. $27.50; $14.00pa. ISBN 0-06-275002-X; 0-06276051-3pa.

Since Major Henry M. Robert first published his handbook in 1876, *Robert's Rules of Order* has been the standard guide to conducting meetings in an orderly and effective manner. The work is arranged in 20 parts, further divided into topical chapters. Although at first glance the sheer volume of information presented in the handbook seems daunting, an excellent index eases the way for novices.

A less intimidating approach to the same information, however, is provided by Alice Sturgis's clearly written, user-friendly *Standard Code of Parliamentary Procedure* (3d ed., McGraw-Hill, 1988, 275p., $9.95pa., ISBN 0-070623099-6), which translates the formalities of parliamentary rules into language more accessible to the beginning meeting organizer. The two works complement each other, and are recommended purchases for all public libraries.

411. **Statesman's Year-Book [yr.]: Statistical and Historical Annual of the States of the World.** New York, St. Martin's, 1864- . Annual. 1v. $75.00/yr. (1994 ed.). ISSN 0081-4601.

Statesman's Year-Book has long been considered the first source for descriptive and statistical information about the world's governments. Arrangement is alphabetical by individual country, and coverage includes ruler, constitution and government, area, population, religion, social welfare, education, justice and crime, state finance, defense, production and industry, agriculture, commerce, navigation, communications, banking and credit, money, weights and measures, diplomatic representatives, and other information as appropriate. Excellent selective bibliographies accompany each country's entry, and the yearbook's person, product, place, and international organizations indexes enable readers to find specific information quickly. A necessary acquisition for all libraries, regardless of size.

412. **Yearbook of the United Nations.** New York, United Nations Publications, 1946/47- . Annual. 1v. Price varies. ISSN 0082-8521.

The Yearbook of the United Nations documents the main activities of the UN during a calendar year (not necessarily the one directly preceding its publication date). The work is arranged in two parts. The first reviews the activities and engagements of the United Nations, including its departments and special agencies. The second part describes the activities and organization of related intergovernmental groups such as the World Health Organization. Appendixes identify UN member countries, provide directory listings for UN information centers, present the UN charter and information regarding the UN's organizational structure, and note the agenda for the year under review. The yearbook is indexed by subject, name, and resolution/decision.

U.S. GOVERNMENT

General Works

Almanacs

413. Barone, Michael, and Grant Ujifusa. **The Almanac of American Politics [yr.]: The Senators, the Representatives and the Governors .…** Washington, DC, National Journal, 1972- . Biennial. 1v. $59.95; $48.95pa. ([1994 ed.). No ISSN available.

It is difficult to imagine the amount of research and analysis that must go into this essential, influential reference work. The almanac provides state-by-state and district-by-district assessments of each state's representatives, senators, and governor as to the individual's record, political background and constituencies, and political interests. The authors consistently deliver perceptive assessments of trends and influences at national, state, and local levels, as well as including more specific information on topics such as demographic changes and campaign finances. Lists of each state's governor and congressional delegations, rosters of congressional committees, and congressional district maps complement the main text. This work cannot be surpassed for insightful and objective analysis of the nation's elected representatives and what they're up to.

414. **Congressional Quarterly's Politics in America [yr.].** Washington, DC, Congressional Quarterly, 1981- . Biennial. 1v. $79.95; $49.95pa. (1994 ed.). ISSN 1064-6809.

Although the *Almanac of American Politics* (entry 413) provides a broader survey of national and regional politics, the presidency, Congress, governors, demographic trends, and campaign finances, *Politics in America* is a valuable and authoritative reference for its coverage of the nation's political players. Arranged alphabetically by state, each section presents statistics for the state, concise information on the governor, a map of congressional districts, and extensive information on the state's senators and representatives. Entries for Congress members include an analysis of background and political issues, a list of committee assignments, election results, campaign finances, key votes and voting record, and ratings by various special-interest groups. The guide offers a generous amount of supplemental information, including a table of seniority by party and a helpful guide to the pronunciation of members' names, but it is most relied upon for its excellent profiles and analyses of congressional legislators.

415. **CQ Almanac.** Washington, DC, Congressional Quarterly, 1945- . Annual. 1v. $205.00 (1994 ed.). ISSN 0095-6007.

The *CQ Almanac* is an annual cumulation and synthesis of information drawn from the *CQ Weekly Report* for the congressional session most recently completed. The almanac leads off with a chapter on topics related to congressional organization, such as congressional ethics or campaign finance reform; the rest of the work is organized into topical chapters that survey legislative activity within specific arenas, for example, economic or foreign policy. Charts and sidebar notes frequently accompany the text. In addition, there are summaries of legislation, results of roll-call votes, the text of communications from the president, and a list of lobby registrations. A standard reference from a well-respected publisher.

Biographies

416.   **American Leaders 1789-1991: A Biographical Summary.** Washington, DC, Congressional Quarterly, 1991. 534p. index. $37.95. ISBN 0-87187-594-2.

The American leaders referred to herein are presidents, vice presidents, Supreme Court Justices, members of Congress, and state governors. Profiles are arranged according to office held; entries include very basic biographical information for the individual in question. The strength of this work, however, is in its fascinating anecdotes about the individuals profiled and useful comparative statistical information. Although enjoyable for browsing, the book is able to fulfill a ready-reference role as well, because of its detailed table of contents and excellent index.

Parts of *American Leaders* are drawn from an earlier CQ publication, *Members of Congress Since 1789* (3d ed., Mary Ames Booker, ed., 1985), which is unfortunately now out of print. *American Leaders* should not be considered a replacement or even update of the earlier work, as their focuses and formats are substantially different; thus, those libraries still in possession of *Members of Congress* will want to hold onto their copies.

417.   O'Brien, Steven G. **American Political Leaders from Colonial Times to the Present.** Santa Barbara, CA, ABC-Clio, 1991. 473p. illus. $65.00. ISBN 0-87436-570-8.

American Political Leaders is an excellent source of biographical information on more than 400 key American political figures. The sketches range from a few hundred to well over a thousand words, depending on the importance of the individual discussed. Portraits are included in many of the entries, as are short bibliographies of important titles about each person. O'Brien's engaging writing style and ability to interpret the meaning and significance of each individual's life sets this work apart from similar titles. Although intellectual, scientific, cultural, or social reform movement leaders are not included, such was not the book's purpose; instead, it has successfully brought to life hundreds of men and women whose contributions and influence have in some manner shaped American politics.

418.   **Who's Who in American Politics [yr.].** New Providence, NJ, R. R. Bowker, 1967- . Biennial. 2v. index. $225.00/set (1994 ed.). ISSN 0000-0205.

This standard reference brings together 26,000 entries that list the biographee's party affiliations; birth date and place; names of parents, spouse, and children; education; political, governmental, and business positions held; military service; honors and awards; publications; memberships; religion; voting residence; and mailing address. Separate sections identify the president, cabinet members, U.S. Courts of Appeals judgeships, and each state's and territory's congressional delegation, governor, and party chairs. Also available online and on magnetic tape.

419.   **Who's Who in Congress [yr.].** Washington, DC, Congressional Quarterly, 1991- . Biennial. 1v. $14.95pa. (1994 ed.). ISSN 0095-6007.

For each member of Congress, this biographical directory provides birth date, educational background, occupation, political background, office address, telephone number, key staff positions, committee assignments, CQ voting analysis, key interest-group ratings, and basic election statistics. It also contains lists of all congressional committees and their members, a list of the leadership of both houses, and a breakdown of how each member voted on key issues in the previous session. Although not nearly as extensive as, say, *The Congressional Staff Directory* (entry 421), *Who's Who in Congress* is a well-executed, useful, and very reasonably priced resource.

Dictionaries and Encyclopedias

420. Plano, Jack C., and Milton Greenberg. **The American Political Dictionary.** 9th ed. Fort Worth, TX, Harcourt Brace, 1993. 672p. $21.75pa. ISBN 0-15-500-281-3.

Plano and Greenberg define more than 1,200 alphabetically arranged entries in this standard guide to the terminology of American politics. The authors have continued their successful format, namely, briefly defining each term and then commenting in more detail on its significance in American history and politics. Words and phrases are drawn from all areas of political enterprise and governance, whether at the local, state, or federal level. A detailed index rounds out the work.

Although *The American Political Dictionary* should probably be the first purchase in this subject area, if libraries are considering supplementing it with other references the best alternative would probably be Jay M. Shafritz's *HarperCollins Dictionary of American Government & Politics* (HarperCollins, 1993, 704p., $50.00; $10.00pa. ISBN 0-06-270031-6; ISBN 0-06-461021-7pa.). Although designed more for academic than public library use, this encyclopedic work nevertheless provides a tremendous amount of information for a very reasonable price. It defines roughly 5,000 terms and concepts used in the executive, legislative, and judicial branches of the American government; in addition, there are descriptions of major federal laws and landmark decisions of the Supreme Court, brief biographies of significant political figures, and chronologies of important events in American history.

Directories

421. Brownson, Ann L., ed. **Congressional Staff Directory [yr.].** Mount Vernon, VA, Staff Directories, 1959- . Annual. 1v. illus. index. $69.00 (1994 ed.). ISSN 0069-8938.

This directory provides 3,200 detailed biographies of the staffs of both individual members and the various committees and subcommittees of Congress. In addition, it lists the addresses of field representatives, staffs of the Library of Congress and the General Accounting Office, and congressional party organizations.

Much of the information in the *Congressional Staff Directory* can also be found, although certainly much less easily or rapidly, in the GPO's biennial *Official Congressional Directory* (1809- , $25.00 [1994 ed.], S/N 052-070-06543-5). As in so many things, the tradeoff is cost versus time and convenience.

422. **Federal Regulatory Directory.** 7th ed. Washington, DC, Congressional Quarterly, 1994. 1000p. illus. index. $119.95. ISBN 0-87187-811-9.

Federal regulations are having an increasingly large impact on all of our lives; thus, there is increasing patron demand to know who's responsible for what. The *Federal Regulatory Directory* is a good source for such information. It provides informative overviews of the history, powers and authority, functions, and organization of more than 100 federal regulatory agencies; brief biographies of key personnel; and addresses for regional as well as national offices. In addition, there are reviews of the regulatory process, texts of important laws, and explanations of how to use the *Federal Register* and the *Code of Federal Regulations*. Subject/agency and personal name indexes conclude the directory.

423. **Washington Information Directory [yr.].** Washington, DC, Congressional Quarterly, 1976- . Annual. 1v. index. $94.95 (1994 ed.). ISSN 0887-8064.

The *Washington Information Directory* has long been a favored place to start when tracking down information on federal executive branch offices and departments, congressional committees and subcommittees, and nonprofit and special-interest organizations with headquarters or regional offices in Washington, DC. It's all here, in entries that include the name, address, and telephone number of the organization; the organization's director or other appropriate contact person; and a description of the organization's purpose and activities. Also included are public information and press telephone numbers, locator numbers, information on foreign embassies, state and local government officials, labor unions, and federal regional offices.

The twin publications that compete with the *Washington Information Directory* are the quarterlies published by Monitor, *Congressional Yellow Book: A Directory of Members of Congress, Includes Their Committees and Key Staff Aides* (1976- , $215.00 [1994 ed.], ISSN 0191-1422) and *Federal Yellow Book: A Directory of Federal Departments and Agencies* (1976- , $215.00 [1994 ed.], ISSN 0145-6202). Both of these works are excellent and offer much more comprehensive information on the federal and legislative branches than does the CQ publication; however, they are vastly more expensive as well. Yet a third alternative commenced publication fairly recently, and that is *The Government Directory of Addresses and Telephone Numbers: Your Comprehensive Guide to Federal, State, County, and Local Government Offices …* (Omnigraphics, 1992- , annual, $150.00 [1994 ed.], ISSN 1062-1466). It provides comprehensive listings of government offices and positions, from city level to federal agencies and most areas in between. A typical entry in the directory gives the address, a list of top administrative positions by title only, and telephone numbers. Because the scope of each of these government directories differs in breadth and depth, libraries will have to determine which level of coverage best meets their unique needs.

Handbooks and Yearbooks

424. **The Book of the States.** Lexington, KY, Council of State Governments, 1935- . Biennial. 1v. index. $79.00 (1994 ed.). ISSN 0068-0125.

The focus of this well-known publication is the political environment and activities as they are played out within the 50 states, the District of Columbia, American Samoa, Guam, the Northern Mariana Islands, Puerto Rico, and the U.S. Virgin Islands. *The Book of the States* offers informative articles (many accompanied by extensive bibliographies) written by the Council of State Governments staff on such topics as intergovernmental affairs and state management and administration. In addition, there is basic statistical and directory data for each state, including principal officials, nickname, motto, flower, bird, song, and tree. State-specific information is provided by the states themselves, so statistics are not always as current or complete as one might wish. Nevertheless, this remains an important purchase for most libraries.

The Book of the States has also created several spin-off publications that libraries may also want to consider for purchase. These are *State Elective Officials and the Legislatures* (biennial, 1v., $35.00pa. [1994 ed.], ISSN 0191-9466); *State Legislative Leadership, Committees and Staff* (biennial, 1v., $30.00pa. [1994 ed.], ISSN 0195-6639); and *State Administrative Officials Classified by Function* (biennial, 1v., $30.00pa. [1994 ed.], ISSN 0191-9423).

425. **Congressional Quarterly's Guide to Congress.** 4th ed. Washington, DC, Congressional Quarterly, 1991. 1185p. illus. index. $189.95. ISBN 0-87187-584-5.

Encyclopedic in its scope and format, this work has become the standard resource for impartial, thorough information on the history, development, and current workings of the United States Congress. In addition to its excellent overviews of Congress's origins and procedures, it provides a wealth of supplemental materials, including glossaries, bibliographies, biographies, and texts of important congressional documents. The guide also offers a detailed index.

Although well worth the price, *Guide to Congress* is expensive. For libraries not able to justify such an expenditure, *Congress A to Z: CQ's Ready Reference Encyclopedia* (2d ed., Congressional Quarterly, 1993, 547p, $110.00, ISBN 0-87187-826-7) offers a handy, reliable, and much less costly alternative. It covers the workings of the U.S. Congress, legislative terminology, historical information, and biographical sketches in 280 clearly written entries ranging in length from one paragraph to two pages. There are in addition 30 extended essays on subjects such as the budget process, impeachment powers, and the legislative process. Although it cannot approach the breadth and comprehensiveness of *Guide to Congress*, *Congress A to Z* easily stands on its own as an outstanding ready-reference source, and libraries able to afford both will find that the two publications complement each other.

426. Scammon, Richard M., and Alice V. McGillivray, comps. and eds. **American Votes 20: A Handbook of Contemporary American Election Statistics.** Washington, DC, Congressional Quarterly, 1993. 537p. $132.00. ISBN 0-87187-784-8.

Published since 1951, *America Votes* has long been a key resource for voting statistics. County-by-county voting patterns in every state, for president and for every governor, senator, and representative, with accompanying registration figures, vote totals, percentages, and pluralities for the years 1991 and 1992 are recorded in *America Votes 20*. In addition, the handbook lists state-by-state vote totals for presidents from Coolidge to Clinton. Not only is this the preeminent reference choice in this subject area, it is also a fascinating read for those interested in the political voice of America.

427. **United States Government Manual.** Washington, DC, Government Printing Office, 1935- . Annual. 1v. $30.00 (1994 ed.). S/N 069-000-00015-1. ISSN 0092-1904.

The official handbook for the federal government, this annual contains brief descriptions of the functions of many government agencies, departments, and other organizations. Quasi-official agencies (the Smithsonian Institution) and international organizations in which the United States participates (the Organization of American States) are treated in separate sections. Entries note the agency or department's purpose and activities, programs, history and development, names, addresses, and telephone numbers of key officials, and regional offices. Some entries include a "Sources of Information" section that provides information on related publications, contracts, grants, and other items. Five appendixes—abolished or transferred agencies and functions, abbreviations and acronyms, organizational charts, standard federal jurisdictions for agency and department offices, and a listing of agencies that notes where they appear in the *Code of Federal Regulations*—conclude the manual.

The Presidency

428. **Congressional Quarterly's Guide to the Presidency.** Michael Nelson, ed. Washington, DC, Congressional Quarterly, 1989. 1521p. illus. index. $189.95. ISBN 0-87187-500-4.

Guide to the Presidency reflects the same high standards of objectivity adhered to in its two related publications, *Guide to the U.S. Supreme Court* (entry 345) and *Guide to Congress* (entry 425). This work covers the historical development of the presidency, presidential powers, and the presidency as it relates to the public, the executive branch, and the federal government. Although historical coverage is not slighted, more space is devoted to recent events and presidents than to those of the past. Brief biographies are included for presidents and vice presidents through the Bush administration. The well-written, readable articles are often accompanied by bibliographies and notes, and there is a generous number of cross references, tables and charts, illustrations, and photographs. Although the guide could benefit from a more detailed index, this is nevertheless an outstanding resource for information on the presidents and their role in America, both historical and current.

Where there is strong patron interest in the presidency, another excellent CQ title is Michael Nelson's *The Presidency A to Z: A Ready Reference Encyclopedia* (1992, 574p, $115.00, ISBN 0-87187-667-1), which comprises more than 300 alphabetically arranged entries on such topics related to the presidency as constitutional powers, the budget process, the Cabinet, and the relationship of the presidency to Congress and the Supreme Court. Biographies are provided for all presidents and vice presidents, as well as for others who have had an impact on the office. There are many informative charts and tables, useful appendixes, and detailed indexes, all of which enhance this work's value as a complement to *Guide to the Presidency*.

428A. Levy, Leonard W., and Louis Fisher, eds. **Encyclopedia of the American Presidency.** New York, Simon & Schuster, Academic Reference Division, 1994. 4v. index. $355.00/set. ISBN 0-13-275983-7.

Spearheaded by two highly respected constitutional scholars, *Encyclopedia of the American Presidency* comprises just over 1,000 entries/articles written by 335 contributors, each of whom specializes in a specific area of the presidency. The articles, ranging in length from one to ten pages, are purposely written to avoid the dusty, dry prose of typical encyclopedias, and instead offer engaging narratives that present the opinions, judgment, and interpretations of their contributors. Articles conclude with excellent selective bibliographies; a synoptic outline of topics, a general index, and a case index are found in volume 4.

13

Psychology and Parapsychology

PSYCHOLOGY

Bibliographies

429.   Baxter, Pam M. **Psychology: A Guide to Reference and Information Sources.** Englewood, CO, Libraries Unlimited, 1993. 219p. index. $36.50. ISBN 0-87287-708-6.

Baxter describes 600 sources, published primarily after 1970, that include resource guides, comprehensive retrospective bibliographies, indexing tools and online databases, handbooks, dictionaries, encyclopedias, journals, biographical sources, and organizations. The resources are grouped within four broad categories: general social science and reference works, specific resources in social science disciplines, general psychology reference sources, and special topics in psychology. Works are listed alphabetically within sections; materials in the special topics sections are further grouped by classification headings similar to those used in *Psychological Abstracts* (American Psychological Association, monthly). Entries include complete bibliographical information and a descriptive annotation.

Baxter is also the co-author (with Jeffrey G. Reed) of another psychology title, *Library Use: A Handbook for Psychology* (American Psychological Association, 1992, 179p., $19.95pa., ISBN 1-55798-144-2), a topically organized introduction to college-level library research in psychology. Although it tends to slight electronic research, the handbook's coverage of print materials is authoritative and thorough. A good complement to *Psychology: A Guide to Reference and Information Sources.*

430.   Bernstein, Joanne E., and Masha Kabakow Rudman. **Books to Help Children Cope with Separation and Loss: An Annotated Bibliography.** 4th ed. New Providence, NJ, R. R. Bowker, 1994. 514p. index. $49.00. ISBN 0-8352-3412-6.

Bernstein published the first issue of this valuable bibliography in 1977; fortunately, especially given the dire circumstances so many children face today, she has continued her involvement in this important subject area. In 1983, Bowker published the second edition of *Books to Help Children Cope with Separation and Loss* (439p., $39.95, ISBN 0-8352-1484-2), and in 1989, the third edition arrived; both are still in print (and on the shelves of most public and school libraries).

This fourth iteration deals with publications appearing from 1989 to 1993. The authors provide an annotated bibliography of fiction and nonfiction works dealing with all varieties of separation and loss (ranging from the first day in school to death, divorce, sexual abuse, AIDS, suicide, and homelessness) that are appropriate for children ages 3 to 16. The first part of the work presents materials for adults that discuss the meaning of separation and loss to children, the therapeutic use of books (bibliotherapy), and writers' comments on how they tackle problems of separation and loss in their works. The second part, arranged in eight broad subject areas and then further subdivided by topic, comprises descriptions of about 600 recommended titles, complete with bibliographic citation, interest/reading levels, and evaluative annotations for each. Two extensive bibliographies—one on the topic of separation and loss, the other on bibliotherapy—are found in the third section, as well as a list of appropriate helping organizations. The work is indexed to provide five separate access points: author, title, subject, interest level, and reading level. *Books to Help Children Cope with Separation and Loss*, in all its iterations, belongs in every library that serves children or adults who care about them.

Dictionaries and Encyclopedias

431. Corsini, Raymond J., ed. **Encyclopedia of Psychology.** New York, John Wiley, 1984. 4v. illus. bibliog. index. $440.00/set. ISBN 0-471-865-94-X.

When it was first published, the *Encyclopedia of Psychology* was hailed for its comprehensiveness; its high standards of scholarship; the clear, well-organized, and accessible manner in which its information was presented; and the world-class intellectual and professional abilities of its editor and contributors. A decade later, it is still relied upon for those same reasons. The encyclopedia addresses 10 major subject groups as they relate to psychology: "Applied," "Clinical," "Cognitive," "Developmental," "Educational," "Measurement," "Personality," "Physiological," "Social," and "Theoretical." Within these subject parameters, there are roughly 1,500 entries, with an additional 650 entries devoted to biographical profiles of individuals, both living and deceased, eminent in the field of psychology. The bibliography found in volume 4 cumulates the approximately 15,000 references cited throughout the encyclopedia's articles; the 24,500-item index, a model of exhaustive detail, facilitates rapid access to any information sought.

If at all possible, libraries would do well to purchase the four-volume encyclopedia. However, for libraries that simply cannot afford such an expenditure, an excellent alternative is the *Concise Encyclopedia of Psychology* (Wiley, 1987, 1242p., $125.00, ISBN 0-471-01068-5), also edited by Corsini. Its 2,150 articles are much less exhaustive than those found in the unabridged work, but they nevertheless uphold its high standards of scholarship and readability.

432. Doctor, Ronald M., and Ada P. Kahn. **The Encyclopedia of Phobias, Fears, and Anxieties.** New York, Facts on File, 1989. 487p. index. $45.00. ISBN 0-8160-1798-0.

Doctor and Kahn not only cover descriptions of fears, anxieties, and phobias, but also provide brief biographies of noted theorists, theoretical notes, and historical information about the topic. There are, in addition, examples of fear surveys, suggestions as to how some phobias might be treated, and descriptions of various medications currently used to treat anxiety. Topics are easily located; cross references facilitate finding an item either under its technical name or the fear (say, of heights) that relates to it. A bibliography and solid index conclude the work.

433. Pettijohn, Terry, ed. **The Encyclopedic Dictionary of Psychology.** 4th ed. Guilford, CT, Dushkin, 1991. 304p. illus. $17.95; $12.95pa. ISBN 1-56134-043X; 0-87967-885-2pa.

This work discusses roughly 1,400 terms, people, or concepts central to the field of psychology. The alphabetically arranged entries are written by subject specialists, although only the longer articles (one-half to a full page) are signed. The volume leads off with three brief indexes that list biographical entries, "topic guides," and "subject maps." (*Topic guides* are boxed overviews of related articles found through-out the dictionary; *subject maps* are extended lists of articles grouped by subtopic.) The writing is clear, concise, and easily understood by the educated lay reader.

Handbooks

434. **Diagnostic and Statistical Manual of Mental Disorders: DSM-IV.** 4th ed. Washington, DC, American Psychiatric Association, 1994. 886p. index. $42.95; $39.95pa. ISBN 0-89042-061-0; 0-89042-062-9pa.

The stated purpose of *DSM-IV* is "to provide clear descriptions of diagnostic categories in order to enable clinicians and investigators to diagnose, communicate about, study, and treat the various mental disorders." To this end, the work provides the following: an overview of the *DSM-III-R* classification scheme used to categorize more than 200 mental illnesses and disorders; a section on using the book; diagnostic categories with text and criteria; and appendixes that include an annotated listing of changes in *DSM-IV*, decision trees for differential diagnosis, a glossary of technical terms, symptom and diagnostic indexes, and several other codes and classifications listings. Although intended primarily for professionals, this work is also an excellent resource for patrons seeking to understand what a professional's diagnosis may mean in plain English.

435. Gregory, Richard L., with O. L. Zangwill, eds. **The Oxford Companion to the Mind.** New York, Oxford University Press, 1987. 865p. illus. index. $49.95. LC 87-1671. ISBN 0-19-866124-X.

Reflecting the traditional high intellectual and professional standard of the Oxford Companion series, the 1,001 entries offered here address concepts and ideas related mainly to numerous branches of psychology, philosophy, and the physiology of the higher nervous system. The diversity of these entries is stunning, ranging from such traditional areas as consciousness and language to more esoteric topics such as "Clever Hans" (the thinking horse) and iconic imagery. The work also includes biographies of psychologists, philosophers, and scientists from a broad range of countries and cultures who have contributed to our understanding of the mind throughout history. In addition to the articles, *The Oxford Companion to the Mind* offers a 20-page tutorial on the nervous system. Whether for reference or simply the sheer joy of browsing through its fascinating articles, this is a wonderful resource for all libraries to have on hand.

436. Kramer, Jack J., and Jane Close Conoley, eds. **The Eleventh Mental Measurements Yearbook.** Lincoln, NE, University of Nebraska Press, 1992. 1183p. index. $125.00. ISBN 0-910674-33-7.

This handbook deals with the new and revised tests that have appeared in print since publication of the *Tenth Mental Measurements Yearbook* in 1989; it updates, but does not replace, that work. Of the 477 tests identified, more than 80 percent are reviewed. The citations are arranged alphabetically and note test title, group for whom the test is intended, date of publication, acronym, validity and reliability data, forms, length, time of administration, publisher, and other information as appropriate. A list of literature citations pertaining to the test and reviews of the test follows. Included among the handbook's appendixes and indexes are a test title index, an index of acronyms, a subject index that indicates under which subject areas the tests are applicable, a test publisher directory, and a subscore index.

PARAPSYCHOLOGY

437. Bletzer, June G. **The Donning International Encyclopedic Psychic Dictionary.** Norfolk, VA, Donning, 1986. 875p. bibliog. $29.95; $19.95pa. ISBN 0-89865-372-X; 0-89865-371-1pa.

This fascinating, encyclopedic treatment of parapsychology and holistic philosophy is written by an author whose life has been devoted to "occult philosophy"; thus, the definitions found here are not objective and scholarly but rather lively, intelligent, insightful, and often magical. There are more than 9,000 entries, ranging in length from several lines to several paragraphs. Cross references abound. In addition to the main body of definitions, there are appendixes (a usage section, an overview of 166 "occult laws," and a 122-term list of forms of divination) and a 48-lesson tutorial on psychic skills.

438. Drury, Nevill. **Dictionary of Mysticism and the Esoteric Traditions.** Rev. ed. Santa Barbara, CA, ABC-Clio, 1992. 328p. illus. $49.50. ISBN 0-87436-699-2.

The more than 1,000 alphabetically arranged entries in Drury's illustrated sourcebook cover not only Eastern and Western mysticism, but also the occult, aspects of parapsychology, astrology, and cultism. Illustrations include photographs of notables in the fields covered and line drawings from various elements included. Drury has done an especially good job of identifying the noteworthy individuals, both living and dead, who have contributed to these areas. Extensive cross references and a selective, unannotated bibliography supplement the text.

439. Guiley, Rosemary Ellen. **The Encyclopedia of Witches and Witchcraft.** New York, Facts on File, 1989. 421p. illus. index. $45.00. ISBN 0-8160-1793-X.

Witches and Witchcraft covers every aspect of its subject in an objective manner, neither affirming nor denying the reality of witchcraft. Balanced in tone, the work's more than 400 alphabetically arranged entries deal with animals, beliefs, events, legends, myths, people, places, and other aspects of witchcraft from ancient through contemporary times. Guiley carefully describes historical events, profiles individuals associated with witchcraft, outlines practices and rituals, and provides a diverse range of information appropriate to students at all levels. An excellent bibliography and a detailed index conclude the encyclopedia.

440. Opie, Iona, and Moira Tatem, eds. **A Dictionary of Superstitions.** New York, Oxford University Press, 1989. 494p. index. $35.00. ISBN 0-19-211597-9.

More than 1,500 superstitions—including spells, cures, charms, omens, rituals, and taboos, excluding witchcraft, the evil eye, herbal remedies, and local beliefs—are described in Opie and Tatem's dictionary. Although most of the superstitions identified originally hail from Great Britain and Ireland, many will be familiar to Americans as well. Entries are arranged alphabetically by keywords or key phrases; within each entry, there are chronologically arranged quotations and selections, from many sources, that illustrate the superstition in practice. Researchers will especially appreciate the work's generously cross-referenced analytical index.

441. Shepard, Leslie, ed. **Encyclopedia of Occultism & Parapsychology: A Compendium of Information on the Occult Sciences, Magic, Demonology, Superstitions, Spiritism, Mysticism, Metaphysics, Psychical Science, and Parapsychology** ... . 3d ed. Detroit, Gale, 1991. 2v. index. $295.00/set. ISBN 0-8103-4907-8.

The first edition (1978) of this highly respected encyclopedia was based on the merger of two works, Lewis Spence's *Encyclopedia of Occultism* (1920) and Nandor Fodor's *Encyclopedia of Psychic Science* (1934). Interpreting *occult* in its widest sense, this two-volume third edition includes within its purview (to name but a few) magic, miracles, witchcraft, and paranormal and psychic phenomena, as well as people, gods and goddesses, groups and organizations, periodicals, plants, animals, superstitions, and legends. There are well over 4,000 entries, ranging in length from several lines to 12 pages. Many of the longer articles include bibliographical references. An exhaustive general index as well as a detailed topical index are located in volume 2.

Recreation and Sports

GENERAL WORKS

Bibliographies

442. Burns, Grant. **The Sports Pages: A Critical Bibliography of Twentieth-Century American Novels and Stories Featuring Baseball, Basketball, Football, and Other Athletic Pursuits.** Metuchen, NJ, Scarecrow, 1987. 274p. index. $27.50. ISBN 0-8108-1966-X.

Burns's selective bibliography is as delightful to read as it is informative, drawing on the author's experience as a reference librarian as well as his thoughtfulness, wit, excellent writing skills, and obvious love of sports. Annotations describe not only plot and character elements, but thematic issues as well. The emphasis on a thematic approach is furthered by use of a thematic index that classifies stories by theme (for example, adolescence, aging, father-son relationships, marriage). Intended as a guide to good reading for sports fans of all ages, *Sports Pages* will also function well as a selection tool for librarians.

443. Davis, Lenwood G., and Belinda S. Daniels. **Black Athletes in the United States: A Bibliography of Books, Articles, Autobiographies, and Biographies on Black Professional Athletes in the United States, 1800–1981.** Westport, CT, Greenwood Press, 1981. 265p. index. $65.00. ISBN 0-313-22976-7.

Leading off with an objective survey of the substantial contributions of Black athletes from the 18th century forward, *Black Athletes in the United States* identifies almost 4,000 books and articles on the accomplishments of African-American athletes in the fields of baseball, basketball, boxing, football, golf, and tennis. Materials are arranged in reference, monographic, biographic, and article subdivisions. Books are accorded one-line annotations, articles (two-thirds of the titles included) are simply cited. In addition to the citations, there are a list of vertical file materials, a chronological list of officially recognized champions and most valuable players, a filmography, and an extensive index.

444. Herron, Nancy L., ed. **The Leisure Literature: A Guide to Sources in Leisure Studies, Fitness, Sports, and Travel.** Englewood, CO, Libraries Unlimited, 1992. 181p. index. $28.50. ISBN 1-56308-062-1.

The leisure-related materials Herron covers here are divided into four categories: leisure studies, fitness, sports, and travel and tourism. Each section leads off with an introductory essay. Within chapters, brief annotations describe guides and handbooks; standard and classic sources; noteworthy books; dissertations; bibliographies and catalogs; dictionaries and encyclopedias; directories; indexes, abstracts and databases; core journals; conference proceedings; and statistical sources. The work concludes with appendixes that list degree programs in U.S. colleges and universities, important publishers in each area, and a list of leisure-related organizations, as well as author/title and subject indexes.

445. Remley, Mary L. **Women in Sport: An Annotated Bibliography and Resource Guide 1900-1990.** Boston, G. K. Hall, 1991. 210p. index. $35.00. ISBN 0-8161-8977-3.

This useful guide to monographs treating women in sports organizes its materials into four chapters: "Timid Beginnings, 1900-1930," "Play Days and Olympic Medals, 1931-1960," "The Winds of Change, 1961-1975," and "Women's Sports Comes of Age, 1976-1990." Brief essays introduce each chapter; within chapters, the annotated entries are arranged chronologically then alphabetically by author rather than topic. Coverage encompasses a broad range of sports, including automobile racing, golf, gymnastics, aviation, marksmanship, and self-defense. Periodicals that cover women's sports, national organizations open to or dedicated to women's sports, and halls of fame that recognize outstanding women athletes are described in a concluding chapter. Author, subject, and title indexes conclude the bibliography.

Biographies

446. Page, James A. **Black Olympian Medalists.** Englewood, CO, Libraries Unlimited, 1991. 190p. illus. index. $27.50pa. ISBN 0-87287-618-7.

Page's biographical dictionary profiles 465 Black Olympians (primarily American) dating back to 1904. In addition to providing such basic information as name, date and place of birth, country represented, events, medals won, and competition times and distances, the entries also highlight the major achievements of each athlete both on and off the field. A number of useful statistical tables (broken down by event and, when applicable, gender), tables of medalists by place and date, and a full list of sponsoring countries follow the biographical sketches.

Dictionaries and Encyclopedias

447. Considine, Tim. **The Language of Sport.** New York, Facts on File, 1982. 355p. index. $17.95. ISBN 0-87196-653-0.

The Language of Sport defines approximately 5,000 terms drawn from 9 of the Western world's most popular sports—baseball, basketball, bowling, boxing, football, golf, ice hockey, soccer, and tennis. Both the "official" words and phrases and the insiders' jargon are included, making for a dictionary that is as engaging as it is informative. The entries are arranged alphabetically by sport, with brief but lively histories of each sport preceding its terms. The definitions range beyond just the literal meanings of the terms by providing background lore and anecdotes that demonstrate the terms' usage "on the field." This is a useful, delightful, well-rendered work that cries out for a new edition—until then, make sure the 1982 edition is at the reference desk.

448. Hickok, Ralph. **The Encyclopedia of North American Sports History.** New York, Facts on File, 1992. 516p. illus. index. $50.00. ISBN 0-8160-2096-5.

Although Hickok covers virtually all sports, including college and professional, in this solid encyclopedia, the focus is on the major ones: football, baseball, basketball, hockey, and golf. Canadian sports, but especially hockey and football, are included as well. More than 1,600 entries provide both historical and current information, with cross references, numerous photographs, and a thorough index complementing the main text. Addresses for organizations, names of award winners, and a wealth of similarly useful details are embedded in relevant entries throughout the encyclopedia.

449. White, Jess R. **Sports Rules Encyclopedia.** 2d ed. Champaign, IL, Leisure Press/Human Kinetics, 1990. 732p. illus. $44.95. ISBN 0-88011-363-4.

Widely considered the best resource on the "official" rules of sports (especially team sports), White's encyclopedia covers 51 of the most popular athletic games. In addition to describing the rules for a given sport, *Sports Rules Encyclopedia* also lists the journals covering that sport, as well as the organizations that oversee it (with organization addresses).

Directories

450. Bast, Carol J., and others, eds. **Masters Guide to Sports Camps.** Grand Rapids, MI, Masters Press, 1987. 1v. (various paging). maps. index. $24.95pa. ISBN 0-940279-00-2.

Nearly 4,000 U.S. and Canadian summer sports camps in 48 major and minor sports are profiled in this helpful directory. The camps are geared toward kids (youngsters up to age 18) who may or may not be involved in organized school sports. Information provided for each camp includes a description of the program, staff (with names, titles, and experience often noted), site (including housing and meal facilities), dates, and cost. Each entry also covers application data, with addresses and telephone numbers. Arrangement is by region (Northeast, Midwest, South, and West), with indexes by camp name in each section; regional editions are available as well.

Handbooks and Yearbooks

451. Arlott, John, ed. **Oxford Companion to World Sports and Games.** New York, Oxford University Press, 1975. 1143p. $35.00. ISBN 0-19-211538-3.

This well-written compendium of information, a standard title in most secondary school libraries, explains how the world's major sports are played. Historical background, rules, and famous athletes are described as well. Board, table, folk, and children's games are excluded, as are blood sports.

452. Boehn, David A., Jim Benagh, and Cyd Smith, eds. **Guinness Sports Record Book [yr.].** New York, Facts on File, 1972- . Annual. 1v. illus. index. $21.95 (1994 ed.). ISSN 1054-4178.

Record-setting facts and figures for 93 different kinds of competition—from recognized international sports (e.g., basketball) to minor sports (e.g., footbag) to standard games (e.g., bridge) to minor games (e.g., Twister)—are featured in this popular Guinness annual. The work is arranged alphabetically by sport, and each entry provides brief information about the sport's origins and an eclectic selection of important, representative, and/or unusual records. Although the work needs a name index, it does have a topical subject index.

453. Loeffelbein, Robert L. **The Recreation Handbook: 342 Games and Other Activities for Teams and Individuals.** Jefferson, NC, McFarland, 1992. 237p. illus. $24.95pa. ISBN 0-89950-744-1.

The 342 games described in this handbook range from surf hockey to Frisbee volleyball to billiard baseball to hopscotch rope jumping and everything in between. All are "pickup games," meaning that players pick up whatever is handy and play a game on a field, a street, a vacant lot, an empty wall, a spare table, a driveway, a patio ... whatever is available and free. Although the handbook provides rules, space needed, number of players, age levels, and equipment needs, Loeffelbein encourages players to make up new rules or change them as desired so that imagination and spontaneity can have free rein. Despite the lack of an index, this is still an excellent purchase for all public and school libraries.

454. Meserole, Mike, ed. **The Information Please Sports Almanac. [yr.].** Boston, Houghton Mifflin, 1988- . Annual. 1v. illus. $9.95pa. (1994 ed.). ISSN 1046-4980.

A delight for sports fans of almost any persuasion. *Sports Almanac* is also an excellent source of ready-reference information. The book begins with an update of the most recent year in sports, including a month-by-month chronology through the previous October. Most of the book consists of essays by noted sportswriters, covering individual sports as well as sports-related issues. Especially helpful for quick reference information, a "Through the Years" section of facts, records, and statistics follows many of the essays. Although the focus is on American sports, there is nevertheless substantial coverage of soccer and other international athletic games.

455. Paciorek, Michael J., and Jeffrey A. Jones. **Sports and Recreation for the Disabled: A Resource Handbook.** 2d ed. Carmel, IN, Cooper Publishing Group, 1994. 550p. illus. index. $45.00pa. ISBN 1-884125-4-2.

Every public library should make this wonderful sourcebook available to its patrons. It provides information on more than 50 major sports and recreational activities (including all-terrain vehicle riding and wilderness experiences) for people with disabilities. Each chapter focuses on one sport, providing information on rule modifications, organizations that sponsor competitive events, the rationale behind offering the sport to disabled persons, adapted equipment, suppliers, and additional resources. A reference list and bibliography conclude each chapter. Seven appendixes—equipment sources, lightweight wheelchair manufacturers, sports organizations, national handicapped sports and recreation chapters, national wheelchair chapters and organizations, American Athletic Association for the Deaf chapters, and Special Olympics international chapters and directors—round out the work.

BASEBALL

456. **The Baseball Encyclopedia: The Complete and Official Record of Major League Baseball.** 9th ed. New York, Macmillan, 1993. 2857p. $55.00. ISBN 0-02-579041-2.

The *Baseball Encyclopedia* is generally considered to be the essential reference for statistics on our national pastime and those who have played it. The ninth edition continues to provide chronological listings, beginning with the first official game in

1876, in addition to statistics and background information on pitching and hitting; players, managers, and teams; playoff, World Series, and all-star games; and a broad spectrum of special records and awards. An overwhelming amount of very detailed information, much of it cross-referenced, can be located within the covers of *The Baseball Encyclopedia*.

457. Hoppel, Joe, and Craig Carter, eds. **The Series**. St. Louis, MO, Sporting News, 1992. 392p. illus. $12.95pa. ISBN 0-89204-444-6.

The Series provides a good, concise history of baseball's annual fall classic, the World Series. Arranged chronologically, starting with the first games in 1903, the book provides a year-by-year description of the competition. Each year's entry consists of a brief narrative history and a game-by-game box score; similar information is provided for the American and National League championships beginning with 1969. In addition to the Series statistics, there is also a listing of all-time batting and pitching leaders.

458. Sloan, Dave, ed. **Official Baseball Guide**. St. Louis, MO, Sporting News, 1940- . Annual. 1v. $11.95pa. (1994 ed.). ISSN 0078-3838.

Sporting News publishes a number of respected annuals in the baseball arena as well as for other major sports such as basketball and football. This publication looks at pitching and batting statistics, individual team statistics, league championships, the World Series, all-star games, and major and minor league drafts and player moves. There is also an obituary section that lists the deaths of individuals noteworthy for their contributions to baseball. The companion publication to the *Guide* is Sporting News' *Official Baseball Register* (Barry Siegel, ed., annual, 1v., $11.95pa. [1994 ed.], ISSN 0067-4281), which contains complete major- and minor-league career statistics for every player who played in at least one major-league game during the previous year, regardless of where they were before or where they ended up.

459. Smith, Myron J., Jr., comp. **Baseball: A Comprehensive Bibliography**. Jefferson, NC, McFarland, 1986. 915p. index. $65.00. ISBN 0-89950-222-9. **Supplement**. 1993. 437p. index. $45.00. ISBN 0-89950-799-9.

Smith's mammoth bibliography is organized into seven sections: "Reference Works," "General Works, History, and Special Studies," "Professional Leagues and Teams," "Youth League, College, and Amateur/Semi-Pro Baseball," "Baseball Rules and Techniques," "Collective Biography," and "Individual Biography." The 21,251 entries (some of which are duplicates) are primarily to books and periodical articles that could easily be obtained at most public libraries; the majority of the citations are bibliographic only, although a few have brief annotations. The supplement brings coverage current through mid-1992, and adds another 8,000 sources to what was already the best place to start for researching this popular subject.

BASKETBALL

460. Neft, David S., and Richard M. Cohen. **The Sports Encyclopedia: Pro Basketball**. 3d ed. New York, St. Martin's Press, 1990. 589p. $17.95pa. ISBN 0-312-05162-X.

Primarily a statistical compendium, the third edition of this familiar resource extends coverage through the end of the 1989–1990 NBA season. Its mix of annual narrative summaries and statistics is arranged chronologically, with complete player and team summaries for the past 53 seasons. Rather than providing a master index for the entire chronology, the more than 3,200 players and their statistics are indexed by 10-year period. Reliable and inexpensive, this is a slam-dunk reference for basketball fans and reference librarians.

461. Sachare, Alex, and Dave Sloan, eds. **Official NBA Guide.** St. Louis, MO, Sporting News, 1958- . Annual. 1v. index. $10.95pa. (1994 ed.). ISSN 0078-3862.

Official NBA Guide, designed more for the individual fan than as a library reference tool, nevertheless functions admirably as a ready-reference source of both current and retrospective statistical information on this popular sport. The guide provides a statistical summary of the previous season, current season team records and schedules, NBA records and award winners, and season-by-season team records since the 1946-1947 season (including team and individual records). As with most of the Sporting News publications, much of the information is repeated from year to year.

462. Taragano, Martin. **Basketball Biographies: 434 U.S. Players, Coaches and Contributors to the Game, 1891-1990.** Jefferson, NC, McFarland, 1991. 318p. illus. index. $45.00. ISBN 0-89950-625-9.

Taragano considered high career scores, All-Star selections, career top-10 leaders in one or more statistical categories, longevity, number of games played, defensive abilities, leadership in assists, or other unique contribution when selecting the 434 individuals included in his biographical compendium. (For college players, the criteria were primarily All-American status and being a significant member of a championship team.) The resulting profiles, arranged alphabetically, provide career information, statistics, and an assessment of the individual's contribution to the sport. Although obviously not a comprehensive source, *Basketball Biographies* provides a good starting place for identifying and learning about individuals who have made outstanding contributions to the sport.

FOOTBALL

463. Bollig, Laura E., ed. **NCAA Football's Finest: All-Time Great Collegiate Players and Coaches.** Chicago, Triumph Books, 1991. 232p. illus. $21.95; $7.95pa. ISBN 1-880141-03-5; 0-9264436-8-9pa.

According to NCAA statistics, collegiate sports are now a billion-dollar business, a large part of which is devoted to college football. Given the popularity of this spectator sport, Bollig's review of the achievements of 343 All-Americans and the men who coached them should prove a useful addition to many public libraries. The book divides its materials into two sections: those who played from 1904 to 1969, and those who played from 1970 through 1989. Mysteriously, only offensive players are profiled, but for these Bollig lists complete collegiate records, including rushing yardage, passing yardage, percentages, kick return yardage, touchdowns, kicking points, punting yardage, and games played. Position played, high school attended, size, brief post-season bowl notes, and year AA honors were achieved are also noted for each player. Separate sections list all players by school and describe coaches' regular-season coaching records and bowl game scores. This is a useful work that could be improved by higher standards of editing and the inclusion of defensive players in the next edition.

464.   **Football Register.** St. Louis, MO. Sporting News, 1966- . Annual. 1v. illus. $10.95pa. (1994 ed.). ISSN 0071-7258.

Football Register is an alphabetically arranged biographical compendium of active NFL players that provides general biographical information as well as current and previous team affiliations and yearly statistics. Facts such as age, weight, birth place, education, awards, honors, and records are combined with detailed, year-by-year performance statistics for each player's entire pro career. There are also entries on additional active players, rookie rosters, player movements, NFL head coaches, new Hall of Fame inductees, and recently retired players.

465.   Jarrett, William S. **Timetables of Sports History: Football.** New York, Facts on File, 1989. 82p. illus. index. $17.95. ISBN 0-8160-1919-3.

Covering both collegiate and professional football, this slim chronology spans the years from the late 1800s through 1988. Events prior to 1920 are covered as eras; the years from 1920 through 1988 are each represented by a single page divided into three columns (college, professional, and post-seasonal football). A few photographs of notable players and coaches supplement the listings. Although the price seems high relative to the amount of information provided, this is nevertheless a handy resource for libraries looking for a football chronology. The publisher has also published similar titles for baseball (1989, 90p., $17.95, ISBN 0-8160-1918-5) and basketball (1990, 96p., $17.95, ISBN 0-8160-1920-7).

466.   Neft, David S., Richard M. Cohen, with Rick Korch. **The Sports Encyclopedia: Pro Football. The Modern Era 1960-1990.** 8th ed. New York, St. Martin's Press, 1990. 672p. $17.95pa. ISBN 0-312-04429-1.

As with the other titles in The Sports Encyclopedia series (basketball and football), this work represents a triumph of statistical compilation by Neft and his associates. The book is divided into chapters that represent every season from 1960 to 1989. Each year is further subdivided into sections on the two league conferences, listing team rosters, statistical leaders, records, and playoff results. A separate 35-page section lists all players alphabetically, indicating the team(s) they played for and their professional statistics. A concluding section chronicles team and individual records.

There are so many recreational activities, and so many books devoted to them, that it would be impossible to adequately describe them all here. However, most libraries will want to offer at least basic resources—dictionaries, guides, directories, and other references as available—on the topics of bicycling, camping and hiking, card and board games, golf, hockey, hunting and fishing, skiing, soccer, tennis, track and field, and water sports. These subjects should be supplemented with coverage of regional pursuits (for example, ice fishing) as appropriate.

Social Science, Sociology, and Social Welfare

SOCIAL SCIENCES

467. Herron, Nancy L., ed. **The Social Sciences: A Cross-Disciplinary Guide to Selected Sources.** Englewood, CO, Libraries Unlimited, 1989. 287p. index. $36.00; $27.50pa. ISBN 0-87287-725-6; 0-87287-777-9pa.

Herron's work is intended as a text/bibliography for the social sciences. It comprises chapters on the social sciences in general, anthropology, communications, economics and business, education, geography, history, law and legal issues, political science, psychology, sociology, and statistics and demographics. Topical essays and annotations of the nearly 800 items cited are provided by either Herron or other subject specialists. Both print and online resources are included, with print materials published as recently as 1988. Because it includes online databases as well as more recent titles, Herron also functions well as an update/supplement to William H. Webb's *Sources of Information in the Social Sciences* (3d ed., American Library Association, 1986, o.p.).

468. Kuper, Adam, and Jessica Kuper, eds. **The Social Science Encyclopedia.** New York, Routledge & Kegan Paul/Methuen, 1989. 916p. $75.00; $29.95pa. ISBN 0-7102-0008-0; 0-415-04081-7pa.

The Social Science Encyclopedia contains more than 700 signed articles, contributed by 500 scholars, on the topics of anthropology, biology, business, communication and media studies, demography, economics, education, geography, history, industrial relations, law, linguistics, Marxism, medicine, methodology, philosophy, political theory, psychiatry, social problems and criminology, and sociology. Arranged alphabetically, the articles range in length from several hundred words to eight pages. The readership is assumed to be educated but not expert. Strengths include broad introductory essays on all the major social science disciplines, biographical data on key scholars and theoreticians, and excellent bibliographies that accompany each entry. The major drawback of this work is its lack of a systematic subject index. Nevertheless, it is a comprehensive and easily used reference for social science questions.

The publisher has produced a series of spin-off titles ("Social Science Lexicons") from the encyclopedia that excerpt specific kinds of information from the main volume, and these works might be of interest to libraries that do not feel they need quite as much coverage as is provided in the original work. An example is *Key Thinkers, Past and Present* (1987, 276p., $13.95pa., ISBN 0-7102-1173-2), which is made up of 111 biographical essays of key social theorists, both living and dead. Each essay of approximately 500 to 2,000 words in length includes a brief bibliography of books by and about the subject.

469. Mitchell, G. Duncan, ed. **A New Dictionary of the Social Sciences.** 2d ed. New York, Aldine/Routledge & Kegan Paul, 1979. 244p. $42.95. ISBN 0-202-30285-7.

Intended to meet the needs of the interested lay reader as well as the beginning sociology student, Mitchell's dictionary comprises approximately 350 terms drawn from sociology and the related disciplines of cultural and social anthropology, social psychology, and political science. Entries range in length from four lines to four pages, depending on importance or complexity of the item being defined. Many of the entries are signed; a few include bibliographic references. In addition to the terms defined, there are also biographical profiles for key individuals (no longer living) in the social sciences.

470. Sills, David L., ed. **International Encyclopedia of the Social Sciences.** New York, Free Press/Macmillan, 1968–1979. 8v. index. $325.00/set. ISBN 0-02-897396-8.

The *International Encyclopedia of the Social Sciences* was first published by Macmillan as a 17-volume encyclopedia from 1930 to 1935. It was hailed as a landmark of scholarly achievement, both for its breadth of scope and for its successful integration of the myriad avenues of endeavor that together make up the social sciences.

The eight-volume set is intended to build on, rather than replace, the original work. Arranged alphabetically, the 1,716 signed articles (and their accompanying bibliographies) attempt to update readers regarding developments during the decades between the 1930s and the 1970s. As in the earlier work, the bulk of the articles address concepts, theories, and methodologies drawn from the disciplines of anthropology, economics, geography, history, law, political science, psychiatry, psychology, and sociology. Although statistics was not included in the first work, it has been here. In additional to the topical articles, there are biographical profiles of approximately 600 individuals born before 1890 who were deemed to have made significant contributions to the social sciences. The editors have made generous use of cross references in addition to providing an exhaustive index, both attributes that greatly enhance the value of an already outstanding resource. Although expensive, the *International Encyclopedia of the Social Sciences* provides such a vast amount and scope of information that it provides tremendous benefit for its cost.

471. **Social Sciences Index.** Bronx, NY, H. W. Wilson, 1974- . Annual. Sold on service basis. ISSN 0094-4920.

Formerly known as *International Index* and *Social Sciences and Humanities Index*, *SSI* has been described as an "indispensable tool for access to the periodical literature of the social sciences," and as such is an important purchase for all libraries with strong patron interest in this area. The publication currently indexes 342 periodicals drawn from a broad range of disciplines, including anthropology, area studies, community health and medical care, economics, ethnic studies, geography,

SOCIOLOGY

Bibliographies

472. Aby, Stephen H. **Sociology: A Guide to Reference and Information Sources**. Littleton, CO. Libraries Unlimited, 1987. 231p. index. $36.00. ISBN 0-87287-498-2.

Aby's guide provides descriptions of 659 of the major reference sources in sociology, its subdisciplines, and the related social sciences. The materials are arranged in three sections: "General Social Science Reference Sources," "Social Science Disciplines," and "Sociology," which comprises the bulk of the bibliography. The focus is on English-language indexes, bibliographies, dictionaries, and other reference sources published from 1970 through 1986, with annotations ranging in length from approximately 60 to 200 words. Author/title and subject indexes round out *Sociology*.

Dictionaries and Encyclopedias

473. Borgatta, Edgar F., ed. **Encyclopedia of Sociology**. New York, Macmillan, 1992. 4v. index. $340.00/set. ISBN 0-02-897051-9.

This encyclopedia's 370 articles, written by scholars and subject experts in language that is clear and accessible to the lay reader, deal with both traditional concepts and theories and newer theoretical approaches (for example, feminist theory, new structuralism). Coverage includes social problems (homelessness, incest, organized crime, AIDS), subfields of sociology (urban, applied), various area studies (Africa, the Middle East, Latin America), multicultural studies (Native-American, African-American, Asian-American), and the sociology of other disciplines (law, education). Articles, ranging in length from 2 to 18 pages but averaging about 5 or 6, lead off with background information that places the topic in context within the discipline, and then discuss issues, theory, and research findings. Most articles conclude with a list of cross references and a substantial bibliography.

Although the *Encyclopedia of Sociology* is a highly recommended purchase for all libraries that can afford it, it is expensive. A much less costly (and comprehensive) alternative is Richard Lachman's reliable reference, *The Encyclopedic Dictionary of Sociology* (4th ed., Dushkin, 1991, 321p, $12.95pa, ISBN 0-87967-886-0). The fourth updated and revised edition of what was originally the *Encyclopedia of Sociology* (1974), this work defines more than 1,350 terms drawn from the terminology, concepts, research, institutions, and fundamental processes and practices of sociology. Although written by 120 subject specialists, the alphabetically arranged entries are geared toward the general reader rather than the scholar or professional. Many entries contain cross references that serve either to connect interrelated concepts or to deepen comprehension of a topic. More encyclopedic in its approach than dictionary-like, this work provides a good overview of sociology's themes and topics.

gerontology, international relations, and law and criminology. Access is by subject, author, and article title. As with other Wilson indexes, title enhancement, which offers additional clarifying information within brackets, is provided when the title of the article is somewhat ambiguous. Also available online, on disk, on CD-ROM, and on magnetic tape.

474. DiCanio, Margaret. **The Encyclopedia of Marriage, Divorce and the Family.** New York, Facts on File, 1989. 607p. $45.00. ISBN 0-8160-1695-X.

The assumption underlying DiCanio's encyclopedia is that marriage is the core concept around which lifestyle and family are defined. Within this context, the volume presents more than 500 alphabetically arranged entries that deal with such topics as aspects of the family cycle, problems affecting the family, cross-cultural practices, controversies, practical advice, and medical procedures. Entries are essentially brief essays that review current literature and/or provide a brief history of the topic; cross references are generous and helpful. Supplementary materials include a bibliography and appendixes that offer practical advice on issues such as family counseling and mental health services, divorce procedures, and child-support enforcement.

475. Jary, David, and Julia Jary. **The HarperCollins Dictionary of Sociology.** New York, HarperPerennial/HarperCollins, 1991. 601p. $15.00pa. ISBN 0-06-461036-5.

This is the U.S. version of a British publication, *The Collins Dictionary of Sociology* (London, HarperCollins, 1991), which inexplicably includes many more definitions and short biographies than the stateside edition. Nevertheless, the entries contained in this work are clearly written, current, and reflect the authors' expansive approach as to what disciplines fall within the purview of "sociology." There are many cross references and, although the individual entries do not include citations, a 40-page bibliography concludes the dictionary.

476. Kastenbaum, Robert, and Beatrice Kastenbaum, eds. **Encyclopedia of Death.** Phoenix, AZ, Oryx Press, 1989. 295p. illus. index. $74.50. ISBN 0-89774-263-X.

The 130 articles on all aspects of death and dying that make up this encyclopedia were written either by Robert or Beatrice Kastenbaum, both eminent in this area, or by equally authoritative contributors known for their expertise in related fields of study. The articles, ranging in length from one to several pages, range across a broad spectrum of disciplines, including the humanities (historical events and trends in attitudes toward death, its representation in literature and mythology, etc.), the social sciences (violent death, bereavement counseling and hospice care, cross-cultural aspects of funerary rites, etc.), legal issues, and biomedical concerns. Several articles treat organizations or major periodicals in the field of death studies. Generous cross-referencing, a thorough subject index, and a topical guide to all the encyclopedia's articles contribute to the overall value of this useful work.

SOCIAL WELFARE

General Works

477. Dumouchel, J. Robert. **Government Assistance Almanac [yr.]: The Guide to All Federal Financial and Other Domestic Programs.** Washington, DC, Foggy Bottom, and Detroit, Omnigraphics, 1985- . Annual. 1v. index. $125.00 (1994 ed.). ISSN 0883-8690.

Based on information found in the federal catalog, *Government Assistance Almanac* describes about 1,100 federal programs for those needing federal assistance. The work is arranged in three parts, the first of which presents a helpful, user-friendly overview of how to use the book's information to seek federal assistance. The second part provides basic information on all federal assistance programs,

478. Kipps, Harriet Clyde. **Volunteerism: The Directory of Organizations, Training, Programs, and Publications.** 3d ed. New Providence, NJ, R. R. Bowker, 1991. 1164p. index. $119.00. ISBN 0-8352-2739-1.

Volunteerism is a guide to information on volunteer involvement in specific areas of human services and the physical environment, and to resource groups and training events that assist volunteer managers. It is arranged in three parts further subdivided into numerous subsections. The primary areas are administrative/organizational resources, subject-specific resources, and an annotated bibliography. The first two of these sections provide information in three distinct fields of concern to volunteer managers: national, federal, state, and regional resource groups; training courses and events on and off college and university campuses; and individual local volunteer programs. The third section, the bibliography, describes more than 2,000 titles organized alphabetically by subject and by title within subject. Indexed by organization and by geographic designation.

479. Paul, Ellen, ed. **Adoption Choices: A Guidebook to National and International Adoption Resources.** Detroit, Visible Ink Press/Gale, 1991. 590p. index. $24.95pa. ISBN 0-8103-9403-0.

Intended as an aid to prospective parents, birth parents, adoption professionals, counselors, physicians, attorneys, and support groups, this directory identifies public and private adoption organizations at the county, state, national, and international levels. The work is organized into several topical sections. The first section, an alphabetical, state-by-state listing of public, private, and independent agencies, associations, and support groups for adoptive parents, includes agency profiles, procedures, fees, and home study protocols. The second section focuses on adoption exchanges, whereas the third and fourth sections cover Canada and selected foreign countries. A final section addresses foster care. An organization index concludes this comprehensive sourcebook.

For libraries that can afford broader coverage in this subject area, Paul's resource is nicely complemented by *The Encyclopedia of Adoption* (Christine Adamec and William L. Pierce, Facts on File, 1991, 382p. $45.00, ISBN 0-8160-2108-2), which in some 400 entries addresses the entire scope of adoption from agencies to zygote adoption. Some of the important topics discussed are who adopts and why, drug-addicted babies, gay and lesbian adoption, surrogate parenthood, teenage parents, and transracial adoption. An introduction presents a concise overview of the history of adoption, while extensive appendixes provide, through tables and charts, information on the demographics of adoption in the United States.

480. Treboux, Dominique, with Elizabeth I. Lopez. **T.A.P.P. Sources: A National Directory of Teenage Pregnancy Prevention Programs.** Metuchen, NJ, Scarecrow, 1989. 557p. $42.50. ISBN 0-8108-2277-6.

Organized by state, then city within state, *T.A.P.P. Sources* describes more than 500 teenage pregnancy prevention programs based in a variety of clinical, community, and educational settings. In addition to basic information, such as address, telephone number, type of agency, scope, target population, fees, and parental notification, the description of each program includes goals; direct, indirect, and special services; and funding sources. Two introductory sections further enhance the value of this directory: the first discusses the major types of pregnancy prevention programs and their strategies, the second the importance of incorporating an understanding of the function of teenage sex role stereotyping into prevention strategies. Given that the United States currently has the highest rate of teenage pregnancy among industrialized nations, the *T.A.P.P.* directory should be a priority purchase for all public libraries.

Abuse

481.   Clark, Robin E., and Judith Freeman Clark. **The Encyclopedia of Child Abuse.** New York, Facts on File, 1989. 328p. index. $45.00. ISBN 0-8160-1584-8.

This encyclopedia comprises more than 500 entries, ranging in length from one sentence to several paragraphs, on perhaps one of the most heart-breaking areas of public concern. The descriptions cover clinical medical terms; legal issues (laws, technical legal expressions, and important court cases and their decisions); names of advocacy groups and child-protection organizations; categories of abusers and forms of abuse and neglect; psychological concepts; treatment programs; and geographical and political entities (with regard to their response to child abuse). Supplementary materials include statistical charts and tables, a lengthy bibliography, and 15 appendixes that list organizations, state-by-state reporting laws, funding patterns, child welfare statutes, and similar useful information.

482.   Webster, Linda, comp. and ed. **Sexual Assault and Child Sexual Abuse: A National Directory of Victim/Survivor Services and Prevention Programs.** Phoenix, AZ, Oryx Press, 1989. 353p. index. $55.00pa. ISBN 0-89774-445-4.

Designed to "assist victims, survivors, their families and friends, to find the help they need," this directory profiles 2,700 local agencies. Arrangement is alphabetical by state, and then city within state. Each entry provides the agency's name, address, telephone number, type of agency, contact names, geographical areas served, years in operation, and description of services. Separate sections profile 268 state agencies and 100 national organizations working in the area of sexual assault and child sexual abuse. Indexed by specialized services, clientele, and agencies listed. Unfortunately, this is an important resource to have on hand at all public libraries.

Aging

483.   Brazil, Mary Jo. **Building Library Collections on Aging: A Selection Guide and Core List.** Santa Barbara, CA, ABC-Clio, 1990. 174p. index. $45.00. ISBN 0-87436-559-7.

Brazil's helpful guide is arranged in two parts. The first provides information for people who want to create collections on aging as to what kinds of materials to select, where to get the materials, and how to obtain the least expensive types. The second presents an annotated core list divided into 27 topics, such as alcohol and drug abuse, Alzheimer's disease, caregiving, economics and insurance, and ethics and legal issues. Titles include visual and print materials, including periodicals and government reports. Each entry contains a full bibliographic citation, pagination, cost, ISBN, and a brief descriptive and evaluative annotation. A 19-page subject/author/title index concludes the guide.

484. Cheney, Walter J., William J. Diehm, and Frank E. Seeley. **The Second 50 Years: A Reference Manual for Senior Citizens.** New York, Paragon House, 1992. 445p. illus. index. $21.95pa. ISBN 1-55778-531-7.

The critical issues faced by retirees—retirement planning, living on a fixed income, health care, insurance, nutrition and fitness, housing, and personal security, among others—are the focus of this basic reference manual for senior citizens. The work is organized by about two dozen broad categories, each further subdivided into a number of constituent essays written by one of the manual's three authors. All essays are clearly written and are accompanied by addresses and telephone numbers for important organizations and services. A thorough subject index, which includes organization names and book titles, provides additional access to information. Seniors will especially appreciate the work's large page size and 12-point type.

485. Maddox, George L., and others, eds. **The Encyclopedia of Aging.** New York, Springer, 1987. 893p. illus. bibliog. index. $96.00. ISBN 0-8261-4840-9.

The intent of this highly regarded, interdisciplinary encyclopedia is to provide "comprehensive, authoritative, but concise coverage of gerontology" (from the preface). Articles, ranging in length from one-half to several pages, appear under more than 400 headings representing major issues, topics, and events concerned with aging humans. Topics include such areas as economics, public policy, geriatrics, sociology, human services and mental health, and psychology. Although the encyclopedia meets the highest standards of scholarship (the reference list alone runs to 130 pages), it is written to be accessible to the nonspecialist, and thus is a comprehensive and valuable resource for public libraries.

A good complement to *The Encyclopedia of Aging* is Diana K. Harris's *Dictionary of Gerontology* (Greenwood Press, 1988. 20p., $37.95. ISBN 0-313-25287-4), which provides brief definitions of approximately 800 terms, theories, research methods, statistical techniques, organizations/agencies, drugs, medical conditions, and other key concepts in the study of gerontology.

486. Vierck, Elizabeth. **Fact Book on Aging.** Santa Barbara, CA, ABC-Clio, 1990. 199p. index. $45.00. ISBN 0-87436-284-9.

This reference is a compilation of one-line statistics covering such topics as health, crime, transportation, and demographics related to older adults. Chapters are organized by broad subject area (for example, seniors and money), and then further subdivided and organized within the chapter to focus on such topics as attitudes about money, income, and assets. All statistics are documented, with both source and bibliographic information provided. A good resource for a broad range of statistics on our aging society.

Community Life

487. **The Better Community Catalog: A Sourcebook of Ideas, People, and Strategies ... .** By Partners for Livable Places. Washington, DC, Acropolis Books, 1989. 375p. illus. index. $24.95pa. ISBN 0-685-25302-3.

Social innovation—coming up with new ways to address social and community problems—is the subject of this fascinating sourcebook, which charts the combined civic efforts of public, private, and government sectors that have led to more humane habitats. The book is arranged alphabetically by topic, such as adaptive reuse or fundraising. Topics lead off with a brief introduction, followed by an ideas section that describes in practical detail accomplishments in specific communities.

Bibliographies of books, reports, and articles and a list of sources for consultation conclude each topical entry. A state-arranged list of individuals and organizations concerned with community development and an index round out *The Better Community Catalog*, a work that deserves a place in all public libraries.

488. Hombs, Mary Ellen. **American Homelessness.** 2d ed. Santa Barbara, CA, ABC-Clio, 1994. 300p. index. $39.50. ISBN 0-87436-725-5.

Designed as an information sourcebook for nearly all aspects of homelessness in the United States, Hombs's guide includes a chronology of events related to advocacy for the homeless; biographies of individuals central to this issue; information on key documents, reports, federal legislation, and court cases; a directory of private and federal organizations; a bibliography of print and nonprint reference materials; and a brief glossary of terms and acronyms encountered in working with the homeless and the agencies that deal with them. Subject, name, and title indexes complete the handbook.

Disabilities

489. Abrams, A. Jay, and Margaret Ann Abrams. **The First Whole Rehab Catalog: A Comprehensive Guide to Products and Services for the Physically Disadvantaged.** White Hall, VA, Betterway, 1990. 240p. illus. index. $16.95pa. ISBN 1-55870-131-1.

This catalog contains information about commercial products designed to help those with physical disabilities live independent lives. Arranged topically, the book covers home management, personal care, access, mobility, transportation, health and fitness, and recreation aids. In addition, the authors have included information on catalogs, books, information centers, databases, and government and advocacy organizations of interest to the intended audience. Entries provide a description of the product or service, note price range, and give the manufacturer's name, address, and telephone number; often the descriptions are accompanied by illustrations of the aids in use. An important purchase for public libraries, this publication will be very helpful to individuals with physical disabilities as well as those who work with them.

490. **AFB Directory of Services for Blind and Visually Impaired Persons in the United States and Canada.** New York, American Foundation for the Blind, 1926- . Biennial. 1v. index. $75.00 (1994 ed.). Spiralbound. ISSN 0899-2533.

Describing programs and services for impaired persons from children through the elderly, this directory is organized to enable the blind and visually impaired, their families, and their friends to locate needed services quickly and with a minimum of effort. It provides information on federal agencies, national nonprofit organizations, and state, local, and regional services. Low-vision clinics are also identified. Entries note the organization's name, address, telephone number, and key official, as well as program services, accreditation, and membership information. In addition, a section entitled "How to Find Services" includes several tables of statistics about the visually impaired population of the United States, definitions of visual terms, and a quick reference guide to major federal programs. The work is extensively indexed.

491. Eckstein, Richard M., ed. **Handicapped Funding Directory [yr.]: A Guide to Sources of Funding in the United States for Programs and Services for the Disabled.** 7th ed. Margate, FL, Research Grant Guides, 1990. 250p. index. $39.50pa. ISBN 0-945078-02-1.

This well-known directory cites 835 foundations and corporations and 28 federal sources of grants for the disabled, defined herein to encompass the blind, deaf, emotionally disturbed, and physically disabled. Among the types of programs and services included are construction, education, equipment, eye research, mental health, operating costs, recreation, rehabilitation, research, sheltered workshops, speech improvement, vocational training, and youth services. Arranged alphabetically by state, entries for foundations and corporations include name, address, telephone number, contact person, and area of interest. Federal entries also cover eligibility, fiscal, regulatory, and program information. Supplementary materials include advice on grantsmanship; a list of 21 associations that serve the disabled; listings of area grantmakers; regional and local federal offices and information centers; state agencies involved with hiring of the handicapped, vocational rehabilitation, and special education; and Foundation Center information collections. Indexes by associations, foundations, and corporations (both alphabetically and by area of service), as well as federal programs by agency, conclude the directory.

492. Mackenzie, Leslie, ed. **The Complete Directory for People with Disabilities.** Lakeville, CT, Grey House, 1992. 800p. index. $99.95. ISBN 0-685-60585-X.

Intended as a one-stop resource for persons with disabilities, their families, friends, and the professionals who provide services for them, this directory organizes its materials into sections on associations, media, products, and programs. Additional categories (e.g., hearing impaired, hotlines, mentally disabled, physically disabled, visually impaired) are provided under associations. Under the products section, each of the items has a brief description and price code. In the program section, addresses, telephone numbers, and directors/administrators are included along with a brief description of the program. Indexes to entry/organization/name, disability/need, and geographic location of institutions and organizations round out the directory.

493. Moore, Cory. **A Reader's Guide for Parents of Children with Mental, Physical, or Emotional Disabilities.** 3d ed. Rockville, MD, Woodbine House, 1990. 248p. index. $14.95pa. ISBN 0-933149-27-1.

The goal of this annotated bibliography is to identify and describe information sources about living with a disabled child, as well as those addressing specific disabilities. The work is arranged in five sections. The first lists public and private agencies that serve disabled children, and gives for each the name, address, and program focus. The second section provides information about specific disabilities; for each is provided a list of basic readings, information about the child at home, school, and growing up, personal accounts from those who have the disability, and where to write for information. The third section explores topics of special interest to families dealing with disabilities, such as advocacy or dealing with siblings. The fourth section comprises an annotated bibliography of books for younger children that provide realistic views of disabilities and of children who are living with them. Journals, newsletters, and directories useful to parents of disabled children are described in the final section. This is a well-done and very useful guide that deserves to be in all libraries, regardless of size.

Sex Studies

494.   The Alyson Almanac: A Treasury of Information for the Gay and Lesbian Community. Boston, Alyson, 1989- . Biennial. 1v. illus. index. $9.95pa. (1994 ed.). No ISSN available.

Bringing together a diverse array of information about lesbians and gays, *The Alyson Almanac* covers history, books, periodicals, films, theater, music, organizations, awards, AIDS, hotlines, sports, finances, relationships, health, safer sex, pen pals, slang, symbols, travel, religion, politics, and famous people. Brief biographies of more than 175 individuals are also included. A detailed, thorough index completes the almanac.

495.   Frayser, Suzanne G., and Thomas J. Whitby. Studies in Human Sexuality: A Selected Guide. 2d ed. Englewood, CO, Libraries Unlimited, 1995. 600p. index. $85.00. ISBN 1-56308-131-8.

A guide to monographic works on human sexuality, Frayser and Whitby's annotated bibliography identifies selected resources in the areas of biology, medicine, psychology, sociology, anthropology, and the arts. Although most of the more than 1,000 works cited were published in the 1980s and 1990s, older classics were included as appropriate. Entries are grouped according to a topical classification schedule, and include full bibliographic citations, lengthy evaluative annotations, and an indication of reading level.

Substance Abuse

496.   Drug, Alcohol, and Other Addictions: A Directory of Treatment Centers and Prevention Programs Nationwide. 2d ed. Phoenix, AZ, Oryx Press, 1993. 646p. $68.50pa. ISBN 0-89774-623-6.

This is the most comprehensive directory available for coverage of drug, alcohol, and behavior addiction facilities and programs. The 12,000 facilities listed include programs supported by schools, hospitals, prisons, and state and local governments. Entries are arranged by state; within state, facilities are alphabetized by city and name. Each entry includes the usual name, address, and telephone number, as well as information on addictions treated, treatment type, setting, statistics, special programs, payment method, and accommodations.

Oryx has also published a similar, well-regarded title for teenagers with addiction problems, *Substance Abuse Residential Treatment Centers for Teens* (1990, 286p., $55.00pa., ISBN 0-89774-585-X). An important and helpful resource for those—especially parents—needing to find programs for troubled youths ages 9 to 19, this title covers about 1,000 government, nonprofit, and for-profit programs and agencies, providing address, telephone number, crisis hotline number, name of contact person, and a description of the various programs. Although the work's focus is on teenage alcohol and drug abuse, programs for high risk-taking behaviors, eating disorders, codependency, sexual assault victims, and suicidal behaviors are also included. There are an organization name index, a listing of programs under approximately 40 categories in an addiction/disorder index, and a similar number of therapeutic methods and services in the treatment method index.

497. Myers, Sally, and Blanche Woolls, eds. **Substance Abuse: A Resource Guide for Secondary Schools.** Englewood, CO, Libraries Unlimited, 1991. 167p. index. $28.50. ISBN 0-9-87287-805-8.

A compilation of resources and information on substance abuse, this work includes fiction and nonfiction books, filmstrips, films, videos, and computer programs. Each entry notes author, title, publisher, dates, notes, pagination, number of disks or frames included, cost, LC and ISBN numbers, and format. The accompanying annotations are thoughtful and informative. In addition to the entries, there are source lists of free and inexpensive materials; a list of periodical titles; and appendixes that provide information on such items as search strategies, state agency addresses, and substance abuse curricula. An author/title index rounds out the bibliography.

PHILANTHROPY

498. Murphy, C. Edward, and Joan Seabourne, eds. **Guide to U.S. Foundations, Their Trustees, Officers, and Donors.** Compiled by the Foundation Center. New York, Foundation Center, 1993. 2v. index. $195.00pa./set. ISBN 0-87954-488-0.

Murphy and Seabourne's reference is a comprehensive list of some 34,000 private, community, and operating nongovernmental and nonprofit organizations that offer grants to outside applicants or charitable programs or that allocate their funds to their own research. It replaces the familiar *National Data Book of Foundations,* which was published by the Foundation Center from 1973 to 1992, and includes additional information: contact person and telephone number; geographical limitations; application information; and foundation trustees, officials, and donors. The most comprehensive source of information related to sources of funding, this set will serve as a first step in identifying prospective funding sources in a local community or geographical area and potential connections between an organization and a grant funding source.

499. Olson, Stan, and Margaret Mary Feczko, eds. **The Foundation Directory.** Compiled by the Foundation Center. New York, Foundation Center, 1978- . Annual. 1v. index. $185.00; $160.00pa. (1994 ed.). ISSN 0071-8092.

The Foundation Directory is the standard reference source for information about private and community grantmaking foundations in the United States. It includes descriptive entries of about 6,300 foundations with assets of at least $2 million or annual giving of at least $200,000. Foundation information is arranged alphabetically by states, and within states by foundation name. Entries for each foundation include areas of foundation giving, types of grants and other types of support, specific limitations on foundation giving by geographical area, subject focus or types of support, and application information. Includes a glossary of terms used in the grantmaking process. A companion publication, *The Foundation Directory: Part 2: A Guide to Grant Programs $50,000–$200,000* (annual, 1v., $160.00pa. [1994 ed.], ISSN 1058-6210), provides similar information for about 4,300 private and community foundations in the United States that make annual grants within these financial parameters.

16

Statistics, Demography, and Urban Studies

STATISTICS AND DEMOGRAPHY

500. Ambry, Margaret. **The Official Guide to Household Spending: The Number One Guide to Who Spends How Much on What.** 2d ed. Ithaca, NY, New Strategist, 1993. 428p. index. $69.95. ISBN 0-9628092-3-3.

Ambry has compiled a work that is both informative and fascinating, as it answers that age-old question, "So how much do other families spend on groceries?" In fact, this reference work provides tables detailing how much household consumers spend for approximately 1,000 products and services—everything from homes and cars to pies, tarts, and turnovers. The statistics cited are based on the 1992 Consumer Expenditure Survey conducted by the Bureau of the Census and analyzed and published by the Bureau of Labor Statistics. The guide is organized into 10 chapters of broad spending categories, such as shelter or utilities; each chapter includes sections on spending trends and spending by age, income, household type, and household size. An 11th chapter offers a summary and supplemental tables, and the appendix includes information on the survey used to compile the data. There are also a glossary of expenditure items and terms used and a detailed index to specific items.

501. Garwood, Alfred N., and Louise L. Hornor, eds. **Dictionary of U.S. Government Statistical Terms.** Palo Alto, CA, Information Publications, 1991. 247p. $50.00; $45.00pa. ISBN 0-931845-25-4; 0-931845-24-6pa.

Especially helpful to nonspecialist users of U.S. government publications such as the Census, *Dictionary of U.S. Government Statistical Terms* provides convenient access to more than 1,000 terms with specialized meanings used extensively in government publications. Each alphabetical entry includes the term, the defining agency or agencies, brief collection methodology, and related terms connected by cross references. In addition to the definitions, a bibliography of source publications from which definitions were taken and a list of abbreviations are included.

502. Morgan, Kathleen O'Leary, Scott Morgan, and Neal Quinto, eds. **State Rankings, [yr.]: A Statistical View of the 50 United States.** Lawrence, KS, Morgan Quinto, 1967- . Annual. 275p. $43.95pa. (1994 ed.). ISSN 1057-3623.

A familiar work in most public libraries, this statistical compendium ranks states by 274 categories, including agriculture, education, crime, and social welfare. Data are current through 1988. A large majority of the data series are drawn from Census Bureau reports, and although most of the information presented in *State Rankings* is much more accessible that government agency, its presentation in *State Rankings* is much more accessible and easy to use. All tables note sources of data for those wishing to track down more information.

503. O'Brien, Jacqueline Wasserman, and Steven R. Wasserman, eds. **Statistics Sources: A Subject Guide to Data on Industrial, Business, Social, Educational, Financial, and Other Topics for the United States and Internationally.** 10th ed. Detroit, Gale, 1960- . Irreg. 2v. biblig. $385.25 (1994 ed.) ISSN 0585-198X.

Intended as a "finding guide" for locating statistics on a mind-boggling array of topics, *Statistics Sources* provides access to U.S. and international statistical data available from some 2,000 national and international sources, both published and unpublished. The work is arranged alphabetically by subject and topically within subject; source documents in which specific statistical information can be found are listed for each subject section. The selective bibliography of key statistical sources, listing more than 300 general governmental and nongovernmental print and nonprint resources, is especially useful.

Two other good resources in this area are Oryx's *Federal Statistical Source: Where to Find Agency Experts & Personnel* (29th ed., William R. Evinger, 1991, 161p., $37.50pa. ISBN 0-89774-673-2), which identifies roughly 4,000 key federal personnel (plus their telephone and fax numbers) identified by department/division and area of expertise; and Gale's *State and Local Statistics Sources: A Subject Guide to Statistical Data on States, Cities, and Locales . . .* (2d ed., 1993, 1912p., $135.00, ISBN 0-8103-5468-3), which, in its 60,000-plus citations, provides a comprehensive guide to standard and specialized sources of state and local data.

504. **State and Metropolitan Area Data Book [yr.]: A Statistical Abstract Supplement: Regions, Divisions, States, Metropolitan Areas (SMSAs); SMSAs by Population-Size Class.** Washington, DC, Bureau of the Census; distr., Government Printing Office, 1979- . Annual. 1v. index. Price varies. S/N 003-024-01638-9.

A supplement to the *Statistical Abstract of the United States* (entry 505), the *Data Book* presents more than 2,000 statistics for each state and in excess of 200 for each Standard Metropolitan Statistical Area (SMSA). Statistics chosen are those deemed "generally useful summary measures," including such standard areas as crime, education, elections, employment, housing, income, manufacturing, and population. Although most information is drawn from the official census, statistics from other government agencies and several nongovernmental organizations have also been included. For data covering even smaller geographic areas, libraries may also want to have on hand this publication's companion volume, *County and City Data Book* (1988, $36.00, S/N 003-024-06709-9) and its annual update, *County and City Extra [yr.]* (Courtenay M. Slater and George E. Hall, eds., Bernan Press, 1992- , 1v., $89.95 [1994 ed.], ISSN 1059-9096), which provide similar information for counties, cities, and other small communities.

505. **Statistical Abstract of the United States.** Washington, DC, Bureau of the Census; distr., Government Printing Office, 1878- . Annual. 1v. index. Price varies. S/N 003-024-03619-3.

Stat Abs is the standard compendium of statistics on the social, political, and economic organization of the United States. Arranged by 31 topical sections, materials are selected from a diverse range of statistical publications, both governmental and commercial/private. Statistics are usually retrospective over a period of 15 to 20 years, although some data series go back as far as 1789. Presentation is primarily tabular, with occasional graphs and charts. Especially useful is the compendium's references to other statistical works and resources in each of the section introductions, as well as in an appendix that functions as a guide to statistics sources. A very detailed index concludes *Stat Abs*. Also available online, on microfiche, and on microfilm.

Depending on patron interest and budget concerns, libraries may also wish to consider Tom Biracree and Nancy Biracree's *Almanac of the American People* (Facts on File, 1988, 336p., index, $29.95, ISBN 0-8160-1821-9), an interesting, primarily narrative overview of statistical information drawn from such diverse sources as the Gallup Poll, Clairol, and the Census Bureau.

506. **Statistical Yearbook [yr.].** Paris, UNESCO; distr., UNIPUB, 1948- . Annual. 1v. $115.00 (1994 ed.). ISSN 0082-8459.

This authoritative United Nations publication is a massive compilation of internationally comparable data on education, educational expenditures, science and technology, libraries, book production, newspapers and other periodicals, cultural communication, film and cinema, and radio and television broadcasting. Statistical tables are grouped into three broad parts: a world summary, general socioeconomic statistics, and statistics of basic economic activities. Although somewhat unwieldy due to size and organization, the *Statistical Yearbook* is nevertheless the best source for international data on educational institutions, science, culture, and mass media. No index, but an extensive table of contents.

URBAN STUDIES

507. Boyer, Richard, and David Savageau. **Places Rated Almanac: Your Guide to Finding the Best Places to Live in America.** New York, Prentice-Hall, 1993. 435p. maps. $20.00pa. ISBN 0-671-84947-6.

Ever since Alexis de Tocqueville noted that Americans were perhaps the most mobile people on earth, we have been proving him right by moving from place to place with amazing regularity. Thus, a work like *Places Rated Almanac* finds a ready audience in the thousands who at any given moment are contemplating greener pastures in Des Moines, Seattle, Winnemucca, Little Rock, or any of the other 333 cities rated in this popular resource. The work compares metropolitan areas on factors judged most important in selecting a place to reside: costs of living, jobs, crime, health care, environment, transportation, education, the arts, recreation, and climate. Each of the areas is described, scored, and ranked in terms of these key factors. A summary chapter pulls all of the rankings together.

Area ratings have become a popular item in publishing, and thus there are now more and more publications along this line available to libraries, should patron interest warrant. Among the best are Norman Crampton's *The 100 Best Small Towns in America* (Prentice-Hall General Reference, 1993, 392p., $12.00pa., ISBN 0-671-84671-X), which rates 100 small towns (cities of 5,000–10,000 population) by criteria such as per-capita income, racial diversity, number of physicians, and crime rate; *50 Fabulous Places to Retire in America* (Lee Rosenberg and Saralee Rosenberg, Career Press, 1992, 251p., $14.95pa., ISBN 0-934829-29-2), a terrific book that profiles (with great detail) such varied locales as college towns, military towns, state capitals, and golf and ski meccas, with climates that range from tropical to desert to year-round mild; *50 Fabulous Places to Raise Your Family* (Career Press, 1993, 320p., $17.95pa., ISBN 1-56414-034-2), also by the Rosenbergs, which provides five-page profiles for the 50 towns (large and small) deemed most conducive to family life; *The Livable Cities Almanac* (John Tepper Marlin and others, HarperPerennial/HarperCollins, 1992, 416p., $30.00; $14.00pa., ISBN 0-06-270035-9; 0-06-273134-3pa.), which considers environmental factors—both natural and social—that contribute to or detract from the quality of life in more than 100 individual communities; and George Thomas Kurian's *World Encyclopedia of Cities: North America* (ABC-Clio, 1994, 2v., $150.00/set, ISBN 0-87436-649-6), which provides comprehensive demographic, cultural, economic, historical, social, and climate information for 136 cities, most of which have a population of 100,000 or greater. With the exception of this last title, in general these works are so inexpensive that libraries may want to have several on hand if patron interest warrants.

17 Women's Studies

BIBLIOGRAPHIES

508. Carter, Sarah, and Maureen Ritchie. **Women's Studies: A Guide to Information Sources.** Jefferson, NC, McFarland, 1990. 278p. index. $39.95. ISBN 0-89950-534-1.

The 1,076 resources annotated in *Women's Studies* were published primarily between 1978 and 1988; children's literature materials and bibliographic works on individual women writers have been excluded. The bibliography is divided into three sections: general reference materials (including sections on libraries, the book trade, publishing, and bookshops as well as women's organizations and nonbook materials); "Women in the World," in which citations are organized geographically; and a section devoted to special subjects such as the arts and sciences and social issues. In addition to the women's materials, the authors have also included bibliographies on men's studies. Indexed by proper name, subject, and selected titles (primarily of periodicals).

509. Loeb, Catherine R., and others. **Women's Studies: A Recommended Core Bibliography 1980–1985.** Littleton, CO, Libraries Unlimited, 1987. 538p. index. $55.00. ISBN 0-87287-472-9.

This work is a continuation of Stineman's well-received earlier work, *Women's Studies: A Recommended Core Bibliography* (Libraries Unlimited, 1982), which is now out of print. *Women's Studies 1980–1985* evaluates more than 1,200 English-language titles published during the early- to mid-1980s, including 645 titles recommended as essential for smaller library collections. Chapters are arranged by broad subject areas such as general reference, art and material culture, law, religion and philosophy, literature, sports, the women's movement, and feminist theory. Author, title, and subject indexes identify not only the main citations but also all materials mentioned within the annotations.

There are a number of excellent special-topic women's studies bibliographies that libraries may also wish to consider. One of these is *Women and Aging: A Selected, Annotated Bibliography* (Greenwood Press, 1989, 135p, $45.00, ISBN 0-313-26021-4), which covers roles and relationships, economics, employment, retirement, health, sexuality, religion, housing, racial and ethnic groups, policy issues, international concerns, middle age, and general concerns, and identifies appropriate books, articles, films, documents, and dissertations within these subjects. Another is *Women in the World: Annotated History Resources for the Secondary*

BIOGRAPHIES

510. Bataille, Gretchen M., ed. **Native American Women: A Biographical Dictionary.** Hamden, CT, Garland, 1993. 333p. index. $40.00. ISBN 0-8240-5267-6.

Bataille's biographical dictionary, prepared with the help of more than 60 expert contributors, describes the lives of 231 women born between 1595 and 1960. Most entries are between 400 and 600 words long and provide basic biographical information and some sense of the person's life and contributions. In addition, there are several appendixes: a list of entries by specialization of the biographees (e.g., activism, law, social work), breakdowns of the entries by decades of birth, breakdowns by state or province of birth, and breakdowns by tribal affiliation. A detailed index completes the work.

511. Griffin, Lynne, and Kelly McCann. **The Book of Women: 300 Notable Women History Passed Over.** Holbrook, MA, Bob Adams, 1992. 160p. $10.95. ISBN 1-55850-106-1.

Griffin and McCann's delightful resource profiles the lives and achievements of women who have been largely ignored throughout the centuries. Included among the 69 categories are rodeo stars, sting artists, daredevils, founding mothers, women who took male identities, agricultural pioneers, and spies. A bibliography and an index conclude the resource.

512. Sicherman, Barbara, and others, eds. **Notable American Women, The Modern Period: A Biographical Dictionary.** Cambridge, MA, Belknap Press, Harvard University Press, 1980. 773p. $50.00; $24.95pa. ISBN 0-674-62732-6; 0-674-62733-4pa.

This outstanding work is an update of the now out-of-print *Notable American Women, 1607–1950* (Edward T. James, Janet Wilson James, and Paul S. Boyer, eds., Belknap/Harvard University Press, 1972, 3v.); both are patterned after their parent publication, the internationally known Belknap/Harvard University Press *Dictionary of American Biography* (entry 37). Biographies of 442 women constitute *The Modern Period*, with selection based on "the individual's influence on her time or field; important or significant achievements; pioneering or innovative quality of her work; and the relevance of her career on the history of women." The scholarly profiles, all signed, range in length from one-and-a half to two pages, and include crucial dates, ancestry, birth order, education, marital status, children, and cause of death. Focus is on the woman's life, her personality, and her career or contribution placed in a historical context.

513. Smith, Jessie Carney, ed. **Notable Black American Women.** Detroit, Gale, 1992. 1334p. $49.95. ISBN 0-8103-4749-0.

The 501 Black American women described by Smith are drawn from colonial (Lucy Terry Prince, poet, 1730) through contemporary times, although more than 400 are from the latter period. The range of talents and contributions covers some 200 categories, and includes writers, politicians, religious leaders, scientists, artists, teachers, and civil rights activists, among others. Entries range from brief to lengthy

Student (Llyn Reese and Jean Wilkinson, comps. and eds., Scarecrow, 1987, 220p., $27.50, ISBN 0-8108-2050-1), which is especially useful for guiding students toward resources that highlight the vast range of contributions women have made and roles they have played throughout history.

depending on how much information was available. Photographs accompany many of the biographies, and each of the entries concludes with a list of references directing readers to further resources. A thorough subject index rounds out this excellent resource.

There is another excellent, though more expensive, source of biographical information on Black American women that libraries will also want to consider. That is *Black Women in America: An Historical Encyclopedia* (Darlene Clark Hine, Elsa Barkley Brown, and Rosalyn Terborg-Penn, eds., Carlson, 1993, 2v., $195.00/set, ISBN 0-926019-61-9). This exhaustive, authoritative work is as much encyclopedic as it is biographical; not only are the lives of historically significant Black women presented in signed articles, but there are also more than 150 topical treatments (e.g., the abolitionist movement, Black feminism, the Harlem Renaissance) found through-out the two volumes. In addition, the set offers a wealth of supplementary material that further enhances the richness of the text. If at all possible, libraries should purchase both of these volumes for their complementary coverage; however, if cost is the driving consideration, the Jessie Carney Smith work will provide substantial coverage for a reasonable price.

514. Telgen, Diane, and Jim Kamp, eds. **Notable Hispanic American Women.** Detroit, Gale, 1993. 448p. illus. index. $59.95. ISBN 0-8103-7578-8.

The 300 Hispanic women profiled here are individuals of Mexican, Puerto Rican, Cuban, Spanish, Central American, and South American heritage who, although achieving success in all walks of life, have not abandoned their Hispanic roots. Often accompanied by photographs, biographical sketches range from 500 to 2,500 words in length and focus on personal, career, and family influences that contributed to the successes of the women profiled. A 19-page subject index con-cludes the work.

515. **Who's Who of American Women, [yr.].** Chicago, Marquis Who's Who, 1958- . Biennial. $225.00 (1994 ed.). ISSN 0083-9841.

This standard reference work includes brief biographical sketches for more than 28,000 women currently prominent in their chosen field or profession. Entries note occupation, vital statistics, education, writings and creative works, civic contribu-tions, and political activities. Although this work is regularly (and appropriately) criticized for various editorial inconsistencies and flaws, no other publication comes close to its sheer volume of coverage. Also available on CD-ROM.

DICTIONARIES AND ENCYCLOPEDIAS

516. **Encyclopedia of Feminism.** New York, Facts on File, 1986. 399p. bibliog. $35.00. ISBN 0-8160-1424-8.

Written from a feminist perspective, *Encyclopedia of Feminism* encompasses titles, figures, slogans, terms, and events relevant to the women's movement in the United States and other countries of the world. Entries range from a few sentences to a few paragraphs, with key topics given lengthier (several pages) treatment. Although clearly written from a strong (and stated) point of view, the encyclopedia is balanced and informative. Generous cross references and a extensive, 20-page bibliography supplement the main text.

517.   Walker, Barbara G. **The Woman's Encyclopedia of Myths and Secrets.** San Francisco, Harper San Francisco, 1983. 1124p. illus. bibliog. $27.00pa. ISBN 0-06-250925-X.

The stated intent of this fascinating work is to compile in one place the facts, practices, myths, and legends surrounding the "process of transition from female oriented to male oriented religions in western civilization." Many of the 1,350 alphabetically arranged articles are drawn from paganism, whereas others are from biblical myths written and rewritten during the centuries of transition from matriarchal to patriarchal societies. Supplementing the text are numerous cross references, margin notes, article footnotes and references, and full bibliographic information for sources.

DIRECTORIES

518.   Brennan, Shawn, ed. **Women's Information Directory: A Guide to Organizations, Agencies, Institutions, Programs, Publications, Services, and Other Resources ...** . Detroit, Gale, 1993. 795p. index. $75.00. ISBN 0-8103-8422-1.

The 10,800 organizations, agencies, institutions, and other groups described here are arranged into 26 chapters according to type of information provided. Most of the entries contain contact data and descriptive information about the association or product, such as the date of its founding and the purpose or service it performs. In addition to the organization listings, there are also entries for libraries, museums, and galleries with special collections of interest to women; women's colleges, research centers, and women's studies programs; publications, publishers, and booksellers that focus on topics for, by, and about women; and scholarships, fellowships, loans, awards, and prizes that are available to women.

519.   Schlachter, Gail Ann. **Directory of Financial Aids for Women [yr.]: A List of Scholarships, Fellowships, Loans, Grants, Awards, and Internships ...** . San Carlos, CA, Reference Service Press, 1978- . Biennial. 1v. index. $45.00 (1994 ed.). ISSN 0732-5215.

This well-known reference continues to provide women with valuable information on all sources of financial aid. Loans, scholarships, internships, awards, and grants are among the more than 1,700 sources identified and described. There are also a state listing of educational benefits for women; a bibliography of 75 financial aid directories; and a detailed index that lists entries by sponsoring organization, topic, location, and application calendar. An essential purchase for all public libraries.

520.   Tulloch, Paulette P., comp., and Susan A. Hallgarth, ed. **NWO: A Directory of National Women's Organizations.** New York, National Council for Research on Women, 1992. 664p. index. $40.00pa. ISBN 1-880547-10-5.

In addition to describing national nonprofit organizations whose primary focus is women, NWO also includes coverage of professional organizations for traditionally women-intensive occupations (for example, nursing), reproductive rights coalitions, and family planning organizations. Organizations are arranged alphabetically by name. The entries include address, telephone number, name of contact person, description, area of focus, services offered, publications, user access, target population, and organization meeting. In addition to the main entries, there are five very useful appendixes: a listing of women's funds, women's political action committees (PACs), federal agencies and offices, state commissions on women, and National Council for Research on Women member centers. Indexed by keyword and by state.

The other title in this subject area, Gale's *Encyclopedia of Women's Associations Worldwide: A Guide to Over 3,400 National and Multinational Nonprofit Women's and Women-Related Organizations* (Jacqueline K. Barrett and Jane A. Malonis, eds., 1993, 471p., $80.00, ISBN 1-873477-25-2), follows the familiar format of the Gale's *Encyclopedia of Associations* volumes. Its 6,000 entries are broken down by region into 8 chapters and then alphabetically by country within each chapter, with indexes by name of organization and by subject providing access to the directory listings. Although certainly more extensive in its coverage than *NWO*, the Gale publication may be more information than many libraries need for their patrons.

HANDBOOKS

521. Buck, Claire, ed. **The Bloomsbury Guide to Women's Literature.** New York, Prentice-Hall General Reference, 1992. 1171p. illus. $40.00; $20.00pa. ISBN 0-13-689621-9; 0-13-089665-9pa.

Women's literature of all times and languages, from early Greece to the modern world (including the often underrepresented countries of the Far East, Middle East, and Africa) is comprehensively surveyed in this encyclopedic resource. It is divided into two parts: an opening section of essays (brief overviews of the literatures and literary history of various countries or regions) followed by the main body of encyclopedic entries, which briefly discuss authors, works, genres, styles, and movements. Numerous cross references are interwoven throughout both the essays and the main entries; unfortunately, the work lacks any references to secondary sources.

522. Read, Phyllis J., and Bernard L. Witlieb. **The Book of Women's Firsts: Breakthrough Achievements of Almost 1,000 American Women.** New York, Random House, 1992. 511p. illus. index. $24.00; $16.00pa. ISBN 0-679-40975-0; 0-679-74280-8pa.

Read and Witlieb's handy compendium documents the breakthrough achievements of nearly 1,000 American women from the 17th century to the present. These women are a highly diverse lot, including athletes, reformers, criminals, the first woman chosen as principal chieftain of a major Native American tribe, and the first woman to go over Niagara Falls in a barrel. The alphabetically arranged entries, ranging in length from several sentences to more than a page, note reason for inclusion, provide a biographical sketch, and often include a photograph. A brief index concludes the handbook.

523. Taeuber, Cynthia, comp. and ed. **Statistical Handbook on Women in America.** Phoenix, AZ, Oryx Press, 1991. 385p. index. $54.50. ISBN 0-89774-609-0.

Taeuber's handbook brings together statistical data on American women gathered, for the most part, between 1985 and mid-1990. The data, presented in 437 tables and charts, is drawn from a variety of United States government publications, such as the Bureau of the Census. Where possible, historical and/or international statistics are included for comparison. Topical areas include population, births, marriage and divorce, voting and political involvement, labor force issues, economic issues (including child support, public assistance, and food stamps), and alcoholism and drug abuse, among others. Introductory narrative summaries, a detailed list of contacts for both the Bureau of the Census and the Bureau of Labor Statistics, a glossary of terms, and a list of sources cited further enhance the usefulness of the handbook.

The competing publication in this area is Gale's *Statistical Record of Women Worldwide* (Linda Schmittroth, comp. and ed., 1991, 763p., $89.50, ISBN 0-8103-8349-7), which splits its coverage of national and international statistics roughly half-and-half. The data are drawn from a wide variety of sources, ranging from government, research, and international organizations to periodicals. In addition, its breadth of topical coverage is greater than that found in *Statistical Handbook on Women in America*. Optimally, libraries that can afford to do so will want to buy both publications for their complementary coverage; however, if price is the primary consideration, Taeuber does a good job of providing basic statistics.

QUOTATION BOOKS

524.   Partnow, Elaine, comp. and ed. **The New Quotable Woman.** Rev. ed. New York, Facts on File, 1992. 714p. index. $40.00. ISBN 0-8160-2134-1.

Partnow's *The New Quotable Woman* is a revision of two earlier volumes, arranged, as they were, chronologically by author. The more than 15,000 quotations start with Eve and move forward through women who flourished in the 1970s and 1980s. Four indexes cover biography, subject, career and occupation, and ethnicity and nationality. Because as Partnow points out in her preface, only one-half of 1 percent of the statements quoted in the new edition of John Bartlett's *Familiar Quotations* (entry 91) were made by women, *The New Quotable Woman* should be considered a necessary accompaniment to Bartlett's for all libraries.

Part III
HUMANITIES

BIBLIOGRAPHIES

525. Blum, Eleanor, and Frances Goins Wilhoit. **Mass Media Bibliography: An Annotated Guide to Books and Journals for Research and Reference.** 3d ed. Champaign, IL, University of Illinois Press, 1990. 344p. $49.95. ISBN 0-252-01706-4.

This is the third iteration of Blum's well-known *Basic Books in the Mass Media*, and it continues its predecessors' standards of comprehensiveness and usefulness. Nearly 2,000 titles are briefly described, often in an evaluative manner. Citations are arranged alphabetically by author under broad subject areas such as general communications, broadcast media, and film, and provide author, title, place, publisher, and pagination. An extensive subject index as well as an author-title index enhance access to the entries.

Blum's work is complemented by Eleanor S. Block and James K. Bracken's *Communication and the Mass Media: A Guide to the Reference Literature* (Libraries Unlimited, 1991, 198p. $40.00, ISBN 0-87287-810-4), an annotated bibliography that covers 483 English-language titles published since 1970. Focusing on the disciplines of journalism, mass media, and communication, entries are divided into 10 broad categories: bibliographies; dictionaries, encyclopedias, and handbooks; indexes and abstracts; biographical sources; library catalogs; directories and year-books; online and CD-ROM databases; core periodicals; research centers and archives; and societies and associations.

526. Cates, Jo A. **Journalism: A Guide to the Reference Literature.** Englewood, CO, Libraries Unlimited, 1990. 214p. index. $38.00. ISBN 0-87287-716-7.

Covering Canadian items as well as those from the United States, Cates's annotated bibliography treats journalism in both its print (newspapers and magazines) and broadcast (radio and television) forms. The 728 entries include such standard sources as bibliographies, encyclopedias, and dictionaries as well as more unusual items such as libraries, style books, associations, wire services, and government bodies. Titles cited have been published primarily between the late 1960s and the late 1980s. Entries include complete bibliographic data (except price) and brief but informative (and often engaging) annotations. Author/title and subject indexes conclude the work.

527. Garay, Ronald. **Cable Television: A Reference Guide to Information.** Westport, CT, Greenwood Press, 1988. 177p. index. $49.95. ISBN 0-313-24751-X.

Cable Television is an extended bibliographic essay on approximately 400 print resources available regarding cable television topics. The five chapters cover general resources; business and industry/system economics; program services, program content, uses and effects, viewing habits, and criticism; cable law and regulations; and videotex. With the exception of the general sources section, each chapter begins with a survey of its topic, followed by a source overview that identifies subject-related books and book chapters, government documents, and periodical articles. Each chapter concludes with a bibliography that provides brief, unannotated bibliographic citations (publisher and date only) for the publications mentioned.

528. Shuman, R. Baird. **Resources for Writers: An Annotated Bibliography.** Pasadena, CA, Salem Press, 1992. 167p. index. $40.00. ISBN 0-89356-673-X.

Shuman's bibliography focuses on works likely to be available in one's local small- to medium-sized public library. The materials are organized into the categories of short fiction, novels, nonfiction, drama, poetry, film and television, juvenile literature, autobiography/biography/family history, magazines and journals, and preparing/marketing/promoting manuscripts and books. In addition to the briefly annotated entries, the final chapter provides the names of post-secondary writing programs (arranged by state), writer's conferences and workshops (also arranged by state), writers' colonies, and additional print sources.

DICTIONARIES AND ENCYCLOPEDIAS

529. Brown, Les. **Les Brown's Encyclopedia of Television.** 3d ed. Detroit, Gale, 1992. 723p. illus. index. $39.95. ISBN 0-8103-88715.

In a bit more than 800 entries, Les Brown provides a good overview of the who, what, why, and when of the television business. The encyclopedia is international in scope, with entries that range from brief, dictionary-type definitions to longer, multiple-page articles on major topics such as regulatory issues. There is a general subject index (which could benefit from improved cross-referencing) as well as a bibliography newly expanded for the third edition. In addition, appendixes list top-rated network programs, commissioners of the Federal Communications Commission (FCC), and worldwide television advertising expenditures.

530. Diamant, Lincoln, ed. **The Broadcast Communications Dictionary.** 3d ed. Westport, CT, Greenwood Press, 1989. 255p. $49.95. ISBN 0-313-26502-X.

Diamant's dictionary includes more than 6,000 terms drawn from the areas of radio and television programming and production; network and local station operations; broadcast equipment and engineering; cable television technology; satellite communications technology; audio and videotape production; advertising; media usage; communications research; and defense, government, trade, and allied groups. Definitions range from short (two words) to expansive (the definition for cable television includes the number of U.S. cable subscribers and annual industry revenues). Extensive cross references guide the reader to similar or related terms, as well as to equivalent British terminology. Although Diamant makes no claim to comprehensive coverage of any discipline represented, there are helpful suggestions for further reading.

531. Jones, Glenn R. **Jones Cable Television and Information Infrastructure Dictionary.** 4th ed. Englewood, CO, Jones Interactive, 1994. 216p. ISBN 0-885400-00-4.

More than 2,900 terms drawn from cable television, telephony, computers, multimedia, and the regulatory arena are defined in the Jones dictionary. Entries are brief—one or two sentences—and are accompanied by more than 750 cross references. Also included are more than 500 industry-related agencies, associations, and services, both national and international. Given the community impact of local cable television company decisions, this will be an especially useful purchase for public libraries.

532. Watson, James, and Anne Hill. **A Dictionary of Communication and Media Studies.** 3d ed. New York, Edward Arnold/Routledge, Chapman, & Hall, 1993. 224p. $17.95pa. ISBN 0-340-57425-9.

Although intended to serve communications and media studies students, this dictionary will also enable libraries to respond to the increased popular interest in the effects of media on the political process. The work is arranged alphabetically, and encompasses interpersonal communication, public address, information technology, communication theory, and myriad other key topics in communications/media studies. Entries range from brief, several-sentence descriptions to multiple-column topic explanations. Cross references guide the reader to related entries, and the text is occasionally supplemented by helpful line drawings.

533. Wiener, Richard. **Webster's New World Dictionary of Media and Communications.** New York, Prentice-Hall, 1990. 533p. $29.95. ISBN 0-13-969759-4.

Wiener defines roughly 30,000 communications-related terms and phrases in this excellent resource. Broadcast radio and television, print and electronic journalism, public relations, and cable television are among the communications disciplines covered, although many other related fields are included as well. Definitions range in length from a sentence to a paragraph, include phonetic pronunciations as appropriate, and are written in language easily understood by the lay reader but still informative to the communications professional. Industry data and specific communications companies are also mentioned, enhancing the dictionary's usefulness to both industry professionals and those who would like to pursue careers in one of the media/communications fields.

DIRECTORIES

534. **Broadcasting & Cable Yearbook [yr.].** New Providence, NJ, R. R. Bowker, 1992- . Annual. 2v. index. $169.95 (1994 ed.). ISSN 0000-1384.

Formerly published by Broadcasting magazine as *Broadcasting Yearbook* from 1935 to 1991, this addition to the Bowker family of annuals organizes its material into 10 sections: radio; broadcast television; cable television; satellites and other carriers; market statistics, advertising, and marketing services; programming services; general services and suppliers (technology and professional services); associations, events, education, and awards; books, periodicals, and videos; and law and regulation, government agencies, and ownership. The index section includes nearly 600 pages of "yellow pages" listings for the radio, television, and cable industries; an index to radio and television by state/possession/province; and indexes to sections and advertisers. Supplementary materials include a trade show calendar, annotated bibliographies of books and periodicals, a glossary, industry histories and overviews, and a chronology of key events from 1931 to date.

The primary competition to *Broadcasting & Cable Yearbook* is Warren Publishing's expensive, two-volume annual, *Television & Cable Factbook* (1945- , $345.00/set [1994 ed.], ISSN 0732-8648). *Television & Cable Factbook* covers most of the information presented by its competitor, but adds a nearly overwhelming amount of other, industry-related information as well. Although the *Factbook* is well worth its hefty price tag for companies in the broadcasting, cable, or related industries, *Broadcasting & Cable Yearbook* represents a more cost-effective choice for the majority of small and medium-sized libraries.

535. Brooks, Tim, and Earle Marsh. **The Complete Directory to Prime Time Network TV Shows 1946-Present.** 5th ed. New York, Ballantine, 1992. 1216p. index. $19.00pa. ISBN 0-345-37792-3.

This outstanding resource offers an alphabetical listing of every regular series ever carried on commercial networks (including Fox) during prime time; network series carried in the early evening and late night hours; and top syndicated programs that were aired primarily in the evening hours. Each entry includes the dates of the first and last broadcasts, as well as the days, times, and networks on which the series was broadcast. In addition, the names of regular cast members and guests are listed, followed by an informative description of the series. Appendixes list prime-time network schedules for each season from 1946-1947 through 1991-1992, Emmy Award winners, the top 100 series of all times, and hit theme songs from series. In addition, an index to personalities and performances traces the particular programs in which specific actors have appeared.

536. Neff, Glenda Tennant, and Mark Kissling, eds. **Writer's Market, [yr.]: Where & How to Sell What You Write.** Cincinnati, OH, Writer's Digest Books, 1926- . Annual. 1v. illus. index. $26.95 (1994 ed.). ISSN 0084-2729.

Chock-full of business and professional as well as writing tips, this hardy annual continues to offer a tremendous amount of useful information for a reasonable price. Market information for freelance writers—including submission, style, payment, and, frequently, editors' tips—is provided for more than 4,000 potential publishing opportunities, ranging from magazines to greeting card publishers. In addition to providing a general index covering all of the entries in the book, the work is also indexed by subject for book publishers and agents. Although *The Writer's Handbook* (Sylvia K. Burack, ed., Boston, The Writer, 1938- , annual, 1v, $29.95, ISSN 0084-2710) covers roughly similar territory, *Writer's Market* is broader in scope, describes 1,500 more publishing markets than its competitor, focuses more tightly on practical, business-oriented information, and even costs a few dollars less. Only libraries with very strong patron interest in freelance writing opportunities would need to have both on hand.

The "Market" approach has proven so successful that there seems no end to the spin-offs; several of these might be useful purchases for public libraries if demand warrants. These titles include the *Writer's Digest* annuals, all priced at roughly $22.00: *Novel and Short Story Writer's Market* (ISSN 0897-9790); *Writer's & Illustrator's Market* (ISSN 0897-8912); *Children's Writer's & Illustrator's Market* (ISSN 1043-240); *Humor and Cartoon Markets* (ISSN 1043-240); *Poet's Market* (ISSN 0883-5470); *Mystery Writer's Marketplace and Sourcebook* (ISSN 1068-8528); and *Fiction Writer's Market* (ISSN 0275-2123). A similar work from the same publisher that is highly recommended for all public libraries is Kathy Henderson's excellent, encouraging *Market Guide for Young Writers* (1993, 304p., $16.95pa., ISBN 0-89879-606-7), which provides just the right amount of practical, easily understood advice and information to youngsters and teenagers who are aspiring writers. Libraries should also consider a fairly recent entrant in this genre, Meera Lester's *Writing for the Ethnic Markets* (Writer's Connection, 1991, 259p., $14.95pa., ISBN 0-9622592-4-1), an excellent resource for this rapidly expanding market.

537. Winklepleck, Julie, Eric J. Restum, and Scott Stange, eds. **Gale Directory of Publications and Broadcast Media [yr.]: An Annual Guide to Publications and Broadcasting Stations ...** . Detroit, Gale, 1869- . Annual. 3v. With update. maps. index. $340.00/set (1994 ed.). ISSN 1048-7972.

Gale's media directory provides detailed information about 43,000 radio, television, and cable stations and systems as well as newspapers, magazines, journals, and periodicals. Entries encompass 29 different kinds of data, including the standard directory-type information (name, address, etc.) plus such items as printing method, trim size, advertising rates, and circulation statistics. The master index is arranged alphabetically; subject indexes are organized geographically and by subject. The directory contains detailed information for making comparisons between advertising alternatives as well as information for finding key personnel such as newspaper feature editors. Also available online, on disk, and on magnetic tape.

HANDBOOKS, YEARBOOKS, AND GUIDES

538. Gee, Robin, ed. **Guide to Literary Agents & Art/Photo Reps, [yr.].** Cincinnati, OH, Writer's Digest Books, 1991- . Annual. 1v. index. $16.95 (1994 ed.). ISSN 1055-6087.

Gee's work leads off with 10 essays about literary agents (what they do, how to choose one, etc.), and then proceeds with sections on non-fee and fee-charging literary agents, script agents, commercial art and photography representatives, and fine art representatives. Within these sections, entries for the 500 agents listed are dense with data; up to 20 types of information (date of agency establishment, member agents, areas of interest, etc.) may be given for each. A separate resources section lists recommended publications and professional organizations for writers and artists, and a glossary and indexes round out the book.

The primary competitor to Gee's guide is Arthur Orrmont and Leonie Rosenstiel's *Literary Agents of North America: The Complete Guide to U.S. and Canadian Literary Agencies* (5th ed., Author Aid/Research Associates International, 1993, 249p., $33.00, ISBN 0-911085-12-2). *Literary Agents* lists 1,000 individuals in contrast to the *Guide's* 500, but the *Guide* goes into more depth in specific areas and also discusses art/photography representatives. Although there is some duplication between entries, there is not enough to warrant passing up either title if libraries can afford both.

539. **World Radio and TV Handbook.** Andrew G. Sennitt, ed. New York, Billboard Books/Watson-Guptill, 1947- . 1v. Annual. $29.95pa. (1994 ed.). ISSN 0144-7750.

The material in this short-wave listener's bible, organized by continent and country, provides detailed information on international short-wave radio and television activities, organizations, companies and officials, and broadcasting stations (including frequencies, mandatory new wavelengths, transmitter power, call signs, and station names) throughout the world. A typical country entry lists the medium-, long-, and short-wave stations along with addresses, frequencies, and times of operation, program identification (international signal), and method of verification of signal reception. Although there is extensive coverage of television data, international radio broadcasting, especially English-language broadcasts, is the main focus of the annual.

INDEXES

540. Transcript/Video Index, [yr.]: A Comprehensive Guide to Television News and Public Affairs Programming. Denver, CO, Journal Graphics, 1990- . Annual. 1v. $24.95pa. (1994 ed.). ISSN 1057-0764.

Since 1900, Journal Graphics has transcribed selected network, syndicated, and public television programs and made those transcripts available to the public for very reasonable prices. Their annual index provides access to roughly 7,000 shows that appeared in the previous year on about 80 "hard news" and "tabloid television" programs, such as "Wall Street Report," "Nightline," "Geraldo," and all the CNN programs. Entries are chronologically arranged by air date under 250 broad subject headings (e.g., abortion, weather, women). Information contained in each entry includes abbreviated show title, episode number, broadcast date, a brief episode summary, and availability on video. The only drawback to this excellent resource is the lack of an index, which severely hinders the reader's ability to locate needed information quickly. Despite this criticism, the *Transcript/Video Index* is highly recommended for all types of libraries.

STYLE MANUALS

541. The Chicago Manual of Style. 14th ed. Chicago, University of Chicago Press, 1993. 921p. $40.00. ISBN 0-226-10389-7.

The 14th edition of this authoritative guide for writers, editors, and publishers enhanced the work's already outstanding reputation for coverage of grammar, usage, style, copyediting, and numerous other writing concerns. The 14th edition has expanded by some 200 pages the previous edition, incorporating new information on current usage. It continues its familiar three-part organization: bookmaking, style, and production and printing. Because it is the authority to which most style questions are referred, no library should be without *The Chicago Manual of Style.*

542. Turabian, Kate L. A Manual for Writers of Term Papers, Theses, and Dissertations. 5th rev. ed. Chicago, University of Chicago Press, 1987. 300p. illus. index. $20.00; $7.95pa. ISBN 0-226-81624-9; 0-226-81625-7pa.

"Turabian" has long been a standard resource for high-school and college students charged with writing well-organized and thoroughly documented papers. It offers chapters dealing with parts of the paper, abbreviations and numbers, spelling and punctuation, capitalization, quotation marks, tables, and illustrations. Sample page layouts further clarify the narrative instructions for page composition. The fifth edition includes expanded coverage of footnotes, bibliographies, and public documents, but it is the new material regarding the use of computers in the paper-writing process that is most noteworthy (and helpful).

Applied Arts

GENERAL WORKS

543. Ehresmann, Donald L. **Applied and Decorative Arts: A Bibliographic Guide.** 2d ed. Englewood, CO, Libraries Unlimited, 1993. 629p. index. $75.00. ISBN 0-87287-906-2.

Covering ornaments, folk art, arms and armor, ceramics, clocks and automata, costumes, enamels, furniture, glass, leather, metalwork, musical instruments, textiles, dolls, and other decorative arts, the second edition of Ehresmann's familiar guide describes 3,000 books written in Western European languages. The bibliography is arranged alphabetically by media type; within each media category, entries are listed alphabetically by author and title. In addition to including standard bibliographical data, entries also offer brief evaluative abstracts of about 75–100 words. An author/title index and a subject index complete the volume.

544. Fleming, John, and Hugh Honour. **Penguin Dictionary of Decorative Arts.** New York, Viking Press, 1990. 976p. illus. $40.00pa. ISBN 0-670-82047-4.

Fleming and Honour's popular dictionary is a compact, highly authoritative, single-volume reference work that defines nearly 4,000 terms and phrases related to the furniture and furnishings of European and American homes. The time span covered is roughly from the Middle Ages to the present for Europe, and from the Colonial era forward for the United States. Entries include definitions of terms, schools, styles, and periods, descriptions of materials and processes, histories of important manufacturers and factories, and biographies of leading craftspersons and designers. More than 1,000 illustrations supplement the text; in addition, brief bibliographies are appended to many of the entries.

545. Osborne, Harold, ed. **The Oxford Companion to the Decorative Arts.** New York, Oxford University Press, 1975; repr., New York, Oxford University Press, 1985. 865p. illus. $22.50pa. ISBN 0-19-281863-5.

Essentially a reprint of the 1975 hardcover volume of the same name, *The Oxford Companion to the Decorative Arts* provides authoritative—though unsigned— articles on all facets of the decorative arts, considered herein to be those pursuits whose creations are valued primarily for their workmanship and beauty of appearance. Within these parameters, the *Companion* presents information on specific crafts, historic periods and cultures, techniques and materials, design elements, and individuals who have made noteworthy contributions in the various decorative-arts fields. Taking the broadest possible approach to the topic, the work's alphabetically arranged entries encompass woodworking and papermaking, glassmaking, enamel and ceramics, landscape gardening, costuming, bookbinding and typography, and many other endeavors requiring both artistic skills and craftsmanship. Although theoretically international in scope, the majority of the entries reflect a British, European, or United States focus. An extensive bibliography concludes the work.

COLLECTING

546. Kovel, Ralph, and Terry Kovel. **Kovels' Antique and Collectibles Price List [yr.].** New York, Crown, 1967- . Annual. 1v. illus. index. $13.00pa. (1994 ed.). No ISSN available.

Published previously as *Kovels' Antiques Price List* and *Kovels' Complete Antiques Price List*, this annual publication provides current price information (based on sales recorded during the previous 12 months) for a diverse range of antiques and collectibles. The items are listed alphabetically by category or object; a brief description followed by price quotes is provided for each, with occasional "insider" comments added as well. The guide's usefulness is further enhanced by more than 500 clear, black-and-white photographs plus many small line drawings, and by a thoroughly cross-referenced index. This is the best known, and most widely used, price guide in the area of antiques and collectibles. The Kovels are widely known as experts in this area, and have published an extensive family of related works (*Books in Print* lists more than 20 titles beginning with "Kovel's . . . ").

In addition to the Kovel price guides, there are several other similar, reliable works that libraries may want to have on hand as well, depending on patron interest. These include (among others) Harry L. Rinker's two biennial publications, *Warman's Antiques and Their Prices* (Warman, $14.95pa. [1994 ed.], ISSN 0-196-2272) and *Warman's Americana & Collectibles: A Price Guide Devoted to Today's Collectibles* (Warman, $15.95pa. [1994 ed.], ISSN 0739-6457), and the annual *Miller's Collectibles Price Guide* (Judith Miller and Martin Miller, Antique Collectors' Club, $25.00 [1994 ed.], no ISSN available).

FASHION AND COSTUME

547. Calasibetta, Charlotte Mankey. **Fairchild's Dictionary of Fashion.** 2d ed. New York, Fairchild, 1988. 749p. illus. (part col.). $50.00. ISBN 0-87005-635-2.

"Fashion" is given its widest possible meaning in this exhaustive guide to the terminology of clothing. The material covers 11 centuries from classical to modern and goes beyond historical costume terminology to include cultural, nationalist, stylistic, and artistic terms as well. The more than 15,000 terms are arranged alphabetically, and are supplemented by numerous entry cross-references, some 500 black-and-white drawings, and 16 pages of full-color illustrations cross-referenced to the text. In addition to the brief (often one-line) definitions, *Fairchild's* includes an index of biographical entries of famous fashion designers, with photographs of the individual and his or her works.

Libraries may also wish to consider a more narrowly focused but still noteworthy publication, Georgina O'Hara's *The Encyclopedia of Fashion* (Abrams, 1986, 272p., $34.95, ISBN 0-8109-0882-4), which surveys fashion from the 1840s through the mid-1980s. O'Hara provides more than 1,000 entries that encompass the contributions of fashion and costume designers, clothing manufacturers, notable store owners, art directors, illustrators, fashion photographers, couturiers, magazine reporters and editors, and even hairdressers. Entries also define art movements, types of clothing and fabric, fashion terms, and styles of dress. An exceedingly broad range of excellent illustrations and a four-page bibliography further recommend this useful resource.

548. Peacock, John. **The Chronicle of Western Fashion: From Ancient Times to the Present Day.** New York, Harry Abrams, 1991. 224p. illus. $29.95. ISBN 0-8103-3953-3.

A good representative of the development of dress through recorded Western history, Peacock's work contains examples of costumes from all major historical periods, including ancient Egypt, the Middle Ages, the Renaissance, and the 16th through 20th centuries. Especially helpful is the fact that although most of the costumes are from upper-class fashion, the book does include the dress of people from all walks of life. The materials, primarily color plates, are organized by periods. Detailed descriptions accompany each plate. An illustrated glossary that defines many obscure or archaic fashion terms accompanies the main text.

Another excellent title for fashion history is Jack Cassin-Scott's *The Illustrated Encyclopaedia of Costume and Fashion 1550–1920* (Blandford Press; distr., Sterling, 1986, 160p, $24.95, ISBN 0-7137-1811-0). As fun to browse as it is informative to use, Cassin-Scott's encyclopedia comprises 150 full-color plates that depict more than 300 costumes in minute detail, including period dress for men and women, children, soldiers, nobility, peasants, and musicians. Each costume is dated and described, and fabric and country of origin are noted for almost all entries. Coverage ranges from the late Renaissance through modern times.

549. Stegemeyer, Anne. **Who's Who in Fashion.** 2d ed. New York, Fairchild, 1988. 243p. illus. index. $27.50. ISBN 0-87005-574-7. **Supplement.** 1991. 72p. illus. index. $15.00pa. ISBN 0-87005-746-4.

Who's Who in Fashion focuses on established designers as well as influential individuals in related fields, with a few "up-and-comers" thrown in for good measure. Both Americans and non-Americans are among the 200 individuals profiled. The entries are usually several paragraphs or less in length (although some of the better-known designers are represented by a page or more), and are accompanied by black-and-white photographs of the individuals and their creations. A bibliography and 16 pages of full-color plates supplement the biographical profiles. The supplement provides similar information for another 55 individuals.

FURNITURE

550. Aronson, Joseph. **The Encyclopedia of Furniture.** 3d rev. ed. New York, Crown, 1986. 202p. illus. index. $27.50. ISBN 0-517-03735-1.

International in scope, this encyclopedia explores furniture design from its earliest days through contemporary times. Aronson has employed a two-pronged approach, wherein major topical articles are supplemented by approximately 2,500 narrower definitions and descriptions, which gives the reader both a broad overview of the discipline's important subjects as well as more targeted information on specific items. The work is nearly equally balanced between text and photographs, and is further enhanced by an extensive and thorough index.

551. Butler, Joseph T. **Field Guide to American Antique Furniture.** New York, Henry Holt, 1986. 399p. illus. bibliog. index. $18.95pa. ISBN 0-8050-0124-7.

Leading off with a 60-page "History of American Furniture" written by Butler, a well-known expert in this field, this handy visual resource then presents 1,700 detailed drawings of furniture objects arranged by purpose and historical period. Chairs, beds, tables, chests, desks, and a multitude of other furniture items are presented, with their myriad historical distinctions and stylistic variations. Several sections supplement the text; among these are an "anatomy of furniture" that presents easy-to-read diagrams of common furniture types and appropriate terms; a listing of museum locations for the objects illustrated and for outstanding collections; a lengthy glossary; a selected bibliography; and a 20-page index.

INTERIOR DESIGN

552. Pegler, Martin. **The Dictionary of Interior Design.** New York, Fairchild, 1983. 217p. illus. $28.50. ISBN 0-87005-447-3.

This guide to the terminology of interior design describes roughly 4,300 words, phrases, and individuals. Arranged alphabetically, the entries encompass furniture, design motifs and concepts, textiles and other materials, and individuals such as architects or designers who have made notable contributions. The brief definitions are accompanied by black-and-white line drawings that further clarify the term in question, and numerous cross references facilitate a broader contextual understanding for the lay reader. International in scope, Pegler's dictionary also includes many Italian, French, German, and Spanish terms.

20

Fine Arts

GENERAL WORKS

Bibliographies

553. Best, James J. **American Popular Illustration: A Reference Guide.** Westport, CT, Greenwood Press, 1984. 171p. index. $49.95. ISBN 0-313-23389-6.

Best's engaging and informative guide to the information resources in American popular illustration leads off with a historical overview of its development from the 1800s forward. This narrative survey is followed by critical analyses of the discipline's major works, including histories, illustrated works, bibliographies, biographies of American illustrators, and works dealing with the technique, illustration media, and the social/artistic context of illustration. Each section ends with a comprehensive bibliography of the key articles and books mentioned. Three appendixes—"Magazines and Periodicals," "Research Collections," and "Bibliography of Illustrated Books"—conclude the work.

554. Ehresmann, Donald L. **Fine Arts: A Bibliographic Guide to Basic Reference Works, Histories, and Handbooks.** 3d ed. Englewood, CO, Libraries Unlimited, 1990. 373p. index. $55.00. ISBN 0-87287-640-3.

International in scope, this annotated bibliography of more than 2,000 titles covers fine art topics from prehistoric times through the late 1980s. The work is arranged in two parts, "Reference Works" and "Histories and Handbooks." The former covers bibliographies, library catalogs, indexes, directories, iconography, and historiography of art history; the second section comprises chapters on prehistoric and primitive art, periods of Western art history, national histories and handbooks of European art, Oriental art, New World art, and the art of Africa and Oceania. Although most titles cited are in English, there is substantial representation of non-English (especially German and French) works. Entries provide basic bibliographic data (though price and ISBN are not included) as well as a brief (one- or two-sentence), primarily descriptive annotation. The work concludes with author/title and subject indexes.

Biographies

555. Marks, Claude. **World Artists 1980-1990.** Bronx, NY, H. W. Wilson, 1991. 432p. illus. index. $55.00. ISBN 0-8242-0802-1.

A companion to Marks's highly regarded *World Artists 1950–1980* (H. W. Wilson, 1984. 928p., $80.00. ISBN 0-8242-0707-6), which is still in print, this work explores the lives of artists considered to have been influential during the 1980s. The 118 profiles, generally four pages in length and accompanied by a small black-and-white photograph, are arranged alphabetically by artist's surname. Entries include a chronology of the artist's life and significance in the 1980s, excerpts from reviews of exhibitions, lists of past exhibitions and of collections that house the artist's work, and citations to additional biographical and critical literature about the artist. Given their reasonable price and extensive coverage, both *World Artists 1950–1980* and *World Artists 1980–1990* should be considered standard acquisitions for almost all libraries.

556. Opitz, Glenn B., ed. **Mantle Fielding's Dictionary of American Painters, Sculptors, and Engravers.** 2d ed. Poughkeepsie, NY, Apollo Books, 1986. 1081p. bibliog. $95.00. ISBN 0-938290-04-5.

Originally written and privately published by Mantle Fielding in Philadelphia in 1926, the current iteration of this well-known resource profiles nearly 13,000 American artists who lived and created from colonial through contemporary times. Encompassing both major and minor artists, the biographies are arranged alphabetically and note biographical data, awards, exhibitions, commissions, and latest known address, when all of this information is available. (Because many of the individuals profiled are decidedly "minor" figures in the art field, information is occasionally quite scanty.) The publication concludes with a useful, though now somewhat out-of-date, eight-page bibliography.

557. Petteys, Chris, and others. **Dictionary of Women Artists: An International Dictionary of Women Artists Born before 1900.** New York, Macmillan, 1985. 851p. $75.00. ISBN 0-8161-8456-9.

This biographical dictionary, international in scope, profiles more than 21,000 women painters, sculptors, printmakers, and illustrators born prior to 1900. Entries include full name, married name, and pseudonym; birth and death dates; the media in which the artist worked; subject matter for which she is known; place of residence; other artists in the family; formal education and teachers with whom she studied; exhibitions and awards; and a list of further bibliographical references. *Dictionary of Women Artists* does an admirable job of providing both ready-reference information and a starting point for further research in this increasingly important field. Equally strong coverage for American female sculptors is provided by Charlotte Streifer Rubinstein's *American Women Sculptors: A History of Women Working in Three Dimensions* (G. K. Hall, 1990. 638p. $49.95, ISBN 0-685-38164-1).

558. **Who's Who in American Art [yr.].** New Providence, NJ, R. R. Bowker, 1936/37– . Biennial. 1v. index. $176.00 (1994 ed.). ISSN 0000-0191.

A standard purchase for almost all libraries, *Who's Who in American Art* encompasses all segments of the art world in its profiles of those who happen to hail from (or be creating in) the United States, Canada, or Mexico. The biographical entries (more than 11,000) cover vital statistics; professional classifications; education and training; work in public collections; commissions; exhibitions; publications; positions held with schools, museums, or organizations; membership in art societies; honors and awards; interest or research statement; media; dealer; and mailing address. Arranged alphabetically, the biographies are indexed by geographic location and professional classification. Also available online.

The two other sources that offer somewhat similar biographical information on artists are Paul Cummings's less extensive, and consequently less expensive, *Dictionary of Contemporary American Artists* (6th ed., St. Martin's Press, 1993, 786p., $85.00, ISBN 0-312-08440-4), which profiles about 900 living and deceased artists who have been influential during this century; and *Contemporary Artists* (3d ed., Colin Naylor, ed., St. James Press, 1989, 1059p., $145.00, ISBN 0-912289-96-1), a reliable reference source for information on about 850 individuals prominent in the contemporary international art scene. Because all three of these publications are well executed and reliable, patron interest and budget considerations will be the determinants of which best meet the needs of individual libraries.

Dictionaries and Encyclopedias

559. Chilvers, Ian, and Harold Osborne, eds. **The Oxford Dictionary of Art.** New York, Oxford University Press, 1988. 548p. $49.95; $17.95pa. ISBN 0-19-866133-9; 0-19-280022-1pa.

Drawing on the materials found in the three well-known Oxford Companion titles dealing with art, decorative arts, and 20th-century art, the dictionary focuses primarily on Western and European art and artists. The entries are brief—two or three paragraphs—but provide authoritative information and assessments, especially of the significance of various artists' contributions. In addition to profiling artists and their works, the dictionary also covers both traditional and contemporary art terms, major art institutions (e.g., the Prado), key art historians, and architects and architecture as they relate to other media.

Although Chilvers has also produced a condensed version of the dictionary, *The Concise Oxford Dictionary of Art and Artists* (Oxford University Press, 1990, 517p., $9.95pa., ISBN 0-19-282676-X), its size and the brevity of its coverage (2,000 entries on painting, sculpture, and graphic arts) render it more suited to the needs of students and the circulating collection for all but the smallest of libraries.

560. Diamond, David, ed. **The Bulfinch Pocket Dictionary of Art Terms.** 3d ed. New York, Little, Brown, 1992. 1v. (unpaged). illus. $8.95pa. ISBN 0-8212-1905-7.

This title replaces *Pocket Dictionary of Art Terms* (New York Graphic Society, 1979), a standard reference work in many libraries. Designed as a portable guide to art and architecture terms, the dictionary specializes in short, informative definitions in easy-to-read format. Although the work's hundreds of entries do a good job of providing up-to-date coverage of today's art and architecture worlds, no biographies of those working in these fields have been included.

For coverage of art supplies, techniques, and terms, another good resource is *The HarperCollins Dictionary of Art Terms and Techniques* (2d ed., Ralph Mayer and Steven Sheehan, HarperCollins, 1991, 474p., $15.00pa., ISBN 0-06-461012-8), which is based on the initial work Mayer published in 1969, 10 years before his death. Long considered a classic in the field, this is an especially useful reference for libraries fielding questions from novice (or seasoned) artists.

561. **Encyclopedia of Visual Art.** Chicago, Encyclopaedia Britannica Educational, 1989. 10v. $279.00/set. ISBN 0-85229-187-6.

Many small libraries may rightly feel that the cost (in both dollars and shelf space) of this multi-volume art reference is prohibitive. However, for those libraries wishing to acquire a comprehensive resource in the area of the visual arts, *Encyclopedia of Visual Art* should be given first consideration. Written for lay readers, its in-depth articles are accessible, informative, and accompanied by beautiful illustrations. The work encompasses historical developments, genres, individual art objects, and significant artists, from classical through contemporary times. Most helpful is the chronological survey of the entire range of visual arts that helps place the articles in a broader, more encompassing context. The encyclopedia's glossary, bibliography, and index further enhance the usefulness of this outstanding set.

Directories

562. **American Art Directory [yr.]** New Providence, NJ, R. R. Bowker, 1898- . 1v. Biennial. index. $186.00 (1994 ed.) ISSN 0065-6968.

First published in 1898 as *The American Art Annual*, *American Art Directory* has become the standard reference work of its type for libraries. It provides basic information for more than 7,000 U.S., Canadian, and overseas art institutions; identifies collections, funding sources, exhibitions, key personnel, and the like for more than 2,500 art museums, libraries, and other relevant organizations; and describes enrollment, entrance requirements, degree programs, and other salient items for approximately 1,700 art schools. In addition, the directory provides information on major museums and schools abroad, state art councils, art education administrators, selected U.S. art magazines, newspaper art editors and critics, art scholarships, and exhibition booking agencies. Subject, personnel, and institutional indexes guide the reader through the mass of information to be found herein.

563. **The Official Museum Directory [yr.].** Wilmette, IL, National Register, 1961- . Annual. 1v. index. $185.00 (1994 ed.). ISSN 0090-6700.

This directory describes more than 7,000 museums to be found throughout the United States and its territories. For each, it gives the institution's name, address, telephone number, and fax number; date of establishment; key personnel; governing authority; a profile of collections; research fields; a description of facilities; an overview of educational activities offered; publications; hours of operation; admission costs; and membership fees. The entries are arranged alphabetically by city within state. In addition to museum-specific information, the directory describes relevant professional organizations, regional museum associations and state representatives, federal agencies providing museum support, state museum organizations, regional arts organizations, state humanities councils, and other related organizations.

Although *The Official Museum Directory* should certainly be considered the first purchase in this subject area, there are many good, often inexpensive, special-focus museum directories and guides that also merit attention. These include Joanne Cleaver's *Doing Children's Museums: A Guide to 265 Hands-On Museums* (Williamson, 1992. 229p., $13.95pa. ISBN 0-913589-63-2); *Access to Art: A Museum Directory for Blind and Visually Impaired People* (Irma Shore and Beatrice Jacinto, comps., American Foundation for the Blind and Museum of American Folk Art, 1989, 127p., $19.95pa., ISBN 0-89128-156-8); and *Corporate Museums, Galleries, and Visitor*

Centers: A Directory (Victor J. Danilov, Greenwood Press, 1991, 211p, $55.00, ISBN 0-313-27658-7).

Handbooks

564. Miller, Lauri, ed. **Artist's Market, [yr.]: Where & How to Sell Your Artwork.** Cincinnati, OH, Writer's Digest Books, 1979– . Annual. 1v. illus. index. $22.95 (1994 ed.). ISSN 0161-0546.

Artists' Market is a comprehensive guide to the market opportunities available to the freelance fine or commercial artist. The bulk of the annual consists of coverage of key markets, including advertising agencies, art/design studios, art and book publishers, businesses, galleries, greeting card and paper products producers, magazines, newspapers and newsletters, performing arts groups, record companies and syndicates, and clip-art firms. Each chapter opens with a brief overview of the particular market under discussion, followed by an alphabetical list of agencies, companies, publishers, and/or galleries. The entries include address, telephone and fax numbers, contact information, date of establishment, company description, and submission requirements. Supplementing the market entries are informative articles on business concerns, profiles of professional freelancers of interest to freelance writers, recommended publications, a list of organizations of interest to freelance writers, recommended publications, a glossary, and an index. An excellent resource, this is a standard purchase for almost all public libraries.

565. Osborne, Harold, ed. **Oxford Companion to Art.** New York, Oxford University Press, 1970. 1277p. illus. $49.95. ISBN 0-19-866107-X.

Intended for the lay reader, this comprehensive, general guide to the visual arts comprises articles that range in length from short definitions of terms and brief biographies of major artists to lengthy articles on periods, styles, civilizations, and special aspects of the study of the fine arts. The author also addresses places, significant buildings, and museums. (Handicrafts and the practical arts have been excluded.) Entries include bibliographical references to the nearly 3,000 titles cited in the general bibliography that concludes the volume. Osborne has also authored a highly recommended related work, *The Oxford Companion to Twentieth-Century Art* (Oxford University Press, 1981, 656p., $22.50pa., ISBN 0-19-282076-1), which profiles artists working between 1900 and 1975 and provides information on the schools, movements, and concerns of the art world during this dynamic period.

566. Oxenhorn, Douglas, ed. **Money for Visual Artists.** New York, American Council for the Arts, 1993. 238p. index. $14.95pa. ISBN 1-879903-05-9.

The roughly 200 organizations that support professional visual artists in the United States and Canada described here by Oxenhorn, offer assistance that includes grants and fellowships, artists' colonies, artist-in-residence programs, emergency assistance and health-care programs, technical assistance, and other essential services. In addition, groups are listed that offer studio or exhibition space, travel grants, loans, legal assistance, international exchange programs, and marketing assistance. Arranged alphabetically by organization name, the entries lead off with address, telephone number, and contact person, and then provide three sections for quick reference: a profile of financial support to artists, direct support programs, and technical assistance programs and services. Indexes of organizations, listed alphabetically, by geographical area, and by types of support, conclude the volume.

Indexes

567. **Art Index.** Bronx, NY, H. W. Wilson, 1929- . Quarterly; annual cumulations. Sold on service basis. ISSN 0004-3222.

Art Index provides a subject/author index to some 225 domestic and foreign periodicals, yearbooks, and museum bulletins. Coverage encompasses advertising art, antiques, archaeology, architecture and architectural history, art and art history, city planning, computers in archaeology, architecture and art, crafts and folk art, graphic arts, industrial design, jewelry, landscape architecture, motion pictures, photography, pottery, television, textiles, video, and woodwork. Complete biblio-graphic information is provided for each article cited, including notation of illustra-tions, portraits, diagrams, plans, and charts. Articles are indexed by subject heading, while reproductions of specific works of art are indexed by the artist's name. Book reviews are indexed separately.

ARCHITECTURE

568. Harris, Cyril M., ed. **Dictionary of Architecture & Construction.** 2d ed. New York, McGraw-Hill, 1993. 924p. illus. $59.50. ISBN 0-07-026888-6.

The second edition of this highly regarded reference features some 22,500 definitions and 2,000 illustrations. Definitions are clear and concise; for some terms, there are several definitions when they are used in a variety of related fields, as well as cross references within a field. Many of the entries reflect terminology, symbols, and abbreviations used by the American Institute of Architects (ASTM) and Ameri-can National Standards Institute (ANSI) standards.

A good (and inexpensive) complement to the *Dictionary of Architecture & Construction* is the fourth edition of *The Penguin Dictionary of Architecture* (John Fleming, Hugh Honour, and Nikolaus Pevsner, Penguin Books, 1991, 497p., $12.00pa. ISBN 0-14-051241-1). The brief entries cover architecture in general but are also especially strong in their coverage of history and biography. About 90 line drawings of plans and details accompany the text, and bibliographical citations are appended to many of the entries.

569. Maddex, Diane, ed. **Landmark Yellow Pages: Where to Find All the Names, Addresses, Facts and Figures You Need.** 2d ed. By National Trust for Historic Preservation. Washington, DC, Preservation Press, 1992. 416p. illus. index. $19.95pa. ISBN 0-89133-169-7.

An expansion of the National Trust's 1983 *Brown Book,* the *Landmark Yellow Pages* identifies about 5,000 individuals and organizations "working to instill preservation values in the United States and abroad" (from the preface). The directory leads off with a lengthy overview of the what, why, how, and who of the preservation effort. The bulk of the work, however, consists of directory-type listings by state and territory of key preservation contacts (for example, state historic preservation offices). Although coverage focuses primarily on the United States, brief information is included for Australia, Canada, New Zealand, and South Africa.

Another recommended publication in this subject area that may be appropriate for purchase, depending on patron interest, is *Historic America: Buildings, Struc-tures, and Sites* (recorded by the Historic American Buildings Survey and the Historic American Engineering Record, Alicia Stamm, comp., C. Ford Peatross, ed., Government Publishing Office, 1983, 708p., $29.00, S/N 030-000-00149-4), which documents by state those buildings, structures, and sites we have designated for preservation as historical landmarks.

570. Morgan, Ann Lee, and Colin Naylor, eds. **Contemporary Architects.** 2d ed. Chicago, St. James Press, 1987. 1038p. illus. $145.00. ISBN 0-912289-26-0.

International in scope, the roughly 600 individuals profiled in *Contemporary Architects* include not only architects, but also planners, structural engineers, landscape architects, and the theorists whose ideas shaped the movement and forward progress of contemporary architecture. Each entry is made up of five parts: a summary of the individual's life, with honors and awards; a chronological listing of works, included design work that never made it to the building stage; a list of publications by and about the individual; a signed critical essay about the individual's work and philosophy; and a black-and-white photograph illustrative of the designer's work. This work is especially recommended for its outstanding overview of the architects and architecture of Germany, Japan, Italy, China, Australia, and Canada, as well as its thorough coverage of the United States and Great Britain.

571. Norwich, John J. **The World Atlas of Architecture.** Boston, G. K. Hall, 1984; repr, Outlet Books, 1988. 408p. illus. maps. bibliog. index. $34.99. ISBN 0-517-66875-0.

Including in its lofty purview nothing less than the entire history of architecture, this monumental resource include photographs of structures, maps that indicate locations of monuments, detailed charts, comparative timelines, building plans, isometric and perspective drawings, and a diverse assortment of diagrams. The physical production is outstanding, and includes 53 cutaway views that give the reader a concept of both interiors and exteriors of scores of major buildings. There is extensive coverage of the architecture of non-European countries and civilizations, including China, Korea, Japan, India, Southeast Asia, Black Africa, pre-Hispanic America, the Pacific Ocean areas, and Islam. The authoritative text, color illustrations, cutaway reconstructions, maps, time charts, glossary, and outstanding visual appeal recommend this atlas as an essential reference work for all libraries that can afford it.

PHOTOGRAPHY

572. Marshall, Sam A., ed. **Photographer's Market, [yr.]: Where & How to Sell Your Photographs.** Cincinnati, OH, Writer's Digest Books, 1979- . Annual. 1v. illus. index. $22.95 (1994 ed.). ISSN 0147-247-X.

Another in this publisher's successful series of "Market" guides, this annual directory provides information on stock agencies, print publications, public relations firms, corporate clients, and galleries in the market for still, film, and video photography. Although coverage is worldwide, most of the entries describe U.S. publications and companies. The guide notes current and projected needs as indicated by individual photograph buyers; describes how (and with whom) to make contact; provides payment, terms, and submission information; and offers a professional "tips" section that may include a summary of the philosophy of the publication or client or provide candid advice on what the candidate looks for in photographs. Separate sections are devoted to listings of workshops, professional organizations, and contests, as well as such business information as copyright, insurance, client-photographer contracts, and model release forms.

573. Naylor, Colin, ed. **Contemporary Photographers.** 2d ed. 1145p. Chicago, St. James Press, 1988. $145.00. ISBN 0-912289-79-1.

Based on the recommendations of a distinguished editorial board as well as the signed contributions of 155 experts and scholars, *Contemporary Photographers* provides biographical profiles of 650 noteworthy photographers, including both living and recently deceased individuals. The profiles lead off with personal biographical information, exhibitions, galleries and museums holding the individual's works, and a bibliography of works (both books and articles) by and about the person. Signed critical essays and a sample of the photographer's work complete the profiles.

574. Stroebel, Leslie, and Hollis N. Todd. **Dictionary of Contemporary Photography.** Dobbs Ferry, NY, Morgan & Morgan, 1974. 217p. $15.00. ISBN 0-87100-065-2.

Although clearly in need of an updated edition, Stroebel and Todd's reasonably priced work is the best single-volume photography dictionary available. It offers 4,500 definitions that are written for clarity and accessibility to the lay reader; drawings and photographs accompany many of the entries, and cross references guide readers to related terms.

575. Stroebel, Leslie, and Richard Zakia, eds. **Focal Encyclopedia of Photography.** 3d ed. Stoneham, MA, Butterworths, 1993. 914p. illus. $125.00. ISBN 0-240-80059-1.

The *Focal Encyclopedia of Photography* comprises scholarly, signed articles that encompass the broad range of subjects—including economics, law, and education—that contribute to the study of photography. (Only three areas have been excluded: cinematography, video, and electronic still photography.) The encyclopedia also offers biographical profiles of individuals noteworthy in this field. Entries are alphabetically presented, and range in length from a few lines to up to 60 pages. A familiar and reliable resource of use to both the lay reader and the professional, this work functions well as both a dictionary and an encyclopedic treatment of the field of photography.

Language and Linguistics

GENERAL WORKS

576. Comrie, Bernard, ed. **The World's Major Languages.** New York, Oxford University Press, 1987. 1025p. index. $29.95pa. ISBN 0-19-506511-5.

Fifty major languages and language families—including such better known ones as Turkic and Indo-European as well as their lesser-known counterparts such as Vietnamese and Swahili—are thoroughly described in this scholarly yet accessible work. The languages are explored within a very broad context that includes historical, sociological, and linguistic information. Most chapters also include extensive descriptions of the phonological and graphic systems, morphology, word formation, syntactic patterns, and characteristic features of the lexicon. Bibliographic notes and an extensive list of references accompany most chapters.

For coverage of the English language only, libraries will be well served by the same publisher's *The Oxford Companion to the English Language* (Tom McArthur and Feri McArthur, eds., 1992, 1184p, $45.00, ISBN 0-19-214183-X), which it bills (appropriately) as "everything you always wanted to know about the English language but were afraid to ask." The *Companion* contains more than 3,500 signed entries from nearly 100 scholars on all aspects of our changing language, including grammar, history, pronunciation, usage, education, literature, culture, linguistics, politics, and technology, with numerous related articles on tangential subjects. Well-written and informative, this engaging work is also a delight to browse.

577. Crystal, David. **The Cambridge Encyclopedia of Language.** New York, Cambridge University Press, 1987. 472p. illus. index. $54.95; $27.95pa. ISBN 0-521-26438-3; 0-521-42443-7pa.

Written by world-renowned linguist David Crystal, *The Cambridge Encyclopedia of Language* is an encyclopedic survey of knowledge about language and of the many kinds, schools, and branches of linguistic science. The work is divided into 11 parts that are further subdivided into 56 independent thematic sections, each of which focuses on a major area of language study. The topical sections comprise detailed yet succinct essays (cross-referenced to related sections) that are complemented by hundreds of tables, maps, data charts, photographs, drawings, newspaper clippings, and cartoons that further clarify the text. Appendixes include a 1,000-word glossary, a table of the world's hundreds of living languages, a list of recommended resources for further study, and a list of references.

Libraries that can afford to may also wish to consider Kirsten Malmkjaer's *The Linguistics Encyclopedia* (Routledge, Chapman & Hall, 1991, 575p., $120.00, ISBN 0-415-02942-2), a scholarly but accessible work designed to guide its readers—educated laypeople as well as students and scholars of linguistics—through the complex world and history of the study of language. Each article covers a single topic of linguistics. Well-defined segments, such as acoustic phonetics, are treated in detail; broader subjects, such as sociolinguistics, are broken up into several subareas to ensure adequate coverage. Numerous cross references, illustrations, an extensive index, and a 40-page bibliography supplement the text.

578. DeMiller, Anna L. **Linguistics: A Guide to the Reference Literature.** Englewood, CO, Libraries Unlimited, 1991. 256p. index. $45.00. ISBN 0-87287-692-6.

DeMiller's work annotates more than 700 references sources, published primarily between 1957 and 1989, that are organized within 31 chapters clustered into 3 parts. The 12 chapters on general linguistics that constitute the first part contain most of the general reference works, such as bibliographies, encyclopedias of linguistics, indexes, abstracts, and biographies of linguists. Part 2 focuses on interdisciplinary areas and applications such as applied linguistics, anthropological linguistics, psycholinguistics, sociolinguistics, and other overlapping fields. Part 3 has specific information on reference works that focus on individual languages or language groups. Three detailed indexes—author, title, and subject—complete the reference.

ENGLISH LANGUAGE DICTIONARIES

579. Kister, Kenneth F. **Kister's Best Dictionaries for Adults & Young People: A Comparative Guide.** Phoenix, AZ, Oryx Press, 1992. 438p. index. $39.50. ISBN 0-89774-191-9.

Intended as a consumer guide to a wide variety of English-language dictionaries, Kister's guide evaluates 132 adult (unabridged, college desk, family and office, and pocket and paperback) and 168 young people's (high-school, junior-high, upper elementary, primary, and preschool) dictionaries. Each review leads off with the standard bibliographic information, then proceeds to assess the merits of the work, including quotations from other reviews if useful. An especially helpful introductory essay discusses the many different uses of dictionaries, their history, how they are compiled, the ongoing and spirited debate about whether they should prescribe or describe how the language is used, whether offensive words should be included, major publishers, how dictionaries are bought and sold, and selection criteria. A must-buy for all libraries.

Abridged Dictionaries

580. Allen, R. E., ed. **The Concise Oxford Dictionary of Current English.** 8th ed. New York, Clarendon Press/Oxford University Press, 1990. 1454p. $27.50. ISBN 0-19-861200-1.

Based on the latest edition of the scholarly, multi-volume *Oxford English Dictionary* (also known as the *OED*), the *Concise Oxford Dictionary* encompasses English as it is currently spoken and written around the world. Definitions for the 120,000 entries and 190,000 vocabulary items tend to be descriptive rather than prescriptive; where multiple definitions occur for a given term, those definitions are numbered and appear in order of familiarity. Separate sections are provided after the definitions of single words for phrases and idioms, which are also clearly indicated in boldface type. Although the focus of this work is British English, it nevertheless does a thorough job of indicating American variations and usage.

581. **The American Heritage Dictionary of the English Language.** 3d ed. Boston, Houghton Mifflin, 1992. 2184p. illus. maps. $39.95. ISBN 0-395-44895-6.

This work provides pronunciation, spelling, syllabication, and definitions for more than 200,000 terms. Within entries, the usual arrangement is headword (syllabicated), pronunciation, part of speech, inflections, definitions (in order of frequency of use), and a brief etymology. Definitions, many with examples, are generally clear, and are often supplemented by some of the approximately 4,000 well-chosen black-and-white photographs and line drawings. A distinctive feature of this dictionary is its usage panel, composed of 173 writers, editors, scholars, and distinguished members of various professions, which rules, via periodic ballots, on questions of current English usage. With its wealth of supplementary materials, including informative essays, hundreds of cross references, tables, charts, and diagrams, this excellent and reasonably priced dictionary is recommended for all libraries.

582. **Webster's Tenth New Collegiate Dictionary.** Springfield, MA, Merriam-Webster, 1993. 1559p. illus. index. $29.00. ISBN 0-87779-711-0.

Although directed toward students, office employees, and home users, *Webster's Tenth* is also an excellent abridged dictionary for public libraries and secondary school libraries. Definitions are descriptive rather than prescriptive, and the strong emphasis on currency is reflected in both the inclusion of many recently coined terms and in the addition of new definitions for existing terms. Entries include synonyms, word origins, and dates of first recorded usage; where there are numerous definitions for a given term, they are listed in historical order. Supplemental materials include listings of biographical and geographical names and foreign words and phrases, as well as a rudimentary style manual that will answer many term-paper questions for students. Reliable and authoritative, this is a must purchase.

Unabridged Dictionaries

583. Gove, Philip Babcock, ed. **Webster's Third New International Dictionary of the English Language.** Springfield, MA, Merriam-Webster, 1986. 2662p. $99.95. ISBN 0-87779-201-1.

Webster's Third has long been considered the most authoritative and prestigious single-volume dictionary of the American language available. Although many have criticized the publisher's decision to move from the prescriptive approach of the *Second* to the more descriptive approach of the *Third* (another change is the exclusion of biographical and geographical names), this work is still the first choice for wordsmiths and others who strive to preserve linguistic standards of clarity. Presented in historical order, definitions are clearly written and often include illustrative quotations and word histories. A must purchase for all libraries.

Although new words have been listed in a 55-page addendum in recent printings, libraries that own earlier printings of the *Third* will probably want to purchase the update publication, *12,000 Words: A Supplement to Webster's Third New International Dictionary* (Merriam-Webster, 1986, 212p., $13.95, ISBN 0-87779-207-0), which includes additions through 1985 to Americans' vocabularies.

584. **The Random House Unabridged Dictionary.** 2d ed. New York, Random House, 1993. 2550p. illus. (part col.). maps. index. $100.00. ISBN 0-679-42917-4.

This update of a work first published nearly three decades ago provides up-to-date, easily understood descriptive definitions for some 315,000 terms, including biographical entries. Although not as comprehensive or scholarly as *Webster's Third, The Random House Dictionary of the English Language* is nonetheless an excellent resource, jammed with supplementary materials that make this a one-stop reference for a vast range of information in addition to its definitions. Several essays that treat linguistic topics (e.g., changes in usage) as well as a "how to use this dictionary" section precede the main body of definitions; back matter includes a list of signs and symbols drawn from the sciences, business, computers, mathematics, medicine, road signs, and the like; a directory of U.S. and Canadian colleges and universities; copies of the Declaration of Independence and the U.S. Constitution; brief Italian, German, French, and Spanish dictionaries; a very basic style manual with information on writing term papers; a list of commonly confused and misspelled words; a full-color atlas that includes pictures of national flags; a weights-and-measures chart; and a chart of foreign alphabets. Also available on CD-ROM.

Visual Dictionaries and Sign Language

585. Butterworth, Rod R., and Mickey Flodin. **The Perigee Visual Dictionary of Signing: An A-to-Z Guide ...** . Rev. ed. New York, Perigee Books/Berkley, 1991. 480p. illus. index. $13.00pa. ISBN 0-399-51695-6.

This dictionary provides the basic vocabulary of American Sign Language (ASL) and includes signs that are commonly known and accepted by people who use signs to communicate with the deaf. Basic hand positions are described, and arrows are used with each illustration to indicate correct hand movements. The main body of the work is a guide to more than 1,200 signs of ASL arranged in alphabetical order by the word to be signed. Each entry has a clear illustration of the sign, a narrative description for making it, a memory aid intended to help a student recall the sign, and an example of the word used in a sentence. A supplemental signs section includes 48 signs new to the revised edition; about one-third of these represent geographic proper names. Entries for these signs are integrated into the main entry and synonym index.

586. Corbeil, Jean-Claude, ed. **The Macmillan Visual Dictionary.** New York, Macmillan, 1992. 862p. illus. maps. index. $45.00. ISBN 0-02-528160-7.

The 25,000 terms, the 3,500 stunning, computer-generated color illustrations, and the 600 subjects treated in *The Macmillan Visual Dictionary* encompass almost all of the physical world. In addition to contemporary materials, the scope of the dictionary includes historical objects such as the parts of a castle, the elements of ancient costumes, types of sailboats, and ancient weapons. Useful and fascinating for both children and adults, this is a recommended purchase for all libraries.

THESAURI AND RELATED WORD BOOKS

587. Chapman, Robert L., ed. **Roget's International Thesaurus.** 5th ed. New York, HarperCollins, 1992. 1141p. index. $18.95. ISBN 006-270014-6.

Roget's International Thesaurus uses a traditional topical arrangement of 15 broad categories to organize its more than 300,000 words and phrases. (It is, in fact, the book that most patrons have in mind when they ask for a thesaurus.) Some 1,000 subcategories further subdivide the broad topics. Within each section, words are grouped by part of speech in the following order: nouns, verbs, adjectives, adverbs, prepositions, conjunctions, and interjections. Helpfully, an alphabetical index expedites access to *Roget's* vast number of synonyms and antonyms. The classic work in this field, *Roget's International* is a must for all libraries.

588. Kay, Maire Weir, and others, eds. **Webster's Collegiate Thesaurus.** Springfield, MA, G&C Merriam, 1976, 1988. 944p. $15.95. ISBN 0-87779-069-8.

Noted for its comprehensiveness and ease of use, the *Collegiate Thesaurus* features roughly 23,000 entries that encompass more than 100,000 synonyms and antonyms, related and contrasted words, phrases and idiomatic equivalents, glosses (restating the meaning of words), and idioms. The thesaurus is arranged alphabetically, and is geared toward individuals unwilling or unable to deal with the organizational complexities of *Roget's International Thesaurus* (entry 587).

589. **Roget's II: The New Thesaurus.** By the editors of the *American Heritage Dictionary.* Boston, Houghton Mifflin, 1988. Unpaged. $16.95; $14.95pa. ISBN 0-395-48317-4; 0-395-48318-2pa.

Roget's II offers an unusual approach to thesaurus organization. Forgoing the traditional, unwieldy index access, it instead arranges main entries alphabetically, followed by indented subentries of related words. Entries comprise brief dictionary-style definitions of words, labels indicating parts of speech, synonyms, near-synonyms, antonyms, near-antonyms, and idioms. Sample sentences illustrate context and usage. Secondary entries are used mainly to cross-reference words to main entries. Although many patrons may be more comfortable with the "traditional" thesaurus arrangement, most who use *Roget's II* will quickly adapt to its innovative—and effective—organization.

NON-ENGLISH DICTIONARIES

Chinese

590. Corbeil, Jean-Claude, and Mein-ven Lee. **The Facts on File English/Chinese Visual Dictionary.** New York, Facts on File, 1988. 823p. illus. index. $35.00. ISBN 0-8160-2043-4.

According to the authors, this dictionary is "meant for the active member of the modern industrial society who needs to be acquainted with a wide range of technical terms from many assorted areas, but not to be a specialist in any." Like similar visual dictionaries from this publisher, the *English/Chinese Visual Dictionary* is the tool to turn to when the reader knows what something looks like, but not what it is called (and vice versa). The work's division into two main sections—the first comprises illustrations depicting the entries, the second contains alphabetically arranged general indexes—allows the reader to search with either the illustration or the word as a starting point. Approximately 25,000 English and Chinese terms are named (but not described).

591. **A New English-Chinese Dictionary.** Rev. ed. Compiled by The Editing Group of *A New English-Chinese Dictionary*. Seattle, WA, University of Washington Press, 1988. 1769p. $19.95. ISBN 0-295-96609-2.

Assembled by a group of more than 70 Chinese scholars, the dictionary defines more than 80,000 English words, including general-use terms, science and technology terms, foreign words, and geographic names. Entries include pronunciation, part of speech, derivation, usage, knowledge, definition, compounds and phrases including the word, and illustrative sentences. A supplement defines more than 4,000 new words added since the 1975 edition. In addition to the definitions, there are nine appendixes: a list of irregular English verbs, lists of ranks in the U.S. and British armed forces with Chinese equivalents, tables of weights and measures (metric and U.S./British), lists of common marks and symbols with Chinese names, and conversion tables of complex-to-simplified-to-complex Chinese characters.

French

592. Atkins, Beryl T., and others. **Collins-Robert French-English, English-French Dictionary.** 2d ed. New York, HarperCollins, 1993. 570p. $20.00. ISBN 0-06-275513-7.

Intended for use by students, teachers, business people, and the general public, this concise bilingual dictionary comprises about 200,000 terms roughly divided between headwords and compounds and currently used phrases and idioms. General usage notes are a special strength of this work, and subtle variations in meaning are carefully illustrated by sample phrases. Mild colloquialisms, very slangy words, and old-fashioned terms are consistently identified, and variant forms and meanings are clearly marked. Although efforts have been made throughout to incorporate American usage, the dictionary does reflect an underlying British tone.

593. Corbeil Jean-Claude, and Ariane Archambault. **The Facts on File English/ French Visual Dictionary.** New York, Facts on File, 1987. 924p. illus. index. $35.00. ISBN 0-8160-1545-7.

A bilingual version of the familiar *Facts on File Visual Dictionary*, this work has identical entries and illustrations, but identifies its more than 3,000 terms in both French and English. Separate general, thematic, and specialized indexes in French and English are thorough and easy to use. This dictionary will be especially useful for students of French, or for others attempting to identify and name objects encountered in everyday life but rarely found in standard French-English dictionaries.

594. Girard, Denis, and others, eds. **Cassell's French Dictionary: French-English; English-French.** New York, Macmillan, 1977. 1440p. $24.95. ISBN 0-02-522610-X.

This popular, highly regarded dictionary encompasses the various iterations of the French language, including French-Canadian terms, among its more than 100,000 items. Entries note American usage, figurative expressions, pronunciation, specialized vocabulary, mode of verb, parts of speech, grammatical information, idiomatic usage, examples of use, and current technical applications. Separate appendixes cover conversion tables for weights and measures, French and English irregular verbs, and common French and English abbreviations.

German

595. Betteridge, Harold T. **Cassell's German Dictionary: German-English, English-German.** Rev. ed. New York, Macmillan, 1978. 1580p. $26.00. ISBN 0-02-522930-3.

In addition to the broad range of terms found in this reliable dictionary, there are phonetic transcriptions of German keywords and a key to German pronunciation; an indication of whether verbal prefixes are separable or not; a new bibliography of technical and specialist dictionaries; and proper names included in the main text. Especially helpful is the enlarged type that has been incorporated in the revised edition.

596. **The Oxford Duden German Dictionary: German-English, English-German.** Edited by the Dudenredaktion and the German Section of the Oxford University Press Dictionary Department. New York, Clarendon Press/Oxford University Press, 1990. 1696p. $29.95. ISBN 0-19-864171-0.

The Oxford Duden German Dictionary is respected not just for the comprehensiveness and currency of its coverage, but also for the fact that its definitions so accurately reflect the subtleties of both German and English, which allows users to move between the two languages with much greater clarity of meaning. The text includes frequent examples of actual usage, with words inserted into the context of phrases or full sentences. Subject labels are used to indicate specialized vocabulary of fields such as medicine or engineering, and stylistic labels designate language levels such as colloquial, slang, or formal speech. Appendixes include brief outlines of grammar and punctuation; lists of irregular verbs; and guides to letter writing, weights and measures, numbers, and expressions for times of the day (all for both languages).

Greek

597. Pring, J. T., comp. **The Oxford Dictionary of Modern Greek: English-Greek.** New York, Clarendon Press/Oxford University Press, 1986. 370p. $13.95. ISBN 0-19-864148-6.

The Oxford Dictionary of Modern Greek is a good resource for those interested in learning contemporary—rather than classic—Greek. Its more than 20,000 terms emphasize conversational and written communication, an approach that makes it especially well-suited to the needs of travelers as well as students.

Italian

598. **Cassell's Italian Dictionary: Italian-English, English-Italian.** New York, Macmillan, 1977. 1096p. $24.00. ISBN 0-02-522530-8.

Cassell's Italian Dictionary reflects current terminology and colloquialisms; in addition, some obsolete terms appearing in classical Italian literary works are included. Entries provide parts of speech, examples of use, pronunciation, figurative expressions, and specialized vocabulary. A separate section addresses Italian verbs.

599. **HarperCollins Italian Dictionary: Italian-English, English-Italian.** College ed. New York, HarperCollins, 1990. 391p. $12.00pa. ISBN 0-06-276508-6.

Intended for use by students, teachers, business people, and the general public, this concise bilingual dictionary encompasses some 70,000 entries and 100,000 translations, with emphasis on current American usage. A good supplementary purchase to the *Cassell's* dictionary.

Japanese

600. Vance, Timothy J. **Kodansha's Romanized Japanese-English Dictionary.** New York, Kodansha America, 1993. 666p. $25.00pa. ISBN 4-7700-1603-4.

This dictionary is a completely rewritten version of *The New World Japanese-English Dictionary for Juniors* (Kodansha America, 1990). It comprises 16,000 entries that include useful sample sentences in both romanized and Japanese script, followed by English translations. They also contain brief yet comprehensive explanations about particles; labels to particular speech levels, such as formal or colloquial; and cross references to synonyms, antonyms, and other locations in the dictionary. Two appendixes, which cover inflections of verbs and adjectives and Japanese numerals, counters, and numbers, conclude the work.

Latin

601. Simpson, D. P. **Cassell's Latin Dictionary: Latin-English, English-Latin.** New York, Macmillan, 1977. 883p. $24.95. ISBN 0-02-522570-7.

First published in 1854, this work continues to be relied upon by students as well as laypersons interested in the language that gave birth to so many others. It incorporates contemporary English terminology as well as geographical and proper names in its 30,000 entry words, which for the most part reflect classical Latin. Entries indicate parts of speech, include etymological notes, and are clarified by illustrative quotations.

Russian

602. Wheeler, Marcus. **The Oxford Russian Dictionary.** 2d ed. New York, Clarendon Press/Oxford University Press, 1984, 1990. 930p. index. $85.00; $27.50pa. ISBN 0-19-864154-0; 0-19-864167-2pa.

Designed for English-speaking users (more British than American), *The Oxford Russian-English Dictionary* contains about 70,000 entries. These encompass colloquial vocabulary, standard idioms, and some general scientific and technological vocabulary, along with everyday, standard terminology. Explanatory glosses and appendixes that give official abbreviations and Russian geographical names further enhance the dictionary's value to users.

This work is nicely supplemented and updated by Stephen Marder's *A Supplementary Russian-English Dictionary* (Slavica, 1992, 522p, $27.95pa, ISBN 0-89357-2284). This work provides definitions for 29,000 terms not found in Wheeler's dictionary. Most are neologisms that consist of both new coinages and older words with new meanings. The remaining third of the work consists of extant words not found in the standard dictionaries.

Spanish

603. **The American Heritage Larousse Spanish Dictionary: Spanish/English, English/Spanish.** Boston, Houghton Mifflin, 1986. 1152p. $21.95; $3.59pa. ISBN 0-395-32429-7; 0-317-65694-5pa.

This dictionary's emphasis on Latin American—as distinct from European—Spanish makes it an especially valuable reference for public libraries. It provides a number of very useful enhancements to the main entries, including a reference of all irregular verbs keyed to a Spanish verb table at the beginning of the dictionary and the provision of synonyms in the language of the entry word to differentiate the senses. The same publisher also offers *The Concise American Heritage Larousse Spanish Dictionary* (1989, 616p., $14.45, ISBN 0-395-43412-2), a good alternative for libraries that cannot afford the parent work.

604. Peers, Edgar A., ed. **Cassell's Spanish Dictionary: Spanish-English, English-Spanish.** New York, Macmillan, 1977. $24.00; $13.95pa. ISBN 0-02-522910-9; 0-02-522660-6pa.

Like all Cassell foreign-language dictionaries, this one is thorough, reliable, and contemporary in its terminology. Iberian Spanish is emphasized, but some coverage is accorded to Spanish-American terminology. The dictionary focuses on the words and phrases most likely to be encountered in everyday usage; consequently, technological terms will usually have to be checked in one of the more specialized Spanish dictionaries.

605. Smith, Colin, and others. **Collins Spanish-English, English-Spanish Dictionary.** 3d ed. New York, HarperCollins, 1993. 1v. (various paging). $27.50. ISBN 0-06-275504-8.

A welcome revision and expansion of the second (1989) edition, this excellent unabridged dictionary presents more than 230,000 entries and 440,000 translations. Its entries indicate usage level and reflect a high degree of currency. An 80-page section on language in use, with phrases and expressions grouped according to the function being performed when they are used in communication, rounds out the work.

COLLOQUIALISMS, IDIOMS, AND SPECIAL USAGE

606. Partridge, Eric. **A Dictionary of Slang and Unconventional English: Colloquialisms and Catch-phrases, Solecisms and Catachreses, Nicknames and Vulgarisms.** 8th ed. New York, Macmillan, 1984. 1400p. $75.00. ISBN 0-02-594980-2.

Partridge's monumental work has delighted wordsmiths (and assisted reference librarians) for decades, and the more than 100,000 entries found in the eighth edition continue to do so. Although it remains primarily a dictionary of British usage, there is sufficient coverage of terms of interest to Americans to merit its inclusion in all reference collections. The work is arranged alphabetically and is abundantly cross-referenced. Entries provide type of speech, definition, type of term (colloquialism, nickname, etc.), and the group most likely to employ the term (e.g., military).

Historical information—date of term, source, and an example of the term's use in print—concludes the entries.

In a budgetary pinch, libraries that cannot afford the complete work can make do with its abridged publication, *A Concise Dictionary of Slang and Unconventional English* (Paul Beale, ed., 534p., Macmillan, 1990, $35.00, ISBN 0-02-605350-0). If budget allows, other recommended works of "unconventional English" to consider are Robert L. Chapman's *New Dictionary of American Slang* (Harper & Row, 1986, 485p., $32.50, ISBN 0-06-181157-2) or its abridgment, *American Slang* (Perennial Library/Harper & Row, 1987, 499p., $12.00pa., ISBN 0-06-096160-0), based on Harold Wentworth and Stuart Berg Flexner's *Dictionary of American Slang* (Crowell, 1975); and Esther Lewin and Albert E. Lewin's *The Thesaurus of Slang: 150,000 Uncensored Contemporary Slang Terms, Common Idioms, and Colloquialisms ...* (Facts on File, 1988, 435p., $50.00, ISBN 0-8160-1742-5), which lists slang equivalents for approximately 12,500 terms drawn from standard English.

607. Rogers, James. **The Dictionary of Clichés.** New York, Facts on File, 1985; repr., Outlet Books, 1992. 305p. index. $7.99. ISBN 0-517-06020-5.

Roughly 2,000 clichés, ranging in length from one word to extended phrases, are collected and annotated in this delightful compendium of overused, overwrought, but wonderfully familiar sayings. Entries are arranged alphabetically, and each features a brief paragraph that explains both the term's figurative meaning and current use while also exploring its origin and history. Many entries include citations from printed texts, with names of authors, titles, and years of publication. A nine-page index of cross references makes it easy to locate specific words and phrases.

ETYMOLOGY

608. Barnhart, Robert K., ed. **The Barnhart Dictionary of Etymology.** Bronx, NY, H. W. Wilson, 1988. 1284p. $64.00. ISBN 0-8242-0745-9.

Tracing "the origins of the basic vocabulary of modern English," this dictionary comprises more than 20,000 entries that together encompass the development of primarily American English. Entries give pronunciation for words deemed difficult or unusual, part of speech, definition, date, language(s) from which the term derived, variant forms of the word, and cross references. The scope of this work is extremely broad, ranging from words dating from the Middle Ages and earlier through the buzzwords of the 1980s.

609. **A Dictionary of American Idioms.** 2d ed. Rev. and updated by Adam Makkai. Hauppauge, NY, Barron's Educational Series, 1987. 398p. $11.95pa. ISBN 0-8120-3899-1.

This dictionary will be especially useful to those for whom English is a second language. It includes slang, clichés, and proverbial and informal regional expressions, providing for each a definition of the phrase, a sentence to illustrate the meaning in standard English, and parts of speech and restrictive use labels (is it considered slang, vulgar, or a cliché?). Numerous cross references guide the reader to variant ways in which the idiom might be listed. Given the increasing importance of ESL programs in communities all across the country, *A Dictionary of American Idioms* should be considered an important acquisition for all public libraries.

610. Morris, William, and Mary Morris. **Morris Dictionary of Word and Phrase Origins.** 2d ed. New York, Harper & Row, 1988. 669p. index. $28.00. ISBN 0-06-015862-X.

Aiming to entertain a lay audience rather than edify a scholarly one, the current edition of the *Morris Dictionary of Word and Phrase Origins* incorporates the several thousand entries from the previous (1977) edition as well as adding a substantial number of new entries. Although informative, the brief descriptions have been written to engage the reader; thus, the Morris work offers a good alternative to the drier, more scholarly etymological works such as *The Barnhart Dictionary of Etymology* (entry 608).

Works like the Morrises' are popular for both reference and browsing. Depending on patron interest, several other similar titles libraries may want to have on hand are *The Merriam-Webster New Book of Word Histories* (Merriam-Webster, 1991, 526p., $9.95pa., ISBN 0-87779-603-3); Robert Hendrickson's *Facts on File Encyclopedia of Word and Phrase Origins* (Facts on File, 1987, 581p., $50.00, ISBN 0-8160-1012-9), a dictionary-like compendium of 7,500 words and phrases; and the compendium of the late John Ciardi's erudite and witty works, *The Complete Browser's Dictionary: The Best of John Ciardi's Two Browsers' Dictionaries in a Single Compendium of Curious Expressions & Intriguing Facts* (HarperCollins, 1988, 400p., $22.95, ISBN 0-06-016008-X).

611. Onions, C. T., and others, eds. **Oxford Dictionary of English Etymology.** New York, Oxford University Press, 1966, 1982. 1024p. $60.00. ISBN 0-19-861112-9.

A companion work to the authoritative *Oxford English Dictionary* (*OED*), this scholarly, comprehensive dictionary traces the history and development of everyday English words back from their current usage to their Indo-European beginnings. There are about 24,000 entries; provided for each are pronunciation, a chronologically arranged selection of meanings that trace the general developmental trend, and an indication of the century in which the word or meaning was first recorded. The focus is on British, rather than American, English, thus making this work a good complement to the *Barnhart* dictionary.

FOREIGN WORDS AND PHRASES

612. Ehrlich, Eugene, ed. **The Harper Dictionary of Foreign Terms.** 3d ed. New York, Harper & Row, 1987. 423p. $20.00. ISBN 0-06-181576-4.

More than 15,000 foreign expressions—drawn from more than 50 languages—are defined in this well-known dictionary, which builds on the work done in previous editions by C. O. Sylvester Mawson (1934) and Charles Berlitz (1975). The definitions are succinct and indicate usage by region and/or field of endeavor. Access to the material is enhanced by cross references and by an English index; unfortunately, no pronunciation guidance is included in this otherwise excellent source of information on foreign expressions used in English.

613. Guinagh, Kevin. **Dictionary of Foreign Phrases and Abbreviations.** 3d ed. Bronx, NY, H. W. Wilson, 1983. 261p. $42.00. ISBN 0-8242-0675-4.

The third edition of this useful and by now standard reference work defines approximately 5,250 foreign phrases, proverbs, and abbreviations (derived from 15

614. Follett, Wilson. **Modern American Usage.** Completed by Jacques Barzun, ed., with Carlos Baker and others. New York, Hill and Wang, (c1966) 1979. 528p. $14.95pa. ISBN 0-8090-0139-X.

This outstanding lexicon of American usage is a treasure for individuals concerned that language be used precisely and correctly. The "Inventory of Main Entries in the Lexicon" contained in the prefatory material indicates the four-part arrangement of the work: diction, idiom, syntax, and style. Sections treating "shall (should)," "will (would)," and punctuation are appended. Regardless of size or budget, all libraries should have this classic work in their reference collections.

615. Fowler, Henry Watson. **A Dictionary of Modern English Usage.** 2d rev. ed. Ernest Gowers, rev. New York, Oxford University Press, 1965. 725p. $24.95. ISBN 0-19-869115-7.

First published in 1926, Fowler's *Dictionary of Modern English Usage* has for decades been considered the definitive work on this subject. Coverage includes etymology, usage, and comparative British and American interpretations, pronunciation, and usage. The topical entries are arranged alphabetically. A six-page "Classified Guide to the Dictionary" is included in the prefatory material, but there is no index.

616. Maggio, Rosalie. **The Dictionary of Bias-Free Usage: A Guide to Nondiscriminatory Language.** Phoenix, AZ, Oryx Press, 1991. 293p. $25.00pa. ISBN 0-89774-653-8.

Maggio has compiled a reference list of some 5,000 sex- and gender-specific words and phrases with preferred words and phrases used in common with both sexes. She does not advocate such awkward constructions as *s/he, chairperson, herstory,* or *authoress,* but instead guides the writer in how to use normal, standard, literate English while avoiding unthinking, unneeded distinctions as to sex—either one. This is a welcome, practical guidebook that will be of use to writers, speakers, and all others who seek to avoid sexist or otherwise biased terminology in their communications.

617. Urdang, Laurence, and others, eds. **Ologies & Isms: A Thematic Dictionary: A Unique Lexicon of More than 15,000 English Words Used of and about Theories, Concepts, Doctrines, Systems, Attitudes, Practices, States of Mind, and Branches of Science ... .** Detroit, Gale, 1986. 795p. index. $99.00. ISBN 0-8103-1196-8.

This familiar compendium identifies and defines about 17,000 -ologies and -isms. Entries are arranged in 430 thematic sections, preceded by a 35-page table of categories and a list of all cross-references. The thematic arrangement, supplemented by an excellent index, is especially helpful when looking for a word that one suspects exists, but cannot guess the beginning of.

GENERAL USAGE

major languages, including Latin) that occur frequently in English. Entries are listed alphabetically, are brief but clear, and include an elementary sound transcription in square brackets to aid in pronunciation. An index of phrases arranged by language follows the dictionary listing; a pronunciation guide and an overview of the several competing pronunciations of Latin further assist the reader.

618. Wilson, Kenneth G. **The Columbia Guide to Standard American English.** New York, Columbia University Press, 1993. 482p. $24.95. ISBN 0-231-06988-X.

With about 6,500 alphabetically arranged entries covering many aspects of word choice, pronunciation, grammar, and idiomatic usage, this new guide covers both prescriptive and descriptive contemporary American (rather than British) usage. Alternative pronunciations and spellings are given where appropriate, and the entries are generously cross-referenced. In his informative introduction, Wilson describes the five levels of Standard American English writing (intimate, casual, impromptu, planned, and oratorical) and the three levels of Standard American English writing (informal, semi-formal, and formal) referred to throughout the book.

If there is room in the budget for more usage books, there are a number of good, fairly recently published titles from which to choose. Two of these are *Webster's Dictionary of English Usage* (Merriam-Webster, 1989, 978p., $18.95, ISBN 0-87779-032-9), which takes a historical approach in its article-length entries exploring usage questions; and *The World Almanac Guide to Good Word Usage* (Martin H. Manser with Jeffrey McQuain, eds., World Almanac/St. Martin's Press, 1989; repr., Avon Books, 1991, 274p., $8.95pa., ISBN 0-380-71449-3), a practical, down-to-earth guide to five main language areas: spelling, pronunciation, grammar and punctuation, usage, and buzzwords. Geared to the needs of the general public, this is a reliable and worthwhile handbook whose credibility is vetted by none other than the venerable Edwin Newman, who wrote its introduction.

Literature

GENERAL WORKS

Biographies

619. Combs, Richard E., and Nancy R. Owen. **Authors: Critical & Biographical References.** 2d ed. Metuchen, NJ, Scarecrow, 1993. 478p. index. $49.50. ISBN 0-8108-2679-8.

Authors consists of three parts. The first lists about 3,300 authors (writers of prose, poetry, fiction, or nonfiction) alphabetically, and provides for each brief coded citations to materials that contain biographical or critical information about the author in question. The second part lists all 1,158 books analyzed and provides bibliographical information (author/editor, publisher, and place and date of publication) for each of them. Part 3 is an alphabetical list of all authors and editors whose works are cited. Reference works treating a single author have not been included, and passages are listed only if the entry cited is at least six pages long.

620. **Contemporary Authors.** Detroit, Gale, 1962- . Irregular. 1v. $119.00/v. (1994 volumes). ISSN 0010-7768.

A veritable cottage industry, the Contemporary Authors series (at 142 volumes in 1994) and its spin-offs continue to offer reliable bio-bibliographical information on writers in the fields of fiction, nonfiction, poetry, journalism, drama, motion pictures, and television. A typical profile includes personal information (birth date and place, family, education, politics and religion, avocations); addresses (personal and professional); a career overview; a bibliography of writings by the individual; information on projects "in progress"; and a listing of biographical sources (books and magazine articles) for further information.

In addition to the main CA series, there are also ongoing updating series: the Contemporary Authors First Revision Series and its successor, the Contemporary Authors New Revision Series, both of which update information found in the original volumes; the Contemporary Authors Permanent Series, a two-volume set that contains bio-bibliographical sketches for 3,500 authors who were deceased or inactive in 1975; the Contemporary Authors Bibliographical Series, which provides bibliographical checklists of works by and about each featured author and then describes and evaluates the most significant secondary sources (so far only two volumes here,

American Novelists and American Poets); and the Contemporary Authors Autobiography Series, wherein are found 10,000- to 15,000-word essays by the writers themselves (approximately 20 per volume) describing their lives and works.

All of these volumes are standard, reliable sources of information on our most influential writers; however, at $119.00 per volume, libraries will have to carefully consider whether they want to maintain the entire CA family, or purchase just the specific volumes that best suit patrons' more immediate needs. Some alternatives to consider would be *Major 20th-Century Writers: A Selection of Sketches from Contemporary Authors* (Bryan Ryan, ed., Gale, 1991, 4v., $295.00/set, ISBN 0-8103-7766-7), which contains more than 1,000 biographical essays culled from the CA series; *Hispanic Writers: A Selection of Sketches from Contemporary Authors* (Bryan Ryan, ed., Gale, 1990, 514p, $90.00, ISBN 0-8103-7688-1), which treats 400 authors "who are part of twentieth-century Hispanic literature and culture in the Americas"; and *Black Writers: A Selection of Sketches from Contemporary Authors* (2d ed., Sharon Malinowski, Gale, 1994, $89.00, ISBN 0-8103-7788-8), which covers more than 400 of the most-studied Black authors from the Harlem Renaissance, social and political writers, and foreign Black writers of interest to American audiences. All of these materials are also available on a single CD-ROM.

621. Henderson, Lesley. **Contemporary Novelists.** 5th ed. Chicago, St. Martin's Press, 1991. 1053p. $120.00. ISBN 1-55862-036-2.

The fifth edition of *Contemporary Novelists* continues the format and scope of its predecessors, addressing 589 novelists writing in English, regardless of their country of residence. For the most part, the novelists profiled are drawn from Great Britain, the Commonwealth countries, and the United States. The entries are arranged alphabetically by author, and contain a biographical paragraph; a primary bibliography that identifies best-known, easily accessible titles; and a signed, critical essay on the body of the author's work. Many of the profiles include remarks from those subject individuals who chose to comment on their own work. The biographical dictionary concludes with a very helpful title index that includes all novels and short story collections cited in the primary bibliographies.

622. Kunitz, Stanley J., and Howard Haycroft, eds. **Twentieth Century Authors: A Biographical Dictionary of Modern Literature ...** Bronx, NY, H. W. Wilson, 1942. 1577p. $92.00. ISBN 0-8242-0049-7. **Supplement.** 1955. 1123p. $82.00. ISBN 0-8242-0050-0.

This standard reference provides biographical profiles of 1,850 20th-century authors, poets, dramatists, philosophers, and biographers writing in the English language, although some international coverage is provided. The biographical sketches include a listing of each writer's major works and suggestions for sources of more detailed information.

Twentieth Century Authors is supplemented and updated by John Wakeman's *World Authors, 1950–1970* (1975, 1594p, $95.00, ISBN 0-8242-0419-0) and *World Authors, 1970–1975* (1980, 894p, $95.00, ISBN 0-8242-0641-X), and Vineta Colby's *World Authors, 1975–1980* (1985, $82.00, ISBN 0-8242-0715-7), and *World Authors, 1980–1985* (1991, 938p, $82.00, ISBN 0-8242-0797-1). Each supplement contains between 300 and 400 biographical or autobiographical sketches of writers who came to prominence during the era covered. Libraries may also wish to consider the recently published *Gay and Lesbian Literature* (Sharon Malinowski, ed., St. James Press, 1994, 488p, $85.00, ISBN 1-55862-174-1), which provides detailed biographical, bibliographical, and critical information on 200 authors whose work has contributed to the field of gay and lesbian literature.

Dictionaries and Encyclopedias

623. **Benet's Reader's Encyclopedia.** 3d ed. New York, HarperCollins, 1987. 1091p. $45.00. ISBN 0-06-181088-6.

Benet's Reader's Encyclopedia is a one-volume literary reference designed to encompass the entire spectrum of world literature and the arts. Its more than 9,000 alphabetically arranged entries vary in length from several lines to several columns and include information on authors; principal characters; literary movements; allusions; literary terminology; individuals involved in the arts, religion, philosophy, and other related disciplines; myths and mythological characters; and specific literary works. Not only an outstanding reference source, *Benet's Reader's Encyclopedia* is also a delight for browsers.

624. Klein, Leonard S., ed. **Encyclopedia of World Literature in the 20th Century.** 2d ed. New York, Frederick Ungar, 1981-1984. 4v. illus. index. $125.00/v. ISBN 0-804-3148-5. **Volume 5: Supplement and Index.** New York, Crossroad/Continuum, 1993. 732p. illus. index. $150.00. ISBN 0-8264-0571-1.

This authoritative, international survey of 20th-century writers and national literatures is best known for its coverage of European and North American writers, although it does address African, Asian, and South American writers to a lesser extent. The encyclopedia is especially strong in its treatment of important international developments in 20th-century literature, and its articles on national literatures, especially of Third World countries, are unrivaled. Arrangement of the author and topical articles is alphabetical, with extensive cross-referencing in the survey articles. Bibliographical sources—including articles in English, German, French, and Spanish—are cited, and black-and-white photographs have been provided for most authors. An extraordinarily detailed and well-organized index comprises the entirety of volume 5.

625. Urdang, Laurence, and Frederick G. Ruffner, Jr., eds. **Allusions—Cultural, Literary, Biblical, and Historical: A Thematic Dictionary.** 2d ed. Detroit, Gale, 1986. 634p. bibliog. index. $89.00. ISBN 0-8103-1828-8.

Urdang and Ruffner have compiled 8,700 allusions (organized in 712 thematic categories) to inform the inquisitive and delight the browser. *Allusions* is not a quotation finder, but rather a source for identifying allusions to actual or mythical persons, places, or things that might puzzle a reader and which might not be found in a general dictionary. Allusions are drawn from the Bible, famous authors, various mythologies, music, the arts, industry, movies, television, radio, the comics, and other sources. Generous use of cross references enable the reader to find related categories, and a bibliography lists contemporary editions of books containing the allusions cited.

Handbooks and Digests

626. Baker, Nancy L. **A Research Guide for Undergraduate Students: English and American Literature.** New York, Modern Language Association, 1985. 61p. bibliog. $6.50pa. ISBN 0-87352-147-1.

Intended to ease the way for freshmen English students, Baker's brief but excellent guide provides information about the library's wealth of literature research materials, including bibliographies, indexes, handbooks, online databases, stylebooks, and other useful resources. Chapter 2, which explores the intricacies of both manual and computerized card catalogs, is especially helpful for the many students (and patrons) intimidated by yet another technological interface. Although not nearly as broad or comprehensive as Harner's *Literary Research Guide* (entry 627), this work serves beautifully as a user-friendly introduction to the library and its literary reference works.

627. Harner, James L. **Literary Research Guide: A Guide to Reference Sources for the Study of Literatures in English and Related Topics.** 2d ed. New York, Modern Language Association, 1993. 766p. index. $37.00; $19.50pa. ISBN 0-87352-558-2; 0-87352-559-0pa.

Although the predecessor to this work—Margaret C. Patterson's *Literary Research Guide*, 2d ed.—was intended for beginning students, Harner's guide is for serious researchers, ranging from advanced undergraduates to practicing scholars. His focus is on reference sources essential to the study of literature in English, limiting coverage of literatures in other languages to a brief section that describes guides to reference works and significant bibliographies. The entries are arranged within 21 sections that encompass general literary reference sources, national literatures (Irish, American, etc.), and topics relating to literature. Annotations are both evaluative and descriptive. Cross references are used between both entries and sections. Indexed by name, title, and subject.

Although Harner's guide is a valuable work, its focus and approach are so different from that of Patterson's MLA guide that libraries that own the earlier (now out-of-print) publication—*Literary Research Guide: An Evaluative, Annotated Bibliography of Important Reference Books and Periodicals on English, Irish, Scottish, Welsh, Commonwealth, American, Afro-American, American Indian, Continental, Classical, and World Literatures, and Sixty Literature-related Subject Areas* (Margaret C. Patterson, 2d ed., Modern Language Association)—will most likely want to keep it available for patrons new to literary research.

628. Holman, C. Hugh, and William Harmon. **A Handbook to Literature.** 6th ed. New York, Macmillan, 1992. 624p. index. $30.00. ISBN 0-02-553440-8.

Known to hundreds of thousands of English students as "Thrall and Hibbard" since it was first published in 1936, *A Handbook to Literature* contains 1,600 words and phrases related to English and American literature. The entries, which range in length from one line to several pages, are arranged alphabetically and include helpful cross references designed to link related terms for those just beginning English studies. In addition to an extensive outline of literary history and an index of proper names, the book also provides information on Nobel Prizes for literature since 1901, and Pulitzer Prizes for fiction, poetry, and drama since 1917.

629. Kaplan, Fred, ed. **The Reader's Adviser: A Layman's Guide to Literature.** 14th ed. New Providence, NJ, R. R. Bowker, 1994. 6v. index. $500.00/set. ISBN 0-8352-3320.

The Reader's Adviser was created in 1921 to guide independent learners to the best works in a particular subject area. It evolved from its initial one-volume format to an enlarged three-volume set to its current six-volume iteration. The six volumes, which may each be purchased individually for $110.00, are: volume 1, *The Best in Reference Books, British Literature, and American Literature* (ISBN 0-8352-3321-9); volume 2, *The Best in World Literature* (ISBN 0-8352-3322-7); volume 3, *The Best in the Social Sciences, History, and the Arts* (ISBN 0-8352-3323-5); volume 4, *The Best in Philosophy and Religion* (ISBN 0-8352-3324-3); volume 5, *The Best in Science, Technology, and Medicine* (ISBN 0-8352-3325-1); and volume 6, *Indexes*

(ISBN 0-8352-3326-X). The materials are arranged from the general to the specific; written by subject specialists, each chapter begins with an introductory essay, followed by general reading lists and then topical ones. Major authors are covered in brief essays followed by a bibliography of works by and about the individual. Each item listed is given a brief evaluative description. Works cited contain complete bibliographic information. Subject, title, and author indexes conclude each volume; volume 6 cumulates all of the indexes of the previous five volumes. Given the renewed interest in independent learning and the increased ease of interlibrary loan, this will continue to be an important reference for libraries.

630. Magill, Frank N., ed. **Magill's Survey of World Literature.** North Bellmore, NY, Marshall Cavendish, 1993. 6v. illus. index. $389.95/set. ISBN 1-85435-482-5.

This six-volume ready-reference set summarizes and analyzes more than 740 works by 215 significant world writers. These authors, drawn from antiquity to the late 20th century, include Homer, Sophocles, Dante Alighieri, Miguel de Cervantes, Daniel Defoe, Jane Austen, George Eliot, Virginia Woolf, Salman Rushdie, and P. D. James, and represent virtually all genres and 30-plus nationalities. American writers are excluded because they are covered in *Magill's Survey of American Literature* (entry 663).

Arranged alphabetically by author, each signed essay includes a one-sentence note about the author's literary significance; a biography; general analyses that discuss such characteristics as the writer's plots, themes, styles, and settings; specific analyses of principal works, organized by genre, then chronologically within each genre; a one- or two-paragraph summation of the author's literary achievements and place in world literature; and an unannotated bibliography of some 6 to 12 secondary sources. Author and title indexes and a glossary of literary terms conclude each volume.

631. Ousby, Ian, ed. **The Cambridge Guide to Literature in English.** 2d ed. New York, Cambridge University Press, 1994. 1061p. illus. $49.95. ISBN 0-521-44086-6.

Originally published as *The Cambridge Guide to English Literature* (1983), this scholarly work includes writers in English from the United Kingdom and the United States, as well as from such countries as India, Africa, Australia, and Canada. It describes authors and their works, defines literary terms and allusions, provides information about literary movements and schools of literary criticism, and describes various genres. Entries are arranged alphabetically and are supplemented by numerous cross references and approximately 300 illustrations.

CLASSICAL LITERATURE

632. Howatson, M. C., ed. **The Oxford Companion to Classical Literature.** 2d ed. New York, Oxford University Press, 1989. 615p. maps. $49.95. ISBN 0-19-866121-5.

Written for the general reader rather than the classical scholar, this work covers the period from the first appearance of the Greeks around 2200 B.C. to the closing of the Athenian philosophy schools in A.D. 529. The articles, which are authoritative, clearly written, and literate, discuss authors, major works, historical and mythological figures and topics of literary significance, and literary and linguistic topics. Most early Christian writers have been excluded, except for a few such as Augustine or Boethius whose works fall within the classical tradition. Although there is no index, the liberal use of cross references helps facilitate access to related materials. For libraries that would like a less expensive but similarly authoritative resource, this work is shortened and slightly revised by *The Concise Oxford Companion to Classical Literature* (M. C. Howatson and Ian Chilvers, eds., 1993, 575p, $14.95pa., ISBN 0-19-282708-1).

633. Luce, T. James, ed.-in-chief. **Ancient Writers: Greece and Rome.** New York, Scribner's, 1982. 2v. bibliog. index. $180.00/set. ISBN 0-684-16595-3.

The 47 scholarly articles in Luce's biocritical handbook are, for the most part, devoted to the Greek and Roman writers considered most influential in classical literature. The arrangement is chronological. Articles range in length from 10 to more than 50 pages, and comprise a brief biographical sketch followed by an extensive critical evaluation of the writer's works; a bibliography of currently available editions in the original Greek or Latin, as well as recommended modern translations; and a list of primarily English-language critical studies.

For libraries seeking something a bit less expensive than *Ancient Writers*, Michael Grant's *Greek and Latin Authors, 800 B.C.–A.D. 1000* (H. W. Wilson, 1980, 490p., $65.00, ISBN 0-8242-0640-1) offers an excellent alternative. Part of the Wilson Author series, it profiles approximately 300 classical authors in articles that vary in length in proportion to the importance of the author. Bibliographies accompany each entry, and include titles appropriate for both the lay reader and the classical scholar.

FICTION

General Works

634. Husband, Janet, and Jonathan F. Husband. **Sequels: An Annotated Guide to Novels in Series.** 2d ed. Chicago, American Library Association, 1990. 576p. index. $50.00. ISBN 0-8389-0533-1.

The second edition of this well-received, standard reader's advisory resource provides readers and reference librarians with access to bibliographic, plot, and related information on novels in series. A *series* is defined as books that show progressive plot or character development from book to book, share a common set of characters or setting, or were originally conceived as a series by the author. (Most juvenile and nonfiction series are excluded, as are short stories.) Entries are arranged alphabetically by author. Within each author listing, the series and the books that comprise them are arranged in preferred reading order. Each series entry has an explanatory paragraph followed by the book entries; each book entry gives title, publisher, date, and a brief annotation. A title index and a subject index that includes genres and main characters round out the work.

635. Rintoul, M. C. **Dictionary of Real People and Places in Fiction.** New York, Routledge, Chapman & Hall, 1993. 1184p. $99.95. ISBN 0-415-05999-2.

Covering approximately 1,000 English-language novels and short stories, Rintoul's dictionary consists of four sections. The heart of the work is an alphabetical list of more than 4,000 real people, places, publications, groups, and other entities that have served as the basis for fictional counterparts. Entries provide brief biographical or other descriptive information and note the name of the fictional counterpart and the author, title, and publication date of the work in which the reference appeared. The other major section is arranged first by author and then by titles of works from which characters are identified. Under each title, fictional names are paired with their real counterparts. Additional sections provide access by fictional names and titles of works.

636. Rosenberg, Betty, and Diana Tixier Herald. **Genreflecting: A Guide to Reading Interests in Genre Fiction.** 3d ed. Englewood, CO, Libraries Unlimited, 1991. 345p. index. $35.00. ISBN 0-87287-390-5. (Note: 4th edition forthcoming.)

Six types of genre fiction are explored in Rosenberg's guide: western, thriller, romance, science fiction, fantasy, and horror. Within each topical chapter, works are divided into subgenres such as spy/espionage or historical romance, and best-selling, significant, or especially popular authors are identified. Subsections provide selective, annotated lists of anthologies, bibliographies, biographies, encyclopedias, history, criticism, manuals, periodicals, associations, conferences, awards, publishers, atlases, and films. Indexes cover genre authors, genre themes, and secondary materials.

Another useful guide, which lacks Rosenberg's wit and charm but is nevertheless packed with helpful information, is Mary K. Biagini and Judith Hartzler's *A Handbook of Contemporary Fiction for Public Libraries and School Libraries* (Scarecrow, 1989, 247p, $25.00, ISBN 0-8108-2275-X). The handbook lists more than 1,100 contemporary American, British, and world authors, as well as their noteworthy titles, within categories such as romance, mystery, science fiction, westerns, and historical fiction. A topical bibliography concludes each genre section, and an author index concludes the work.

637. Seymour-Smith, Martin. **Dictionary of Fictional Characters.** Rev. ed. Boston, The Writer, 1991. 598p. $18.95pa. ISBN 0-87116-166-4.

An update of William Freeman's original 1963 edition and Fred Urquhart's 1973 revision of that work, Seymour-Smith's *Dictionary of Fictional Characters* identifies some 50,000 characters drawn from the world's most beloved works of fiction. Each character's entry provides the author and title of the work from whence the character came, and the names and relationships of the other main characters in the book. An appendix offers explanations of terms used in the annotations; indexes by author and by title conclude the dictionary.

638. Yaakov, Juliette, and John Greenfieldt. eds. **Fiction Catalog.** 12th ed. Bronx, NY, H. W. Wilson, 1991. 943p. index. $98.00. ISBN 0-8242-0804-8.

The primary purpose of this standard reference source is to list novels and novelettes likely to be of interest to adult readers. Among its 5,159 titles, it lists both established writers, such as Charles Dickens, and contemporary ones, such as Margaret Atwood. *Fiction Catalog* also contains a representative selection of English translations of the world's finest writers, such as Aleksandr Solzhenitsyn and Gabriel García Márquez. Although most of the works identified are in print, out-of-print works are also listed if considered significant. The purchase price includes four annual paperback supplements that update the main edition.

Mystery, Detection, and Crime

639. Cassiday, Bruce, comp. and ed. **Modern Mystery, Fantasy and Science Fiction Writers.** New York, Continuum, 1993. 673p. index. $75.00. ISBN 0-8264-0573-8.

A work of literary criticism, this book covers 88 authors in its 800 entries, which have been excerpted from 112 publications. The majority of the authors represented are 20th-century writers, but in order to adequately reflect the beginnings of a genre, certain 19th-century authors (for instance, Jules Verne) have been included. Authors are arranged alphabetically, although most of the excerpts dealing with them appear chronologically. A separate listing of works mentioned and an index to critics provide alternative access to the entries.

640. Henderson, Lesley, ed. **Twentieth-century Crime and Mystery Writers.** 3d ed. Chicago, St. James Press; distr., Gale, 1991. 1294p. $132.00. ISBN 1-55862-031-1.

The third edition of this familiar work offers brief biographies of more than 700 writers, followed by a bibliography of books, short stories, plays, screenplays, manuscript collections, theatrical and recording activities, and works about the authors. Many of the signed critical essays are quite extensive, and, whenever possible, entries include comments by the author. A title and character index concludes the book.

641. Menendez, Albert J. **The Subject Is Murder: A Selective Subject Guide to Mystery Fiction.** New York, Garland, 1986–1990. 2v. index. $25.00 (v.1); $29.00 (v.2). ISBN 0-8240-8655-4 (v.1); 0-8240-2580-6 (v.2).

The Subject Is Murder identifies just over 3,800 titles, dating primarily from the 1930s to 1985, of interest to mystery readers and the librarians who work with them. The titles are arranged under 25 mystery genres such as medicine, archaeology, politics, newspapers, the sea, Hollywood, and (yes!) libraries. A brief topical overview precedes each chapter; in addition to the topical sections, the work includes a listing of mystery bookshops and book dealers. Indexed by author.

For similar coverage from 1985 through 1991, libraries can turn to Tasha Mackler's *Murder ... by Category: A Subject Guide to Mystery Fiction* (Scarecrow, 1991, 470p., $52.50, ISBN 0-8108-2463-9), which organizes its titles according to subject matter and provides engaging synopses for each.

Science Fiction

642. Barron, Neil, ed. **Anatomy of Wonder: A Critical Guide to Science Fiction.** 4th ed. New Providence, NJ, R. R. Bowker, 1994. 874p. index. $52.00. ISBN 0-8352-3288-3.

Anatomy of Wonder is widely considered the standard reference work on science fiction. It evaluatively annotates approximately 2,100 adult and juvenile science fiction titles. The articles are written by recognized experts, and include overviews that trace the emergence of science fiction, examine its development from 1918 through 1993, and discuss science fiction for children and young adults and in 13 countries besides the United States and Great Britain. The chapters on research aids cover general reference works, history and criticism, biographical studies, television, film and illustration, magazines, and notable library and private collections. A core collection checklist is also provided. Barron has also published two other bibliographic works in related areas, *Fantasy Literature: A Reader's Guide* (Garland, 1990, 586p., $55.00, ISBN 0-8240-3148-2) and *Horror Literature: A Reader's Guide* (Garland, 1990, 596p., $55.00, ISBN 0-8240-4347-2), both of which provide exhaustive coverage of their subjects in clearly written, annotated citations.

643. Clute, John, and Peter Nicholls, eds. **The Encyclopedia of Science Fiction.** New York, St. Martin's Press, 1993. 1370p. $75.00. ISBN 0-312-09618-6.

A revision, update, and expansion of Nicholls's highly regarded *Science Fiction Encyclopedia* (1979), this work is now current through 1992. New thematic entries, such as those on cyberpunk, steampunk, poetry, virtual reality, and technothrillers, reflect current trends; new entries on feminism, women as portrayed in science fiction, and women science fiction writers illustrate the growing importance of these topics. Although the lively, opinionated language that so engaged readers of Nicholls's first work has been toned down in this new edition, the encyclopedia nevertheless remains an outstanding resource in the area of science fiction.

644. Watson, Noelle, and Paul E. Schellinger. **Twentieth-Century Science-Fiction Writers.** 3d ed. Chicago, St. James Press; distr, Gale, 1991. 1016p. index. $123.00. ISBN 1-55862-111-3.

More than 600 English-language science fiction writers are profiled in Watson and Schellinger's update of Curtis Smith's highly regarded bio-bibliography. Entries contain detailed biographical information, a critical analysis of major works, and a full listing of each writer's science fiction and other book publications. The essays are signed and run about 1,000 words in length. Although the primary focus of the work is on English-language writers, a number of foreign authors have also been profiled.

The other standard work in this subject area, *Science Fiction Writers: Critical Studies of the Major Authors from the Early Nineteenth Century to the Present Day* (E. F. Bleiler, ed. Scribner's, 1982. 623p. $95.00. ISBN 0-684-16740-9), examines 76 notable science fiction authors—primarily contemporary writers—from a perspective of thematic analysis and critical evaluation. Whereas Smith's work surveys a much broader range of writers, Bleiler's brings together detailed and judicious literary assessments of the genre's most noteworthy authors.

POETRY

645. Chevalier, Tracy. **Contemporary Poets.** 5th ed. Chicago, St. James Press, 1991. 1179p. index. $135.00. ISBN 0-558-62035-4.

Eight hundred of the most prominent poets currently writing in the English language are featured in *Contemporary Poets*. Each entry includes a summary of biographic data; a full bibliography covering the poet's own works as well as major critical works published by the poet; a signed critical essay by a senior critic; and, whenever possible, the poet's own comments on his or her works. In addition to the main entries, *Contemporary Poets* provides a listing by title of all poems included in the main body of the work; an appendix treating deceased, major post-war poets; an explanatory note on poetic movements current in the 1980s; and a selection of major poetry anthologies.

646. Hazen, Edith P., ed. **The Columbia Granger's Index to Poetry.** 10th ed. New York, Columbia University Press, 1993. 2150p. $199.00. ISBN 0-231-08408-0.

First published 90 years ago, *Granger's* remains the standard work for those attempting to locate English-language poems (or those translated into English) in anthologies. The work is organized into indexes that provide access by title, first line, author, and subject; a list of anthologies with their symbols is included as well. The more than 100,000 poems that make up this tenth edition are drawn from about 400 anthologies, including some 150 that are new to the tenth edition. Although expensive, most libraries will want to purchase this standard resource. Also available on CD-ROM.

A related publication is *The Columbia Granger's Dictionary of Poetry Quotations* (Edith P. Hazen, ed., Columbia University Press, 1992, 1132p., $99.00, ISBN 0-231-07546-4), which includes quotations selected from the 4,000 most-anthologized poems (as drawn from the same 400 volumes on which *Granger's Index* is based). Arrangement is alphabetical by poet, and alphabetical by title under each name. Nearly 700 poets spanning history and nationalities are included, although English-language poets predominate. Subject and keyword indexes make up more than half the volume.

647. Kalasky, Drew. **Poetry Criticism**. Detroit, Gale, 1987- . Annual. 1v. $83.00/v. (1994 ed.). ISSN 1052-4851.

Each annual volume of *Poetry Criticism* provides critical excerpts and biographical information on 8 to 10 major poets drawn from all eras (for example, Robert Burns and Wallace Stevens). Entries include an introductory biographical sketch of the poet, excerpts of a wide variety of critical analyses of major poems, and sources for additional reading. Comments from the poets themselves and excerpts from interviews are included when available. Title, author, and nationality indexes conclude the volumes.

648. Preminger, Alex, and T. V. F. Brogan, eds. **The New Princeton Encyclopedia of Poetry and Poetics**. 3d ed. Princeton, NJ, Princeton University Press, 1993. 1383p. $125.00; $29.95pa. ISBN 0-691-3271-8; 0-691-2123-6pa.

Like the first edition (1965) of this standard reference, the third edition is an authoritative and scholarly encyclopedia. International in scope, it is intended for anyone "interested in the history of any poetry in any national literature of the world, or in any aspect of the technique or criticism of poetry." Terms used in criticism are defined, including some used in prose and in the fine arts; articles on individual poets or poems and allusions are omitted. As in previous editions, its more than 1,000 articles are thoughtful, clearly written, and accessible to the lay reader.

Preminger has also produced a somewhat abbreviated and updated version of the *Encyclopedia* at a lower cost, *The Princeton Handbook of Poetic Terms* (1986, 309p., $44.50; $12.95pa. ISBN 0-691-06659-0; 0-691-01425-6pa.). It includes 402 entries on poetic forms, prosody, rhetoric, genre, and topics such as poetry reading and the relationship of linguistics to poetry.

SHORT STORIES

649. **Short Story Index: An Index to Stories in Collections and Periodicals.** Bronx, NY, H. W. Wilson, 1974- . Annual. 1v. $90.00/yr. (1994 ed.). ISSN 0360-9774.

This publication indexes short stories published in collections or in periodicals indexed for Wilson's *Readers' Guide* or *Humanities Index* in the preceding year. Using a single-alphabet approach, the work indexes entries by author or editor's name, title of story, and subject. There are numerous cross references, and in addition to the index entries *Short Story Index* also offers a list of indexed collections, a directory of periodicals cited, and a directory of publishers and distributors. In addition to the annual volume, Wilson publishes numerous multiple-year cumulative indexes at varying prices.

NATIONAL LITERATURE

United States

Bibliographies

650. Gerhardstein, Virginia Brokaw. **Dickinson's American Historical Fiction.** 5th ed. Metuchen, NJ, Scarecrow, 1986. 368p. index. $35.00. ISBN 0-8108-18667-1.

Since 1956, *Dickinson's* has been a first stop for individuals wishing to use fiction to bring American history to life, either for themselves, their students, or their children. This basic annotated bibliography classifies more than 3,000 novels published from 1917 to 1984, plus a few older standard titles in American history, into chronological periods beginning with colonial times and continuing through the turbulent years of the 1960s and 1970s. A separate section lists individual, family, social, economic, biographical, and autobiographical works, and other chronicles of larger time periods. Extensive author/title and subject indexes round out the bibliography.

651. Newby, James Edward. **Black Authors: A Selected Bibliography.** New York, Garland, 1991. 720p. index. $80.00. ISBN 0-8240-3329-9.

The more than 3,000 entries in Newby's comprehensive bibliography chronicle significant writings by African-Americans published between 1773 and 1990. (There are also works by several writers who are African and Caribbean but are living or publishing in the United States.) The bibliography is divided into nine chapters categorized by subject or genre, for example, history, juvenile literature, and auto-biographies. Some entries are briefly annotated, but many are not. Title and author indexes.

For works on African-American women writers, there are a number of good choices. Two of the best are Casper LeRoy Jordan's *A Bibliographical Guide to African-American Women Writers* (Greenwood Press, 1993, 387p., $65.00, ISBN 0-313-27633-1), which covers about 900 creative writers, biographers, essayists, and critics whose works range chronologically from the 18th-century poet Lucy Terry to today's notable writers; and *Black American Women in Literature: A Bibliography, 1976 through 1987* (Ronda Glikin, McFarland, 1989, 251p., $35.00, ISBN 0-89950-372), which identifies some 4,300 works published between 1976 and 1987 by and about 300 Black American women writers.

652. Ruoff, A. LaVonne Brown. **American Indian Literatures: An Introduction, Bibliographic Review, and Selected Bibliography.** New York, Modern Language Association, 1990. 200p. index. $45.00, $19.75pa. ISBN 0-87352-187-0; 0-87352-188-9pa.

Ruoff has created a highly readable bibliographic essay on oral and written works produced by American Indians. The three sections of the work are an intro-duction to American Indian literature, a bibliographic review of the major works on the subject, and a selected bibliography of works about American literature (though not necessarily by Native Americans).

653. Zimmerman, Marc. **U.S. Latino Literature: An Essay and Annotated Bibliography.** Chicago, MARCH/Abrazo Press, 1992. 156p. $10.95pa. ISBN 1-877636-01-0.

Zimmerman's book is a critical-historical study of U.S. Latino literature, with its lengthy bibliographic annotations distributed among seven categories. An initial essay addresses U.S. Latino culture, the history and development of Latino literature in the United States, and a review of the models and theories that drive present-day critical approaches to Latino literature. The bibliographic entries follow. These are grouped under Chicano literature, U.S. Puerto Rican literature, U.S. Cuban literature, Latino-tending U.S. Latin American writing, Latino children and young adult books, Chicanesque literature, and secondary materials. With its comprehensive coverage and thoughtful detailed annotations, Zimmerman's work will be a valuable resource for all libraries.

Biographies

654. Baechler, Lea, and A. Walton Litz, eds. **African American Writers.** New York, Scribner's, 1991. 544p. index. $95.00. ISBN 0-684-19058-3.

This volume presents 34 critical essays on the lives and works of African-American writers (both men and women) from Olaudah Equiano to Alice Walker. The articles are written by established scholars and offer not only bio-bibliographical data but also some original literary criticism. Each essay includes a discussion of the author's life and contributions to literature, as well as some treatment of literary reception and a selected bibliography of primary and secondary works. An authoritative work that is sufficiently well written to also be an engaging read.

655. Bruccoli, Matthew J., and Richard Layman, eds. **Contemporary Authors: Bibliographical Series. Volume 1: American Novelists.** Detroit, Gale, 1986. 431p. index. $115.00. ISBN 0-8103-2225-0.

This series is yet another spin-off from Gale's Contemporary Authors undertaking. Focusing on writers of a particular nationality and genre, each volume is designed to complement the biographical portraits found in the Contemporary Authors series. The *American Novelists* volume covers 10 major American writers: James Baldwin, John Barth, Saul Bellow, John Cheever, Joseph Heller, Norman Mailer, Bernard Malamud, Carson McCullers, John Updike, and Eudora Welty. For each, a subject expert has provided a primary bibliography listing works by the author; a secondary bibliography listing bibliographies, biographies, interviews, and critical studies; and a lengthy bibliographic essay comparing and evaluating the critical material. Although this is a fairly expensive work for coverage of only 10 writers, one can easily argue that the authors included are probably among the most-studied by contemporary American literature students.

A related title is Ronald Baughman's *Contemporary Authors Bibliographical Series. Volume 2: American Poets* (Gale, 1986, 387p., $115.00, ISBN 0-8103-2226-9), which focuses on 11 major post-World War II poets: John Berryman, Elizabeth Bishop, James Dickey, Robert Hayden, Randall Jarrell, Robert Lowell, Howard Nemerov, Charles Olson, Theodore Roethke, Anne Sexton, and Richard Wilbur.

656. **Concise Dictionary of American Literary Biography.** Detroit, Gale, 1987–1989. 6v. illus. index. $70.00/v.; $380.00/set. ISBN 0-8103-1819-9 (v.1); 0-8103-1821-0 (v.2); 0-8103-1824-5 (v.3); 0-8103-1820-2 (v.4); 0-8103-1822-9 (v.5); 0-8103-1823-7 (v.6); 0-8103-1818-0 (set).

The six volumes in this outstanding set are *Colonization to the American Renaissance, 1640–1865; Realism, Naturalism, and Local Color, 1865–1917; The Twenties, 1917–1929; The Age of Maturity, 1929–1941; The New Consciousness,*

1941–1968; and *Broadening Views, 1969–1988.* Among them, they provide biographical and critical information for 200 of America's most noteworthy and influential writers. Although updated and revised as appropriate, the essays are essentially reprints (rather than excerpts or condensations) of those found in the larger work on which the six-volume set is based, Gale's *Dictionary of Literary Biography*, now up to 135 volumes ($120/v.). The concise version is geared to meet the needs of students, school libraries, and smaller public libraries; consequently, the individuals profiled are those considered to be "most frequently studied in high school and college literature courses." Information provided for each includes the subject's life, work, and a critical evaluation.

657. Kanellos, Nicolas, ed. **Biographical Dictionary of Hispanic Literature in the United States: The Literature of Puerto Ricans, Cuban Americans, and Other Hispanic Writers.** Westport, CT, Greenwood Press, 1989. 357p. index. $49.95. ISBN 0-313-24465-0.

This work profiles 50 contemporary Puerto Rican, Cuban, Central American, and South American novelists, poets, and dramatists. (Mexican-American authors have been excluded on the assumption that they are thoroughly covered in other resources.) Arrangement is alphabetical by name; the signed entries include a two-to three-page biographical sketch, an overview of major themes in the writer's works, a brief review of criticism, and a listing of works by and about the writer. In addition to the profiles, the dictionary also offers an overview of Puerto Rican and Cuban America/Cuban exile literature, a three-page general bibliography on Hispanic literature in the United States, an author-title index, and a list of contributors. Although obviously a very selective overview of those working in this dynamic literary area, the *Biographical Dictionary of Hispanic Literature* provides a good starting point for further exploration and study.

658. Kunitz, Stanley J., and Howard Haycraft, eds. **American Authors 1600–1900: A Biographical Dictionary of American Literature.** Bronx, NY, H. W. Wilson, 1938. 846p. $72.00. ISBN 0-8242-0001-2.

Now in its eighth reprinting (1977), this standard title provides biographies of nearly 1,300 authors whose work influenced the development of American literature from the first English settlement at Jamestown through the close of the 19th century. Entries range in length from 150 to 2,500 words and include selective bibliographies of works by and about the author in question. The text is supplemented by about 400 portraits.

659. Levernier, James A., and Douglas R. Wilmes, eds. **American Writers before 1800: A Biographical and Critical Reference Guide.** Westport, CT, Greenwood Press, 1983. 3v. index. $295.00/set. ISBN 0-313-22229-0.

Perhaps the most important strength of this authoritative and scholarly work is its thorough coverage of lesser-known early American writers. Among the 786 writers profiled in the dictionary's biographical/critical overviews, students will find information not only on the period's major literary lights (e.g., the redoubtable Cotton Mather), but also on many less-publicized writers, such as Anthony Benezet and Gilbert Imlay. The signed entries provide primary bibliographical references to the author's publications, a brief but thoughtful biography that considers influential factors in the individual's life, a critical appraisal of the writer's works, and a list of selected readings. Separate appendixes list the writers by date of birth, place of birth, and primary residence, while a fourth appendix offers a chronology of the era. A 40-page index rounds out the dictionary.

660.   Mainiero, Lina, ed. **American Women Writers: A Critical Reference Guide from Colonial Times to the Present.** New York, Frederick Ungar, 1979–1983. 4v. index. $380.00/set. ISBN 0-8044-3150-7.

American Women Writers has gained recognition as an indispensable source of bio-bibliographical and critical information about the contributions more than 1,000 American women have made to this country's literary heritage. Scholarly and thoughtful, the entries are arranged alphabetically by author, range in length from one to four pages, and include a selective bibliography of recommended resources. If price is a constraint, however, a good alternative is the abridged edition (same title as the four-volume set) edited by Langdon Lynne Faust (1983, 1988, 899p., $59.50, ISBN 0-8044-3157-4).

Although certainly in need of updating (coverage ranges from colonial times through the mid-1970s), this set should be considered an important purchase for all libraries. For more recent coverage, libraries will want to purchase Lea Baechler and A. Walton Litz's *Modern American Women Writers* (Scribner's, 1991, 583p., $95.00, ISBN 0-684-19057-5), a collection of excellent essays on 41 20th-century writers, from Frances Ellen Watkins Harper (1825–1911) to Alice Walker. The essays, averaging about 14 pages in length, are comprehensive, thoughtful, critical surveys of the writers' lives and works.

Dictionaries and Encyclopedias

661.   Perkins, George, Barbara Perkins, and Phillip Leininger, eds. **Benet's Reader's Encyclopedia of American Literature.** New York, HarperCollins, 1991. 1176p. $45.00. ISBN 0-06-270027-8.

Encompassing Canada, the United States, and Latin American, *Benet's Reader's Encyclopedia of American Literature* comprises thousands of signed articles that range from brief identifications to extensive surveys—the latter treating major and minor authors, concepts, individual works, and more. Examples of lengthier essay entries include Native American poetry and prose, Jewish-American literature, children's literature, and motion pictures. Although cross references are adequate, the lack of an index detracts from the work's ease of access.

Handbooks

662.   Hart, James D. **The Oxford Companion to American Literature.** 5th ed. New York, Oxford University Press, 1983. 896p. $49.95. ISBN 0-19-503074-5.

A joy for librarians as well as all other lovers of American literature, this standard reference tool presents dictionary-style entries on an amazingly broad range of topics of relevance to the study and enjoyment of American letters. It contains biographies of American authors with lists of their major writings (including comments on style and subject matter); descriptions of significant novels, poems, stories, and essays; definitions of literary societies, magazines, anthologies, and literary awards; and discussions of social, economic, aesthetic, political, and scientific topics that have shaped American action and thought over the past four centuries. In addition to the main entries, the compendium also provides a parallel-column chronology detailing the social history and cultural events that provided the backdrop to the writers' works.

The Oxford Companion to American Literature should be considered a key purchase for all libraries. However, those unable to afford it have a good alternative choice in its sibling publication, *The Concise Oxford Companion to American*

Literature (Oxford University Press, 1986, 497p., $30.00, $15.95pa., ISBN 0-19-503982-3, 0-19-504771-0pa.). *Concise* offers about 2,000 alphabetically arranged entries that include brief biographies of authors and summaries and critiques of their works, definitions of literary terms, overviews of literary schools and movements, and similar information. Particular emphasis has been placed on more recent authors. The chronological index (1577–1974) has been included, along with the wealth of cross references so helpful in the unabridged publication.

663. Magill, Frank N. **Magill's Survey of American Literature.** North Bellmore, NY, Marshall Cavendish, 1991. 6v. illus. index. $389.95/set. ISBN 1-85435-437-X.

Nearly 200 noteworthy American authors from the 17th to the late 20th centuries are profiled in this Magill survey, which treats writers of long and short fiction, poetry, drama, and nonfiction. Coverage includes Native American, African-American, Asian-American, Hispanic, immigrant, and women writers, as well as authors of young adult, science fiction, detective, and western stories. The work is organized to support ready-reference inquiries. Entries, arranged alphabetically by author's name and averaging several pages in length, present information in three sections: biography, analysis (the author's style, themes, and literary characteristics), and an overview of the writer's major work (organized chronologically within genres). Each entry concludes with a paragraph summary of the writer and his or her position within the American literary arena, and an unannotated bibliography of five to ten titles.

664. Magill, Frank N. **Masterpieces of African-American Literature.** New York, HarperCollins, 1992. 593p. index. $40.00. ISBN 0-06-270066-9.

This Magill survey features critical summaries of 149 literary works by 96 African-American authors from the 18th century to the present. Works include novels, plays, poetry, short stories, biographies, autobiographies, and essays; authors include such notables as Maya Angelou, James Baldwin, Malcolm X. W. E. B. Du Bois, Alice Walker, and Alex Haley. Averaging 2,500 words in length, summaries offer brief analyses of stylistic devices such as themes, characters, and settings, and place the studied work in its literary and historical context. Author and title indexes provide access.

665. Magill, Frank N. **Masterplots II: American Fiction Series.** Englewood Cliffs, NJ, Salem Press, 1986. 4v. index. $365.00/set. ISBN 0-89356-456-7.

Another of the ubiquitous Masterplots sets, *American Fiction Series* provides plot digests of 383 titles not found elsewhere in the Masterplots family. In this work, according to the editors, "along with summarization of plot, narrative devices are often explored and characterization studied in more depth than [in other Masterplots series] ... . In addition, the major themes of the novel at hand are identified and analyzed, and the overall success of the author's effort is usually discussed in an interpretive summary." The scope is quite broad, encompassing the entire 20th century through 1985 both in this country and in Latin America. The 198 authors treated include 53 women, 32 Black Americans, and 34 Latin Americans; unfortunately, there is only negligible coverage of Canadian writers. As usual, a good starting point for students, who should be encouraged, entreated, and cajoled to explore further.

666. Salzman, Jack, ed. **The Cambridge Handbook of American Literature.** New York, Cambridge University Press, 1986. 286p. bibliog. $29.95. ISBN 0-521-30703-1.

With roughly 750 brief, alphabetically arranged entries, this Cambridge handbook is an authoritative, informative guide to American writers, literary movements, and magazines. Entries include brief plot summaries, overviews of literary movements, concise biographies, and explanations of a multitude of literary terms encountered in the exploration of the American literary tradition. A chronology of American history and American literature are presented side-by-side, and a selective bibliography of important critical works published during the 50-year period prior to 1983 round out the handbook. This work makes an excellent complement to the *Oxford Companion to American Literature*, and most libraries will want to own both.

British

667.   **Concise Dictionary of British Literary Biography.** Detroit, Gale, 1992. 8v. illus. index. $65.00/v.; $410.00/set. ISBN 0-8103-7981-3 (v.1); 0-8103-7982-1 (v.2); 0-8103-7983-X (v.3); 0-8103-7984-8 (v.4); 0-8103-7985-6 (v.5); 0-8103-7986-4 (v.6); 0-8103-7987-2 (v.7); 0-8103-7988-0 (v.8); 0-8103-7980-5 (set).

This eight volumes in this outstanding set are *Writers of the Middle Ages and Renaissance Before 1660*; *Writers of the Restoration and 18th Century, 1660–1789*; *Writers of the Romantic Period, 1789–1832*; *Victorian Writers, 1832–1890*; *Late Victorian and Edwardian Writers, 1890–1914*; *Modern Writers, 1914–1945*; *Writers After World War II, 1945–1960*; and *Contemporary Writers, 1960–Present*. Among them, they provide biographical and critical information for 200 of Britain's most noteworthy and influential writers. Although updated and revised as appropriate, the essays are essentially reprints (rather than excerpts or condensations) of those found in the larger work on which the eight-volume set is based, Gale's *Dictionary of Literary Biography*, now up to 135 volumes ($120.00/v.). The concise version is geared to meet the needs of students, school libraries, and smaller public libraries; consequently, the individuals profiled are those considered to be "most frequently studied in high school and college literature courses." Information provided for each includes the subject's life, work, and a critical evaluation.

668.   Drabble, Margaret, ed. **The Oxford Companion to English Literature.** 5th ed. New York, Oxford University Press, 1985. 1155p. $49.95. ISBN 0-19-866130-4.

Intended to be "quite precisely a reader's companion to English literature" since its first publication in 1932, no more felicitous companion could be wanted than this delightful guide through the vast and varied pages of English letters. It provides detailed, engaging biographies of some 3,000 authors born before 1939, giving special attention to 20th-century authors; offers thoughtful overviews of tried-and-true genres (e.g., detective fiction) as well as more contemporary trends (structuralism); and explains the influence of various classical and foreign authors and artistic movements on English literature. Drabble's personal love of English literature permeates the work, transforming it from a dry reference suitable only for the most determined of English scholars into a true companion-in-arms, ready to join in the next literary adventure at a moment's notice.

669.   Kirkpatrick, D. L., ed. **Reference Guide to English Literature.** 2d ed. Chicago, St. James Press, 1991. 3v. index. $295.00/set. ISBN 1-55862-078-8.

Covering all time periods, the second edition of *Reference Guide to English Literature* focuses on prominent English-language writers from Great Britain, Ireland, Canada, Australia, New Zealand, Africa, Asia, and the Caribbean. The 894 alphabetically arranged author entries found in volumes 1 and 2 range in length from

300 to 1,500 words and include critical overviews of the author's writings. Volume 3 contains signed essays (i.e., critical, contextual analyses) on approximately 570 English novels, poems, plays, short stories, and other works judged by the editors to be "the best-known works in English literature." Volumes 1 and 2 include alphabetical and chronological lists of all authors treated, and volume 3 concludes with a title index to all primary publications cited in the author bibliographies. Each index entry also notes the genre, author, and date of the work.

Canadian

670. ECW's Biographical Guide to Canadian Novelists. Toronto, ECW Press, 1993. 252p. illus. $25.00pa. ISBN 1-55022-151-5.

This work and its companion, *ECW's Biographical Guide to Canadian Poets* (1993. 282p., $25.00pa., ISBN 1-55022-152-3), provide a good introduction to Canadian literary figures. *Novelists* identifies 49 individuals, *Poets* 48. Each biographee merits a short essay that notes birth date and place, career highlights, awards, and important works. Arrangement is chronological by period of literary endeavor. Although each of the guides could be improved with an overall index and a general bibliography for further reading and study, they nevertheless offer a good starting point for those just beginning to explore Canadian literature studies.

671. Toye, William, ed. **The Oxford Companion to Canadian Literature.** New York, Oxford University Press, 1983. 843p. $60.00. ISBN 0-19-540283-9.

The 750 signed entries that make up this guide to Canadian literature range from short bio-bibliographies to lengthy essays on both English- and French-language literary works. Although the primary focus is on contemporary literature, coverage is also provided for early eras of Canadian literature. Arranged in dictionary format, the compendium offers broad coverage of such topics as ethnic, period, and regional literatures; foreign writers in Canada; religion and theology themes; notable literary works and magazines; and critical assessment. Entries run from less than a page to several pages in length. A list of contributors and their affiliations is provided at the beginning of this handy reference.

Other National Literatures

There are many excellent guides to the various national literatures that, taken together, reflect the universal human experience. Depending on patron and community interest, the following titles might also be good resources to have on hand.

Arabic: *Modern Arabic Literature* (Roger Allen, comp. and ed. Ungar/Crossroad/Ungar/Continuum, 1987, 370p., $75.00, ISBN 0-8044-3024-1).

Australian: *The Oxford Companion to Australian Literature* (William H. Wilde, Joy Hooton, and Barry Andrews, Oxford University Press, 1985, 1991, 760p., $59.00; $29.95pa., ISBN 0-19-554233-9; 0-19-553273-2pa.).

Chinese: *The Indiana Companion to Traditional Chinese Literature* (William H. Nienhauser, Jr., and others, eds., Indiana University Press, 1986, 1050p., $75.00, ISBN 0-253-32983-3).

French: *The Oxford Companion to French Literature* (Sir Paul Harvey and J. E. Heseltine, comps. and eds., Oxford University Press, 1959, 1984, 771p., $55.00, ISBN 0-19-866104-5); *Guide to French Literature: 1789 to the Present* (Anthony Levy, St. James Press; distr., Gale, 1992, 884p., $115.00, ISBN 55862-086-9).

German: *The Oxford Companion to German Literature* (2d ed., Henry Garland and Mary Garland, eds., Oxford University Press, 1986, 1020p., $55.00, ISBN 0-19-866139-8); *A Companion to Twentieth-Century German Literature* (Raymond Furness and Malcolm Humble, Routledge, Chapman, & Hall, 1991, 305p., $49.95, ISBN 0-415-01987-7).

Japanese: *The Princeton Companion to Classical Japanese Literature* (Earl Miner, Hiroko Odagiri, and Robert E. Morrell, Princeton University Press, 1985, 570p., $55.00; $18.95pa., ISBN 0-691-06599-3; 0-691-00825-6pa.); *John Lewell's Modern Japanese Novelists: A Biographical Dictionary* (Kodansha America, 1993, 497p., $50.00, ISBN 4-7700-1649-2).

Latin American: *Handbook of Latin American Literature* (David William Foster, comp., Garland, 1992, 799p., $95.00; $18.95pa., ISBN 0-8153-0343-2; 0-8153-1143-5pa.).

Spanish: *The Oxford Companion to Spanish Literature* (Philip Ward, ed., Oxford University Press, 1978, $55.00, ISBN 0-19-866114-2).

Russian and Eastern European: *Handbook of Russian Literature* (Victor Terras, ed., Yale University Press, 1985, 558p., $24.95pa., ISBN 0-300-04868-8; Robert B. Pynsent and S. I. Kanikova's *Reader's Encyclopedia of Eastern European Literature* (HarperCollins, 1993, 605p., $50.00, ISBN 0-06-270007-3).

23

MUSIC

GENERAL WORKS

Bibliographies

672. Duckles, Vincent H., and Michael A. Keller. **Music Reference and Research Materials: An Annotated Bibliography.** 4th rev. ed. New York, Schirmer Books/Macmillan, 1994. 740p. index. $39.95. ISBN 0-02-870822-9.

An exhaustive bibliography, *Music Reference and Research Materials* contains 3,074 entries noted for the completeness of their citations and the authoritative, analytical nature of their annotations. Topical coverage is most complete for those areas of interest to the serious-minded musicologist (be it graduate student, researcher, or librarian), while somewhat scanty for more "popular" interests. The arrangement is first by format (catalogs, dictionaries, discographies, etc.), then by specific topic under format. Entries are presented alphabetically by author within these subdivisions. An extensive—if less than consistent—index concludes this music reference standard.

Biographies

673. **Baker's Biographical Dictionary of Musicians.** 8th ed. Revised by Nicolas Slonimsky. New York, Schirmer Books/Macmillan, 1992. 2115p. $125.00. ISBN 0-02-872415-1.

This delightful and informative biographical dictionary offers some 13,000 entries (ranging in length from a few lines to a few pages) that encompass a broad range of individuals who have contributed to music through the centuries. Composers, conductors, scholars, performers, educators, and librarians can all be found among those profiled and/or pilloried in Slonimsky's opinionated entries. Coverage extends to contemporary musicians as well as those of historical standing, and popular musicians are not slighted.

Although an unwieldy tome that would greatly benefit from a two-volume format, Baker's remains a key resource for ready-reference work. However, for libraries in need of a less expensive alternative, there is *The Concise Baker's Biographical Dictionary of Musicians* (8th ed., Nicolas Slonimsky, Schirmer

Books/Macmillan, 1993, 1407p., $50.00, ISBN 0-02-872416-X), which offers about half the entries of the parent volume. Focus in *Concise* is on the most important musicians; for those individuals, the entries have been provided nearly intact from the eighth edition (1992) of the main work.

674.   Ewen, David. **American Songwriters**. Bronx, NY, H. W. Wilson, 1987. 489p. illus. index. $64.00. ISBN 0-8242-0744-0.

American Songwriters describes 146 composers and lyricists and, between them, more than 5,500 songs. Although coverage extends from the early 19th century through contemporary times, the bulk of the material is devoted to those who rose to fame during the 1920s through the 1950s. Portraits and brief bibliographies accompany the articles. A song index is included; there is, however, no performer index. This work is an update and revision of Ewen's *Popular American Composers* (1962) and its supplement (1972), so libraries that relied on those two works will find *American Songwriters* an important addition to their music collections.

Now deceased, Ewen was known as an authoritative and prolific author of musical reference works, and libraries that can afford them may want to also add to their collection two of his other biographical guides: *Great Composers, 1300–1900: A Biographical and Critical Guide* (H. W. Wilson, 429p., c1966, 1986, $58.00, ISBN 0-8242-0018-7) and *Composers since 1900: A Biographical and Critical Guide* (H. W. Wilson, 1969, 639p., $65.00, ISBN 0-8242-0400-X; *Supplement 1*, 1981, 328p., $45.00, ISBN 0-8242-0664-9). Both provide informative profiles of the world's most noteworthy composers, including lists of principal works by and about each of them.

675.   LaBlanc, Michael L. **Contemporary Musicians: Profiles of the People in Music**. Detroit, Gale, 1983- . Irregular. 1v. $63.00/v. (1994 ed.). ISSN 1044-2197.

Each new volume of *Contemporary Musicians* profiles about 85 musical artists from all genres, including pop, rock, rap, jazz, rhythm and blues, folk, New Age, country, gospel, and reggae. The musicians' entries provide vital statistics, detailed biographical source information, critical essays, photographs, personal sidelights, selected discographies, and, occasionally, addresses. Photographs accompany each profile. The work is indexed by both musician's name and subject.

Dictionaries and Encyclopedias

676.   Cohen, Aaron I. **International Encyclopedia of Women Composers**. 2d ed. New York, Books & Music (USA), 1987. 2v. illus. $130.00/set. ISBN 0-9617485-2-4.

Nearly 6,200 composers—who also happen to be women—are described in this valuable reference work. Drawing from historical through contemporary times and from throughout the countries of the world, Cohen provides birth and death dates, place of birth, education, areas of specialization, musical compositions, and a list of references for each composer. In addition, the encyclopedia offers a wealth of supplementary materials: composers arranged by country, century, instrument, and occupation; a list of operas by women; compositions influenced by Shakespeare; pseudonyms; a discography of LPs; an extensive bibliography; and myriad other bits and pieces of useful information.

677. Kennedy, Michael. **The Oxford Dictionary of Music.** New York, Oxford University Press, 1985. 824p. $49.95. ISBN 0-19-311333-3.

The bulk of the 11,000 entries in this single-volume musical reference are devoted to biographical profiles, although musical terms and specific works have also been included. Coverage is especially strong for contemporary composers and performers. The dictionary-style entries are arranged alphabetically, facilitating easy use for its intended audience of music lovers, concert- and opera-goers, and ready-reference librarians. A good complement to *Norton/Grove* (entry 680).

678. Morehead, Philip D., with Anne MacNeil. **The New American Dictionary of Music.** New York, E. P. Dutton, 1991. 608p. illus. $24.95. ISBN 0-525-93345-X.

By being quite brief in its hundreds of definitions, this dictionary manages to gather an incredible breadth and quantity of musical information within its pages. Despite its title, coverage is nearly universal (both geographically and chronologically). Readers will find short entries on such topics as specific instruments, terms, and people (composers, impresarios, and performers) from music history and classical, folk, and popular music, plus extended entries for the more important concepts, names, or instruments (for example, "fugue," "Haydn," "Benny Goodman," "pianoforte"). Translations are provided for non-English terms, and a glossary of musical terms in English, French, Italian, and German completes the work. A perfect resource for ready-reference questions.

679. Randel, Don Michael, ed. **The New Harvard Dictionary of Music.** Cambridge, MA, Belknap Press/Harvard University Press, 1986. 942p. illus. $37.50. ISBN 0-674-61525-5.

Leaving biographies to the other major music reference works, *New Harvard Dictionary of Music* chooses instead to focus its nearly 6,000 articles on all other aspects, terms, and subjects of music. Randel and his 70 contributing scholars have done an excellent job of presenting their information in a manner that is easily understand by the work's intended audience: music lovers, musicians, teachers, students, and librarians. Entries range in length from a few sentences to (occasionally) a few pages, although the majority are brief, dictionary-style treatments. Some 220 instrument drawings and 250 musical examples supplement the text. A must purchase for all libraries.

680. Sadie, Stanley, and Alison Latham, eds. **The Norton/Grove Concise Encyclopedia of Music.** New York, W. W. Norton, 1988. 850p. illus. $40.00. ISBN 0-393-02620-5.

The wonderful, monumental, and very expensive *New Grove Dictionary of Music and Musicians* (6th ed., Stanley Sadie, ed., Grove's Dictionaries of Music, 1980, 20v., $2,300/set, ISBN 0-333-23111-2) will always be first choice for those libraries fortunate enough to be able to afford its budgetary and shelf-space requirements. However, for small and many medium-sized libraries, a good alternative is Sadie's *Norton/Grove Concise Encyclopedia of Music*, which uses the *New Grove* as its primary source of information. Intended for music lovers and students, the encyclopedia provides about 10,000 brief entries for composers, performers, instruments, musical terms, genres, musical works, music publishing, instrument makers, acoustics, and non-Western music. In addition, there are extended entries for such major topics as criticism, opera, and the symphony. Line drawings for families of instruments and selective lists of works for major composers are also included. Although similar in scope to *The Oxford Dictionary of Music* (entry 677), the two works are complementary rather than competitive.

Directories

681. Rabin, Carol Price. **Music Festivals in America.** Stockbridge, MA, Berkshire Traveller Press, 1990. 286p. illus. bibliog. index. $10.95pa. ISBN 0-930145-01-1.

The festivals described in Rabin's handy reference for musically inclined travelers are arranged into six categories: classical, opera, jazz, pop, folk, and country. Within these categories, the festivals are arranged by state. Each festival's description includes its location and approximate date, origin and development, the types of music performed, where to write for tickets, and information on local accommodations, restaurants, public transportation, and points of interest.

682. **Songwriter's Market, [yr.]: Where & How to Market Your Songs.** Cincinnati, OH, Writer's Digest Books, 1979- . Annual. 1v. illus. index. $19.95 (1994 ed.). ISSN 0161-5971.

Using a directory-style format, this popular annual provides insiders' insights and practical information on how and where to place songs in more than 2,000 song markets. Each listing includes current submission requirements and tips from the buyer. In addition, articles and interviews explore the business side of songwriting and focus on trends in the songwriting industry. Separate sections list organizations of interest to songwriters as well as contests, competitions, and workshops.

Discographies

683. Erlewine, Michael, Scott Bultman, and Stephen Thomas Erlewine, eds. **All Music Guide: The Best CDs, Albums & Tapes.** San Francisco, Miller Freeman, 1992. 1176p. index. $19.95pa. ISBN 0-87930-264-X.

As the popularity of CDs continues to grow, the importance of collection development tools such as this work will also. Its goal is to provide a guide to the 23,000 "best" recordings in all formats—cassette, vinyl, and compact disc—from a database of 100,000, reviewed by music writers or others with expertise in the field. Arrangement is by music genre, beginning with rock, pop, and soul and ending with jazz. In between are listings for rap, blues, country, classical, Christmas, children's, women's, and gay music. Within genres, entries are arranged by artist or composer, each of whom is given a short biography, followed by a listing of the best recordings with the date of release and a short comment on each. Symbols by selected album titles indicate either a landmark recording, an essential collection, or a recommendation that this be a first purchase of a particular artist.

Handbooks and Yearbooks

684. Arnold, Denis, ed. **The New Oxford Companion to Music.** New York, Oxford University Press, 1983. 2v. illus. $135.00. ISBN 0-19-311316-3.

The focus of this well-known work is succinct factual entries for composers and their works, opera synopses, musical terms, and important musical institutions. Also included are more expansive articles that address theory, form, style, aesthetics, instruments, acoustics, and musical notations; suggestions for further reading and cross references to related articles are appended. Coverage ranges from the earliest known music through contemporary times, and embraces both Western and non-Western musical experiences. Black-and-white photographs, line drawings, and musical examples supplement the text.

Librarians should also consider acquiring a spin-off publication, the well-received *Oxford Companion to Musical Instruments* (Anthony Baines, 1992, 404p., $35.00, ISBN 0-19-311334-1). Intended for the general reader, *Musical Instruments* consists of short articles for individual concepts, techniques, and instruments; families of instruments; and characteristic groupings of instruments. Although emphasis is on European instruments, those from non-Western cultures have been included as well. Entries range from a sentence or two to the 12 pages devoted to the organ. In addition to its engagingly written text, the work is heavily illustrated with drawings and photographs.

685. Fuld, James J. **The Book of World-Famous Music: Classical, Popular and Folk.** 3d ed. New York, Dover Publications, 1985. 714p. index. $15.95pa. ISBN 0-486-24857-7.

This reasonably priced paperback provides the history of a large number of our most popular melodies. For each, Fuld identifies the composer and lyricist, date of first publication, and salient or simply interesting facts about its use or performers. In addition, he discusses techniques for dating music, a history of foreign currency, copyright (by country), and plate numbers (by selected publishers). A detailed name/title index concludes this versatile work, which will be useful to lay music lovers, professional musicians, and librarians alike.

686. Reed, W. L., and M. J. Bristow, eds. **National Anthems of the World.** 8th ed. London, Cassell; distr. Sterling, 1993. 561p. $75.00. ISBN 0-304-34218-1.

By now a familiar reference for librarians, *National Anthems of the World* presents about 180 anthems, including those of countries newly independent in the mid-1980s as well as new or revised anthems of countries already established during this period. The arrangement is alphabetical by country. The words and music are printed for voice and piano, with non-English lyrics translated and printed as text following the music. Lyricists and composers are named, and brief historical statements note the date the piece was adopted as a national anthem.

FORMS AND PERIODS

Classical

687. **Best Rated CDs: Classical [yr.].** Voorheesville, NY, Peri Press, 1992- . Annual. 1v. $19.95pa. (1994 ed.). No ISSN available.

Best Rated CDs is based on information found in the publisher's *CD Review Digest*, published quarterly as well as in annual compilations. The purpose of the guide is to provide information (in the form of reviews excerpted from 38 music magazines) about the best classical music CDs published within a given year. Although the quality and value of the reviews are somewhat inconsistent, and the work's arrangement into eight broad categories rather than by composer makes finding specific pieces a bit problematic, it is hoped that future editions may correct these shortcomings, resulting in a very useful resource. With these caveats, this reasonably priced guide can be recommended as a handy checklist for updating classical CD collections. Peri Press also publishes a similar annual for jazz and popular music.

688. Rosenberg, Kenyon C. **A Basic Classical and Operatic Recordings Collection on Compact Discs for Libraries: A Buying Guide.** Metuchen, NJ, Scarecrow, 1990. 375p. index. $39.50. ISBN 0-8108-2322-5.

An outstanding collection development tool for all public libraries and their musically inclined patrons, Rosenberg's buying guide is distinguished by a valuable introductory essay on musical criticism, its highly opinionated (and engaging) descriptions, and a rating system that indicates core purchases for all libraries, purchases for medium-to-large public libraries, and purchases recommended only for academic and large public libraries. The work describes roughly 1,200 recordings from more than 600 composers, providing for each all the data necessary for ordering except—surprisingly—price. Arrangement is by type of music, with composers listed in the table of contents; good cross-referencing and an index provide alternative access points.

Folk, Country, and Western

689. Miller, Terry E. **Folk Music in America: A Reference Guide.** New York, Garland, 1986. 424p. index. $40.00. ISBN 0-8240-8935-9.

Miller's wide-ranging guide encompasses some 1,900 scholarly articles, books, doctoral dissertations, and even important encyclopedia articles related to the study of American folk music. Within nine broad subject chapters, the materials are arranged by topical category (e.g., the music of American Indians and Eskimos, Anglo-American folksongs and ballads, instruments and instrumental music, and singing school and shape-note traditions). Entries note author, title, publisher or journal, date, and pagination. Annotations are brief (one or two sentences) and descriptive; titles published from the 1950s through the mid-1980s predominate. Author and subject indexes conclude the guide.

690. Roland, Tom. **The Billboard Book of Number One Country Hits.** New York, Billboard Books/Watson-Guptill, 1991. 584p. illus. index. $19.95pa. ISBN 0-8230-7553-2.

This book documents the shift over the past 21 years from the Nashville Sound to Urban Cowboy to the present "New Traditionalism," especially the flow of new artists in the 1980s that became a flood in 1986. Like its sibling, Fred Bronson's *The Billboard Book of Number One Hits* (entry 699), each entry presents the story behind the song, along with listing song title, artist, writer, producer, date song became number one, and weeks spent in that position. In addition to a large number of cross references, there are author and song-title indexes.

691. Sandberg, Larry, and Dick Weissman. **Folk Music Sourcebook.** New York, Da Capo, 1989. 260p. $16.95pa. ISBN 0-306-80360-7.

This reasonably priced work offers an excellent survey of American folk music, from both scholarly and popular vantage points. Sandberg and Weissman chart the industry's origin and development; describe the instruments used; define terms likely to be encountered; and identify important and lesser-known folk music artists, recordings, books, magazines, associations, retail outlets, and film archives. A good introduction and overview for those interested in this aspect of American music.

Jazz and Blues

692. **Best Rated CDs [yr.]: Jazz, Popular, Etc.** Voorheesville, NY, Peri Press, 1992- . Annual. 1v. $19.95pa. (1994 ed.). No ISSN available.

Best Rated CDs is based on information found in the publisher's *CD Review Digest*, published quarterly as well as in annual compilations. Criteria for selection in *Best Rated CDs* include notice by at least two reviewers and an award for excellence from at least one. Along with excerpts from reviews and a list of honors and awards, a rating of 1 to 5 stars is assigned to each recording as a general indication of its level of recognition. Arrangement is by broad category: blues, jazz, pop/rock, and show music. Peri Press publishes a similar annual for classical music, *Best Rated CDs: Classical* (entry 687).

693. Feather, Leonard G. **Encyclopedia of Jazz.** New York, Da Capo Press, c1960, 1984. 527p. $19.95pa. ISBN 0-306-80214-7. **Encyclopedia of Jazz in the Sixties.** c1966, 1986. 312p. $14.95pa. ISBN 0-306-80263-5. **Encyclopedia of Jazz in the Seventies.** c1976, 1987. 393p. $16.95pa. ISBN 0-306-80290-2.

Feather's jazz series remains an unsurpassed resource for biographical information. The first of these biographical dictionaries covers jazz from its beginnings through the mid-1950s, the second from 1956 through 1966, and the last from 1967 through 1975. Entries for each musician provide name/nickname, instruments played, birth date, key dates in school and career, compositions, albums released, primary influences, favorite performers and recordings, and critical commentary (often using quotations from the subject, other musicians, or reviewers). Each volume leads off with a thoughtful essay on the state of jazz by a well-known artist, and includes, in addition to the main entries, more than 350 black-and-white photographs, listings of jazz organizations and record companies, poll results from the leading jazz magazines, and filmographies, discographies, and bibliographies. Although obviously in need of an "eighties" edition, this series should nevertheless be considered an important acquisition for all libraries.

Another excellent resource for coverage of jazz musicians is *Jazz Lives: 100 Portraits in Jazz* (Gene Lees, Firefly Books, 1992, 216p. $39.95, ISBN 1-895565-12-X), which incorporates Lees's valuable insights, based on his personal acquaintance with his subjects, into the biographical profiles of such jazz luminaries as Benny Carter, Dave Brubeck, Bill Challis, Bill Holman, and the Modern Jazz Quartet.

694. Kernfeld, Barry, ed. **The Blackwell Guide to Recorded Jazz.** Cambridge, MA, Basil Blackwell, 1991. 474p. index. $29.95; $15.95pa. ISBN 0-631-17164-9; 0-631-18531-3pa.

This book is intended to "suggest a starter collection" of jazz recordings selected from "among the first and best of jazz." Authoritative writers have selected 125 records, tapes, or compact discs from 11 stylistic categories, ranging from "The First Hot Bands" to the latest fusion. Within categories, contributors present an overview of the style and a discussion of recommended recordings, including discographical information. A valuable addition to the reference literature on recorded jazz.

695. Oliver, Paul, ed. **The Blackwell Guide to Blues Records.** Cambridge, MA, Basil Blackwell, 1991. 347p. index. $15.95. ISBN 0-631-18301-9.

This work combines a historical overview of blues music with a guide to the best blues recordings in 12 categories. Each chapter details a particular style of blues or a specific time period. Following Oliver's excellent opening chapter, the remaining 11 chapters chronicle the evolution of the blues, including "Piano Blues and Boogie-Woogie," "Rhythm and Blues," "Down-Home Postwar Blues," "Louisiana, New Orleans and Zydeco," and "Soul Blues and Modern Trends." Within each chapter, an expert contributor lists 10 "essential" recordings and then another 30 "basic" recordings.

Both a history lesson and a recording overview, Oliver's reasonably priced guide is an important part for all music reference collections. It is perfectly complemented, however, by a much less scholarly work, *The Down Home Guide to the Blues* (Frank Scott and the staff of Down Home Music, A Capella Books; distr., Independent Publishers Group, 1991, 250p., $14.95pa., ISBN 1-55652-130-8), which is based on the inventory of Down Home Music, one of the largest mail-order retail suppliers of blues recordings. Including more than 3,500 entries drawn from 12 years' worth of the company's sales catalogs, this guide is essentially a cumulative catalog of records, cassettes, and CDs that were commercially available at press time. Citations are divided into two sections that cover individuals and groups (arranged alphabetically) and anthologies. Entries include brief historical and/or evaluative overviews plus informed annotations. In addition, to help the novice collector, there is a selection of 100 recordings deemed "essential."

Opera

696. Harewood, Earl of, ed. **The Definitive Kobbe's Opera Book.** New York, Putnam, 1987. 1404p. illus. index. $39.95. ISBN 0-399-13180-9.

Three hundred operas—considered those which an English or American traveling opera goer would be likely to encounter at home or abroad—are described in this standard musical reference tool. The venerable Lord Harewood completely revised the 1987 edition to reflect more current trends and changing tastes in the world of opera performance; thus, many lesser-known works by composers such as Verdi, Prokofiev, and Walton are newly included, while others have been dropped. The book is organized into three historical periods: 1600–1800, the 19th century, and the 20th century. These sections are then organized into either country- or composer-specific chapters, under which the operas themselves appear. For each opera, *Kobbe's* provides dates, places, and cast members of premieres and important revivals; a list of characters and their vocal parts; and a detailed plot synopsis with critical comments as appropriate. A concluding index provides access by opera title, composer, librettist, opera company, and various other opera-related topics. Long considered the premiere opera reference.

697. Larue, C. Steven, ed. **International Dictionary of Opera.** Detroit, St. James Press/Gale, 1993. 2v. illus. index. $250.00/set. ISBN 1-55862-081-8.

Assuming that few small libraries can afford the landmark *New Grove Dictionary of Opera* (Stanley Sadie, ed., Grove's Dictionaries of Music, 1992, 4v., $850.00/set, ISBN 0-935859-92-6), the next best bet is Larue's *International Dictionary of Opera.* Its stated goal is to provide "students, teachers, researchers, and opera enthusiasts with a comprehensive source of biographical, bibliographical, and musicological information on people and works important to the history and development of opera." It accomplishes this goal admirably, and is especially strong in its honest and objective coverage of performing artists past and present. Composer entries include a complete list of compositions, with librettist and premiere information attached, and striking illustrations are used generously throughout the text.

For libraries unable to afford this two-volume set, a good alternative would be *The Oxford Dictionary of Opera* (John Warrack and Ewan West, Oxford University Press, 1992, 782p, $40.00, ISBN 0-19-869164-5). Among its 4,500 entries are included 750 composer sketches; 600 opera entries with all relevant cast, premiere, synopsis, and performance details; and 900 performing-artist biographies.

698. Lazarus, John. **The Opera Handbook.** Boston, G. K. Hall, c1987, 1990. 242p. illus. index. $25.00; $15.95pa. ISBN 0-8161-9094-1; 0-8161-1827-2pa.

Especially useful for the opera novice, this handbook successfully approaches what can be an exceedingly dry topic with warmth and wit. The material is arranged by country or region; within sections, an introductory chapter explores the area's unique operatic history and contributions. Entries for individual operas contain plot summaries and brief discussions that concentrate on the operas' characters, musical idioms, and links to other composers and titles. Suggestions for further reading and listening are noted when appropriate. The concluding section, "The Databank," provides a glossary, a list of opera books, information sources by country (e.g., opera magazines, opera companies, and video sources), and a short guide to major opera singers.

Popular Music

699. Bronson, Fred. **The Billboard Book of Number One Hits.** 3d ed. New York, Billboard Books/Watson-Guptill, 1992. 822p. illus. index. $21.95pa. ISBN 0-8230-8298-9.

Bronson's *Number One Hits* gives the stories behind the songs for all the number one pop and rock hits on the *Billboard* charts, starting with July 1, 1955 (Bill Haley's "Rock around the Clock") and ranging all the way to Vanessa Williams's performance of "Save the Best for Last" (number one on March 21, 1992). In addition to the main entries on the individual songs, the book provides a wealth of lists, such as most number one songs by writer, most weeks at number one by artist and by song, and lists of the biggest jumps to number one (the Beatles' "Can't Buy Me Love," from 27 to 1). One of the best books on rock and pop music available, with excellently written entries and comprehensive coverage of the most popular songs and performers of the last 40 years.

700. Clarke, Donald, ed. **The Penguin Encyclopedia of Popular Music.** New York, Viking Penguin, 1989. 1378p. index. $19.95pa. ISBN 0-14-051147-4.

Clarke has attempted a truly daunting undertaking here—namely, documenting the lives and careers of the popular musicians, songwriters, and producers working from the 1930s through the 1980s. The resulting 3,000 entries also include information on such things as significant record labels and popular musical trends. Entries for bands or individual musicians discuss careers, give birth dates, highlight hit records, and recommend material for further reading. Entries about popular musical trends discuss the origins of the style, define its characteristics, and name prominent artists in the field. Entries about record labels describe the companies' histories and note well-known performers who recorded for the various labels. A thorough index and an appendix listing distributors of hard-to-find records round out the encyclopedia.

701. Gammond, Peter. **The Oxford Companion to Popular Music.** New York, Oxford University Press, 1991. 739p. index. $45.00; $19.95pa. ISBN 0-19-311323-6; 0-19-280004-3pa.

Intended as the definitive guide to popular music, this *Oxford Companion* comprises hundreds of articles that cover the history, styles, and important people involved in American, English, and European popular music. Readers will find information on jazz, the blues, ragtime, country, music hall music, operetta, rhythm and blues, brass, military, and folk music here, as well as biographical entries for major composers, singers, librettists, performing artists, band leaders, conductors, and pop groups. In addition, the work covers clubs, impresarios, music publishers, and the plots and favorite songs of famous films and shows. Access to the alphabetically arranged entries is enhanced by abundant cross references and three comprehensive indexes listing people and groups, shows and films, and albums.

702. Havlice, Patricia Pate. **Popular Song Index.** Metuchen, NJ, Scarecrow, 1975. 933p. $59.50. ISBN 0-8108-0820-X. **First Supplement.** 1978. 386p. $37.50. ISBN 0-8108-1099-9. **Second Supplement.** 1984. 530p. $59.50. ISBN 0-8108-1642-3. **Third Supplement.** 1989. 879p. $59.50. ISBN 0-8108-2202-4.

Approximately 300 anthologized song books published between 1940 and 1972, and covering folk songs, hymns, popular music, children's songs, and other types of popular music, are indexed in *Popular Song Index*. The first supplement indexes another 72 anthologies published primarily between 1970 and 1975; the second supplement covers 156 books published mainly from 1974 through 1981 (but including a few books dating back to the 1950s); the third supplement indexes another 181 published through 1986. Each book presents a bibliographic listing of the books indexed, followed by a dictionary arrangement of song titles, first lines of songs, and first lines of choruses. Cross references are included when appropriate. A composer/lyricist index concludes the index.

703. Lax, Roger, and Frederick Smith. **The Great Song Thesaurus.** 2d ed. New York, Oxford University Press, 1989. 774p. $85.00. ISBN 0-19-505408-3.

Few reference books have engendered the kind of reader loyalty this engaging and informative work has. Authors Lax and Smith provide information about more than 11,000 titles ranging from the 16th century through 1987. New to the second edition were about 150 song listings from the years 1980 to 1987, as well as a section on lyric key lines (memorable lines found in the middle of the song). Otherwise, the arrangement has remained the same: the greatest songs by period or year from the Elizabethan era to 1986, with commentary; the award winners by year for both film and theater; themes, trademarks, and signatures; elegant plagiarism; song titles (alphabetical); British song titles (chronological); lyricists and composers; American and British theater, film, radio, and television; and a thesaurus of song titles by subject, keyword, and category. The song's popularity is also noted, including years of popularity, record sales, Hit Parade ranking, and artists who have recorded popular renditions since 1940.

704. Pollock, Bruce, ed. **Popular Music: An Annotated Guide to American Popular Songs ... .** Detroit, Gale, 1985- . Annual. 1v. index. $66.00/v. (1994 ed.). ISSN 0886-442X.

The most comprehensive survey of popular music of the 20th century, *Popular Music* has now become an annual publication that identifies approximately 500 new songs per year. In addition to the annuals, there are three major cumulations: *1900–1919* (1988, 656p, $104.00, ISBN 0-8103-2595-0); *1920–1979* (1985, 3v., 2827p., $270.00, ISBN 0-8103-0847-9); and *1980–1984* (1986, 336p, $81.00, ISBN 0-8103-0848-7). For the series, the works selected for inclusion must have achieved a significant degree of popular acceptance, must have been introduced to the public under especially noteworthy circumstances, or must have been performed by influential musicians and/or dramatic artists. The main body of each of the works is an alphabetical listing by title, followed by composer and lyricist credits; the publisher and date of copyright; and notes relating to performers, recordings, films, and other historical matters. The series now covers more than 20,000 song titles, and includes indexes for lyricists and composers, notable performances, and awards.

705. Robbins, Ira A., ed. **The Trouser Press Record Guide.** 4th ed. New York, Collier Books/Macmillan, 1991. 763p. $20.00pa. ISBN 0-02-036361-3.

The 9,500 records (CDs, cassettes, and a sprinkling of LPs) listed in Robbins's familiar guide are arranged alphabetically by artist or band. Entries include year of release and a signed evaluative review (often quite blunt and/or opinionated) written by one of 46 contributing industry critics. *Trouser Press* is especially useful for identifying changes in a band's personnel, when a specific disc came out, and titles of discs and tracks. Although the guide lacks an index, Robbins has been generous with cross references.

Rock

706. **The Harmony Illustrated Encyclopedia of Rock.** 7th ed. New York, Harmony/Crown, 1992. 208p. $19.00pa. ISBN 0-517-9078-6.

Harmony's biographical dictionary is well written, profusely illustrated, informative, and a good read. It includes hundreds of brief (700 to 1,000 words) entries on today's leading rock musicians, male and female, each accompanied by a color photograph. Entries include (for individuals) country of origin, date and place of birth, real name (if applicable), biographical/career information, and (for groups) original and current line-up of personnel. Especially noteworthy is the inclusion of Peter Frame's 12 "rock family trees," which draw the linkages among various rock groups. Although this publication reflects a noticeable British bias, the work nevertheless is considered the best biographical encyclopedia on rock 'n' roll. It is a good complement to Stambler's similar work (entry 707).

707. Stambler, Irwin. **Encyclopedia of Pop, Rock & Soul.** Rev. ed. New York, St. Martin's Press, 1989. 881p. illus. $35.00; $19.95pa. ISBN 0-312-02573-4; 0-312-04310-4pa.

The bulk of this popular reference comprises biographical essays on artists, promoters, and songwriters. In his more than 500 entries, Stambler has attempted to "reflect all of the pivotal influences in the evolution of today's popular music spectrum" by focusing on the most representative or influential superstars and groups. The alphabetically arranged entries average 800 to 1,000 words; they provide birth date and place, a biographical essay, and selective discographies. Numerous cross references, 157 black-and-white photographs, appendixes listing gold record and Grammy award winners, a list of Oscar nominations and winners in music, and a bibliography documenting Stambler's research supplement the text.

Mythology and Folklore

MYTHOLOGY

708. Bell, Robert E. **Dictionary of Classical Mythology: Symbols, Attributes, & Associations.** Santa Barbara, CA, ABC-Clio, 1982. 390p. $59.00. ISBN 0-87436-305-5.

Bell's handy dictionary, focusing primarily on Greek and Roman mythology, arranges mythological figures according to topic (e.g., wine, repentance); for each, there is a brief description of who they are and what relationship they bear to the subject. Numerous cross references and 16 illustrations accompany the entries. Additional materials include a list of "Surnames, Epithets, and Patronymics" and a "Guide to Persons." This dictionary will be especially helpful to reference librarians attempting to identify allusions for patrons.

709. Bell, Robert E. **Women of Classical Mythology: A Biographical Dictionary.** Santa Barbara, CA, ABC-Clio, 1991. 462p. $59.00. ISBN 0-87436-581-3.

Containing approximately 2,600 names of females associated with Greek and Roman mythology, Bell's biographical dictionary is notable for its discussions of women rarely mentioned in other dictionaries. The entries are engagingly written and include citations to ancient sources, although modern sources are not noted. This is a useful collection of materials for both general and academic audiences, and provides an excellent starting point from which to launch further research.

710. Bulfinch, Thomas. **Bulfinch's Mythology: The Age of Fable; the Age of Chivalry; Legends of Charlemagne.** New York, HarperCollins, 1970. 957p. $22.95. ISBN 0-690-57260-3.

Bulfinch's Mythology is probably the reference best known among students and laypersons interested in mythology. Its coverage of ancient myths and legends is enhanced by numerous well-produced illustrations, plates, and maps. Other supplementary materials include poetry excerpts; an appendix detailing archaeological sites related to myths and legends; and a comprehensive, detailed index that also functions as a dictionary, as each entry is accompanied by a brief definition.

711. Grimal, Pierre. **The Dictionary of Classical Mythology.** New York, Basil Blackwell, 1986. 603p. illus. maps. bibliog. index. $50.00. ISBN 0-631-13209-0.

Originally published in French in 1951, this English translation by A.R. Maxwell-Hyslop is clearly written and engaging to read. It offers variant name spellings, listings of alternate versions of myths, helpful maps, a wealth of attractive illustrations, and 34 pages of genealogical charts. A Concise Dictionary of Classical Mythology (Blackwell, 1990, $34.95, ISBN 0-631-16696-3) offers a good alternative for libraries needing a less expensive choice and willing to forgo the parent publication's photographs, Latin and Greek texts, and index.

712. Jordan, Michael. **Encyclopedia of Gods: Over 2,500 Deities of the World.** New York, Facts on File, 1993. 337p. index. $40.00. ISBN 0-8160-2909-1.

The 2,500 deities profiled by Jordan are from both ancient and contemporary cultures, but exclude figures considered by the author to be demigods, demons, or mythical heroes. Entries are in alphabetical order, rather than by ethnic or cultural group, and each entry notes the modern geographical region in which the deity is recognized. Although the breadth and depth of the entries are based on the perceived significance of the deity under discussion, all entries include the original cultural sources. Also included is the role of the deity in the pantheon and the immediate genealogy. Cross references to other deities are included where deemed appropriate.

713. South, Malcolm, ed. **Mythical and Fabulous Creatures: A Sourcebook and Research Guide.** Westport, CT, Greenwood Press, 1987. 393p. illus. bibliog. index. $49.95. ISBN 0-313-24338-7.

Scholarly in approach but nevertheless engaging to read, Mythical and Fabulous Creatures is organized into two main parts. The first comprises 20 essays, of 10 to 30 pages each, that discuss creatures arranged according to four classifications: "Birds and Beasts" (unicorns, dragons, the phoenix, rocs, griffins, chimeras, and basilisks), "Human-Animal Composites" (manticora, mermaids, sirens, harpies, gorgons/medusas, sphinxes, minotaurs, satyrs, and centaurs), "Creatures of Darkness" (vampires, werewolves), and "Giants and Fairies." Each essay notes the origins of the creature and its treatments in myth, folklore, literature, film, sculpture, and art from classical through contemporary times, and concludes with a three- to four-page bibliography. The second part provides an extensive bibliography, a miscellany of less easily categorized creatures, and a taxonomy of five broad groupings for these creatures. In addition to these two primary sections, prefatory materials include an introduction that defines and classifies the "imaginary creature" and surveys its place in literature and art, and a brief glossary of 63 creatures with accompanying illustrations.

714. Willis, Roy. **World Mythology.** New York, Henry Holt, 1993. 311p. illus. maps. index. $45.00. ISBN 0-8050-2701-7.

More than 500 color photographs, charts, and maps enhance Willis's informative text in World Mythology. The work is organized into two sections. In the first, myths are organized thematically and include such areas as creation, cosmic disasters, supernatural beings, heroes, and tricksters. In the second, the arrangement is by geographical area of origin, including Egypt, the Middle East, Greece, Rome, the Orient, Europe, the Americas, Africa, Australia, and Oceania. Each geographical area's section includes a time chart, a map marking sacred sites and the spread of influence, ruled areas, ornaments appropriate to the country, and other salient information, such as the life of Buddha or a comparative list of the Greek and Roman pantheons. Each major section is divided thematically under headings such as

"Creation," "Gods and Goddesses," or "The Underworld." The volume concludes with an extensive list of books for further reading and a thorough index.

Another good all-around mythology resource, albeit a more expensive one, is Anthony S. Mercatante's *The Facts on File Encyclopedia of World Mythology and Legend* (Facts on File, 1988, 807p., $95.00, ISBN 0-8160-1049-8). This encyclopedia presents more than 3,000 succinct, clearly written entries on the myths and legends of the world. Each entry describes the subject, gives dates and historical facts, and lists works in which the subject appears. Title entries (e.g., *The Odyssey*) merit brief plot summaries, and meanings of names and terms are often included. Supplementary materials include an annotated bibliography of primary and secondary sources, a key to variant spellings that provides direction from the less familiar to the most common spelling, and three indexes: a large general index plus cultural and ethnic ones.

FOLKLORE

715. Evans, Ivor H., ed. **Brewer's Dictionary of Phrase and Fable.** 14th ed. New York, Harper & Row, 1989. 1220p. $35.00. ISBN 0-06-016200-7.

Brewer's includes primarily colloquial and proverbial phrases in a wide range of subjects (archaeology, history, religion, the arts, the sciences, and so forth), as well as biographical and mythological references, fictitious characters, and other hard-to-find information. Both historical and contemporary subjects (Jezebel, glasnost) are to be found among the dictionary's more than 20,000 entries. Definitions are arranged alphabetically in dictionary style, and include the word or phrase's historical and contemporary meanings. In addition to numerous cross references, the 14th edition also includes a selective index that identifies both main entries and cross references. For similar information of a more recent vintage, there is *Brewer's Dictionary of 20th-Century Phrase and Fable* (Houghton Mifflin, 1992, 662p., $30.00, ISBN 0-395-61649-2), which concentrates on "the most evocative and interesting words and phrases" introduced during the 20th century as well as our version of "fables"—the urban legends that have been spun out of the likes of famous murders, military disasters, political scandals, notorious film stars, and other such contemporary fascinations.

716. Ireland, Norma Olin, comp. **Index to Fairy Tales, 1949–1972: Including Folklore, Legends and Myths in Collections.** Metuchen, NJ, Scarecrow, c1973, 1985. 741p. $45.00. ISBN 0-8108-2011-0. **Index to Fairy Tales, 1973–1977.** c1979, 1985. 259p. $29.50. ISBN 0-8108-1855-8. **Index to Fairy Tales, 1978–1986.** 1989. 575p. $49.50. ISBN 0-8108-2194-X. **Index to Fairy Tales, 1987–1992.** Joseph Sprug, comp. 1994. 602p. $59.50. ISBN 0-8108-2750-6.

This index is intended to continue the coverage provided by Mary Huse Eastman's *Index to Fairy Tales, Myths and Legends* (Faxon, 1926; *Supplement*, 1937, 1952), now out of print. The purpose of the series is to assist librarians, teachers, parents, and others who wish to locate a specific fairy tale, legend, myth, or piece of folklore among the many collections published in the United States. There are just over 400 collections indexed in *1949–1972*, 130 in *1973–1977*, 261 in *1978–1986*, and 145 in *1987–1992*. The arrangement is alphabetical by title and subject; the title entry provides the author/title abbreviation symbol that identifies the collection of which it is a part. A separate section—the "List of Collections Analyzed in the Work and Key to Symbols Used"—provides complete bibliographic information for the collections indexed. The work is generously cross-referenced.

717. MacDonald, Margaret Read, ed. **The Folklore of World Holidays.** Detroit, Gale, 1992. 739p. index. $89.00. ISBN 0-8103-7577.

Describing more than 340 festivals and holidays from more than 150 countries and many diverse ethnic groups, *World Holidays* is arranged chronologically according to the Gregorian calendar. Descriptive information is provided for more than 1,800 beliefs, stories, superstitions, proverbs, recipes, games, pageants, fairs, processions, and other lore. Entries range in length from several sentences to several pages, and conclude with a bibliographic notation of sources. The detailed subject index that concludes the book includes ethnic, geographic, and subject entries.

Equally extensive, but local, coverage is provided in a related work, Hennig Cohen and Tristram Potter Coffin's *The Folklore of American Holidays* (2d ed., Gale, 1991, 509p. $89.00. ISBN 0-8103-7602-4), a lively and useful guide to 125 holidays and their associated customs, rituals, stories, and beliefs—the folklore—associated with America's varied set of holidays.

GENERAL WORKS

718. Hubbard, Linda S., and Monica O'Donnell, eds. **Contemporary Theatre, Film and Television.** Detroit, Gale, 1984– . 1v. Annual. $125.00 (1994 ed.). ISSN 0749-064X.

Formerly *Who's Who in the Theatre*, this annual biographical guide covers American and British choreographers, composers, critics, dancers, designers, entertainment executives, producers, and technicians, as well as the standard theater, film, and television performers. There are now 12 volumes in print, providing biographies for nearly 6,000 individuals currently working in the entertainment industry. Entries include birth dates, parental and marriage information, educational data (including professional training), political and religious affiliations, and military service, plus details on writings, recordings, awards and nominations, and memberships. There are both a volume index and a cumulative index in each annual.

719. Loughney, Katharine. **Film, Television, and Video Periodicals: A Comprehensive Annotated List.** New York, Garland. 1991. 431p. index. $50.00. ISBN 0-8240-0647-X.

Loughney's guide annotates more than 1,100 of the most widely used and accessible periodicals devoted to the moving image. International in scope, the work includes serials from the United States and 58 other countries, based on the longevity of their publication and their availability in the United States. Entries are listed alphabetically within country of origin, and include publisher's name, address, and telephone number; frequency of publication; ISSN and OCLC information; span of years during which the periodical has been published; a brief, uncritical content analysis of the publication's scope; its target audience; the nature of its articles; and its Library of Congress and Dewey classification numbers. Nine specialized indexes (e.g., genre, intended audience) conclude this useful bibliography.

720. Palmer, Jean B. **Kliatt Audiobook Guide.** Englewood, CO, Libraries Unlimited, 1994. 237p. illus. index. $34.00pa. ISBN 1-56308-123-7.

Drawing on reviews that appeared in *Kliatt* between January 1990 and November 1993, Palmer has compiled more than 450 signed reviews of recommended fiction and nonfiction audiobooks for personal, business, and educational use. Entries evaluate a broad range of attributes, including narrator's skill, listening level (junior high through adult), quality, depth and scope of content, and associated materials. In addition, those audiobooks considered exceptional are so noted. The reviews are supplemented with topical articles, such as the use and creation of audiobooks as education tools and audiobook collections in libraries; an appendix of audiobook distributors; and indexes that provide access through author/title, narrators and readers, reviewed audiobook subjects, and general subjects.

721. **Words on Cassette [yr.]** New Providence, NJ, R. R. Bowker, 1985- . Annual. 1v. $135.00 (1994 ed.). No ISSN available.

Previously known as the most comprehensive source for spoken-word audiocassettes, *On Cassette* has merged with Meckler's *Words on Tape* to form a new publication, *Words on Cassette*. In its new iteration, the directory provides an annotated list of more than 50,000 recordings of literary, business, historical, political, biographical, and humorous works. Arranged by title, entries identify reader, purchase price, running time, date, contents, live or studio recording, number of cassettes, and rental availability and price. There are author and reader indexes, plus a 124-subject index that repeats all data except content description. The publisher has done a good job of bringing the best of two competing publications into one volume that will be a valuable resource for all libraries.

DANCE

722. Balanchine, George, and Francis Mason. **101 Stories of the Great Ballets.** New York, Doubleday, 1989. 541p. $9.95pa. ISBN 0-385-03398-2.

In 1975 George Balanchine gave us an update of his *Balanchine's New Complete Stories of the Great Ballets* (Doubleday, 1968). This is the most recent iteration of that work. The ballets, presented alphabetically, are divided equally between the older, established favorites (e.g., "Swan Lake") and the most important works debuting between 1968 and 1975. In addition to plot description and occasional critical commentary, each entry notes music, orchestration, choreographer, designers, date and place of premiere, and principal dancers. Although, sadly, Mr. Balanchine's genius is no longer with us, one can only hope that co-author Mason will step forward to update this standard work and keep another part of Balanchine's contribution to the performing arts alive.

723. Bremser, Martha, and Larraine Nicholas, eds. **International Dictionary of Ballet.** Detroit, St. James Press, 1993. 2v. illus. index. $230.00/set. ISBN 1-55862-084-2.

Although a small amount of material is devoted to contemporary dance, the main focus of the *International Dictionary of Ballet* is international coverage of classical ballet as practiced in North America, Europe, and Russia. The work includes biographies of dancers, choreographers, companies, designers, composers, librettists, and teachers. Along with performances, Bremser and Nicholas review dancers, ballet roles, and choreographers' works. Designed to provide access for students, performers, scholars, researchers, and general readers, the compendium lists entries in alphabetical order and includes a generous number of photographs and drawings. The dictionary concludes with a listing of entries by country and by professions and institutions, as well as a separate section giving brief notes on contributors.

724. Koegler, Horst. **The Concise Oxford Dictionary of Ballet.** 2d ed. New York, Oxford University Press, 1982; update 1987. 459p. illus. bibliog. $29.95; $17.95pa. ISBN 0-19-311325-2; 0-19-311330-9pa.

Focusing on the who, what, when, and where of European and American dance, the 5,000 entries that make up this well-known ballet dictionary encompass a time span of some four decades. The brief, alphabetically arranged entries include descriptions of individuals, technical and performance terms, specific ballets, noteworthy events, adaptations from literary works, and nonballet dance forms. Cross references are included where appropriate, and selective bibliographies accompany some of the longer entries.

725. Robertson, Allen, and Donald Hutera. **The Dance Handbook.** Boston, G. K. Hall, c1988, 1990. 278p. illus. index. $25.00; $16.95pa. ISBN 0-8161-9095-X; 0-8161-1829-9pa.

The Dance Handbook is intended as an introductory historical overview of ballet and dance. Its 200 main entries are organized into 8 chronological sections that address romantic, classical, and modern ballet; the Ballets Russes; modern dance; the ballet boom; the dance explosion; and alternative dance (current through Twyla Tharp). Chapters lead off with a two-page introduction, followed by an alphabetical list of the periods' noteworthy choreographers, companies, dancers, and dances. Although all of the major periods and players are adequately represented, the handbook is strongest in its treatment of 20th-century dance. A separate section, "The Databank," provides definitions of terms; a selective list of dance books; information (organized by country) on various dance companies, organizations, magazines, museums, and festivals; and an index.

DRAMA

726. Connor, Billie M., and Helene G. Mochedlover. **Ottemiller's Index to Plays in Collections: An Author and Title Index to Plays Appearing in Collections Published Between 1900 and 1985.** 7th ed. Metuchen, NJ, Scarecrow, 1988. 564p. index. $42.50. ISBN 0-8108-2081-1.

Ottemiller's has long been known as the first place to check when tracking down plays (and especially multiple copies of plays) in collections. The index identifies more than 4,000 plays (by 2,000 playwrights) to be found in roughly 2,000 anthologies. Titles include one-act to full-length plays drawn from all periods, nationalities, cultures, and persuasions, with radio and television dramas occasionally included. An author index, a title index, and a list of analyzed collections provide the access points.

727. **Play Index 1988–1992.** Bronx, NY, H. W. Wilson, 1993. 550p. $80.00. ISBN 0-685-70308-8.

This is the eighth issue of Wilson's respected publication, which indexes English-language (written or translated), published plays for five-year periods. A broad range of dramatic scripts are encompassed, including puppet performances, radio and television plays, and classical Greek drama. A single-alphabet organization interweaves author, title, subject, and "dramatic style" entries for each of the nearly 4,400 plays indexed. Play entries include a brief, descriptive annotation as well as information about the number of acts and scenes, cast size, number of sets, and required dancing or music. In addition, separate sections list plays by the number and sex of cast members needed (men, women, boys, girls); list collections indexed; and provide a directory of publishers and distributors.

For libraries interested in owning all eight of the *Play Index* volumes, the previous publications are: *Play Index 1978–1982* (459p., 1983, $58.00, ISBN 0-685-45835-0); *Play Index 1983–1987* (522p., 1988, $58.00, ISBN 0-685-05422-5); *Play Index 1973–1977* (457p., 1978, $41.00, ISBN 0-685-66661-5); *Play Index 1968–1972* (403p., 1973, $33.00, ISBN 0-686-66660-7); *Play Index 1961–1967* (464p., 1968, $28.00, ISBN 0-686-66659-3); *Play Index 1953–1960* (404p., 1963, $25.00, ISBN 0-686-66658-5); and *Play Index 1949–1952* (239p., 1953, $20.00, ISBN 0-686-66657-7).

728. Salem, James M. **Drury's Guide to Best Plays.** 4th ed. Metuchen, NJ, Scarecrow, 1987. 480p. index. $39.50. ISBN 0-8108-1980-5.

Salem, a well-known drama scholar, has done a thorough job of revising, updating, and expanding this standard reference work. Encompassing plays first performed in ancient Greece through theatrical works performed in the mid-1980s, the fourth edition of *Drury's* surveys approximately 1,500 of the world's "best" plays. Primary organization is alphabetical by playwright, with plays listed within each playwright's entry. Entries for the plays include a brief plot summary, information on the number of acts, male and female cast members, set, text, and royalty payment information. In addition to the main entries, the guide offers a cast index that identifies plays according to the number of characters (from one to more than forty), as well as those that involve all-male or all-female casts; an index of selected topics that arranges the plays according to the subjects they address; a list of award-winning plays; and a list of popular plays for high school and other amateur groups.

729. Trudeau, Lawrence J., and others, eds. **Drama Criticism: Criticism of the Most Significant and Widely Studied Dramatic Works from All the World's Literatures.** Detroit, Gale, 1991- . Annual. 1v. $79.00/v. (1994 ed.). ISSN 1056-4349.

Designed principally for beginning students of literature and theater and for the average playgoer, each annual volume of this drama criticism series covers 10 to 12 important dramatists ranging from Sophocles to Henrik Ibsen to Bertold Brecht. Each author entry includes a biographical sketch, a chronological list of the writer's major works, criticism from major sources on the dramatist's most widely read works, and a bibliography for further research. When movie adaptations exist, they are included. Concluding cumulative author, nationality, and title indexes help significantly in finding specific information about authors, plays, and productions.

FILM AND VIDEO

Dictionaries and Encyclopedias

730. Hunter, Allan, ed. **Chambers Concise Encyclopedia of Film and Television.** New York, Chambers Kingfisher Graham, 1991. 401p. illus. $14.95pa. ISBN 0-550-17253-X.

Hunter's useful resource is based on the idea that television and the film industry, once bitter rivals, are now partners in the entertainment business, each benefiting from the other. Within this context, some 700 technical terms, people, and key films and television programs are described, frequently accompanied by incisive, perceptive annotations. Entries include roughly 400 biographical sketches that have human interest tidbits; about 200 films or television shows, with a brief history of each project, a bit of plot, and the project's critical reception; equipment; and occupational titles (for example, best boy, gaffer, focus puller). Although it lacks an index, the encyclopedia does list winning entries in various film festivals and awards through the years.

731. Katz, Ephraim. **The Film Encyclopedia.** 2d ed. New York, HarperPerennial/HarperCollins, 1994. 1496p. $25.00pa. ISBN 0-06-273089-4.

First published in 1979, this updated edition of Katz's *The Film Encyclopedia* once again may be considered "the most comprehensive encyclopedia of world cinema in a single volume," as claimed in its subtitle. Coverage includes U.S. and foreign actors, directors, screenwriters, composers, producers, cinematographers, film editors, dance directors, and heads of studios, with filmographies included for each. In addition, there are entries for common film terms, film styles, genres, schools of filmmaking, and film-related organizations and studios, as well as a list of Academy Award winners in the major categories from 1927 to 1993.

732. Konigsberg, Ira. **The Complete Film Dictionary.** New York, New American Library, 1987. 420p. illus. $14.00pa. ISBN 0-452-00980-4.

Konigsberg, who occasionally waxes encyclopedic in his treatment of major topics, defines 3,500 terms and phrases drawn from all aspects of motion pictures—their techniques, production, history, criticism, and theory. Entries generally vary in length from single-sentence quickies to paragraph- and page-long definitions; such topics as film, film theory, lighting, sound, and special effects, however, merit multipage articles. All explanations are written in clear, accessible, jargon-free language. Dozens of line drawings further clarify the definitions, and numerous photographs from classic motion pictures are included to illustrate points made regarding film genres and aesthetic techniques. A reliable reference for librarians, film buffs, and the lay reader alike.

733. Slide, Anthony. **The American Film Industry: A Historical Dictionary.** Westport, CT, Greenwood Press, 1986. 431p. index. $55.00; $19.95pa. ISBN 0-313-24693-9; 0-87910-139-3pa.

American Film Industry comprises some 600 entries describing the industry's business organization, industrial techniques, and technology. It includes coverage of producing and releasing companies, technological innovations, film series, genres, organizations, and technical terms. Entries vary in length from a few lines to a few pages, depending on importance of topic. Many include addresses, bibliographies, and lists of repositories of films, photographs, or papers. Numerous cross references, a list of resource libraries and institutions, and a brief bibliography of film history books supplement the text. The work concludes with an index of people, subjects, organizations, and abbreviations.

Directories

734. **Bowker's Complete Video Directory [yr.].** New Providence, NJ, R. R. Bowker, 1990- . Annual. 2v. $205.00/set (1994 ed.). ISSN 1051-290X.

The number of video guides and directories seems to be expanding to reflect the burgeoning interest in this entertainment and information medium. Bowker's entry into the field, basically a *Books in Print* for videos, identifies and describes some

87,000 theatrical and special interest videos. For each, it gives current source and price information, a brief but helpful annotation, full ordering information, and an indication of formats in which the program is available. The two volumes are organized to enable their separate purchase: volume 1, at $99.00, focuses on roughly 35,000 entertainment and performance videos (e.g., movies, cartoons, sports events, concerts, operas); volume 2 ($129.00) covers 52,000 educational and special-interest videos. Volume 1 entries often contain Motion Picture Association of America (MPAA) ratings and important credits; volume 2 entries frequently note public performance rights and availability for rental or preview. In addition to indexes for series, format, and closed caption found in both volumes, the first volume has indexes for cast and director, genre, awards, and Spanish language; the second volume has a subject index that lists titles under 500 broad subject headings. The set also offers a directory of manufacturers and distributors, as well as one for video services and suppliers. Also available on CD-ROM.

The primary competitor to the Bowker *Video Directory* is Gale's annual, *Video Source Book* (2v., $240.00/set [1994 ed.], ISSN 0748-0881). It covers 126,000 videos, with programs arranged alphabetically by title (A–M in volume 1, N–Z in volume 2). For each program, the sourcebook provides technical characteristics, brief descriptions, suggested audience, producer, distributor, and rental/purchase information. A list of program distributors plus subject, credits, videodiscs, 8mm, and captioning indexes are also included. In the best of all worlds, libraries would own both of these complementary directories; however, if budget constraints force a choice between them, the less expensive *Complete Video Directory* should meet most basic needs adequately.

Guides

735. Cella, Catherine. **Great Videos for Kids: A Parent's Guide to Choosing the Best.** New York, Citadel Press/Carol Publishing Group, 1992. 157p. $7.95pa. ISBN 0-8065-1377-2.

The focus of Cella's helpful resource is evaluations of hundreds of animated videos; in fact, no nonanimated movies are included. Reviews are arranged by such categories as book-based, educational, family topics, folk and fairy tales, holidays, instruction, and music; particularly outstanding videos are starred. Entries list producing company, approximate running time, and recommended viewing age, and provide an engaging annotation.

736. Gopen, Stuart. **Gopen's Guide to Closed Captioned Video.** Framingham, MA, Caption Database, 1993. 547p. index. $29.95pa. ISBN 0-9635726-0-1.

Compiled by the father of a deaf child, this work is intended to aid the 26 million hearing-impaired persons in the United States, as well as to assist other potential users such as adults and children learning to read or those learning English as a second language. The guide lists more than 5,000 videos arranged under 23 categories; entries note running time, rating, sources, and price and provide a plot synopsis. For many of the titles in popular categories (e.g., adventure, comedy, horror, romance, and war), Gopen identifies director, stars, and captioning agency. In addition to Hollywood movies, the guide also lists a number of children's, business-oriented, and documentary videos and a handful of instructional, exercise, sports, music, and religious videos. Although much in need of a subject index to enhance access, this work nevertheless is an important purchase for all public libraries.

737. Halliwell, Leslie. **Halliwell's Film Guide.** 7th ed. New York, HarperCollins, 1994. 1312p. illus. $21.00. ISBN 0-06-273241-2.

A mainstay among publications of this sort, Halliwell's guide describes thousands of English-language, feature-length films. Films are listed alphabetically by title. Entries provide country of origin, year of release, running time, whether the film is black-and-white or color, production credits, alternate titles, a synopsis, an assessment, credits (writer, director, photography, music, etc.), cast, comments from critics, additional notes, Academy Awards and nominations, availability on video, and Halliwell's personal rating of the film. An index of alternative titles and a list of English-language titles of foreign films are also included.

Another excellent video guide is Joe Blades's *Viewers' Choice Guide to Movies on Video* (Consumer Reports Books, 1991, 351p., $16.95pa., ISBN 0-89043-476-X). Its 3,500-plus movie ratings are taken from the *Consumer Reports* movie poll, which began in 1947. Those that have earned the highest levels of ratings and are also available on video are listed alphabetically by category. Entries include title, rating, release year, distributor, running time, whether the film is black-and-white or color, directory, cast, and a brief synopsis of plot.

Handbooks and Yearbooks

738. Halliwell, Leslie. **Halliwell's Filmgoer's and Video Viewer's Companion.** 9th ed. John Walker, ed. New York, HarperCollins, 1993. 834p. $60.00; $25.00pa. ISBN 0-06-271570-4; 0-06-273239-0pa.

Since its first publication in 1965, this handbook has contained seemingly a bit of everything a film buff (or reference librarian) could dream of. Entries for actors, writers, producers, directors, cinematographers, major television credits, and about 950 films are here, as well as a delightful interspersing of pithy quotations. In addition, there are about 300 short essays on themes in films and such topics as the Cold War, censorship, and Blacks in film. The main body of the text is followed by alphabetical lists of films, fictional characters and series, themes, variant British/American film titles, and a selective list of some 250 recommended titles on the industry and its players.

739. **Screen World [yr.].** New York, Crown, 1949- . Annual. 1v. illus. index. $19.95 (1994 ed.). ISSN 0080-8288.

Long considered an indispensable chronicle of the American film scene, *Screen World* provides a wealth of data useful to reference librarians and their patrons. Contents include the top 25 box office stars; domestic films released, with full cast and production credits for the more noteworthy films and briefer treatments for the less so; promising new actors; major Academy Awards for the year, accompanied by tabulations for previous years; basic biographical data for performers (real name, place and date of birth, and school attended); obituaries; and an index to names and film titles. Approximately 1,000 black-and-white photographs are interwoven with the text.

Two other annuals that provide complementary coverage to *Screen World* are *International Motion Picture Almanac* (Quigley, 1929- , 1v., $85.00 [1994 ed.], ISSN 0074-7084), which provides more extensive biographical data (including credits); and *Magill's Cinema Annual* (Salem Press, 1982- , $50.00 [1994 ed.], ISSN 0739-2141), which provides plot summaries and critical evaluations of the year's films.

THEATER

Dictionaries and Encyclopedias

740. Packard, William, David Pickering, and Charlotte Savidge, eds. **The Facts on File Dictionary of the Theatre.** New York, Facts on File, 1988. 556p. $35.00; $15.95pa. ISBN 0-8160-1841-3; 0-8160-1945-2pa.

This dictionary sets out to cover the development of world drama from the earliest through contemporary times. In more than 5,000 entries, it provides biographies of performers, playwrights, and figures from all aspects of theater; describes major plays, historical dramatic styles, innovations, and genres; defines technical design terminology; and identifies theatrical companies, schools, and theater organizations. Although the entries are exceedingly brief (35 to 150 words), they provide a good introductory overview of a vast range of theater topics. Although the emphasis is on American and British theater, major European dramatists have been touched on as well. Extensive cross references.

Handbooks and Yearbooks

741. Banham, Martin, ed. **The Cambridge Guide to Theatre.** Updated ed. New York, Cambridge University Press, 1992. 1104p. illus. $24.95pa. ISBN 0-521-42903-X.

Banham's guide is distinguished by its outstanding coverage of all the world's theater, especially that taking place outside Europe and America (for example, in Africa, Asia, Australia, and Latin America). From ancient Japanese drama to West Javanese *sintren* (a trance dance), this Cambridge guide brings hitherto ignored theater topics, practitioners, and traditions into focus. It is equally strong in its treatment of more familiar theater subjects, thus enhancing its utility to an audience that may include students, scholars, and lay readers. The clearly written entries are arranged alphabetically, and include the theater in its historical, contemporary, stage, and televised contexts. Similarly authoritative coverage for the United States is presented in a companion title, Don B. Wilmeth and Tice L. Miller's *Cambridge Guide to American Theatre* (Cambridge University Press, 1993, 547p, $49.95, ISBN 0-521-40134-8), which covers the U.S. theatrical scene from its inception through early 1992.

742. Berney, K. A., ed. **Contemporary Dramatists.** 5th ed. Detroit, St. James Press, 1993. 843p. index. $135.00. ISBN 1-55862-185-7.

The fifth edition of this familiar reference tool includes biographies, bibliographies, and critical essays on nearly 450 living dramatists, including 90 individuals new to this edition. Entries include a brief biography; a complete list of produced or published plays and all other separately published books; the playwright's comments on his or her works, when available; a signed, critical essay; a critical studies list; and information on other published bibliographies and locations of manuscript collections. This work will be useful to both the interested novice and the serious drama scholar.

743. Bordman, Gerald. **The Oxford Companion to American Theatre.** 2d ed. New York, Oxford University Press, 1992. 735p. $49.95. ISBN 0-19-507246-4.

The two outstanding features of this generally excellent reference and its more than 3,000 entries are its large number of biographical profiles not found in other theater resources and the inclusion of nearly 1,000 entries for individual plays, musicals, and revues. For the most part, Bordman has chosen to emphasize detailed but concise factual information rather than provide analytical syntheses or topical overviews. Within these parameters, he has provided a wealth of data sure to warm the hearts and answer the questions of many an American theater buff. For libraries needing a bit less comprehensive (and less expensive) coverage of this topic, *The Concise Oxford Companion to American Theatre* (1987, 451p., $24.95, ISBN 0-19-505121-1), an abridgement based on the earlier (1984) edition of the parent volume, is a good choice.

744. Hartnoll, Phyllis, ed. **The Oxford Companion to the Theatre.** 4th ed. New York, Oxford University Press, 1983. 944p. $55.00. ISBN 0-19-211546-4.

The Oxford Companion to the Theatre has long been considered the best one-volume dictionary treatment of theater throughout the world and throughout history. Coverage includes information on actors, playwrights, directors, set designers, the history of national theater, individual theater companies, important theaters, specific genres, and technical production details. Individual plays are not included. The alphabetically arranged entries are succinct, authoritative, and informative, and are supplemented by 96 black-and-white plates and a guide to further reading. For libraries unable to afford the extensive coverage of this outstanding work, the next best alternative is its reliable abridgement, *The Concise Oxford Companion to the Theatre* (Phyllis Hartnoll and Peter Founds, eds., 1992, 568p., $35.00pa., ISBN 0-19-866136-3).

745. Willis, John. **Theatre World.** New York, Crown, 1944- . Annual. 1v. $25.00 (1993–1994 ed.). ISSN 0082-3856.

A standard performing arts reference tool, *Theatre World* provides complete lists of Broadway, off-Broadway, touring company, and regional theater productions and personnel. Actors, replacements, producers, directors, authors, composers, costume designers, lighting technicians, press agents, and opening and closing dates are all identified for plays presented during each year's season, dated from June 1 through the following May 31. Numerous photographs of the plays and their players and hundreds of short biographies are interspersed throughout. A thorough index concludes the yearbook.

Philosophy and Religion

PHILOSOPHY

746. Angeles, Peter A. **The HarperCollins Dictionary of Philosophy.** 2d ed. New York, HarperPerennial/HarperCollins, 1992. 342p. $25.00; $13.00pa. ISBN 0-06-271564-X; 0-06-561026-8pa.

With the benefit of recency over the other choices in philosophy dictionaries, this work is designed to introduce lay readers and students to the ideas and terminology of philosophy. It comprises more than 3,000 brief definitions of major philosophical concepts, plus a generous number of biographical notes. Rather than being the work of contributors, all the dictionary entries appear to have been written by Angeles, which has resulted in a very uniform style of presentation.

747. Flew, Anthony, ed. consultant. **A Dictionary of Philosophy.** Rev. 2d ed. Jennifer Speake, ed. New York, St. Martin's Press, c1979, 1984. 380p. $13.95pa. ISBN 0-312-20923-1.

Flew's well-organized, easy-to-use dictionary will be useful to both the student and the philosophy scholar. Definitions and a few brief survey articles explain the wealth of terms found in the study of philosophy, its movements, ideas, and key thinkers. Biographical articles ranging up to 4,000 words in length have been included; unfortunately, bibliographies have not.

Flew's dictionary is undoubtedly the best single-volume philosophy dictionary available. However, a strong second choice is A. R. Lacey's *A Dictionary of Philosophy* (2d ed., Routledge & Kegan Paul/Methuen, c1986, 1990, 266p., $15.95pa., ISBN 0-415-05872-4). It contains fewer entries than Flew but often provides more in-depth coverage of the areas that are included. The major advantage of Lacey's dictionary, however, is its excellent and frequently extensive bibliographies. Most libraries will want to have both for reference purposes.

748. Magill, Frank N., ed. **World Philosophy: Essay-Reviews of 225 Major Works.** Ian P. McGreal, assoc. ed. Englewood Cliffs, NJ, Salem Press, 1982. 5v. index. $250.00/set. ISBN 0-89356-325-0.

Another of the Magill family of multi-volume surveys, this set describes virtually all of the famous philosophers and summarizes most of their best-known works. The essays are easily understood by students and lay readers, a clear indication of the contributors' successful efforts to avoid academic jargon and instead focus on accessible meaning. Arranged chronologically from ancient through contemporary times, the essays include reviews of two or three significant commentaries on each work summarized and brief annotated bibliographies of suggestions for further reading. In addition, *World Philosophy* provides both alphabetical and chronological lists of titles, a glossary of common philosophical terms, an author index, and, at the end of volume 5, an index of major works reviewed and an index of recommended readings. An abridgement of this work featuring 100 of the best-known philosophers is available as *Masterpieces of World Philosophy* (Frank Magill, ed., HarperCollins, 1990, 684p., $40.00, ISBN 0-06-016430-1).

RELIGION

General Works

Bibliographies

749. Melton, J. Gordon, and Michael A. Koszegi. **Religious Information Sources: A Worldwide Guide.** Hamden, CT, Garland, 1992. 657p. index. $90.00. ISBN 0-8240-7102-6.

In this major undertaking, the authors have attempted to identify worldwide sources on any given subject area in religion, in whatever form or medium. Thus, sources on Shinto, Taoism, the philosophy of religion, science and religion, church history, Christianity, women and religion, New Age concerns, interfaith dialogs, and a similarly diverse range of topics can be found here. Computer databases are annotated, along with oral histories, CD-ROMs, and professional religious associations. Excellent author, title, subject, and organization indexes are included.

Biographies

750. Bowden, Henry Warner. **Dictionary of American Religious Biography.** 2d ed. Westport, CT, Greenwood Press, 1993. 686p. index. $75.00. ISBN 0-313-27825-3.

The 550 significant American religious figures profiled here all died prior to July 1, 1992. The entries are well written, and are just long enough to summarize the interesting and important facets of the biographees' lives. In addition to a selected general bibliography at the end of the volume, brief biographical references (if available) conclude each article.

Another work of potential interest to libraries is Charles H. Lippy's *Twentieth-Century Shapers of American Popular Religion* (Greenwood Press, 1989, 494p., $85.00, ISBN 0-313-25356-0). The 64 major figures profiled by Lippy include both those directly involved in America's religious life and those who influenced it indirectly. Each entry includes a biography, an assessment of the individual's contribution and importance to the field, a survey of criticism, and a bibliography of writings by and about the person. The writing style is engaging and the commentary astute, making this interesting reading regardless of one's own religious persuasion. A detailed index completes this useful, albeit expensive and narrowly focused, reference.

751. Hinnells, John R., ed. **Who's Who of World Religions.** New York, Simon & Schuster Academic Reference Division, 1992. 560p. maps. index. $75.00. ISBN 0-13-952946-2.

The coverage of Hinnells's ecumenical biographical dictionary ranges from African religions to Zoroastrianism, and includes persons from the mists of legend (for instance, Gilgamesh) to such contemporary religious leaders as the Maharishi Mahesh Yogi, Sun Myung Moon, and Pope John Paul II. Although Christians represent the majority of the entries, the work reflects a conscientious (and successful) effort to provide balance by emphasizing non-Western Christians. Written by religious scholars, entries provide full name, dates, indication of religious subject group, references to the extensive bibliographies, and a biographical sketch. Although expensive, this is a balanced and informative religious resource.

752. Melton, J. Gordon. **Biographical Dictionary of American Cult and Sect Leaders.** New York, Garland, 1986. 354p. index. $50.00. ISBN 0-8240-9037-3.

For the purposes of this dictionary, *sect* is defined as a group engaged in a continuing protest against deficiencies found in a mainline church; a *cult* is a more radical new spiritual option within a culture. To be included here, the individual had to be (1) a founder or major leader of a cult or sect that had (or currently) existed in the United States, and (2) deceased prior to January 1983. Within these parameters, Melton has identified and profiled 213 individuals, arranged alphabetically by name. Each biography includes basic life data, followed by a 300- to 500-word sketch of the person's religious background, experiences, and role in the sect or cult. A brief bibliography of works by or about the individual conclude the profile. In addition to the main entries, there are a list of all individuals included, a detailed index, and three appendixes that list biographees by religious tradition, birthplace, and mainline religious influences. A related work by Melton that libraries may also wish to have on hand is *Encyclopedic Handbook of Cults in America* (rev. ed., Garland, 1992, 407p. $65.00; $18.95pa. ISBN 0-8153-0502-8; 0-8153-1140-0pa.), which provides thorough, unbiased coverage of 33 American cults and sects and their leaders.

Dictionaries and Encyclopedias

753. Bishop, Peter, and Michael Darton, eds. **The Encyclopedia of World Faiths: An Illustrated Survey of the World's Living Religions.** New York, Facts on File, 1987. 352p. illus. (part col.). maps. index. $40.00. ISBN 0-8160-1860-X.

Aimed at students and general readers, this encyclopedia examines religion through six filters: ritual, myth, doctrine, ethics, social, and experiential. The 12 major religions surveyed under these guidelines are Judaism, Zoroastrianism, Christianity, Islam, Babism and the Baha'i Faith, Hinduism, Jainism, Buddhism, Sikhism, Confucianism, Taoism, and Shinto. Articles for each describe the religion's main features from the six aspects noted and include a bibliography and glossary. Separate chapters focus on the general nature of religion, the relevance of religion in the modern world, and "new" (1950s through 1970s) religious movements in modern Western society and among primitive peoples. In addition, eight color sections devoted to the themes of faith and life, gods and gurus, religious leaders, prophets and teachers, death and afterlife, festivals, myths and legends, and life cycles are interspersed throughout the text as visual aids to compare and contrast the practices and beliefs of differing faiths. A generally solid reference, *World Faiths* would greatly benefit from a more detailed and comprehensive index.

754. Crim, Keith, ed. **The Perennial Dictionary of World Religions.** San Francisco, HarperSanFrancisco, 1990. 830p. illus. $26.00. ISBN 0-06-061613-X.

This work, originally published as the *Abingdon Dictionary of Living Religions* (Abingdon Press, 1981), addresses only those religions and religious movements that are practiced throughout the world today. It comprises some 1,600 entries, with longer, signed articles of 7 to 15 pages each for Buddhism, Christianity, Hinduism, Islam, and Judaism. Definitions encompass terminology, persons, places, doctrines and theological concepts, obscure religions and movements, sacred texts, and holy days; pronunciations are provided for appropriate terms. Color maps (8 pages' worth), 150 black-and-white illustrations, an abundance of cross references, and a classified guide to selected entries accompany the main entries. Unfortunately, the index is less than thorough. Even so, this remains a good layperson's reference in an often intimidating subject area.

755. Hinnells, John R., ed. **The Facts on File Dictionary of Religions.** New York, Facts on File, 1984. 550p. illus. maps. index. $40.00. ISBN 0-87196-862-2.

The 1,150 alphabetical entries that make up Hinnells's work focus primarily on the cultural and historical underpinnings of the world's religions: their beliefs and practices, people and places, texts and arts, historical origins, and society and institutions. The bulk of the work is devoted to "living" religions, and includes such diverse movements as astrology, magic, and the occult. Even secular alternatives (e.g., Marxism, existentialism, humanism) find their way into this wide-ranging reference. Varying in length from a few lines to a full column of text, entries define a broad range of words and phrases, including technical terms, general religious concepts, deities, major individual figures, and the vocabularies of specific faiths. Additional materials are a synoptic index that pulls together all the terms demonstrating the facets of a particular faith; scholarly bibliographies for the further study of religion in general and the religions themselves; maps; and a good general index.

756. Melton, J. Gordon, Jerome Clark, and Aidan A. Kelly. **New Age Encyclopedia: A Guide to the Beliefs, Concepts, Terms, People, and Organizations ... .** Detroit, Gale, 1990. 586p. index. $59.50. ISBN 0-8103-7159-6.

Although it is nearly impossible to clearly define (or delimit) what "New Age" encompasses, Melton has made a good attempt here to provide an objective overview of the New Age movement. The encyclopedia leads off with an overview that addresses the history, beliefs, and more important aspects of the movement. The ensuing alphabetically arranged, signed entries cover a broad range of topics, including people, organizations, concepts, beliefs, and opposition to the New Age movement. Cross references, a keyword index, and an appendix that lists educational institutions that offer New-Age related degrees and programs supplement the text.

Directories

757. Melton, J. Gordon. **Directory of Religious Organizations in the United States.** 3d ed. Detroit, Gale, 1993. 728p. index. $125.00. ISBN 0-8103-9890-7.

This work provides contact and descriptive information on 2,489 for-profit and nonprofit organizations headquartered in the United States and engaged in activities for religious purposes. The directory is divided into five sections: the first supplies the main entry information, the next four index the entries by personnel, function (for example, foreign missions, social justice), religious affiliation, and master name/keyword. The main entries found in the first section supply name and address of the organization, chief contact person, telephone and fax numbers, religious affiliation, founding date, size of staff, membership, and mission, goals, purposes, and activities of the organization. When applicable, publications, audio/video, radio and television programs, remarks, and alternate contacts are also noted.

Handbooks and Yearbooks

758. Eliade, Mircea, and Ioan P. Couliano, with Hillary S. Wiesner. **The Eliade Guide to World Religions.** San Francisco, HarperSanFrancisco, 1991. 301p. index. $22.95. ISBN 0-06-0621-45-1.

The last major project of the distinguished religious scholar Mircea Eliade, this guide opens with a brief introduction to religion and its study, followed by 33 alphabetically arranged chapters on major religious traditions, from African religions to Zoroastrianism. More than half of these traditions are from "living religions," actively and somewhat widely practiced today, with Buddhism, Christianity, Islam, and Judaism receiving the most extensive treatment. Although not consistently arranged, most chapters include some history and the essential distinctive features of the particular tradition, and all chapters conclude with bibliographies. A glossary and an annotated subject index round out the guide.

For libraries that would like more extensive coverage of this subject area, an alternative purchase to consider is Ian Harris's *Contemporary Religions: A World Guide* (Longman; distr. Gale, 1992, 511p., $175.00, ISBN 0-582-08695-7). Organized in three parts, the guide offers an overview of key religious traditions (Islam, Christianity, Judaism, etc.) in part 1; more than 750 entries on currently active religious movements in part 2; and, in part 3, a country-by-country, worldwide review that shows the distribution and impact of each religion throughout the world.

Christianity

Dictionaries and Encyclopedias

759. Broderick, Robert C., ed. **The Catholic Encyclopedia.** Rev. ed. Nashville, TN, Thomas Nelson, 1990. 613p. illus. $19.95pa. ISBN 0-8407-3175-2.

Approximately 4,000 alphabetically arranged entries, dealing primarily with Catholic beliefs and practices and ranging in length from 20 to 2,500 words, make up this layperson's encyclopedia. The work includes books and notable persons of the Bible, descriptions of non-Catholic denominations and religions, currently used abbreviations for Catholic organizations, honors and awards, and the more familiar hymns and prayers (often with their words in English). There is very little change (only 35 new articles) in this revision from the 1981 edition; however, most of the changes that have been made are related to changes in the Code of Canon Law promulgated in 1983.

Depending on patron interest, there are several other reference tools that may also be helpful. These include John Deedy's *The Catholic Fact Book* (Thomas More Press, 1986, 412p., $15.95pa. ISBN 0-88347-252-X), a one-volume encyclopedia arranged in seven sections (history, basic tenets, the teaching church, church organizations, saints, modern biography, and dictionary) and containing a diversity of information about church history, beliefs, practices, individuals, events, and documents; James Patrick McCabe's *Critical Guide to Catholic Reference Books* (3d ed., Libraries Unlimited, 1989, 323p., $47.00, ISBN 0-87287-621-7), which describes general works, theology, the humanities, social sciences, and history titles; and

Jovian P. Lang's *Dictionary of the Liturgy* (Catholic Book, 1989, 687p, $9.95, ISBN 0-89942-273-X), intended as a guide to all matters liturgical for the American lay Catholic.

760. Childress, James F., and John Macquarrie, eds. **The Westminster Dictionary of Christian Ethics.** Philadelphia, Westminster Press, 1986. 678p. index. $37.00. ISBN 0-664-20940-8.

A revision of John Macquarrie's *Dictionary of Christian Ethics* (1967), this ecumenical work comprises 620 entries contributed by scholars from the United States, United Kingdom, Canada, and Australia representing Protestant, Anglican, Roman Catholic, Orthodox, and Jewish traditions. The base of contributors was broadened to include not just theologians but also philosophers, lawyers, physicians, and other professionals, to reflect major developments in science, medicine, and health care, among other topics. Traditional ethical concepts are defined, as are biblical ethics from the Old and New Testaments, and theological ethics from major categories such as conscience and natural law. Philosophical traditions such as Aristotelian or Kantian ethics are treated in addition to those of major non-Christian traditions, with coverage of psychological, sociological, and political concepts that affect Christian ethics as well. A name index completes this well-executed work.

761. Cross, F. L., and E. A. Livingstone, eds. **The Oxford Dictionary of the Christian Church.** 2d ed. New York, Oxford University Press, 1974. 1518p. $65.00. ISBN 0-19-211545-6.

This authoritative work is made up of some 6,200 entries (ranging in length from several lines to more than 2,500 words) contributed by 247 subject specialists; 4,500 short bibliographies accompany the entries. Although coverage of American Christianity is not as thorough as might be hoped, the work nevertheless provides the most comprehensive treatment available of the events, people, places, and issues that have shaped the church over the past 2,000 years. A standard purchase for most libraries, regardless of size.

Another alternative in this subject area is *The Westminster Dictionary of Christian Theology* (Alan Richardson and John Bowden, eds., Westminster Press, 1983, 614p., $32.00, ISBN 0-664-21398-7). A revision of the highly regarded *Dictionary of Christian Theology* (1969), this work offers nearly 600 signed articles dealing with a vast range of topics within the broad parameters of biblical, patristic, medieval, Reformation, and modern theology. Roughly three-fourths of the articles include bibliographies; a four-page index of names is also included.

762. Farmer, David Hugh, ed. **The Oxford Dictionary of Saints.** 3d ed. New York, Oxford University Press, 1992. 530p. $13.95pa. ISBN 0-19-283069-4.

Farmer's dictionary aims to identify all the important martyrs and saints of the Christian Church from East and West, a total of more than 1,500 individuals. Entries are arranged alphabetically and range in length from very short (30 words) to essay-length (up to 950 words), depending on the relative obscurity or importance of the saint under consideration. Brief bibliographies accompany all entries. In addition, there are two useful appendixes: the principal patronages of saints and the principal iconographical emblems of the various saints. An index of places in Great Britain associated with particular saints and a calendar of principal feasts of saints venerated on specific days round out the dictionary.

Another alternative in hagiographical references is Donald Attwater's *The Penguin Dictionary of Saints* (2d ed., rev. and updated by Catherine Rachel John, Penguin Books, 1983, 352p., $11.00pa., ISBN 0-14-051-123-7), based on the monumental work originally produced in 1956 by Alban Butler, *Butler's Lives of the Saints* (rev. and suppl. by Herbert Thurston and Donald Attwater, Christian Classics, 1956, 4v., $140.00/set, ISBN 0-87061-137-2). Arranged alphabetically by name, the Attwater work is intended as "a work of quick reference to the lives and legends of notably important and interesting people" among the saints. Despite its tendency toward an English and Irish bias, *The Penguin Dictionary of Saints* provides a reasonably priced complement to *The Oxford Dictionary of Saints*.

763. Reid, Daniel G., ed. **Dictionary of Christianity in America.** Downers Grove, IL, InterVarsity Press, 1990. 1305p. $44.99. ISBN 0-8308-1776-X.

The 2,400 signed articles that make up this resource are intended to provide objective, historical descriptions across a broad spectrum of topics related to the practices of Christian religions in the United States. Denominations, religious movements, ideas, events, traditions, institutions, and biographies are all to be found here, as well as entries on such unusual items as Christian camping and pew rents. Bibliographies accompany many of the articles; numerous cross references are included as well. A useful reference for libraries of all sizes.

Handbooks and Yearbooks

764. Jacquet, Constant H., Jr., ed. **Yearbook of American & Canadian Churches [yr.].** Nashville, TN, Abingdon Press, 1916- . Annual. 1v. index. $29.95pa. (1994 ed.). ISSN 0195-9034.

First published as *Federal Council Year Book,* Abingdon's familiar yearbook provides statistical and other data for more than 250 religious institutions in North America. Information provided for each institution includes names and addresses of headquarters and leadership personnel, geographic and organizational divisions, and brief historical sketches of each denomination. Other sections list theological seminaries, national and international cooperative organizations, service agencies, colleges and universities, and noteworthy periodicals. In addition, a "Calendar for Church Use" notes important events dating three years into the future. A thorough index of topics and church names rounds out the yearbook.

765. Mead, Frank S. **Handbook of Denominations in the United States.** 9th ed. Nashville, TN, Abingdon Press, 1990. 316p. index. $13.95. ISBN 0-687-16572-5.

Mead's handbook sketches the history, doctrines, governance, statistics, and auxiliary institutions of 225 religious groups in the United States. Brief surveys introduce treatments of 16 of the largest religious movements; additionally, there is an "Appendix of Listings" that identifies American Evangelical and Pentecostal groups, a list of denominational headquarters, a glossary, a bibliography, and an index.

Bible Resources

Atlases

766. May, Herbert G., ed. **Oxford Bible Atlas.** New York, Oxford University Press, 1984. 144p. illus. (part col.). $30.00; $16.95pa. ISBN 0-19-143452-3; 0-19-143451-5pa.

This reasonably priced atlas stresses history rather than geography in its black-and-white and color maps. Each map is accompanied by text that relates it to the biblical data and to the wider historical background. In addition, there is an informative, well-illustrated introduction surveying biblical climate and geography considerations and tracing the history of the Israelites from their beginnings in Mesopotamia through the Greek and Roman empires. Further, tables of dates trace the biblical story from the reign of Saul, 1025 B.C., to the fall of Jerusalem in A.D. 70. A very good value for its price.

767. Rasmussen, Carl G. **Zondervan NIV Atlas of the Bible.** Grand Rapids, MI, Zondervan, 1989. 256p. illus. maps. index. $39.95. ISBN 0-310-25160-5.

Stipulating at the outset that information may at times be sketchy or even conflicting, this atlas attempts to depict the historical, archaeological, and geographical details that underlie the biblical stories. Arrangement is geographic and historic, with the latter being the larger. Each section of the historic part leads off with a detailed timeline of events appropriate to the period in question. In addition to being easy to read, informative, and in color, all of the maps are nicely complemented by text that further clarifies the visual information presented. Appendixes include a chronological chart, a bibliography, a brief glossary, scripture and name indexes, and a gazetteer.

Biblical atlases present one of those delightful situations in reference resources where there is a wealth of good materials from which to choose; consequently, for libraries where budget flexibility and patron interest converge to suggest more of an investment in biblical atlases, the massive *Harper Atlas of the Bible* (James B. Pritchard, ed., Harper & Row, 1987, 254p., $49.95, ISBN 0-06-181883-6) is the recommended choice. An incredibly rich presentation of photographs, drawings, and maps, it not only surveys the standard historical eras, but also covers the periods' background details, including color spreads on customs, beliefs, and practices of the times as well as a glimpse into everyday life. Another alternative is the scholarly and highly regarded *Macmillan Bible Atlas* (3d ed., Yohanan Aharoni and others, Macmillan, 1993, 215p., $35.00, ISBN 0-02-500605-3), whose more than 200 maps present a comprehensive overview of biblical history from 3000 B.C. to A.D. 200, emphasizing military and economic events.

Dictionaries and Encyclopedias

768. Achtemeier, Paul J., and others, eds. **Harper's Bible Dictionary.** San Francisco, Harper & Row, 1985. 1178p. illus. (part col.). maps. index. $39.00. ISBN 0-06-069862-4.

The stated goal of this dictionary is to provide "a highly readable, authoritative, and reliable summary of the best of contemporary knowledge about the Bible and the world from which it emerged." The contributors are primarily Protestant and American, although Jewish, Catholic, British, and Israeli scholars have been included as well. Within the parameters of contemporary thought and concerns, the dictionary has successfully striven to objectively present historical and scholarly information derived from new knowledge and discoveries. The basic entries range from one sentence to roughly 500 words; however, major articles on such topics as "Sociology of the Old Testament" or literature may extend to 5,000 words. Bibliographic references are included for the larger articles. Additionally, numerous cross references, 575 illustrations (many in full color), and 91 maps complement the dictionary's 3,700 entries.

Some libraries may also wish to consider the companion volume to this work, *Harper's Bible Commentary* (James L. Mays and others, eds., Harper & Row, 1988, 1326p., $39.00, ISBN 0-06-065541-0). Stressing mainstream biblical scholarship, the commentary covers the biblical story (Genesis to Esther), psalms and wisdom, the prophetic books, the Gospels and Acts, the Pauline letters, and the "General Letters to the Churches." For those seeking other alternatives among bible dictionaries, three titles to consider are the more recent *The Revell Bible Dictionary* (Revell, 1990, 1156p. $29.95, ISBN 0-9220-6651-5), an information-packed work that reflects the authors' and contributors' belief that the Old and New Testaments form a unitary, divinely inspired work; Watson E. Mills's *Mercer Dictionary of the Bible* (Mercer University Press, 1990, 987p. $35.00, ISBN 0-86554-402-6), an authoritative—albeit expensive—students' dictionary that covers books of the Bible, characters, places and geographical features, theological concepts, contemporary history, and culture; and the ecumenical *The Dictionary of the Bible and Religion* (William H. Gentz, ed. Abingdon Press, 1986, 1147p. $18.95, ISBN 0-687-10757-1), which, in roughly 2,800 alphabetically arranged entries ranging in length from 50 to 3,000 words, encompasses an astounding expanse of biblical, Christian, and non-Christian religious topics.

769. Blaiklock, Edward M., and R. K. Harrison, eds. **The New International Dictionary of Biblical Archaeology.** Grand Rapids, MI, Regency Reference Library/Zondervan, 1983. 485p. illus. (part col). maps. index. $34.99. ISBN 0-310-21250-2.

This comprehensive, scholarly dictionary encompasses all facets of the archaeology of Bible places, peoples, and times. More than 800 articles describe cities, sites, persons and peoples, countries, languages, animals, architecture, furniture, and even the science of archaeology (at least 30 articles are devoted to old and new archaeological methods and techniques). Entries range from several columns to 14 pages; most conclude with bibliographies of both English- and foreign-language works. In addition to numerous cross-references, supplementary materials include more than 200 high-quality black-and-white photographs, 28 full-color photographs, 13 adequate black-and-white line maps, plus several other full-color maps that are not as clear or informative as might be hoped.

770. Freedman, David Noel. **Anchor Bible Dictionary.** New York, Doubleday, 1992. 6v. illus. index. $360.00/set. ISBN 0-385-19351-3.

Nearly 1,000 biblical scholars from diverse religious and scholastic backgrounds contributed the 6,200 entries in this landmark work. Coverage includes proper names (person or place) in the Bible, all versions of the Bible, methods of biblical scholarship, and entries on various historical and archaeological subjects. Entries vary in length from a single line to nearly 75 pages, depending on the complexity and/or importance of the topic under consideration, and are written at a level appropriate to an educated lay reader. Almost all articles are signed, and all include well-chosen bibliographies. An excellent purchase for all libraries.

Handbooks

771. Metzger, Bruce M., and Michael D. Coogan, eds. **The Oxford Companion to the Bible.** New York, Oxford University Press, 1993. 874p. maps. index. $45.00. ISBN 0-19-504645-5.

The 700 topical articles found in *The Oxford Companion to the Bible* offer scholarly biblical criticism and historical background on subjects ranging from Aaron to Zion. Introductory material, lists of abbreviations, an index, maps, and a bibliography make this an easily used and understood reference work. Although it includes information about Judaism, Islam, Roman Catholicism, Orthodoxy, and fundamentalism, its orientation leans toward mainstream Protestant theology. Reviewers have correctly noted that coverage of topics is occasionally selective and inconsistent; nevertheless, the *Companion* will still be a good starting point for a vast number of biblical questions.

772.   **Nelson's Quick Reference Bible Handbook.** Nashville, TN, Thomas Nelson, 1993. 383p. $7.99pa. ISBN 0-8407-6904-0.

A revised and enlarged edition of *A Layman's Overview of the Bible* (1987), this handbook is arranged in three parts that reflect the Bible's organization—the Old Testament, the New Testament, and the Apocrypha—plus a fourth part called "Exploring the Bible." Each part is divided into chapters composed of books with similar intent or importance (e.g., books of the law, books of history). In turn, each of these chapters leads off with a brief introduction identifying the books, their basic purposes, and the date line; they then give the reader keys to understanding, accounts of scholarly research on authorship, historicity, theological importance, an outline of contents, and other useful materials. Especially helpful are the summary charts for each book that reflect the book's focus, key references, divisions, topics, locales, and time periods. Although the paperback binding may present problems for heavy reference use, this handbook is nevertheless highly recommended to all public libraries for its reasonable price and wealth of easily understood material.

Buddhism

773.   Prebish, Charles S. **Historical Dictionary of Buddhism.** Metuchen, NJ, Scarecrow, 1993. 387p. $42.50. ISBN 0-8108-2698-4.

The hundreds of concise but informative definitions found in Prebish's dictionary give an excellent sense of the diversity of doctrines and cultures comprising Buddhism. Major historical figures not only from the history of Buddhism but also from the history of Western Buddhist scholarship have been included. A guide to pronunciation, a list of scriptures in the three canonical languages of Buddhism, a chronology of major events in Buddhism, a map showing important Buddhist sites, an excellent 34-page introduction sketching the history of Buddhism, and a 98-page classified bibliography all enhance the reference value of this work; it is to be hoped, however, that the next edition includes an index.

Islam

774.   Glasse, Cyril. **The Concise Encyclopedia of Islam.** San Francisco, San Francisco HarperCollins, 1991. 472p. illus. maps. $24.95pa. ISBN 0-06-063126-0.

Glasse's encyclopedia does a thorough job of explaining the philosophy, metaphysical beliefs, rituals, laws, and observances that together constitute Islamic life. Topics include concepts and beliefs, religious and ritual practices, the law, the calendar, social practices, ethnography, nationhood, languages, history, medicine and the sciences, and major cities and centers of learning. In addition, there are many biographical profiles of Islamic prophets, religious and military leaders, and rulers; quotations from the Koran, prayers, and the Traditions (Hadith); and appendixes that include maps of the pre-Islamic world and the spread of Islam in the modern world, diagrams of the Hajj and the branches of Islam, genealogical tables, and a chronology. Although the book will most likely have to be rebound shortly after purchase, it is nevertheless a useful addition for all libraries.

If budget and patron interest warrant, libraries may also want to consider Farzana Shaikh's *Islam and Islamic Groups: A Worldwide Reference Guide* (Longman; distr., Gale, 1992, 316p, $155.00, ISBN 0-582-09146-2), which focuses less on the religious and more on the political aspects of Islam throughout the world. Country-by-country, it surveys Islam as a political presence in more than 100 countries, considering origins and development, current demographic representation, relationship with the state, and noteworthy political activity in modern times.

Judaism

775. Cohn-Sherbok, Dan. **The Blackwell Dictionary of Judaica.** Cambridge, MA, Basil Blackwell, 1992. 597p. $74.95; $24.95pa. ISBN 0-631-16615-7; 0-631-18728-6pa.

The Blackwell Dictionary of Judaica contains 7,000 well-written, alphabetically arranged entries that together provide an excellent overview of the culture and spiritual underpinnings of the Jewish faith. Although terms derive from many fields of Jewish experience, the work is especially rich in entries for prominent figures and organizations in recent Jewish history. Supplementary materials include a two-page chronology of Jewish history and two maps, one of the ancient Near East and one of ancient Israel. A handy complement to the more extensive encyclopedias on Jewish life and thought.

776. **The New Standard Jewish Encyclopedia.** Rev. ed. New York, Facts on File, 1992. 1001p. illus. (part col.) $59.95. ISBN 0-8160-2690-4.

This authoritative, one-volume reference is composed of 8,000 succinct articles and some 800 photographs and line drawings that describe individuals, settlements, customs, festivals, and other topics (such as Jewish Nobel Prize winners) central to understanding Jewish life and history. It is more comprehensive and its articles are more in-depth than those found in a similarly titled work, Zvi Werblowsky and Geoffrey Wigoder's *The Encyclopedia of the Jewish Religion* (Adama Books, 1986, 415p, $39.95, ISBN 0-915361953391), which is more appropriate to a home or synagogue library.

The standard in this area is, of course, the *Encyclopaedia Judaica* (Jerusalem, Encyclopaedia Judaica; Macmillan, 1972; repr., Coronet Books, 1982. 17v., $895.00/set, ISBN 0-685-36253-1), composed of some 25,000 signed articles and more than 8,000 color and black-and-white illustrations that together provide comprehensive surveys of nearly all aspects of Jewish life, history, and issues. Although somewhat flawed by a less-than-thorough index, this monumental work is recommended for those libraries able to afford both its cost and the requisite shelf space.

777. Entry number not used.

Part IV
SCIENCE AND TECHNOLOGY

General Science and Technology

BIBLIOGRAPHIES

778. Hurt, C. D. **Information Sources in Science and Technology.** 2d ed. Englewood, CO, Libraries Unlimited, 1994. 362p. index. $55.00; $32.00pa. ISBN 1-56308-034-6; 1-56308-180-6pa.

The second edition of Hurt's bibliography covers guides to the literature, abstracts, dictionaries, biographical directories, dissertations, government documents, and literature in the individual disciplines. Descriptive and evaluative annotations define the scope of each work, its intended audience, and special features. Both print and online sources are described for each subject area.

779. Powell, Russell H., ed. **Handbooks and Tables in Science and Technology.** 3d ed. Phoenix, AZ, Oryx Press, 1994. 384p. index. $95.00. ISBN 0-89774-534-5.

Powell's work contains more than 3,000 entries for handbooks and tables drawn from physics, chemistry, engineering, mathematics, astronomy, biology, geology, agriculture, medicine, and dentistry. The focus is primarily on English-language works, with a few German titles included; the bibliography excludes how-to books, dictionaries, encyclopedias, field guides, maps, directories, biographical sources, indexing and abstracting, and current awareness sources. Entries are arranged alphabetically by title, and include full bibliographic data, price, and a summary statement of each publication's content. Author/entry and subject indexes as well as a list of publishers round out the handbook.

780. Walford, A. J., with Marilyn Mullay and Priscilla Schlicke, eds. **Walford's Guide to Reference Material. Volume 1: Science and Technology.** 6th ed. London, Library Association; distr, UNIPUB, 1993. 943p. index. $195.00. ISBN 1-85604-015-1.

The science and technology volume of "Walford" provides descriptions for nearly 7,000 entries in the fields of mathematics, physics, earth sciences, anthropology, natural history, zoology, patents and inventions, engineering, household management, industries, and trades and crafts. Newer topics such as biotechnology, artificial intelligence, robotics, and pollution control are featured as well. Although coverage is international in scope, the works described are primarily English-language. Entries provide full bibliographic citations and a short but comprehensive annotation; no prices are given.

BIOGRAPHIES

781. Aaseng, Nathan. **Twentieth-Century Inventors.** New York, Facts on File, 1991. 132p. illus. index. $16.95. ISBN 0-8160-2485-5.

Twentieth-Century Inventors will lead readers to inventors whose names are not, for the most part, well known, but whose works have dramatically changed the way 20th-century citizens live. Inventors and inventions treated include Leo Baekeland (plastic), Vladimir Zworykin (television), Chester Carlson (xerography), and Wilson Greatbatch (the implantable pacemaker). Aaseng's profiles not only provide insightful information about each inventor's formative years, but also highlight the perseverance, tenacity, and task commitment of each inventor. Although the coverage is broad, unfortunately no women or minority inventors are included.

782. **American Men & Women of Science [yr.]: A Biographical Directory of Today's Leaders in Physical, Biological and Related Sciences.** New Providence, NJ, R. R. Bowker, 1940- . Triennial. 8v. index. $850.00/set (1994 ed.). ISSN 0192-8570.

The 123,000-plus men and women described in this familiar resource are drawn from all the natural science fields in the United States and Canada, with noncitizens included if they have worked in either country for an extended period. Inclusion is limited to the physical and biological sciences, the health sciences, engineering, mathematics, statistics, and computer science. Profiles are based primarily on information provided by the individuals included, and thus reflects the completeness of their responses. A discipline (subject) index is provided in a separate volume. Although an expensive work, especially for smaller libraries, *American Men and Women of Science* does an excellent job of bringing together information valuable in a broad range of circumstances. Also available online, as well as on CD-ROM as part of the publisher's *SciTech Reference Plus* CD-ROM.

783. Asimov, Isaac. **Asimov's Biographical Encyclopedia of Science and Technology: The Lives and Achievements of 1510 Great Scientists from Ancient Times to the Present, Chronologically Arranged.** 2d rev. ed. New York, Doubleday, 1982. 941p. illus. index. $29.95. ISBN 0-385-17771-2.

Scientist/author wunderkind Isaac Asimov wrote many popular works, and this biographical encyclopedia ranks high among them. It provides chronologically arranged biographical profiles for just over 1,500 individuals, focusing primarily on their scientific achievements rather than on their personal lives. Biographies are listed alphabetically in the table of contents; subjects and persons only mentioned in the text can be located through the index. Photographs accompany many of the profiles. For those who particularly enjoy this work, a related reference to consider is Asimov's *Chronology of Science and Discovery* (HarperCollins, 1994, 832p. $35.00. ISBN 0-06-270113-4), which consists of well over a thousand entries starting in 4,000,000 B.C. and concluding in 1993.

784. **Concise Dictionary of Scientific Biography.** American Council of Learned Societies. New York, Scribner's, 1981. 773p. $70.00. ISBN 0-684-16650-X.

Based on Scribner's award-winning, 16-volume *Dictionary of Scientific Biography* (1970–1980, o.p.), *Concise* encompasses all of the 5,000 entries from the original set, but shortens them substantially. The work covers all periods from classical antiquity to the present and draws from more than 90 countries, but includes only deceased scientists.

Another fine alternative for biographies of scientists is the six-volume *The Biographical Dictionary of Scientists*, edited by David Abbott (Peter Bedrick; distr., Harper & Row, 1984–1986, $28.00/v.). The volumes are *Engineers and Inventors* (ISBN 0-87226-009-7); *Mathematicians* (ISBN 0-87226-008-9); *Astronomers* (ISBN 0-87226-008-9); *Biologists* (ISBN 0-911745-82-3); *Chemists* (ISBN 0-911745-81-5); and *Physicists* (ISBN 0-911745-79-3). Each begins with an overview from antiquity to the present, followed by the alphabetically arranged one-half- to two-page biographies. Each volume concludes with a glossary of related scientific terms and a name/subject index.

785. Daintith, John, and others. **Biographical Encyclopedia of Scientists.** 2d ed. Philadelphia, Institute of Physics, 1994. 2v. illus. index. $190.00/set. ISBN 0-7503-0287-9.

Most of the more than 2,000 entries in the well-known *Biographical Encyclopedia of Scientists* are taken from basic sciences such as physics, chemistry, biology, and astronomy, with lesser coverage of medicine, mathematics, engineering, and the social sciences. Ranging from the early Greeks to scientists of current accomplishment, the entries are engagingly written and cover birth and death (if applicable) dates and locations, nationality, major field, and (frequently) personality characteristics and professional controversies. Subject and name indexes complete the encyclopedia.

786. Ogilvie, Marilyn Bailey. **Women in Science: Antiquity through the Nineteenth Century: A Biographical Dictionary with Annotated Bibliography.** Cambridge, MA, MIT Press, c1986, 1990. 254p. index. $14.95pa. ISBN 0-262-65038-X.

Women in Science profiles 186 primarily Western women scientists. Arrangement is alphabetical by name, with entries ranging from one paragraph to more than eight pages in length depending on the importance of the individual. Each profile notes birth and death dates, birth place, parents, branch of science, nationality, education, professional positions held, name of spouse(s), and sources of additional information. A name index and a table of all subjects showing period, field, and nationality supplement the text.

787. **Who's Who in Science and Engineering [yr.].** New Providence, NJ, Marquis Who's Who/Reed Reference, 1992- . Biennial. 1v. $249.95 (1994 ed.). ISSN 1063-5599.

Following the familiar format of the Marquis Who's Who series, this work includes biographies of nearly 22,000 scientists, doctors, and engineers from around the world, although the majority are from the United States. Entries provide up to 20 types of information, such as personal data, address, career information, affiliations, and professional achievements and awards. Specific descriptions of achievements assist the user in identifying the exact area of the biographee's work. A professional area index (including 100 specialties) that is further subdivided geographically, a list of recipients of some 150 awards (arranged by field), and a geographical index round out the volume. Also available on CD-ROM.

CHRONOLOGIES

788. Hellemans, Alexander, and Bryan Bunch. **The Timetables of Science: A Chronology of the Most Important People and Events in the History of Science.** Rev. ed. New York, Simon & Schuster, 1991. 672p. index. $20.00pa. ISBN 0-671-73328-1.

The stated goal of this chronology is to identify "what happened, and who made it happen." Within these parameters, approximately 10,000 events are listed within timetables divided into nine major time periods or sections. Each leads off with an overview that describes the geographical, cultural, and political contexts in which the events of that period took place. Entries vary in length from a few to 80 words, with major topics meriting more extensive coverage. An excellent survey of achievements in astronomy, biology, mathematics, medicine, physics, technology, and general science.

DICTIONARIES AND ENCYCLOPEDIAS

789. Ballentyne, D. W. G., and D. R. Lovett. **A Dictionary of Named Effects and Laws in Chemistry, Physics and Mathematics.** 4th ed. New York, Chapman & Hall, in association with Methuen, 1980. 346p. illus. $44.95. ISBN 0-412-22380-5.

First published in 1958, this well-known dictionary presents brief, alphabetically arranged definitions of equations, laws, theorems, effects, constants, and other effects and laws, and identifies the individuals responsible for their creation or discovery. Typical entries among the 1,200 included are the "Fermi Constant" and the "Riemann Zeta Function."

790. Blackburn, David, and Geoffrey Holister, eds. **Encyclopedia of Modern Technology.** Boston, G. K. Hall, 1987. 248p. illus. (part col.). bibliog. index. $40.00. ISBN 0-8161-9056-9.

"Modern technology" in this case refers to state-of-the-art developments as of 1986, most of which have now been surpassed by events and advances of the past nine years. Nevertheless, this is still an excellent overview of those technology topics that are still making headlines today. Its 34 chapters are organized under nine subject categories: "Recording," "Analyzing," "Measuring," "Seeing," "Powering," "Protecting," "Communicating," "Moving," and "Processing." Within these sections are articles dealing with photography, the atom, computer hardware, and many other topics related to the technology necessary "to create things, to build, to move, to communicate, and to control events." Especially noteworthy are the book's 480 extraordinary illustrations, which include black-and-white and color photographs, computer-generated images, cutaway diagrams, and schematics, among others. Although not especially handy as a ready-reference tool, *Encyclopedia of Modern Technology* provides instead an outstanding overview of an important, dynamic subject.

791. Considine, Douglas M. ed. **Van Nostrand's Scientific Encyclopedia.** 7th ed. New York, Van Nostrand Reinhold, 1989. 2v. illus. index. $199.95/set. ISBN 0-442-21750-1.

This VNR reference has been relied upon through its many editions for authority, currency, and comprehensiveness. The seventh edition continues these strengths in its nearly 6,800 entries. Emphasis is on the physical and technical sciences rather than the natural and human sciences. Following the traditional guidelines, entries present a general overview of a topic followed by a more complex narrative and conclusion. Entry bibliographies, cross references, black-and-white illustrations, and a thorough, detailed index in volume 2 enhance the utility of the encyclopedia.

792. Morris, Christopher, ed. **Academic Press Dictionary of Science and Technology.** San Diego, CA, Academic Press, 1992. 2432p. illus. $115.00. ISBN 0-12-200400-0.

Morris's mammoth dictionary comprises more than 133,000 entries drawn from 124 scientific fields. Short articles about each field, written by distinguished subject experts, provide the discipline's history, scope, and interesting notes about current developments. The layout includes excellent drawings and striking photographs; the 24 color plates contain nearly 100 photographs and images that range from computer graphics to scanning electron and light micrographs of computer chips to images of a human fetus at different stages of development. Appendixes include physical constants, international units and conversions, the periodic table, a geologic timetable, a five-kingdom organism classification, and a chronology of scientific events from 1403 to 1992.

793. Parker, Sybil P., ed. **McGraw-Hill Concise Encyclopedia of Science & Technology.** 2d ed. New York, McGraw-Hill, 1989. 2222p. illus. index. $119.50. ISBN 0-07-045512-0.

An abridgment of the sixth edition of McGraw-Hill's monumental 20-volume *Encyclopedia of Science & Technology* (1987, $1,600/set, ISBN 0-07-079292-5), the *Concise* provides a one-stop, authoritative source for all aspects of scientific information. For the most part, articles have been abridged by omitting whole paragraphs of explanatory material, by rewriting to preserve the sense of the original, and by shortening some articles to mere term definitions. Illustrations, explanatory tables, and the names of original article authors have been retained wherever possible. In addition, there are a number of handy appendixes, including keys to scientists, scientific symbols, element tables, and an index to the volume.

Libraries should be aware that the seventh edition of the *McGraw-Hill Encyclopedia of Science & Technology* (20v., $1,900/set, ISBN 0-07-909206-3) became available in 1992, so it is probable that a new *Concise* will follow soon as well.

794. Parker, Sybil P., ed. **McGraw-Hill Dictionary of Scientific and Technical Terms.** 5th ed. New York, McGraw-Hill, 1993. 2088p. illus. $110.50. ISBN 0-07-042333-4.

With an additional 7,600 entries since the third edition (1984), this standard science reference defines roughly 100,000 terms and phrases and provides pronunciations for each. In addition to providing clear and concise definitions, the entries also identify from which of 102 subject fields they are drawn. There are more than 3,000 sidebar illustrations, along with an extensive appendix that provides the International System of Units, the periodic table, mathematical tables, tables of signs and symbols for various fields, schematic symbols, historical chronologies, and many other supplementary materials. A standard purchase for all libraries.

795. Uvarov, E. B., and Alan Isaacs. **The Facts on File Dictionary of Science.** 6th ed. New York, Facts on File, 1986. 468p. illus. $21.95. ISBN 0-8160-1386-1.

Originally published in earlier editions as the *Penguin Dictionary of Science*, this dictionary defines nearly 7,000 entries drawn from biophysics, biochemistry, physics, medical sciences, chemistry, mathematics, astronomy, and many other scientific disciplines. Entries range from 50 to 100 words in length, and are written in language easily understood (albeit with a British accent) by the lay reader. Cross references are numerous. Emphasis is, as in previous editions, on the general sciences, to the exclusion of technology-related terms.

A similar title of equal value is *The American Heritage Dictionary of Science* (Robert K. Barnhart, Houghton Mifflin, 1988, 740p., $21.95, ISBN 0-395-48367-0). Intended to bridge the gap between simplified and overly technical works of a similar nature, this dictionary defines more than 16,000 entries drawn from the physical and biological sciences. Entries include pronunciation, part of speech, discipline from which the term is drawn, definition, a sentence containing the term to further clarify meaning, word origin, associated terms, and cross references. Either of these dictionaries would be appropriate for small and medium-sized libraries.

DIRECTORIES

796. **Financial Aid for Minorities in Engineering and Science.** Garrett Park, MD, Garrett Park Press, 1992. 1v. (unpaged). index. $4.95pa. ISBN 0-912048-98-0.

The minorities for whom these 327 scholarships, fellowships, and loans (primarily from national or regional organizations) are intended are mainly African-Americans, Hispanic-Americans, and Native Americans. Each entry provides address information and a description of who may qualify, what benefits will be provided, and other details as appropriate (e.g., application deadlines). End matter includes a short list of associations in science and technical areas and a limited bibliography of career information, as well as an index of majors keyed to the entries in the main section.

HANDBOOKS

797. Bunch, Bryan. **The Henry Holt Handbook of Current Science & Technology: A Sourcebook of Facts and Analysis ....** New York, Henry Holt, 1992. 689p. index. $50.00. ISBN 0-8050-1829-8.

This handbook provides a comprehensive review and analysis of the current state of research and discovery in the fields of astronomy and space, chemistry, earth science, environmental issues, life science, mathematics, physics, and technology. Each topic leads off with a short essay on the state of the science (through the early 1990s) followed by a timetable of major developments. The main body of the work has topics, articles, and subtopics that summarize recent advances as reported in the popular scientific press, with appropriate references. In addition to the main text, there are tables and charts, appendixes that list selected books for further references, 1990–1991 obituaries of scientists, various units of measurements, and an extensive index.

798. Macaulay, David. **The Way Things Work.** Boston, Houghton Mifflin, 1988. 384p. $29.95. ISBN 0-395-42857-2.

Intended as a "visual guide to the world of machines," *The Way Things Work* is a fascinating resource for every reader, but is most especially helpful for those of us who are, shall we say, mechanically challenged. Its four-part arrangement groups materials thematically under the mechanics of movement (inclined planes, levers, wheels and axles, gears and belts, etc.); harnessing the elements (floating, flying, pressure power, exploiting heat, nuclear power); working with waves (light and images, photography, printing, sound and music, telecommunications); and electricity and automation (electricity, magnetism, sensors and detectors, computers). Each section leads off with an introductory overview of the topic at hand, then uses nontechnical narrative, clear and often humorous illustrations (many in color), and examples to demonstrate and clarify the principles under review. A brief selective history of mechanical developments, a 175-word glossary, and a name/subject index accompany the text. Appropriate for all age groups, Macaulay's book is a recommended purchase for all libraries.

799. Magill, Frank N., ed. **Magill's Survey of Science: Applied Science Series.** Pasadena, CA, Salem Press, 1993. 6v. index. $475.00/set. ISBN 0-89356-705-1.

This Magill set's 382 articles cover the applied sciences from aerospace to zone refining. The largest number of articles deal with engineering and materials science. Delightfully jargon-free, the articles are written to provide the general reader with basic insights into these scientific topics. Most articles follow a basic format of introduction (plus key definitions), overview, uses of the technology, and context (usually the historical or social environment of the technology). Cross references and a brief annotated bibliography are appended to each article, and an extensive subject index is included in the last volume. An excellent resource for all public libraries that can afford it.

800. Stanley, Autumn. **Mothers and Daughters of Invention: Notes for a Revised History of Technology.** Metuchen, NJ, Scarecrow, 1993. 1116p. index. $97.50. ISBN 0-9108-2586-4.

Divided into general subjects—agriculture, health and medicine, sex and fertility, tools and machines, and computers—*Mothers and Daughters of Invention* presents a wide but detailed view of women's inventions from prehistory through the 20th century. Emphasis is on the diversity and importance of women's inventions, whether officially recognized (i.e., patented) or not. In addition to the descriptions of the individual inventions, Stanley also provides brief biographies of women inventors when such information is available. The 2,000 women inventors featured are drawn mostly from the United States, although some British, French, and Russian women have been included as well. The book closes with an exhaustive 125-page bibliography.

INDEXES

801. **Applied Science & Technology Index.** Bronx, NY, H. W. Wilson, 1913- . Monthly (except July); quarterly and annual cumulations. Sold on service basis. ISSN 0003-6986.

Formerly published as *Industrial Arts Index* from 1913 to 1957, this Wilson publication indexes approximately 400 of the leading English-language science, trade, and technology periodicals. Topics covered include aeronautics and space science, artificial intelligence and machine learning, chemistry, computer technology, construction, engineering (civil, electrical, mechanical), engineering materials, environmental engineering and waste management, food, geology, marine technology and oceanography, mathematics, metallurgy, meteorology, mineralogy, neural networks and optical computing, petroleum and gas, physics, plastics, robotics, solid-state technology, telecommunications, textiles, and transportation. Needless to say, an exhaustive overview of the cutting edge of today's high-technology world. Also available online, on disk, on CD-ROM, and on magnetic tape.

802. **General Science Index.** Bronx, NY, H. W. Wilson, 1978- . Monthly (except June and December); quarterly and annual cumulations. Sold on service basis. ISSN 0162-1963.

General Science Index is intended as a guide to current information in roughly 140 English-language science periodicals. Coverage includes astronomy, atmospheric science, biology, botany, chemistry, earth science, environment and conservation, food and nutrition, genetics, mathematics, medicine and health, microbiology, oceanography, physics, physiology, psychology, and zoology. A separate index that provides reviews of current science books is especially useful to librarians. Also available online, on disk, on CD-ROM, and on magnetic tape.

803. Pilger, Mary Anne. **Science Experiments Index for Young People.** Englewood, CO, Libraries Unlimited, 1988. 239p. $35.00. ISBN 0-87287-671-3. **Update 1991.** 1992. 133p. $21.00. ISBN 0-87287-858-9.

The main volume of Pilger's reference indexes science experiments and demonstrations found in 694 elementary and intermediate science books dating from 1941 through 1988; the update covers an additional 328 titles published between 1964 and 1991. In addition to books specific to the physical sciences, the index includes books dealing with models, math concepts that can be related to the science fields, social science experiments, and food and nutrition experiments. Each of the two works is organized into two parts: the first provides a topically arranged listing of the experiments, with a three- to eight-word description, book number, and book pages where the experiments can be found; the second contains book references arranged by book number.

Another recommended resource in this subject area is Scarecrow's Science Fair Project Index series, intended for students in grades K–8. The original work, *Science Fair Project Index, 1960–1972* (Janet Stoffer, ed., 728p., 1975, o.p.), has been supplemented by *Science Fair Project Index, 1973–80* (Akron-Summit County Public Library, Science and Technology Division, ed., 1983, 729p., $47.50, ISBN 0-8108-1605-9); *Science Fair Project Index, 1981–1984* (Cynthia Bishop and Deborah Crowe, eds., 686p., 1986, $47.50, ISBN 0-8108-1892-2); and *Science Fair Project Index, 1985–1989* (Cynthia Bishop, Katherine Ertle, and Karen Zeleznik, eds., 1992, 555p., $47.50, ISBN 0-8108-2555-4). Among them, these works index thousands of science projects and experiments drawn from books, lab manuals, periodicals, and pamphlets.

AGRICULTURE

804. Herren, Ray V., and Roy L. Donahue. **The Agriculture Dictionary.** Albany, NY, Delmar, 1991. 553p. illus. $19.95pa. ISBN 0-8273-4097-4.

The more than 10,000 words succinctly defined in *The Agriculture Dictionary* are drawn from 18 disciplines. Where terms have a number of different meanings, all are provided. A generous number of illustrations appear in the margins, further clarifying the appropriate definitions. With its very reasonable price, Herren and Donahue's dictionary stands out as a fairly current, affordable resource for basic definitions of agricultural terms.

805. Marti, Donald B. **Historical Directory of American Agricultural Fairs.** Westport, CT, Greenwood Press, 1986. 300p. index. $65.00. ISBN 0-313-24188-0.

Some 2,600 agricultural fairs are held across the United States, and Marti has done an excellent job of describing their history, the important role they have played in the development of American agriculture, and their current manifestations. In addition, for more than 200 specific state, regional, county, and local events, he provides detailed entries about the history of individual fairs, recent attendance, special events, and sources of additional information. A separate section lists all current (as of the mid-1980s) U.S. fairs by state; an index provides access to specific entries.

FOOD SCIENCE AND TECHNOLOGY

Dictionaries and Encyclopedias

806. Herbst, Sharon Tyler. **Food Lover's Companion: Comprehensive Definitions of over 3000 Food, Wine and Culinary Terms.** Hauppauge, NY, Barron's Educational Series, 1990. 582p. illus. $11.95pa. ISBN 0-8120-4156-9.

Food Lover's Companion is a handy reference book that defines more than 3,000 cooking-related terms, including foods; cooking techniques; dishes and sauces; cuts of meat; styles of preparation; equipment; menu terms; and wines, beers, and spirits. Pronunciation is provided for all but the most common terms, as is etymology. Appendixes include an additives directory, a comprehensive table of equivalents and substitutes, measurement conversion tables, candy-making temperatures, charts of cuts of meat, and a quick reference guide to herbs and spices.

807. Lang, Jenifer Harvey, ed. **Larousse Gastronomique.** New York, Crown, 1988. 1193p. illus. (part col.), index. $60.00. ISBN 0-517-57032-7.

Long considered the "world's greatest culinary encyclopedia," this most recent edition of *Larousse* features alphabetically arranged entries on specific dishes, famous chefs, serving, sauces, cooking terms and techniques, utensils, geographic regions and their cuisines (including American regional cuisines), wines and liqueurs (now international in scope), customs, and food preservation, among other topics. Interwoven with the text are not only 1,000 beautifully rendered illustrations and photographs, but also some 4,000 of the world's most wonderful (mostly French) recipes. A recipe index provides access.

808. **The New Frank Schoonmaker Encyclopedia of Wine.** rev. by Alexis Bespaloff. New York, William Morrow, 1988. 624p. maps. $22.95. ISBN 0-688-05749-7.

Providing a basic starting point for investigation of wine-producing regions of the world and the wines for which they are known, this encyclopedia presents more than 2,000 alphabetically arranged definitions for terms, phrases, regions, processes, and specific types of wines found throughout the world. Pronunciation is included for each entry, and the text is supplemented by 120 maps and 50 pages of appendixes that include charts, tables, and lists of recommended wines. The wine labels featured in the earlier edition have been dropped, and there are neither cross references nor index in this edition. Nevertheless, *The New Frank Schoonmaker Encyclopedia of Wine* remains the standard resource in this subject area.

If there is room in the acquisitions budget, libraries may, however, also wish to consider another title, *Alexis Lichine's New Encyclopedia of Wines & Spirits* (5th ed., Alexis Lichine and others, Alfred A. Knopf/Random House, 1987, 771p., $45.00, ISBN 0-394-56262-3) for its complementary coverage. This highly regarded work focuses on various wines, winemaking, wine and food, wine-growing regions, and wine-producing nations, with an emphasis on European (primarily French) wines. To balance this bias, libraries may also want to have Anthony Dias Blue's excellent survey, *American Wine: A Comprehensive Guide* (rev. ed., HarperCollins, 1988, 567p., $37.95, ISBN 0-06-0159-14-6) on hand.

Handbooks and Guides

809. **Bowes and Church's Food Values of Portions Commonly Used.** 15th ed. Rev. by Jean A. T. Pennington. New York, HarperCollins, 1989. 328p. bibliog. index. $24.95. ISBN 0-06-055157-7.

This handy guide, relied upon by nutritionists and other health-conscious readers since its first publication in 1937, provides the nutrient content (calories, cholesterol, fat, vitamins, minerals, and dietary fiber) of everything from whole foods to fast foods to frozen foods to infant formulas. Information is presented in tabular or chart format; the main table, "Nutrient Content of Foods," is arranged alphabetically by 35 food groups (e.g., beverages, fast foods, meats, fruits) and further subdivided as appropriate. Sources are cited, and many useful general-purpose tables are also included, such as the "Recommended Daily Dietary Allowances." Because items are listed only once to conserve space, this work's excellent index is especially appreciated. A standard purchase for all libraries.

810. Garrison, Robert H., Jr., and Elizabeth Somer. **The Nutrition Desk Reference.** rev. ed. New Canaan, CT, Keats, 1990. 306p. index. $17.95pa. ISBN 0-87983-488-9.

The 22 chapters in this handbook are grouped into four broad categories: dietary factors; selected topics on vitamin and mineral research; nutrition and cancer, cardiovascular diseases, drugs, and disease; and dietary recommendations. The authors have done a good job of incorporating advances in nutrition research made since their earlier (1985) edition, and have taken pains to present both sides of controversial issues as objectively as possible. Supplementary materials include 34 tables and figures, a glossary, and an adequate index.

Another useful resource in this area is Lavon J. Dunne's *Nutrition Almanac* (3d ed., McGraw-Hill, 1990. 340p. $15.95pa. ISBN 0-07-034912-6). Although certainly less comprehensive than *Nutrition Desk Reference*, it is good for answering basic questions regarding the interrelationship of food, nutrition, and health. Its eight sections discuss how nutrients work in the body, imbalances caused by lack of nutrients, ailments that benefit from particular vitamin and mineral supplementation, and the benefits of herbs and herbal therapy. In addition, there are a "Table of Food Composition," a nutrient analysis of more than 600 foods, and a "Nutrient Allowance Chart" that breaks down individual nutrient needs by one's body size, metabolism, and caloric requirements.

811. Goodman, Robert L. **A Quick Guide to Food Additives.** 2d ed. San Diego, CA, Silvercat; distr., Publishers Distribution Center, 1990. 62p. $5.95pa. ISBN 0-9624945-1-8.

The major portion of this slim volume is devoted to a discussion of what constitutes a food additive, why additives are used, the types of foods in which they are used, where they come from, and how they are used. A brief section lists selected food categories and the additives they may contain. The remainder of the booklet is a dictionary of the more recognizable additives. A straightforward, easy-to-understand presentation of an often controversial subject.

Indexes

812. Kleiman, Rhonda H. **The American Regional Cookery Index.** New York, Neal-Schuman, 1989. 221p. $59.95. ISBN 0-55570-029-2.

The recipes recounted in Kleiman's well-known reference are drawn from 25 cookbooks dealing with American regional cuisines; although similar in focus, however, these cookbooks reflect widely diverse culinary approaches and styles. Thus, entries range from a Jell-O/Twinkie/vanilla ice cream concoction to a Jerusalem artichoke bisque, with a highly eclectic mix in between. The recipes are indexed by name, type of dish (e.g., salads), main ingredients, methods of preparation, and ethnicity. A popular, informative, and interesting reference work.

FORESTRY

813. Hora, Bayard, consulting ed. **The Oxford Encyclopedia of Trees of the World.** New York, Oxford University Press, 1981. 288p. illus. (part col.). index. $27.50. ISBN 0-19-217712-5.

Both an informative summary of the major genera of trees of the world and an excellent general reference source for native and exotic trees of North America, *The*

Oxford Encyclopedia of Trees of the World has long been relied upon for its authoritative text and its wonderful illustrations. The main part of the book comprises a series of descriptions of trees belonging to the ferns, primitive seed plants (gymnosperms), and the flowering plants (dicots and monocots). The one- to two-page descriptions of individual genera of trees include a summary of distribution, general characteristics, economic importance, and diseases of the genus. Excellent photographs and/or paintings accompany the descriptive narrative. A glossary, small bibliography, and comprehensive indexes to common and scientific names conclude the encyclopedia.

814. Mitchell, Alan. **The Trees of North America.** New York, Facts on File, 1987. 208p. illus. index. $35.00. ISBN 0-8160-1806-5.

Geared toward laypersons and specialists in horticulture and landscape architecture, this publication describes more than 500 species and 250 varieties of trees growing in North America. Arrangement is by common name within a larger grouping of broadleaved trees and conifers. Each species entry provides common name, scientific name, origin, general physical characteristics, geographical range, and, frequently, a specification of preferred location (e.g., park, botanical garden, street, etc.). Outstanding, detailed illustrations of leaf, flower, fruit, bark, and full tree structures (summer and winter) accompany each species entry. In addition, a "Practical Reference Section" describes care of young and mature trees, lists garden trees with specific features and climate information, and provides a set of range maps for 147 of the most popular tree species.

815. Walker, Aidan, ed. **The Encyclopedia of Wood: A Tree-by-Tree Guide to the World's Most Versatile Resource.** New York, Facts on File, 1989. 192p. illus. maps. index. $29.95. ISBN 0-8160-2159-7.

The primary focus of Walker's fascinating compendium is a "directory" section that provides information on the appearance, properties, and uses of 150 of the world's most popular timbers. Entries, arranged alphabetically, are accompanied by a distribution map, a color photograph of the finished wood, and a chart summarizing its most important characteristics (density, workability, etc.). Other chapters discuss general information on wood and the wood industry, processing (logging, milling, and finishing), woodworking craftspeople, tree anatomy and growth, world forests, and deforestation and conservation. A brief glossary and a subject/common name/scientific name index conclude the encyclopedia.

HORTICULTURE (GARDENING)

Dictionaries and Encyclopedias

816. Bagust, Harold, comp. **The Gardener's Dictionary of Horticultural Terms.** London, Cassell; distr., Sterling, 1992. 377p. illus. $29.95. ISBN 0-304-34106-1.

Intended for gardeners, students, writers, and horticulturists, this dictionary includes definitions for gardening tools, growing media, propagation methods, plant organs, soil types, landscaping, and diseases. Definitions are brief and include neither common nor scientific plant names. Hundreds of excellent line drawings enhance the text. A good introductory work appropriate for all public libraries.

817. Bailey, Liberty Hyde, and Ethel Zoe Bailey, comps. **Hortus Third: A Concise Dictionary of Plants Cultivated in the United States and Canada.** Rev. and expanded by the staff of the Liberty Hyde Bailey Hortorium. New York, Macmillan, 1976. 1290p. $150.00. ISBN 0-02-505470-8.

Hortus Third describes all the species and botanical varieties of plants cultivated (as of the mid-1970s) on United States or Canadian soil. Coverage was extended to include Puerto Rico and Hawaii in this edition. Entries note uses (including economic aspects), propagation, and cultivation practices; a separate index lists 10,400 common plant names. Long regarded as the most reliable and comprehensive resource for names and descriptions of North American plants.

818. Bradley, Fern Marshall, and Barbara W. Ellis, eds. **Rodale's All-New Encyclopedia of Organic Gardening: The Indispensable Resource for Every Gardener.** Emmaus, PA, Rodale Press, 1992. 690p. illus. index. $29.95; $17.95pa. ISBN 0-87857-999-0; 0-87596-599-7pa.

Successor to the 30-year-old, beloved *Encyclopedia of Organic Gardening* by J. I. Rodale, this thick volume covers the myriad ways a gardener can prevent and defend against pests and diseases of all kinds. It consists of about 700 medium-length entries on everything from abelia (a type of flowering shrub) to zucchini. Twenty-six longer core articles that provide more extensive treatment of key topics, such as garden design, composting, and pruning and training, are interspersed among the briefer entries. Techniques discussed include recognizing and promoting beneficial insects and animals, arranging and planning a garden to prevent disease and pest problems, and choosing appropriate cultivars.

819. Brickell, Christopher, and Elvin McDonald, eds. **The American Horticultural Society Encyclopedia of Gardening.** New York, Dorling Kindersley, 1993. 648p. illus. index. $59.95. ISBN 1-56458-291-4.

This authoritative how-to gardening guide comprises nearly 600 pages of sound and practical information on subjects ranging from propagation and pests to fences and tools, all organized around basic gardening processes and procedures. Many types of gardens, from rock and container to perennial, are covered. More than 3,000 lavish Dorling Kindersley-style color photographs and drawings enhance the text; in addition, the narrative is supplemented with numerous feature boxes (on specific plant groups or interest areas), plant lists, and cross references.

Another excellent gardening reference by Christopher Brickell is *The American Horticultural Society Encyclopedia of Garden Plants* (Macmillan, 1989, 608p., $49.95, ISBN 0-02-557920-7). Encompassing more than 8,000 garden plants, the book is arranged in two parts. The first comprises a catalog of 4,000 plant photographs accompanied by brief descriptions, with arrangement by type, size, season of interest, and color. The second, larger section is a dictionary of descriptive entries arranged by genus. Each entry provides family name, common name, plant characteristics, cultivation, propagation, pruning techniques, pests and diseases, and cultivation.

820. Kowalchik, Claire, and William H. Hylton, eds. **Rodale's Illustrated Encyclopedia of Herbs.** Emmaus, PA, Rodale Press, 1987. 545p. illus. (part col.). bibliog. index. $24.95. ISBN 0-87857-699-1.

An informative and engaging survey of the world of herbs, this encyclopedia comprises 140 alphabetically arranged entries based on common, rather than scientific, name. Each entry begins with the scientific name of the plant, its family, botanical description, flowering behavior, range of cultivation, and habitat. This information is followed by several sections that describe the herb's history, usages (medicinal, culinary, aromatic, ornamental, cosmetic, dye, etc.), proper cultivation procedures, common pests, and diseases. Frequently, a sketch identifying pertinent features (leaf shape, flowers, berries, etc.) accompanies the text. In addition, numerous color photographs of plants and gardens, as well as other sketches and informative charts, are interspersed throughout. A good bibliography and thorough index conclude the encyclopedia.

Directories

821. Barton, Barbara J. **Gardening by Mail: A Source Book.** 3d ed. Boston, Houghton Mifflin, 1990. 1v. (various paging). illus. index. $16.95pa. ISBN 0-395-52280-3.

Riding the popular wave of mail-order retailing, Barton's mail-order gardening directory is a great idea intelligently executed. It lists plant and seed sources; garden suppliers; professional horticultural, plant, and trade associations; magazines; horticultural libraries; and a bibliography of useful books on plants and gardening. All the essential information is provided for each, including address, telephone number, hours, prices, and so forth. A four-part index provides access by plant source (suppliers by species of plant), by geographical location (suppliers by state), by product source (alphabetically by subject), and by society (organizations listed according to the types of plants they represent).

Handbooks

822. Dean, Jan. **The Gardener's Reading Guide.** New York, Facts on File, 1993. 250p. illus. index. $23.95. ISBN 0-8160-2754-4.

The 3,000 entries that comprise Dean's delightful guide encompass books that range from the practical to the esoteric and from the garden in fiction to gifts and crafts from the garden. Each entry includes a brief annotation, often reflective of the author's personal preferences and opinions. In addition to such expected subjects as container gardening, foliage, and watering methods, the guide also addresses gardens around the world, gardening for the disabled, gardening for the elderly, gardening for profit, and gardening videos. A separate chapter discusses where to find books and provides a list of publishers.

823. Dietz, Marjorie J., ed. **10,000 Garden Questions Answered by 20 Experts.** 4th ed. Originally edited by F. F. Rockwell. Garden City, NY, Doubleday, 1982. 1507p. illus. index. $16.95. ISBN 0-385-18509-X.

Organized by topical chapter, this popular handbook addresses questions about soils and fertilizers, landscaping, trees, shrubs, vines, bulbs, tubers, corms, roses, perennials, annuals, biennials, lawns, vegetables, fruits, house plants, pests and their control, weeds, and regional garden problems. The last section is devoted to recommended reading lists, state agricultural experiment stations, plant societies, botanical gardens, arboreta, public gardens, and commercial sources for plants and seeds. Fortunately, a comprehensive index completes Dietz's information-packed book.

824.   Facciola, Stephen. **Cornucopia: A Source Book of Edible Plants.** Vista, CA, Kampong, 1990. 677p. index. $35.00pa. ISBN 0-9628087-0-9.

Cornucopia includes approximately 3,000 species of higher plants and a few algae, fungi, and bacteria. It comprises a botanical listing section, a list of cultivars (cultivated variety), sources (more than 1,350 firms and institutions), a bibliography, and several indexes. Arranged alphabetically by plant family, the botanical listings includes genus, species, common name, a default code for the type of plant material or product offered, use, distribution, bibliographic citations, and sources. Included for each of the 7,000 varieties described are number of days to maturity, uses, bibliographic citations, and sources of supply. The concluding bibliography includes both technical and popular works.

825.   Smith, Miranda, and Anna Carr. **Rodale's Garden Insect, Disease & Weed Identification Guide.** Emmaus, PA, Rodale Press, 1988. 328p. illus. (part col.). index. $16.95pa. ISBN 0-87857-759-9.

This guide identifies more than 200 common insects, diseases, and weeds that regularly invade America's garden plots. This three-part work describes insects in both their larval and adult/nymph stages, diseases arranged according to the organism causing the problem (fungus, virus, etc.), and weeds grouped by annuals, biennials, perennials, and woody perennials. Thorough descriptive entries, usually accompanied by line drawings, black-and-white illustrations or photographs, or color photographs, are included for each insect, disease, or weed identified.

826.   Wright, Michael. **The Complete Handbook of Garden Plants.** New York, Facts on File, 1984. 544p. $24.95. ISBN 0-87196-632-8.

Essentially a gardener's field guide, this work describes more than 9,000 species and varieties of plants that grow in temperate zones and provides watercolor illustrations of some 2,500 of these. Entries indicate plant sizes, leaf sizes, hardiness and soil needs, how and when to propagate, pruning, and the best varieties of each species for gardening purposes, as well as providing color descriptions of varieties. A glossary is found at the beginning of the book; an excellent index that includes botanical and common names concludes it.

827.   Zucker, Isabel. **Flowering Shrubs & Small Trees.** rev. by Derek Fell. Toronto, Stoddart, 1990. 287p. illus. index. $50.00. ISBN 0-7737-2317-X.

A revision of a classic gardening catalog by Zucker, this volume serves as an encyclopedic list of shrub genera, varieties, and cultivars. It is written in a casual, readable style appropriate to a wide range of people who love gardening, from professionals to home gardeners. In addition to the main shrub and tree entries, there are six appendixes (flowering shrubs for every purpose, bloom time chart, ways of propagating shrubs and small trees, hardiness zone map, where to buy shrubs, and metric conversions) plus subject and plant indexes, the latter of which incorporates Latin, common, and catalog names for complete identification.

VETERINARY SCIENCE

828.   West, Geoffrey P., ed. **Black's Veterinary Dictionary.** 17th ed. Lanham, MD, Barnes & Noble Books; distr., Rowman & Littlefield, 1992. 660p. illus. $67.50. ISBN 0-389-20944-5.

Black's Veterinary Dictionary is intended to be consulted by both lay person and practitioner, so its vocabulary and definitions are practical, straightforward, and primarily nontechnical. As in previous editions, it encompasses terms and phrases related to anatomy, physiology, diseases, diagnosis and treatment, and first aid for large and small animals. Entries range in length from several sentences to more encyclopedic, several-page articles, with a few of the more important topics meriting up to 40 pages of narrative. Line drawings and photographs further clarify many of the definitions; references for further consultation are noted when appropriate; and case reports accompany many of the entries.

If libraries want a second reference in this subject area, Oxford University Press's *Concise Veterinary Dictionary* (1988, 890p., $37.50, ISBN 0-19-854208-9) offers a good complement to *Black's*. Its entries are brief but informative, and often include excellent line drawings. It is more truly a dictionary, in that it focuses on definitions rather than practical information and case reports—but what it does, it does quite well. The two works are complementary, and both are recommended where there is sufficient patron interest.

Engineering

GENERAL WORKS

829. Brady, George S., and Henry R. Clauser. **Materials Handbook: An Encyclopedia for Managers, Technical Professionals, Purchasing and Production Managers, Technicians, Supervisors, and Foremen.** 13th ed. New York, McGraw-Hill, 1991. 1056p. index. $76.50. ISBN 0-07-007074-1.

First published in 1929, this standard reference covers not only engineering materials but also pharmaceuticals, foodstuffs, and historical materials such as bath metal. Both naturally occurring and synthetic substances are included in the work's 15,000 entries. Each material is described in terms of composition, properties, and uses, with related products or subdivisions so noted. There are no comparative data charts or tables, which somewhat lessens the utility of the handbook for those who need the information presented in tabular form.

830. Parker, Sybil P., ed. **McGraw-Hill Encyclopedia of Engineering.** 2d ed. New York, McGraw-Hill, 1993. 1414p. illus. index. $95.50. ISBN 0-07-051392-9.

A spin-off from the seventh edition of the publisher's well-known *Encyclopedia of Science and Technology* (1992), this volume comprises about 700 articles on 11 major engineering specialties: civil, design, electrical, industrial, mechanical, metallurgical, mining, nuclear, petroleum, power, and production. In addition, there are several articles on physical and thermodynamic principles applicable to engineering. Written for the layperson, the signed articles are arranged alphabetically and often include bibliographies. A 6,000-entry index concludes the work. It is important to note that libraries that already own the multi-volume *McGraw-Hill Encyclopedia of Science and Technology* (1992, 20v., $1,700/set) will not need the engineering encyclopedia, as it simply duplicates articles found in the parent work.

CHEMICAL

831. Kent, James A. **Riegel's Handbook of Industrial Chemistry.** 9th ed. New York, Van Nostrand Reinhold, 1992. 1288p. illus. index. $114.95. ISBN 0-442-00175-4.

The U.S. chemical process industry is traditionally the largest user of U.S. scientific and technological resources, the major expender of U.S. commercial research and development funds, and a major contributor to a favorable balance-of-trade position for the United States. Thus, this well-known handbook continues to be an important resource for many professionals, companies, and interested lay readers. New to this edition are chapters that cover waste minimization, safety considerations in plant design and operation, emergency response planning, and statistical applications in quality control and experimental planning. The 50 contributors are all subject specialists, including former executives of the Environmental Protection Agency.

CIVIL

832. Merritt, Frederick S., ed. **Standard Handbook for Civil Engineers.** 3d ed. New York, McGraw-Hill, 1983. 1v. (various paging). illus. index. $124.50. ISBN 0-07-041515-3.

As stated in the preface of this well-known reference, its intent is to "provide in a single volume a compendium of the best of current civil engineering practices," with the goal that the "application of its information will stimulate greater production of cost-effective, energy-efficient and environmentally sound civil engineering work." The 25 sections that make up the handbook cover all aspects of construction engineering, including planning, design, and construction. About one-half of the handbook deals with general topics such as systems design and value engineering, management of design and construction, specifications, geotechnical engineering, and structural engineering. The remainder addresses specific applications, such as bridges, buildings, highways, airports, tunnels, and harbors. A thorough index concludes the handbook.

833. Stein, J. Stewart. **Construction Glossary: An Encyclopedia Reference and Manual.** 2d ed. New York, John Wiley, 1993. 1137p. index. $95.00. ISBN 0-471-56933-X.

The more than 30,000 entries that make up this classic reference are arranged within 16 divisions: general requirements, site work, concrete, masonry, metals, wood and plastics, thermal and moisture protection, doors and windows, finishes, specialties, equipment, furnishings, special construction, conveying systems, mechanical, and electrical. In addition, there are sections on professional services, construction categories, and technical-scientific data; a directory of reference data sources; and three appendixes of abbreviations for scientific, engineering, and construction terms, weights and measures, and carpentry abbreviations. A complete alphabetical index and a detailed table of contents facilitate access to the broad-ranging information packed into this excellent glossary.

ELECTRICAL

834. Ardis, Susan B. **Guide to the Literature of Electrical and Electronics Engineering.** Littleton, CO, Libraries Unlimited, 1987. 190p. index. $37.50. ISBN 0-87287-474-5.

This guide to reference books in electrotechnology categorizes its materials into eight groups: bibliographic sources, ready-reference sources, handbooks and reference texts, journals and newsletters, product literature, patents, standards, and other information sources. In addition to full bibliographic citations, each entry includes a concise, informative annotation. A subject/title/author index provides access.

835. Fink, Donald G., and H. Wayne Beaty, eds. **Standard Handbook for Electrical Engineers.** 13th ed. New York, McGraw-Hill, 1993. 1v. (various paging). illus. index. $110.50. ISBN 0-07-020984-7.

The 13th edition of this familiar reference comprises 28 broad sections covering a vast range of topics. These include, among others, generation, distribution, and control of electric power; nuclear power and its ramifications; energy conservation; project economics; system management; high-voltage transmission systems; and alternative energy sources such as solar, geothermal, and wind power. Many of the sections conclude with short but helpful bibliographies, and diagrams, tables, formulas, line drawings, and graphs are interspersed throughout the text. The index is very general and cites, for the most part, just the major subsections; it is to be hoped that in future editions the index will be enlarged to improve reader access.

836. Gibilisco, Stan, and Neil Sclater, eds. **Encyclopedia of Electronics.** 2d ed. Blue Ridge Summit, PA, TAB Books, 1990. 960p. illus. index. $69.50. ISBN 0-8306-3389-8.

Encyclopedia of Electronics not only defines its more than 3,000 terms and phrases, it also explains them in language that is meaningful to the lay reader. Its scope includes the various subdisciplines within the fields of electricity, electronics, and communications. The text is enhanced with excellent drawings and, when appropriate, equations and formulas are also included. Cross references guide the reader to related terms; a good index provides further access.

837. Jay, Frank, ed. **IEEE Standard Dictionary of Electrical and Electronics Terms.** 4th ed. New York, Institute of Electrical and Electronics Engineers, 1988. 1270p. $65.00. ISBN 1-55937-000-9.

This massive volume briefly defines some 24,000 technical terms derived from all fields of electrical and electronic technology. Almost all of the definitions represent official standards of The Institute of Electrical and Electronics Engineers. Line drawings, diagrams, and formulas are included sporadically; in addition, a valuable appendix defines some 15,000 common acronyms associated with the field. Considered the standard purchase in this subject area.

For libraries that are unable to afford the IEEE publication, a less expensive alternative is Rufus P. Turner and Stan Gibilisco's *The Illustrated Dictionary of Electronics* (5th ed., TAB Books, 1991, 723p., $39.95; $26.95pa., ISBN 0-8306-7345-8; 0-8306-3345-6pa.). The 22,000 brief definitions and hundreds of line drawings that make up this dictionary are geared toward the information needs of the electronics hobbyist and professional, and do a good job of covering the industry jargon.

MECHANICAL

838. Avallone, Eugene A., and Theodore Baumeister III, eds. **Marks' Standard Handbook for Mechanical Engineers.** 9th ed. New York, McGraw-Hill, 1987. 1936p. illus. index. $115.00. ISBN 0-07-004127-X.

Marks has long been relied upon as a primary resource for students and practicing engineers. It is arranged by 19 broad topical sections; within these sections, encyclopedic articles address properties and handling of materials, machine elements, fuels and furnaces, power generation, pumps and compressors, instrumentation, and environmental control. The text is further clarified by nearly 3,000 tables and illustrations. A classic reference recommended for all libraries.

839. Oberg, Erik. **Machinery's Handbook: A Reference Book for the Mechanical Engineer, Designer, Manufacturing Engineer, Draftsman, Toolmaker, and Machinist.** 24th ed. New York, Industrial Press, 1992. 2543p. illus. index. $75.00. ISBN 0-8311-2424-5.

For 75 years, *Machinery's Handbook* has been considered the standard reference work on machines, mechanical products, machine shop practice, and other aspects of practical mechanical engineering. The topically organized materials encompass the broad areas of mathematical tables, logarithms, trigonometric functions, mechanics, strength of materials, gearing, screws, threads, fits, small tools, special feeds, steels, nonferrous materials, and weights and measures. Tables, standards, illustrations, brief text, definitions, formulae, and worked examples are all used to explain the topics under consideration. A thorough index concludes the handbook.

30

Life Sciences

NATURAL HISTORY

840. Allaby, Michael, ed. **The Oxford Dictionary of Natural History.** New York, Oxford University Press, 1985. 688p. bibliog. $49.95. ISBN 0-19-217720-6.

Intended as a resource for amateur naturalists, Allaby's dictionary contains approximately 12,000 short but informative definitions. Coverage includes the various disciplines likely to be encountered in the study of natural history, for example, ecology, cell biology, the earth sciences, genetics, statistics, biochemistry, meteorology, and observational astronomy. The taxa of plants and animals are listed to the family level, with cross references from common names. There are no illustrations.

A less exhaustive (and less expensive) alternative in this subject area is *The Cambridge Illustrated Dictionary of Natural History* (R. J. Lincoln and G. A. Boxshall, Cambridge University Press, 1987, 413p., $39.95, ISBN 0-521-30551-9; ISBN 0-521-39941-6pa.). Aimed at a general audience, this dictionary reflects the more limited view of natural history as the study of the plants, animals, and microorganisms that make up the living world. Its abundance of outstanding line drawings, however, make it a good complement to the Oxford title for libraries that can afford both.

BIOLOGY

841. **Biological & Agricultural Index: A Cumulative Subject Index to Periodicals ...** Bronx, NY, H. W. Wilson, 1916/18- . Monthly (except August); quarterly and annual cumulations. Sold on service basis. ISSN 0006-3177.

This well-known Wilson publication indexes 225 key English-language periodicals in the fields of agriculture, agricultural chemicals, animal husbandry, biochemistry, biology, biotechnology, botany, cytology, ecology, entomology, environmental science, fishery sciences, food science, forestry, genetics, horticulture, limnology, microbiology, nutrition, physiology, plant pathology, soil science, veterinary medicine, and zoology. The periodicals selected have been identified by librarians as sources most frequently cited for general use of students and laypersons. A separate index is devoted to current book reviews.

842. Hollar, David W. **The Origin and Evolution of Life on Earth: An Annotated Bibliography.** Pasadena, CA, Salem Press, 1992. 235p. index. $40.00. ISBN 0-89356-683-7.

Hollar's bibliography covers some 800 books on evolution that date from the 1800s to the early 1990s. After an introductory overview of the history of evolution and genetics and an explanation of chapter contents, the materials are presented by topic and subtopic and then by author. A substantial and informative annotation accompanies each entry. Although an author index is provided, the detailed table of contents provides the most useful access.

843. Margulis, Lynn, and Karlene V. Schwartz. **Five Kingdoms: An Illustrated Guide to the Phyla of Life on Earth.** 2d ed. New York, W. H. Freeman, 1988. 376p. illus. bibliog. index. $37.95; $26.95pa. ISBN 0-7167-1885; 0-7167-1912-6pa.

Intended for science students and laypersons, *Five Kingdoms* presents a broad overview of life on earth and its evolutionary history. It consists of five chapters: "Prokaryotae," "Protoctista," "Fungi," "Animalia," and "Plantae." Within these chapters, 92 phyla are described. The two-page entries for each include a brief descriptive narrative, a typical habitat, and illustrations of one or two species. Illustrations consist of a photograph and a labeled anatomical drawing of the organism. An appendix provides an extensive index, a 734-term glossary, and a list of about 1,000 genera with their respective phylum and common names.

844. Martin, Elizabeth, ed. **Concise Dictionary of Biology.** New York, Oxford University Press, 1985. 256p. illus. $17.95. ISBN 0-19-866144-4.

Drawn from the *Concise Science Dictionary* (Oxford University Press, 1984), Martin's excellent work is intended for the young biologist or lay reader. It defines more than 2,000 terms related to biology and biochemistry, with selected geological, physical, chemical, and medical terms included as appropriate. Definitions are clear, concise, and free from jargon; unfortunately, they do not indicate part of speech, pronunciation, or etymology. The dictionary provides some cross references and includes a number of good line drawings.

845. Tootill, Elizabeth, ed. **The Facts on File Dictionary of Biology.** Rev. ed. New York, Facts on File, 1988. 326p. illus. $24.95. ISBN 0-8160-1865-0; 0-8160-2368-9pa.

This excellent dictionary defines more than 3,000 terms encountered in the life sciences, from the most basic to the most advanced. Coverage is broad, encompassing such traditional fields as botany and anatomy as well as more esoteric areas such as molecular biology, genetics, and immunology. Definitions are written for the lay reader in clear, nontechnical English, and are accompanied by many helpful cross references. The 40 illustrations that have been included are mostly of chemical pathways or cellular anatomy.

BOTANY

General Works

846. Tootill, Elizabeth, ed. **The Facts on File Dictionary of Botany.** New York, Facts on File, 1984. 390p. illus. $24.95. ISBN 0-87196-861-4.

A resource for the student and interested lay reader, Tootill's botanical dictionary comprises 3,000 entries drawn from the pure and applied plant sciences, including taxonomy, anatomy, biochemistry, cell biology, plant pathology, genetics, and ecology. Coverage includes broad general concepts, technical terms, and even major groups of plants down to the level of important families. Definitions range from one or two lines to several paragraphs, and are supplemented by 35 diagrams, line drawings, and charts. Separate appendixes cover scientific terms and recommended chemical names for a number of common organic compounds. Recommended as a good general source for all libraries until a more current alternative is published.

847. **The Visual Dictionary of Plants.** New York, Dorling Kindersley; distr., Houghton Mifflin, 1992. 64p. illus. index. $14.95. ISBN 1-56458-016-4.

There are 25 topics here, each treated in a lavish 2-page picture essay. Topics range from specific parts of the plant (e.g., leaves, flowers) to plant types (e.g., carnivorous plants) to physiological topics (e.g., photosynthesis). Each topic commences with an introductory overview; the heart of the work, however, is found in the series of gorgeous color close-up photographs, micrographs, and color diagrams. In fact, most of the book's information lies in the precise labeling of every part of each illustration. Although no substitute for a good botanical dictionary, this is a wonderful and engaging supplement to one.

Flowers and Flowering Plants

848. Heywood, V.H., and others, eds. **Flowering Plants of the World.** Rev. ed. New York, Oxford University Press, 1993. 335p. illus. (part col.). maps. index. $45.00. ISBN 0-19-521037-9.

The highly regarded *Flowering Plants of the World* aims to appeal to both the general public and the professional. The book is arranged systematically to include 250,000 species in 306 flowering plant groups. Each family is described in regard to its characteristics, distribution, diagnostic features, classification, and economic uses. More than 200 beautifully rendered, full-color plates accompany the text, as do approximately 200 locator/distribution maps, a 20-page, fully illustrated glossary, and an index of English and Latin names.

849. Spellenberg, Richard. **Familiar Flowers of North America: Eastern Region.** New York, Alfred A. Knopf, 1986. 192p. illus. (part col.). index. $4.95pa. ISBN 0-317-56707-1. **Familiar Flowers of North America: Western Region.** 1986. 192p. illus. (part col.). index. $4.95pa. ISBN 0-317-56709-8.

Each of these two pocket guides describes 80 of the most common wildflowers found in their respective regions. The two-page entries are arranged by flower color and shape, and include a full-color photograph of each species on one page; on the opposite are found a description, an overview of habitat and range, and a discussion of look-alike species and relatives. Emphasis is on native plants, although some "immigrant" ones are included. A helpful glossary is found at the back of each guide.

Trees

850. Coombes, Allen J. **Trees.** New York, Dorling Kindersley, 1992. 320p. illus. index. $29.95; $17.95pa. ISBN 1-56458-075-X; 1-56458-072-5pa.

Trees is a photograph-based identification guide to more than 500 trees from around the world. The work begins with about 30 pages of information useful for

851. Petrides, George A. **Peterson First Guide to Trees.** Boston, Houghton Mifflin, 1993. 128p. illus. index. $4.95pa. ISBN 0-395-65972-8.

Although the Peterson field guides are well known to naturalists as excellent resources in a variety of subject areas, they can occasionally be too difficult for beginners; enter the new Peterson First Guide series. The primary focus of this introductory work is on 243 of the most common species of trees existing in North America. Its entries are arranged in six groups by leaf type and arrangement. In addition to brief, nontechnical descriptions, all entries are accompanied by excellent color drawings of leaves, bark, and fruit or flowers. Modest in price and ambition, this guide does a good job of introducing novice naturalists to the trees around them.

ZOOLOGY

General Works

852. Allaby, Michael, ed. **The Concise Oxford Dictionary of Zoology.** New York, Oxford University Press, 1991. 508p. $39.95. ISBN 0-19-866162-2.

This dictionary has definitions for more than 6,000 entries from "aardvark" to "zymogenous," written in a straightforward, understandable style. The terms are primarily taxonomic in nature, although subject terms in ecology, behavior, cell structure and function, physiology, zoo geography, and genetics are covered. Animal groups covered include invertebrates, fishes, reptiles, amphibians, birds, and mammals. Information on each group includes a description of the organism, number of species, and geographic distribution, with the length of each definition varying from a few words to more than a column. A good, reasonably current dictionary that covers the entire field of zoology.

853. **The Grolier World Encyclopedia of Endangered Species.** Danbury, CT, Grolier, 1993. 10v. illus. maps. index. $319.00/set. ISBN 0-7172-7192-7.

The species identified in this stunning Grolier set include those classified as "rare," "vulnerable," "endangered," or "extinct." Accompanied by more than 700 exquisite photographs commissioned specifically for the encyclopedia, the materials are arranged by the geographical regions of Africa, Asia, North America, South America, Oceania, and Europe. Within each region, animals are arranged according to family, order, and class. Their entries note endangered status; provide a map showing current distribution; describe physical characteristics, patterns of feeding, mating, and migration, and natural habitat; and discuss factors threatening the species. Access is provided by two indexes, one by common animal name and one by animal type.

854. O'Brien, Tim. **Where the Animals Are: A Guide to the Best Zoos, Aquariums, and Wildlife Attractions in North America.** Old Saybrook, CT, Globe Pequot Press, 1992. 301p. illus. index. $12.95pa. ISBN 1-56640-077-8.

O'Brien has compiled a very useful introduction to more than 250 of the best zoos, aquaria, wildlife sanctuaries, and other animal exhibits in the United States and

Canada. Information provided for each attraction includes its address and telephone number, general background and history, hours and time of year open, cost, highlights of the exhibits and entertainment, extras (for example, trains and children's zoos), food service, amount of time to allow, directions to the attraction, and other nearby attractions. A great resource for all public libraries.

Another good "where the animals are" guide is Laura Riley and William Riley's *Guide to the National Wildlife Refuges* (rev. ed., New York, Collier Books/Macmillan, 1992, 684p., $16.00pa., ISBN 0-02-063660-1). It describes more than 200 National Wildlife Refuge sanctuaries found throughout the United States. Roughly two pages in length, each sanctuary's entry provides information on the area's natural history (including its plants, mammals, insects, and birds); a general description of the biological importance of the refuge; and a list of the specialty species to be found there. In addition, the Rileys provide details on how to get there, what to look for, places to stay, times to visit, local history, and other nearby attractions. Given their reasonable prices and complementary coverage, these two works are highly recommended for all public libraries.

Birds

855. Harrison, Colin, and Alan Greensmith. **Birds of the World.** New York, Dorling Kindersley, 1993. 416p. illus. maps. index. $29.95; $19.95pa. ISBN 1-56458-296-5; 1-56458-295-7pa.

Birds of the World reflects the outstanding visual presentation style familiar to readers of Dorling Kindersley publications. Drawing on the entire range of bird families, the work briefly describes and stunningly illustrates more than 800 species of birds; in addition, small pictorial keys show distribution and provide information about the species' habitats, body size, and juvenile plumage. Novice bird enthusiasts will especially appreciate the handbook's short introduction to birdwatching and identification and the ornithological glossary.

856. Perrins, Christopher M., and Alex L. A. Middleton, eds. **The Encyclopedia of Birds.** New York, Facts on File, 1985. 445p. illus. (part col). maps. bibliog. index. $45.00. ISBN 0-8160-1150-8.

The world's 180 bird families are profiled (and richly illustrated) in this engaging resource. It includes information on their distribution and ecology, physical characteristics, evolution and classification, diet and feeding habits, social organization, and survival status, as well as covering such special topics as lead poisoning in waterfowl, sexual dimorphism in birds of prey, and water transport in sand grouse. More than 700 color photographs and paintings supplement the narrative, while maps show the worldwide distribution of the bird families in question. Includes a brief glossary and an index.

857. Terres, John K. **The Audubon Society Encyclopedia of North American Birds.** New York, Random House, 1991. 1109p. illus. index. $39.99. ISBN 0-517-03288-0.

The exhaustive *Audubon Society Encyclopedia of North American Birds*, a reprint of the 1980 edition published by Alfred A. Knopf, encompasses nearly 6,000 alphabetically arranged entries that include life histories of 847 species of birds, biographical sketches of more than 120 people for whom American birds have been named, 625 major articles on ornithological subjects, and more than 700 definitions of ornithological terms. In addition, the work includes 1,675 illustrations (including

875 color photos), 4,000 well-chosen cross references, and a comprehensive, alphabetically arranged bibliography.

Fishes, Mollusks, and Seashells

858. Banister, Keith, and Andrew Campbell, eds. **The Encyclopedia of Aquatic Life.** New York, Facts on File, 1985. 349p. illus. index. $45.00. ISBN 0-8160-1257-1.

A useful, reasonably priced introduction to aquatic zoology for general readers, this encyclopedia focuses on life forms (excluding plants) that inhabit the water for their entire life cycle. The materials are arranged within three topical sections: fishes, aquatic invertebrates, and sea mammals. Each section leads off with a brief overview of its topic, then addresses individual taxonomic groups in well-written, informative articles. Insets within articles note classification data and geographic distribution; additional special-topic entries complement the main articles. A bibliography of important references, a three-section glossary, and a detailed index further enhance this well-executed resource.

859. Dance, S. Peter. **Shells.** New York, Dorling Kindersley, 1992. 256p. illus. index. $29.95; $17.95pa. ISBN 1-56458-032-6; 1-56458-060-1pa.

Dance's work serves as an identification guide to more than 500 species of seashells worldwide, with heavy emphasis on gastropods (e.g., snails, limpets, conchs, cowries, tritons, whelks, cones) and bivalves (e.g., clams, oysters, scallops, cockles). Entries for each species include a color photograph, scientific and common names, a brief description, size, habitat and range, region of the world where found, and frequency of occurrence. The work manages both to convey the beauty of shells and to serve as a practical identification guide for hundreds of species.

Insects

860. O'Toole, Christopher, ed. **The Encyclopedia of Insects.** New York, Facts on File, 1986. 160p. illus. index. $24.95. ISBN 0-8160-1358-6.

An introductory survey of arthropods' "success story," with an emphasis on insects, O'Toole's encyclopedia describes insect evolution and classification, common physical features, and life cycles and reproduction. Articles are arranged biosystematically, and are enhanced by more than 160 full-color photographs and illustrations, as well as by numerous insets covering such specialized topics as territoriality in dragonflies, "singing" in cicadas, and the survival of larvae under water. A glossary defines 175 terms found throughout the text; an index concludes the encyclopedia.

Mammals

861. Keienburg, Wolf, ed. **Grzimek's Encyclopedia of Mammals.** New York, McGraw-Hill, 1990. 5v. illus. maps. index. $525.00/set. ISBN 0-07-909508-9.

This classic, comprehensive reference focuses on mammals—including marine mammals, domesticated species such as dogs and cats, and humans—in their natural environment. Volume 1 contains an introductory overview of mammals and their evolution, anatomy, physiology, ecology, and ethology, as well as information about conservation and environmental concerns. The remainder of the set is arranged by orders, grouping together those mammals most closely related. Individual species are described within families, families within orders. Articles are written at a level appropriate to both the interested lay reader and the professional, and are enhanced by standardized comparative charts, diagrams, and photographs. Although hindered somewhat by weak indexing, *Grzimek's Encyclopedia of Mammals* is nevertheless highly recommended as a standard purchase for all libraries.

If libraries are unable to afford *Grzimek's* or would like to have further coverage in this subject area, an excellent alternative is the two-volume *Walker's Mammals of the World* (5th ed., Ronald M. Nowak, Johns Hopkins University Press, 1991, $95.00/set, ISBN 0-8018-3970-X). The arrangement is systematic by order. Each order is introduced with general information on the group and followed by descriptions of each family and genus in the order, including information on threatened or endangered status. Black-and-white photographs accompany most descriptions. Each volume has a complete index to both volumes, and a 113-page bibliography is included in volume 2.

862. Macdonald, David, ed. **The Encyclopedia of Mammals.** New York, Facts on File, 1984. 895p. illus. (part col.). maps. index. $65.00. ISBN 0-87196-871-1.

Macdonald's *Encyclopedia of Mammals* addresses basic evolutionary facts, appearance, social patterns, and environmental concerns for some 700 separate mammals, including all important and many unique species. All of the 800 illustrations are in color and usually show the animal in its habitat. Line drawings illustrate particular aspects of behavior or anatomical distinctions between otherwise similar species. In addition, charts show size relative to humans, give average body sizes, gestation period, longevity, geographic distribution, and other statistics and data. A feast for the eyes as well as the intellect.

Reptiles and Amphibians

863. Cogger, Harold G., and Richard G. Zweifel. **Reptiles & Amphibians.** New York, Smithmark, 1992. 240p. illus. maps. index. $24.98. ISBN 0-8317-2786-1.

Written by 16 noted scholars, the narrative in *Reptiles & Amphibians* is organized into three parts. The first six chapters deal with world amphibians and reptiles in general. Higher taxa are introduced; then classification, origins and historical topics, habitats and adaptations, behavior, and endangered species are sequentially covered. Part 2 comprises three chapters devoted to caecilians, salamanders and newts, and frogs and toads. The third part includes chapters on turtles and tortoises, lizards, snakes, and crocodiles and alligators. Notes on contributors and an index round out the work.

GENERAL WORKS

Atlases

864. Parker, Steve. **The Body Atlas.** New York, Dorling Kindersley, 1993. 63p. illus. index. $19.95. ISBN 1-56458-224-8.

The Body Atlas first illustrates each of the systems of the body, such as the skeletal and nervous systems, then describes specific body parts and organs. Detailed drawings and illustrations show the body part in action; the text includes interesting historical and physiological facts. Although the material in this large-format atlas is written for older elementary students, the information and detailed illustrations will engage and educate interested readers of all ages.

For libraries where a more exhaustive work is needed, the recommended alternative is Anne M. R. Agur and Ming J. Lee's *Grant's Atlas of Anatomy* (9th ed., Williams & Wilkins, 1991, 650p., $50.00pa. ISBN 0-683-03701-3). Although not as well known as the standard medical text, *Gray's Anatomy of the Human Body* (30th ed., Lea & Febiger, 1984), it is more current, easier to use, and contains excellent illustrations, color prints, "overview" drawings, line art, and correlated imaging and photography. An extensive index of more than 20 pages completes the atlas.

Bibliographies

865. Day, Melvin S., ed. **Federal Health Information Resources.** Arlington, VA, Information Resources Press, 1987. 246p. index. $29.50. ISBN 0-87815-055-2.

This guide describes 187 federal agencies that collect and disseminate information on such health concerns as aerospace medicine, orphan drugs, physical fitness, poisons and antidotes, radio-biology, rape, and veterans' medical care. The entries are arranged by subject, and include the basic directory-type information in addition to well-written descriptions of each agency's services, databases, and publications. This main section is preceded by a list of acronyms, followed by an appendix of 66 salient databases. Two indexes—one by agency/organization, the other by subject/title—round out the guide.

866. **Medical and Health Care Books and Serials in Print [yr.]: An Index to Literature in the Health Sciences.** New Providence, NJ, R.R. Bowker, 1972- . Annual. 2v. index. $225.00/set (1994 ed.). ISSN 0000-085X.

This bibliography is the standard guide for identifying what health-related books and journals are currently available for purchase. It contains a list of 70,000 monographic titles and 15,500 serial entries, all arranged alphabetically by author name within 7,200 medical and allied health subject areas and organized by main entry and Library of Congress subject headings. The book titles are works published or distributed in the United States, whereas serial coverage is international in scope. Each main entry provides author, title, ISBN or ISSN, publisher, year of publication, and price. In addition, a separate section lists the names, addresses, and telephone numbers of firms that publish in the health fields.

867. Rees, Alan M., ed. **Encyclopedia of Health Information Sources: A Bibliographic Guide to Over 13,000 Citations for Publications, Organizations, and Databases on Health-Related Subjects.** 2d ed. Detroit, Gale, 1993. 521p. $165.00. ISBN 0-8103-6909-5.

Covering both the popular and scientific literature, the second edition of this handy resource contains more than 13,000 citations from 6,715 unique sources covering the medical specialties, allied health professions, alternative health disciplines, health care administration, and education. The text is arranged alphabetically by subject; within subjects, citations are grouped alphabetically by type, such as abstracting, indexing, current awareness, associations, and journals. Each citation includes title, name and address of publisher, telephone and fax numbers, and frequency of issuance or publication date. Although there is no index, an outline of contents lists subject headings, while extensive cross references in the outline and in the text facilitate access.

A related Gale title libraries may also want to consider is *Encyclopedia of Medical Organizations and Agencies: A Subject Guide to Some 12,200 ...* (5th ed., Karen Backus, ed., 1994, 1200p., $220.00, ISBN 0-8103-8200-8). Focusing on U.S. health-related institutions, organizations, and agencies, the guide covers a wide range of health care (e.g., surgery, pathology, public health, social work) under 69 topical categories. Address, telephone number, membership size, publications, contact person, and a brief description of major research interests and funding priorities are included for each group.

868. Rees, Alan M., and Catherine Hoffman. **The Consumer Health Information Source Book.** 4th ed. Phoenix, AZ, Oryx Press, 1994. 240p. index. $44.50pa. ISBN 0-89774-796-8.

Intended to help health care consumers make informed choices, Rees and Hoffman's sourcebook is organized into three sections. Part 1 addresses the twin issues of health information and medical consumerism. Part 2 comprises chapters on information access, listing health information clearinghouses and information centers, hotlines and toll-free numbers, and other health organizations accessible to the general public. Part 3, the largest section, covers information materials and resources, including excellent evaluations of consumer health books. New to this edition are chapters on health care reform, a recommended core collection of the 44 best consumer-oriented health publications, and a list of 23 electronic publications and databases, for a total coverage of 3,500 health information sources. The sourcebook concludes with author, title, and subject indexes and a directory of publishers' addresses.

Dictionaries and Encyclopedias

869. Bohlander, Richard, and others, eds. **Macmillan Health Encyclopedia.** New York, Macmillan, 1993. 9v. illus. index. $360.00/set. ISBN 0-02-897439-5.

The nine volumes comprising the *Macmillan Health Encyclopedia* cover six broad subject areas: body systems; communicable diseases; noncommunicable diseases and disorders; nutrition and fitness; emotional and mental health; and health care systems. Subjects are arranged alphabetically within each volume. Ranging in length from one paragraph to several pages, the entries are enhanced by the judicious use of color illustrations, diagrams, and charts interwoven throughout. Each volume has its own index, glossary, brief bibliography of sources, and a list of organizations providing information on the topics covered; volume 9 provides a master index. Written in a style that is easy to understand for students and lay readers, the encyclopedia is an informative, if expensive, resource for health information.

870. Hensyl, William R., ed. **Stedman's Medical Dictionary.** 25th ed. Baltimore, MD, Williams & Wilkins, 1990. 1784p. illus. $43.00. ISBN 0-683-07916-6.

Stedman's is organized into five parts, the first of which details how to use the dictionary. The remaining sections are a cursory medical etymology; a "subentry locator," which is essentially a dictionary-within-a-dictionary; the dictionary of approximately 100,000 entries, 24 color plates, 125 tables, and hundreds of illustrations; and a series of appendixes that include comparative temperature scales, temperature equivalents, various weights and measures, laboratory reference range values, and blood groups. Definitions are brief and geared toward the needs of health professionals or knowledgeable lay readers.

Stedman's is less technical than its two closest competitors, *Dorland's Illustrated Medical Dictionary* (27th ed., W. B. Saunders, 1988, 1888p., $41.00, ISBN 0-7216-3154-1) and *Black's Medical Dictionary* (Gordon Macpherson, ed., Barnes & Noble Books/Rowman & Littlefield, 1992, 645p., $67.50, ISBN 0-389-20989-9). However, another work, *Merriam-Webster's Medical Desk Dictionary* (Merriam-Webster, 1993, 790p., $24.95, ISBN 0-87779-125-2) is a good complement to *Stedman's* because of its focus on the information needs—and nontechnical background—of the general user. It defines roughly 55,000 alphabetically arranged terms and phrases, noting parts of speech, pronunciation, illustrative examples of the entry word used in context, and other useful information. It also offers more than 1,000 biographical profiles.

871. Lovejoy, Frederick H., ed. **The New Child Health Encyclopedia: The Complete Guide for Parents.** Boston Children's Hospital. New York, Dell, 1987. 740p. illus. index. $19.95pa. ISBN 0-385-29597-9.

The target audience for this excellent child health resource is parents and child care providers. The book's four sections address "Keeping Children Healthy," "Finding Health Care for Children," "Emergencies," and "Diseases and Symptoms." This last contains current information on signs and symptoms, diagnosis, cause, treatment, and prevention of almost 300 health concerns. The editors suggest that the contents of the first three sections be read by all who care for children, and that that last section be relied upon as a reference tool to be consulted as necessary.

872. Tver, David F., and Percy Russell. **The Nutrition and Health Encyclopedia.** 2d ed. New York, Van Nostrand Reinhold, 1989. 639p. $49.95. ISBN 0-442-23397-3.

Although this work is written at a level appropriate to physicians, scientists, and other health care providers who work with nutritional science, it can still answer questions for an informed public. The text is an alphabetical list of definitions that cover a wide variety of nutrition-related topics, such as food additives, aspects of human physiology, nutritional diseases, food entries, and vitamins. Definitions range in length from a sentence to a page, and occasionally include chemical structures or usage tables. Thirteen appendixes are devoted to special topics.

Two other good sources in this subject area are Kenneth Anderson and Lois Harmon's *The Prentice-Hall Dictionary of Nutrition and Health* (Prentice-Hall, 1985, 257p., $21.95; $9.95pa., ISBN 0-13-695610-6; 0-13-695602-5pa.) and *The Mount Sinai School of Medicine Complete Book of Nutrition* (Victor Herbert and others, St. Martin's Press, 1990, 796p., $35.00, ISBN 0-312-05129-8). The former contains more than 1,200 clearly written, easily understood definitions of terms and phrases encountered by readers trying to understand the nutritional makeup of the foods they eat. The latter emphasizes special nutrition needs and problems and the role of nutrition in common disease. The editors provide basic information and recommendations on each topic, plus evidence to support their advice.

Directories

873. Lesko, Matthew, with Mary Ann Artello and Andrew Naprawa. **What to Do When You Can't Afford Health Care: An "A-to-Z" Sourcebook for the Entire Family.** Kensington, MD, Information USA, 1993. 769. index. $24.95pa. ISBN 1-878346-16-4.

Peripatetic data "compiler" Lesko here provides information on free and low-cost health care and other health care-related services, primarily those available from state and federal agencies. The directory's three main sections address how to obtain free and low-cost medical treatment, including information on obtaining such care from hospitals or through clinical trials; provide topically arranged entries for clearinghouses, hotlines, publications, videos, and the like related to specific diseases, ranging from abetalipoproteinemia to zoonoses; and list consumer resources for free and low-cost legal help to resolve health-related legal issues, such as billing disputes or the right to quality treatment. Additional materials include a section on "The Art of Getting a Bureaucrat to Help You"; sample success stories; and three appendixes covering clinical studies, free medications, and state health statistics.

Two other related titles libraries might want to obtain are Arthur Winter and Ruth Winter's *Consumer's Guide to Free Medical Information by Phone and by Mail* (Prentice-Hall Professional, Technical, and Reference, 1993, 328p., $24.95; $14.95pa., ISBN 0-13-096199-X; 0-13-333535-6pa.) and Elizabeth Vierck's *Paying for Health Care after Age 65* (ABC-Clio, 1990, 291p., $45.00, ISBN 0-87436-095-1). The first title directs the reader to accurate, current information on more than 300 health-related issues, from sports injuries to the latest cancer treatments. The second work does a good job of providing Medicare users with a straightforward guide to and explanation of Medicare, Medicaid, supplemental insurance, and related issues, while also providing access to organizational and print sources of additional information.

PHARMACOLOGY

874. Bindler, Ruth McGillis, Yvonne Tso, and Linda Berner Howry. **The Parent's Guide to Pediatric Drugs.** New York, Harper & Row, 1986. 313p. illus. index. $20.00; $9.95pa. ISBN 0-06-181097-5; 0-06-096073-6pa.

The authors of this guide have done a thorough job of providing information that will help all parents needing to know more about not only specific drugs, but also how children's systems respond to medication in general. The opening chapters discuss how medicines act in children, why maintenance of a therapeutic level of a drug is so important, and the best ways to administer drugs to occasionally resistant young ones. The following chapters are organized by various body systems, with the appropriate over-the-counter drugs described as to trade names, dosage forms, administration methods, unintended effects, contraindications, drug and food interactions, and age limitations. The last three chapters provide similar information for prescription drugs commonly given to children. Concluding materials include a glossary of medical and pharmaceutical terms, a bibliography of books on child rearing and development, and an index that includes generic and brand names, symptoms, and classes of drugs.

875. Harkness, Richard. **Drug Interactions Guide Book.** Englewood Cliffs, NJ, Prentice-Hall, 1991. 288p. index. $24.95; $12.95pa. ISBN 0-13-219601-8; 0-13-219619-0pa.

This guidebook is intended to help readers become active partners in their own health care by avoiding hazardous adverse effects caused by drug interactions. The main section of the book covers basic drug interactions for 314 drugs, providing information for each regarding severity, probability, uses for the drugs, possible adverse effects, and advice on how to handle these bad reactions. Supplemental chapters deal very briefly with potentially dangerous depressants and stimulants that can act as add-on drugs, medications prescribed for 18 common health disorders, and possible bad interactions between basic foods and specific drug groups.

876. Long, James W. **The Essential Guide to Prescription Drugs.** New York, HarperCollins, 1982- . Biennial 1v. $35.00; $17.00pa. (1994 ed.). No ISSN available.

Long's well-known, authoritative guide profiles 219 prescription drugs (and aspirin) commonly prescribed in the United States and Canada. Drugs are listed alphabetically by generic name; for each are given the year introduced, brand names, principal uses, physiology, dosage and dosing, duration of use, adverse effects, precautions for use, possible effects on sexual function, habit-forming potential, effects of overdosage, drug interactions, and discontinuation of use. Supplementary materials include sections on safe usage guidelines, chronic disorder treatments, and drug classes; a glossary of drug-related terms; tables of drug information; and a short bibliography. Brand and generic drug names, as well as names of disorders, are all found in the index.

Although Long's guide should be considered the first purchase in this subject area, there are many other resources that libraries may wish to have on hand for their patrons. These include *The Pill Book* (4th ed., Bantam Books, 1990, 980p., $5.95pa., ISBN 0-553-27934-3), an inexpensive guide that describes more than 1,600 generic and brand-name drugs in nontechnical, user-friendly language; *The Complete Drug Reference* (Consumer Reports Books, 1991- . annual. 1v., $39.95pa. [1994 ed.], no ISSN available), which notes for more than 5,500 drugs their brand names, general description, contraindications, proper usage, precautions while using, and side effects; and the reliable and well-regarded *Complete Guide to Prescription &*

Non-Prescription Drugs (7th ed. H. Winter Griffith, 1232p., Price Stern Sloan, 1990, $25.00; $14.95pa., ISBN 0-89586-860-1; 0-89586-859-8pa.), a work that provides information in a chart format for more than 4,000 brand-name and 490 generic drugs.

877. **Physicians' Desk Reference, [yr.].** Oradell, NJ, Medical Economics Books, 1947- . Annual. 1v. illus. (part col.) index. $57.95 (1994 ed.). ISSN 0093-4461. **Physicians Desk Reference for Non-Prescription Drugs, [yr.].** 1980- . Annual. 1v. illus. (part col.) index. $35.95 (1994 ed.). ISSN 1044-1395.

PDR and its younger sibling are intended for use by medical practitioners, but well-informed laypersons find them useful as well. The text is basically a compilation of the product information package inserts found with all commonly available drugs. Entries for each drug include chemical structure, pharmacological actions, medical indications, contraindications, precautions, adverse reactions, directions for use, and the forms in which it is available. Separate sections list drugs made by each manufacturer, trade names of listed drugs, drugs by product category (for example, antibiotics), and a color reproduction of selected products. Both publications are also available online and on CD-ROM.

878. Yudofsky, Stuart, Robert E. Hales, and Tom Ferguson. **What You Need to Know about Psychiatric Drugs.** New York, Grove Weidenfeld; distr., Ingram, 1991. 646p. index. $35.00. ISBN 0-8021-1281-1.

More than 100 prescription drugs for a wide variety of mental disorders are listed in this work. Entries are arranged alphabetically by generic name, and include brand name; drug group; overdose reactions; precautions for pregnant women, infants/children, people over 60, and patients who drive or operate machinery; general information; benefits; risks; guidelines for users; drug interactions; habit-forming potential; and effects of long-term use. A chart accompanies each drug mentioned and states whether the frequency of a symptom is common or rare. In addition to the drug monographs, there are numerous chapters devoted to each of the drug classes (for example, antidepressants, sedatives and sleeping pills, psychiatric drugs of the future), which explain, in lay terms, the psychiatric disorder, case studies, and various families of drugs used for the disorder.

POPULAR MEDICAL GUIDES

879. Griffith, H. Winter. **Complete Guide to Symptoms, Illness & Surgery for People over 50.** New York, Body Press/Putnam, 1992. 868p. illus. index. $18.95pa. ISBN 0-399-51749-9.

For lay readers who would like more information about specific diseases than is often available from their doctors, this helpful guide discusses common symptoms, illnesses, surgeries, and general information about categories of medications. Each of the alphabetically arranged topics outlines special considerations for older adults, home care and self-treatments, and situations when physician consultation is needed. An appendix offers information on a variety of issues of importance to those over age 50, ranging from health promotion and disease prevention to abuse and driving ability. The guide concludes with a list of references and organizations that can provide additional data on selected health issues, plus an index.

880. Klayman, Charles B., ed. **The American Medical Association Family Medical Guide.** Rev. ed. New York, Random House, 1994. 832p. illus. index. $37.50. ISBN 0-679-41290-5.

Although this guide is aimed primarily at home users, it is equally valuable in public library settings. Its strengths include currency, extensive and clear illustrations, and good indexing and cross-referencing. The handbook is organized into four main sections, each with its own index. The first section deals with the healthy body (stress, diet, exercise, etc.) and includes a 16-page atlas of the body; the second comprises 162 pages of symptom and self-diagnosis charts; the third provides simple explanations of 650 diseases and medical conditions (arranged by body system); the last discusses caring for the sick (health care systems, home care, death and dying). Supplementary materials include a drug index, a section devoted to accidents and emergencies, and a 400-term glossary.

A handy resource to accompany the AMA's reference is the *Complete Guide to Symptoms, Illness & Surgery* (rev. ed., H. Winter Griffith, Price Stern Sloan, 1989, $15.95pa. ISBN 0-89586-798-2), which describes nearly 800 symptoms (listed in chart form), more than 500 illnesses (what they're like, what to expect, how to treat them, and when to call the doctor), and 100 surgeries (general information plus postoperative care indications). Includes a glossary, an index, and a selected bibliography.

881. **The New Our Bodies, Ourselves: A Book by and for Women: Updated and Expanded for the 1990s.** Boston Women's Health Book Collective. New York, Simon & Schuster, 1992. 751p. illus. index. $20.00pa. ISBN 0-671-79176-1.

A familiar, respected resource in all libraries, *The New Our Bodies, Ourselves* continues to offer current, practical information about women's bodies and health care choices. It is organized into seven broad sections: "Taking Care of Ourselves" (body image, food, alcohol, women in motion, etc.); "Relationships and Sexuality" (treating relationships with men as well as lesbianism); "Controlling Our Fertility" (reproduction, birth control, sexually transmitted diseases, etc.); "Childbearing" (pregnancy, childbirth, postpartum, infertility and pregnancy loss); "Women Growing Older" (issues associated with physically and emotionally healthy aging); "Common and Uncommon Health and Medical Problems"; and "Women and the Medical System." Diagrams, illustrations, and wonderful black-and-white photographs accompany the clearly written articles, which also include useful (and current) bibliographies.

882. Starck, Marcia. **The Complete Handbook of Natural Healing.** St. Paul, MN, Llewellyn, 1991. 393p. illus. index. $12.95pa. ISBN 0-87542-742-1.

Starck's handbook provides a broad introduction to nontraditional ways of viewing health and disease, including all natural healing methods used today. Among those discussed are dietary regimens, nutritional supplements, cleansing and detoxification, vitamins and minerals, herbology, homeopathic medicine, traditional Chinese medicine, ayurvedic medicine, and crystal healing. In a section describing 44 specific ailments, the handbook covers their physical, mental, and emotional causes and recommendations for healing using natural treatments of diet, herbs, supplements, and body work. Appendixes list addresses and directory information for consultation and herb sources; homeopathic remedies; flower essences; correspondence courses in ayurvedic medicine, crystals, and aromatherapy; and organizations that provide information about food irradiation.

883. **The Wellness Encyclopedia: The Comprehensive Family Resource for Safeguarding Health and Preventing Illness.** By the editors of the University of California, Berkeley, Wellness Letter. Boston, Houghton Mifflin, 1991. 541p. index. $17.45pa. ISBN 0-395-61330-2.

Designed for family members of all ages, this health care guide presents positive, practical guidelines for maintaining good health. The information is arranged in the five major categories of longevity, nutrition, exercise, self-care, and environment and safety. Illustrations, colored prints, and notes in margins draw attention to important points. Especially helpful for older readers, the encyclopedia has been rendered in large, legible type.

SPECIFIC CONDITIONS AND DISEASES

AIDS

884. Hombs, Mary Ellen. **AIDS Crisis in America: A Reference Handbook.** Santa Barbara, CA, ABC-Clio, 1992. 268p. index. $39.50. ISBN 0-87436-648-8.

AIDS Crisis in America summarizes, abstracts, and extracts key information on this deadly disease and places it in a cohesive and easily accessible format. Chapters present basic definitions, demographics, and policy issues; a selective chronology and biographical sketches; facts, statistics (national, global, states, and specific populations) and public opinion polls pertaining to AIDS; key government and agency reports; legal aspects of AIDS; organizations, hotlines, and government agencies; and a basic bibliography of print and nonprint materials useful for the average reader. A glossary and index conclude the work.

885. Malinowsky, H. Robert, and Gerald J. Perry, eds. **AIDS Information Sourcebook.** 3d ed. Phoenix, AZ, Oryx Press, 1991. 312p. index. $39.95pa. ISBN 0-89774-598-1.

The *AIDS Information Sourcebook* provides both a sound introduction to the subject and a wealth of ready-reference information. The work is organized into four parts: the first is a chronology of the previous 10 years; the second a directory of more than 900 AIDS-related organizations; the third a 1,500-item bibliography of periodical articles, books, bibliographies, and other useful print and nonprint materials; and the last a grouping of selected statistical tables and a glossary of AIDS-related terms. A well-executed, thorough, and valuable reference appropriate for all libraries.

886. Watstein, Sarah Barbara, and Robert Anthony Laurich. **AIDS and Women: A Sourcebook.** Phoenix, AZ, Oryx Press, 1991. 159p. index. $36.50pa. ISBN 0-89774-577-9.

This topically arranged reader is made up of 14 chapters that provide summaries of laboratory, medical, and health research; statistical profiles; directory information; definitions; research methods for continuing education; and bibliographical citations to a broad range of materials. Chapters lead off with introductory overviews, then identify recommended citations and abstracts. Appendixes include a list of audiovisual resources, a directory of agencies and organizations, a glossary, and a brief guide to continuing education. Author, title, and subject indexes round out the work.

Cancer

887. Altman, Roberta, and Michael J. Sarg. **The Cancer Dictionary.** New York, Facts on File, 1992. 334p. index. $35.00. ISBN 0-8160-2608-4.

The 2,500 terms found in Altman and Sarg's encyclopedic dictionary range from succinct one-paragraph explanations to lengthy discussions, particularly for the most common types of cancer. Intended to help patients and their caretakers understand all aspects of the disease, the articles are painstakingly written and cover symptoms, diagnostic tests, risk factors, staging, conventional and alternative treatments, prevention, and many other subjects. Useful appendixes include lists of support organizations for cancer and AIDS; comprehensive cancer centers by state; clinical trial groups; and drugs used in treating cancer and AIDS, arranged by clinical and brand names. A brief bibliography precedes a categorized subject index.

888. Dollinger, Malin, Ernest H. Rosenbaum, and Greg Cable. **Everyone's Guide to Cancer Therapy.** 2d ed. Kansas City, MO, Andrews and McMeel, 1994. 654p. illus. index. $29.95; $19.95pa. ISBN 0-8362-2428-0; 0-8362-2427-2pa.

The guide's intent is to bring much-needed information on diagnosis and treatment to cancer sufferers and their loved ones. Within these parameters, the book presents general information on diagnosis, treatments, supportive care, advances and developments, screening, and prevention. The bulk of the book is devoted to overviews of the numerous common cancers, with descriptions of risk factors, screening, common signs and symptoms, diagnosis, staging, factors that affect prognosis and treatment, treatment overview and follow-up, recurrent cancers, and important questions that patients should ask their doctors. Supplementary materials include a glossary; a list of anticancer drugs and their side effects; a directory of cancer centers, associations, and support groups; a list of suggested readings; and the Physicians Data Query System for Cancer Treatment Information, available through the CompuServe computer network.

889. Fink, John M. **Third Opinion: An International Directory to Alternative Therapy Centers for the Treatment and Prevention of Cancer and Other Degenerative Diseases.** 2d ed. Garden City Park, NY, Avery, 1992. 312p. index. $14.95pa. ISBN 0-89529-503-2.

Clinics, doctors, health practitioners, educators, support groups, and practitioners of alternative medicine and treatments in both the United States and other countries are identified in this unusual directory. The book is divided into four major sections: treatment centers, educational centers, support groups, and information services. Every individual and institute identified was interviewed by the author; the resulting information includes name, telephone number, address, personnel, travel directions, illnesses treated, length of stay, and costs. Appendixes list available services alphabetically by country and region, and a bibliography of books supportive of alternative therapies provides further information. A substantial index rounds out the work.

890. Holleb, Arthur I., ed. **American Cancer Society Cancer Book: Prevention, Detection, Diagnosis, Treatment, Rehabilitation, Cure.** New York, Doubleday, 1986. 650p. index. $24.95pa. ISBN 0-385-17847-6.

Written for the general reader, this comprehensive overview of cancer and its treatment is organized into two parts. The first describes therapies, pain treatments, coping strategies, prevention, and rehabilitation approaches. The second addresses the biology, prevention, diagnosis, and treatment of cancers in various parts of the body. In addition to the main text, there are listings of organizations to contact for further information and of cancer centers, as well as a glossary and index. Although many changes have taken place in cancer studies since this sourcebook was published, it is still valuable for its broad overview of a complex subject.

Heart Disease

891. Goldman, Martin E. **The Handbook of Heart Drugs: A Consumer's Guide to Safe and Effective Use.** New York, Henry Holt, 1992. 297p. index. $29.95; $12.95pa. ISBN 0-8050-1720-8; 0-8050-1721-6pa.

Goldman's handbook is an informative resource for individuals who take heart medications as well as those who care for those individuals. Beginning with a chapter on physician-patient relationships and communications, the work then describes common forms of heart disease and disease symptoms, risk factors, how heart drugs work (including tolerance levels, drug schedules, and possible adverse reactions), and the importance of patient compliance and monitoring. The second half of the guide profiles approximately 90 commonly used heart drugs categorized by function. Each profile lists brand and generic names, explains how the medication works, and gives its purpose, dosage, possible side effects and adverse reactions, and other relevant information.

SUBSTANCE ABUSE

892. O'Brien, Robert, and Morris Chafetz. **The Encyclopedia of Alcoholism.** 2d ed. New York, Facts on File, 1991. 346p. illus. index. $45.00. ISBN 0-8160-1955-X.

The 600 terms found in *The Encyclopedia of Alcoholism* include entries on legislation, medical terms and diseases, well-known reports, organizations, alcoholic beverages, theories, racial and ethnic groups, and other alcoholism-related terms. Definitions range from paragraphs to several pages, and are often enhanced by statistical tables and charts, recommendations for further reading, and cross references. In addition to a lengthy bibliography, the work also provides tables and figures on alcoholism, a list of periodicals related to alcohol abuse, selected sources of information, and a name/title/subject index. A basic purchase for coverage of this important topic.

893. O'Brien, Robert, and others. **The Encyclopedia of Drug Abuse.** 2d ed. New York, Facts on File, 1992. 500p. index. $45.00. ISBN 0-8160-1956-8.

Designed for both lay readers and professionals, the second edition of this highly regarded reference covers a broad range of topics, including medical, physical, psychological, and political aspects of drug abuse. It includes both domestic and international views. Coverage is current, authoritative, and comprehensive in the encyclopedia's more than 1,000 entries, which range in length from a single sentence to several pages. This is a recommended purchase for all libraries, regardless of size.

32

Information Technology

ALMANACS

894. Juliussen, Egil, and Karen Petska Juliussen, eds. **Computer Industry Almanac [yr.].** Austin, TX, Reference Press, 1987- . Annual. 1v. index. $55.00; $45.00pa. (1994 ed.). ISSN 0893-0791.

Self-described as "the complete guide to people, salaries, companies, products, technologies, and forecasts in the fascinating ever-changing computer industry," this engaging almanac lives up to its billing pretty well. Among other things, it surveys important industry trends, technologies, participants, and products; lists rankings, salaries, usage statistics, and awards; summarizes market and technology forecasts for hardware, software, and peripherals; and provides directory-type information for publications, associations, organizations, user groups, companies, and conferences. One is tempted to suggest that the *Computer Industry Almanac* defines the concept "information overload," but its materials are sufficiently well organized and well indexed to be accessible and highly useful. An outstanding overview of an important area.

DICTIONARIES AND ENCYCLOPEDIAS

895. Graham, John. **The Facts on File Dictionary of Telecommunications.** Rev. ed. New York, Facts on File, 1991. 180p. $24.95. ISBN 0-8160-2029-9.

Dictionary of Telecommunications defines 1,500 terms and acronyms drawn from the ever-dynamic data transmission and telecommunications disciplines. Entries are generally concise, but run to more in-depth treatments as necessary, and direct readers to related terms through cross-references. Given the impact of telecommunications and data transmission on emerging electronic library services, all libraries will want a copy of Graham's useful reference.

896. Parker, Sybil P., ed. **McGraw-Hill Encyclopedia of Electronics and Computers.** 2d ed. New York, McGraw-Hill, 1988. 1047p. illus. index. $90.50. ISBN 0-07-045499-X.

This single-volume encyclopedia comprises 520 articles culled from the sixth edition of the *McGraw-Hill Encyclopedia of Science and Technology* (1987). Coverage includes such diverse topics as fabrication methods for integrated circuits, the flow of electricity through semiconducting materials, electromagnetic pulse, and the use of computers in robotics, data management systems, communications, and consumer products. The writing level assumes a technologically informed reader; within articles, keyword subheadings, illustrations, photographs, tables, line drawings, diagrams, and selected bibliographies enhance the text. A standard, authoritative reference for technical terms and concepts.

897. Pfaffenberger, Bryan. **Que's Computer User's Dictionary.** 4th ed. Carmel, IN, Que, 1994. 669p. illus. $12.95pa. ISBN 1-56529-604-4.

The 2,252 terms defined in Pfaffenberger's computer dictionary include "any and all terms relevant to Macintosh and IBM personal computing ... even if some of these terms are not intrinsically computer related." The purpose of such a broad compass is to bring together all the words and phrases a nonprofessional is likely to encounter when attempting to figure out how to use a computer to actually accomplish something productive. Thus, there are entries for desktop publishing terms, word-processing phrases, and accounting processes, among others. Many cross references, diagrams, and "tips and cautions" accompany the clear, concise definitions. The reasonable cost of this dictionary and the usefulness of its definitions make it an excellent resource for all users of personal computers.

898. Potts, William F. **McGraw-Hill Data Communications Dictionary: Definitions and Descriptions ... .** New York, McGraw-Hill, 1993. 268p. index. $34.95. ISBN 0-07-003154-1.

This is a well-organized, comprehensive dictionary of data transmission systems and computer networks. Definitions are concise and, although intended for data communications professionals, are easily understood by lay readers. Sections are devoted to general SNA (Systems Network Architecture) and vendor terms; recommendations and standards; IBM communications products and information display systems; interchange codes; and International System of Units (SI) measure. In addition to the definitions, Potts has included numerous helpful cross references.

899. Raymond, Eric S., ed. **The New Hacker's Dictionary.** 2d ed. Cambridge, MA, MIT Press, 1994. 530p. illus. $30.00; $14.95pa. ISBN 0-262-18154-1; 0-262-68079-3pa.

For the purposes of this dictionary, a *hacker* is "a person who enjoys exploring the details of programmable systems and how to stretch their capabilities, as opposed to most users, who prefer to learn only the minimum necessary." Raymond's work provides an insight into the world of these hardy souls, defining some 1,000 terms such as "angry fruit salad," "flarp," "mouse droppings," "quantum bogodynamics," and "xyzzy." Fortunately, pronunciation is indicated for the more obscure words and phrases. A fascinating counterculture overview, the *Hacker's Dictionary* will wonderfully supplement coverage provided by the more mainstream computer dictionaries.

900. Smith, Raoul. **The Facts on File Dictionary of Artificial Intelligence.** New York, Facts on File, 1989. 211p. illus. $24.95. ISBN 0-8160-1595-3.

Smith's comprehensive dictionary encompasses not just artificial intelligence, but also its many related subdisciplines: expert systems, robotics, natural language programming, intelligent computer-aided instruction, and the like. Roughly a paragraph each, the more than 2,000 entries are written in nontechnical language accessible to the general reader, and often include charts and diagrams that further clarify the term's meaning. Cross references are indicated as appropriate.

Because the AI field is in a constant state of flux, libraries may wish to update their coverage as more recent references become available. Although the Smith title is recommended as a first purchase, two other excellent works for understanding the basic language of artificial intelligence are Dennis Mercadal's *Dictionary of Artificial Intelligence* (Van Nostrand Reinhold, 1990, 334p, $29.95pa, ISBN 0-442-00451-6), which, in addition to its definitions, includes lists of vendors with their types of products, price ranges, company addresses, and phone numbers; and Ellen Thro's *The Artificial Intelligence Dictionary* (Microtrend Books/Slawson Communications, 1991, 407p, $24.95pa, ISBN 0-915391-36-8), which does an excellent job of defining the jargon of the various disciplines (robotics, philosophy, neural networks, etc.) that together contribute to the ongoing development of AI.

DIRECTORIES

901. Bennett, Stephen J., and Richard Freirman, eds. **Microcomputer Market Place [yr.].** New York, Random House, 1992- . Annual. 1v. $30.00pa. (1994 ed.). ISSN 1066-1824.

Aiming to be "the complete guide to PC software and hardware vendors, service providers and information sources," Bennett and Freirman's directory comprises names, addresses, telephone and fax numbers, and main products of huge numbers of companies involved in the small computer business. In addition to listings for hardware and software companies, there are entries on advertising agencies, trade show sponsors, international distributors, venture capital firms, leasing companies, and executive recruiters. Separate sections identify radio and television talk shows, syndicated computer columnists and electronic bulletin boards, lists of universities with accredited computer curricula, and recreational camps with computer programs. Recommended as an information-packed resource at a very reasonable price.

902. **The Software Encyclopedia [yr.].** New Providence, NJ, R. R. Bowker, 1985- . Annual. 2v. index. $229.95pa./set (1994 ed.). ISSN 0000-006X.

More a directory than an encyclopedia, this resource provides annotated listings for more than 16,000 new and established software programs. Entry length varies per title, but in addition to its annotation each entry includes hardware, memory, and operating system requirements, as well as price, availability of manuals, publisher, and warranty information. It accesses entries two ways: by title and by compatible system and application. An index provides a complete list of programs for each publisher. Also available online and on magnetic tape.

HANDBOOKS

903. Chen, C. H., ed. **Computer Engineering Handbook.** New York, McGraw-Hill, 1992. 1v. (various paging). illus. index. $79.50. ISBN 0-07-010924-9.

Taking a tutorial approach, Chen's handbook is organized into major topical areas such as digital logic and design, computer architecture and arithmetic, computer graphics, computer vision, parallel computing, and computer networks. The narrative is well written and current, with contributions from respected authorities. A detailed index rounds out this comprehensive overview of the fundamentals of computer engineering.

INDEXES

904. Jasper, Lisa R., ed. **Microcomputer Index: A Comprehensive Abstracts Journal Covering Microcomputing and Related Subjects.** Medford, NJ, Learned Information, 1980- . Quarterly, with annual cumulation. 1v. $159.00/yr. (1994 ed.). ISSN 8756-7040.

Microcomputer Index covers more than 10,000 articles, abstracts, reviews, and other information resources of use to computer users from novice to professional. (More than 75 English-language journals are covered.) It is arranged into five indexes: authors, company names, product names, compatibility (both hardware and software), and subjects. This is an excellent resource for all libraries (and their patrons) trying to keep up with developments in the computer field. Also available online.

Physical Science and Mathematics

GENERAL SCIENCE

905. Magill, Frank N., ed. **Magill's Survey of Science: Physical Science Series.** Pasadena, CA. Salem Press, 1992. 6v. index. $475.00/set. ISBN 0-89356-618-7.

The 380 general articles found within Magill's six volumes cover the disciplines of astronomy/astrophysics, physical chemistry, computational science, mathematics, and physics. Articles average seven to eight pages, and comprise an introductory classification, a two- to six-line definition, a list of principal terms associated with the topic, a descriptive overview, applications, context, bibliography, and cross references. Each volume has a list of topics discussed in the full set and an overview of categories. Volume six provides a 30-page cumulative index.

906. Parkinson, Claire L. **Breakthroughs; A Chronology of Great Achievements in Science and Mathematics 1200-1930.** Boston, G. K. Hall, 1985. 576p. illus. bibliog. index. $40.00. ISBN 0-8161-8706-1.

Breakthroughs is an ideal resource for grasping quickly the broad sweep of the history of science throughout the world. Grouped under each year or short historical period, the entries are divided into eight main scientific categories and a supplemental one that encompasses related matters, such as the methodology or philosophy of science. Technology, for the most part, is not covered. Parkinson's intent was to create a work that would be general, rather than scholarly, and that would encourage readers "to seek more detailed discussions, especially from primary sources."

ASTRONOMY

907. Audouze, Jean, Guy Israel, and Jean-Claude Falque, eds. **The Cambridge Atlas of Astronomy.** 3d ed. New York, Cambridge University Press, 1994. 431p. illus. maps. index. $75.00. ISBN 0-521-43438-6.

More of an encyclopedia than an atlas, this work is renowned for the outstanding quality of both its text and its more than 1,100 illustrations (including dramatic photographs of recent planetary and space missions), roughly half of which are in color. After an introductory essay on the current state of astronomy, the book organizes its materials into five sections: the sun; the solar system (the largest section, with articles on the planets, our moon, and the asteroids); the stars and our home galaxy; galaxies other than our own; and a concluding overview that addresses such topics as cosmology, the possibility of extraterrestrial life, astronomical observations, and the history of astronomy. New to this edition are sections on clusters of galaxies, gravitational lenses, active galaxies, and the origin of the universe, plus a new chapter on planetary climate change. Rounding out the atlas are a sky map; a brief, subject-arranged list of titles for further reading; a glossary; and an index.

Although the Cambridge atlas is recommended as a first purchase in this area, for libraries that need a less-expensive alternative or simply wish to supplement their coverage, a good choice is Heather Couper and Nigel Henbest's *The Space Atlas* (Harcourt Brace Jovanovich, 1992, 64p., $16.95, ISBN 0-15-200598-6). Intended for the novice astronomer and young adult, the volume is generously illustrated with maps, drawings, and astronomical charts that complement the topical treatment of planets and their satellites, comets, galaxies, and space travel. Coverage of the outermost planets (Uranus, Neptune, and Pluto); the birth, life, and death of a star; "Our Star City," the local group of galaxies; and exploding galaxies is especially noteworthy.

908. Moore, Dianne F. **The HarperCollins Dictionary of Astronomy and Space Science.** New York, HarperCollins, 1992. 338p. $25.00; $13.00pa. ISBN 0-06-271542-9; 0-06-461023-3pa.

Designed to meet the needs of secondary school students or the amateur astronomy enthusiast, Moore's dictionary offers brief, nontechnical, nonmathematical definitions accompanied by cross references as appropriate and occasional illustrations. Ten appendixes include solar system physical and orbital properties, solar and lunar eclipses, data on the nearest and brightest stars, constellations, chronologies of space science and astronomy, and nebulas. Because of its more recent publication date, *The HarperCollins Dictionary of Astronomy and Space Science* makes a good supplement to the Facts on File title.

909. Parker, Sybil P., and Jay M. Pasachoff, eds. **McGraw-Hill Encyclopedia of Astronomy.** New York, McGraw-Hill, 1993. 531p. illus. index. $75.50. ISBN 0-07-045314-4.

A subset of the multi-volume *McGraw-Hill Encyclopedia of Science & Technology* (1992), this work consists of 225 alphabetically arranged topical articles written by prominent astronomers and other specialists from around the world. The focus is on physical rather than descriptive aspects of astronomy, with an underlying theme being the study of the heavens through electromagnetic radiation (for example, visible light, ultraviolet, infrared, radio, etc.). Although the text is presented at a fairly advanced level, it is clearly written and appropriate for an educated lay reader. In addition to a variety of diagrams, charts, and tables of data, the book is also profusely illustrated with both color and black-and-white photographs.

Another excellent work with a bit different focus is Stephen P. Maran's *The Astronomy and Astrophysics Encyclopedia* (Van Nostrand Reinhold, 1992, 1002p., illus., maps, index, $89.95, ISBN 0-442-26364-3). The 400 articles in Maran's comprehensive resource together provide an authoritative summary of current knowledge about astronomy and astrophysics. Despite heavy reliance on mathematics and science terminology, the text manages to be highly readable and informative. Entries generally run from two to four pages and are accompanied by black-and-white photographs or illustrations, as well as brief bibliographies. The intended audience of this work is educated laypeople, teachers, science writers, editors, and scientists, and it does an excellent job of providing the latest information, theories, and data at a writing level appropriate to these groups.

910. Ridpath, Ian, ed. **Norton's 2000.0 Star Atlas and Reference Handbook.** 18th ed. New York, John Wiley, 1989. 179p. illus. maps. index. $44.95. ISBN 0-470-21460-0.

Norton's, a classic work familiar to most amateur astronomers, comprises four chapters: "Position and Time," "Practical Astronomy," "The Solar System," and "Stars, Nebulae and Galaxies." The chapter on practical astronomy is especially noteworthy for its treatment of observation, astronomical instruments, and astrophotography. The writing style is intended for an educated readership, and an understanding of basic mathematics computation is assumed, as is a willingness to spend many nights outside observing the heavens. In addition to its glossary, *Norton's* is packed with charts, tables, illustrations, and other data valuable to anyone interested in astronomy.

911. **The Visual Dictionary of the Universe.** New York, Dorling Kindersley, 1993. 64p. illus. index. $15.95. ISBN 1-56458-336-8.

The goal of this work is to provide the reader "instant access to the specialized vocabulary of astronomy and cosmology in a way that is clear, informative, and easy to understand." In addition to meeting this goal, the dictionary also does an excellent job of explaining the systems of the universe and how the nearly 3,000 specialized terms identified fit into the larger context of these interrelated systems. *Universe* is arranged in 2-page topical sections that present an array of 200 stunning graphics, including photographs, models, and illustrations. Coverage in the 26 sections includes broad system overviews (e.g., the universe, galaxies, the Milky Way, the solar system); specifics (e.g., stars, the Sun, the Earth, Uranus, asteroids and meteoroids); and related topics (e.g., observing space, manned space exploration, lunar exploration). A 60-term glossary and an index to the 3,000 terms identified in the dictionary conclude the work.

CHEMISTRY

Dictionaries and Encyclopedias

912. Budavari, Susan, ed. **The Merck Index: An Encyclopedia of Chemicals, Drugs, and Biologicals.** 11th ed. Rahway, NJ, Merck, 1989. 1v. (various paging). illus. index. $35.00. ISBN 0-911910-28-X.

Intended as a "one-volume compendium of information on the most important chemicals, drugs and biological substances," *The Merck Index* profiles some 10,000 drugs. For each it notes name; identifying number; generic name; *Chemical Abstracts* name; alternate names; molecular formula, molecular weight, and percentage composition; literature references; structure; physical data; derivatives; and therapeutic use. In addition to the basic profiles, there are discussions of special topics such as drugs used against AIDS. A standard resource for chemistry research, this information-packed encyclopedia continues to meet the needs of students, professionals, and librarians.

913. Daintith, John, ed. **The Facts on File Dictionary of Chemistry.** Rev. ed. New York, Facts on File, 1988. 249p. illus. $24.95; $12.95pa. ISBN 0-8160-1866-9; 0-8160-2367-0pa.

Daintith's dictionary comprises approximately 2,500 terms that describe basic chemical terms and reactions, new techniques and applications, and environmental issues such as acid rain and heavy metal pollution. Definitions are nontechnical, provide a clear understanding of the material, and are often accompanied by helpful cross references. Supplementary materials include line drawings; tables of chemical elements with their symbols, proton numbers, and atomic weights; a brief list of physical constants; a list of elementary particles and related information; the Greek alphabet; and the periodic table.

For more extensive (if expensive) coverage in this area, libraries should consider the well-regarded *Hawley's Condensed Chemical Dictionary* (12th ed., Richard J. Lewis, Sr., Van Nostrand Reinhold, 1993, 1275p., $69.96, ISBN 0-442-01131-8). Not only are the definitions current, clear, and understandable, but the clean layout, readable typeface, and extensive use of cross referencing also make it a valuable and easy-to-use resource well worth its purchase price.

914. Parker, Sybil P., ed. **McGraw-Hill Encyclopedia of Chemistry.** 2d ed. New York, McGraw-Hill, 1993. 1236p. illus. index. $95.50. ISBN 0-07-045455-8.

This is a comprehensive encyclopedia of current chemistry that covers, in hundreds of articles, all areas of the subject plus some topics in physics needed to understand modern chemistry. Drawn mainly from the *McGraw-Hill Encyclopedia of Science and Technology* (1992), the articles are authoritative, mostly current, and supplemented by the generous use of diagrams, structural formulas, and a selective list of references. A comprehensive index completes the work.

Handbooks

915. **CRC Handbook of Chemistry and Physics.** Boca Raton, FL, CRC Press, 1913– . Annual. $99.50 (1994 ed.). ISSN 0147-6262.

The *CRC Handbook* has been the standard reference work for the physical sciences for the past 80 years. It provides basic tables in mathematics, physics, and chemistry. Although it is considered somewhat difficult to use for the uninitiated, its wealth of information recommends it to all reference collections in the sciences.

916. Dean, John A., ed. **Lange's Handbook of Chemistry.** 14th ed. New York, McGraw-Hill, 1992. 1v. (various paging). index. $79.50. ISBN 0-07016194-1.

The 14th edition of *Lange's* (a reference first published in 1934), presents values, formulas, facts, and figures within several broad topical sections. These are "Mathematics," "General Information and Conversion Tables," "Atomic and Molecular Structure," "Inorganic Chemistry," "Analytic Chemistry," "Spectroscopy," "Thermal Properties," "Physical Properties," and "Miscellaneous Chemical Information." A 50-page glossary and a 40-page, 2-column index are included. Although specifically intended to meet the needs of working chemists, it is also useful for basic chemistry questions of the sort encountered in libraries.

917. Lewis, Richard J., Sr. **Hazardous Chemicals Desk Reference.** 3d ed. New York, Van Nostrand Reinhold, 1993. 1600p. index. $99.95. ISBN 0-442-01408-2.

More than 6,000 chemicals, many of them used daily in such products as adhesive remover, nail polish remover, and after-bath powders, are described in this daunting—but important—resource. Profiles include hazard rating, molecular formula, synonyms (alternative names), and identification numbers (Department of Transportation, *Chemical Abstracts Service*, and National Institute for Occupational Safety and Health). Chemicals are listed alphabetically. Because so many chemicals have multiple names, a synonym index provides multiple points of access. An important purchase for all libraries.

918. Maizell, Robert E. **How to Find Chemical Information: A Guide for Practicing Chemists, Educators, and Students.** 2d ed. New York, John Wiley, 1987. 402p. illus. index. $74.95. ISBN 0-471-86767-5.

The second edition of this highly regarded guide evaluates both print and electronic sources of chemical information, first describing the resource and then suggesting how it can be used most effectively. Although chemistry is the focus, chemical engineering is given fairly light coverage. Nevertheless, this work's excellent organization, thorough and detailed treatment of both classic and more recent sources, and accessible writing style make it an important reference tool for all libraries.

EARTH AND PLANETARY SCIENCES

919. Allaby, Ailsa, and Michael Allaby, eds. **The Concise Oxford Dictionary of Earth Sciences.** New York, Oxford University Press, 1990. 410p. $39.95. ISBN 0-19-866146-0.

For the purposes of this work, *earth sciences* is defined to include terms for everything from climatology to vulcanology. The philosophy and history of earth sciences are also included, as well as brief biographical notes on important scientists. The work's more than 6,000 terms are provided detailed and descriptive definitions, with lengths varying according to the complexity of the term. Cross references are generously interspersed throughout the text; in addition, an 11-page bibliography at the beginning of the dictionary helps readers locate specific topics. Appropriate for both the specialist and the lay reader, the dictionary should be a useful and reasonably priced addition to most libraries.

920. **The Visual Dictionary of the Earth.** New York, Dorling Kindersley, 1993. 64p. illus. index. $15.95. ISBN 1-56458-335-X.

Included among this work's 25 2-page topical sections are coverage of geological time; the rock cycle; mineral resources; and processes such as faulting and folding, mountain building, and weathering and erosion. In addition, the Earth's waters (rivers, lakes and groundwater, coastlines, oceans, and seas) are addressed, as are the atmosphere and weather. Concise explanatory narratives introduce each topic, placing the exquisitely reproduced photographs, models, and illustrations and their identifying terms within the broader context of the planet's geological system. A text section listing Earth data (e.g., highest, longest, largest, deepest), a single-page glossary that defines some 60 terms, and a 3,000-word index round out the dictionary.

Climatology

921. Bair, Frank E., ed. **The Weather Almanac: A Reference Guide to Weather, Climate, and Air Quality in the United States ...** 6th ed. Detroit, Gale, 1992. 855p. illus. index. $120.00. ISBN 0-8103-2843-7.

Providing both climatic information and a good synopsis of weather and its changes, this standard reference work provides several types of data for each month from 1961 through 1990 for 109 U.S. cities. Explanations address virtually every type of weather phenomena: severe storms, floods, drought, and heat and cold waves; environmental concerns such as acid rain, ozone depletion, and global warming; and related subjects such as earthquakes, volcanic activity, and tsunamis. In addition, the effects of changing climate on agriculture, health, and economics are discussed. A good table of contents and an index facilitate access to the myriad facts presented here.

922. Conway, McKinley, and Linda L. Liston. **The Weather Handbook.** Rev. ed. Norcross, GA, Conway Data, 1990. 548p. maps. index. $39.95. ISBN 0-910436-29-0.

The third revision of a popular work first issued in 1963, *The Weather Handbook* includes the climate summaries of some 850 cities in the world, 250 of which are in the United States. The data are arranged alphabetically by state within the United States and by continent and country in the rest of the world. Each American entry lists by month the averages and all-time extremes for temperature, degree days, cloud cover, (relative) humidity, precipitation and type, and wind. Entries for other countries are limited to temperature, humidity, and precipitation. A weather risk profile, summarizing the frequency of floods, earthquakes, and other natural disasters, is given for each state. In addition to an index that lists all cities alphabetically, another lists a major weather disaster for each.

923. Maunder, W. John., comp. **Dictionary of Global Climate Change.** New York, Routledge, Chapman & Hall, 1992. 240p. $45.00. ISBN 0-412-03901-X.

More than a dictionary, Maunder's reference is a condensed encyclopedia covering such diverse topics as volcanic eruptions and their effects, chlorofluorocarbons, ozone, methane, the carbon cycle, sunspots, the pH scale, and oceans and glaciers. It includes explanations of scientific terms and concepts; meanings of acronyms; and the history, tasks, and findings of many international organizations. The work will be valuable to both the casual reader looking for a definition and to researchers interested in the findings and ongoing work of international groups working on climatic change, its effects, and possible control.

Geology

924. Challinor, John. **Challinor's Dictionary of Geology.** 6th ed. Antony Wyatt, ed. Oxford University Press, 1986. 374p. $35.00; $16.95pa. ISBN 0-19-520505-7; 0-19-520506-5pa.

A revision of Challinor's *A Dictionary of Geology* (5th ed., 1978), this work defines more than 2,000 terms and phrases in entries ranging in length from a few words to short essays. The terms are not only defined, but are also placed in relation to other terms and concepts, as well as being placed in the context of their historical usage—an approach that is helpful to both the geologist and the layperson. Although the text reflects a British origin, and it does not define nearly as many terms as the professional and academic standard, the American Geological Institute's *Dictionary of Geological Terms* (3d ed., Robert Bates and Julia A. Jackson, eds., 1984), at 9,500 entries, *Challinor's* is still recommended over the AGI resource because its definitions are generally more understandable to the lay reader.

925. Parker, Sybil P., ed. **McGraw-Hill Encyclopedia of the Geological Sciences.** 2d ed. New York, McGraw-Hill, 1988. 722p. $90.50. ISBN 0-07-045500-7.

Many of the 500 articles featured here are drawn from the sixth edition of the *McGraw-Hill Encyclopedia of Science and Technology* (1987, 20v.); thus, for libraries that own the larger set, especially in its 1992 edition, *Geological Sciences* will not be a necessary purchase. For those that do not, however, this work provides an excellent and authoritative overview of its subject. Entries are arranged alphabetically, range in length from several sentences to several pages, and are written at a level accessible to the lay reader. Maps, sketches, and numerous other well-executed illustrations complement the text.

Mineralogy

926. Arem, Joel E. **Color Encyclopedia of Gemstones.** 2d ed. New York, Chapman & Hall, 1987. 1v. (various paging). illus. (part col.). index. $49.95. ISBN 0-442-20833-2.

Arem describes approximately 250 gems—minerals that are cut and polished for ornamental purposes—according to the basic properties used to identify them. These include chemical formula, crystallography, color, luster, hardness, density, cleavage, spectra, luminescence, place of occurrence, and size. A separate section is devoted to excellent color photographs of the minerals. Supplementary materials include a brief bibliography, lists of gemstone species and mineral groups, and an index.

927. Pellant, Chris. **Rocks, Minerals & Fossils of the World.** Boston, Little, Brown, 1990. 175p. illus. $17.95pa. ISBN 0-316-69796-6.

Intended for amateur rock enthusiasts, Pellant's handy resource describes 150 of the most commonly encountered rocks plus 250 minerals. Rocks are organized by type (igneous, metamorphic, sedimentary), within which categories they are briefly described as to physical characteristics. The minerals section describes each according to major identifying characteristics (crystal shape, color, luster, cleavage, and hardness). The third section organizes fossils by type (e.g., corals, crinoids, trilobites, fish), and includes a discussion of fossil formation, fossil naming, and the role of fossils in the study of evolution. The text is accompanied by excellent photographs that will be a great help in identifying a particular rock, mineral, or fossil.

Libraries where there is strong patron interest in rocks may also wish to consider Walter Schumann's *Handbook of Rocks, Minerals, and Gemstones* (Houghton Mifflin, 1993, 380p., $35.00; $18.95pa. ISBN 0-395-51138-0; 0-395-51137-2pa.), a well-illustrated guide to 600 of the most common rocks and minerals. It provides general information on such topics as the origin of minerals, with emphasis placed on those properties most useful for identification, including color, hardness, and specific gravity.

Oceanography

928. Couper, Alastair, ed. **The Times Atlas and Encyclopaedia of the Sea.** New York, HarperCollins, 1989. 272p. $65.00. ISBN 0-06-016287-2.

A beautifully executed compilation of maps, photographs, and narrative, *The Times Atlas and Encyclopaedia of the Sea* comprises 17 thematic chapters that encompass nearly every aspect of ocean research, resources, environment, uses, and policies. In addition to the main body of the atlas, there are 11 appendixes, a glossary, a bibliography, and a detailed index. Appropriate for a broad range of readers, from students to naval strategists to marine specialists, this work should be considered the first place to check for information about the world's oceans.

929. Elder, Danny, and John Pernetta, eds. **The Random House Atlas of the Oceans.** New York, Random House, 1991. 200p. illus. maps. index. $39.50. ISBN 0-679-40830-4.

Written under the auspices of the World Conservation Union, this book portrays the immense diversity of the world's oceans, which, the editors point out, are collapsing under the strain of coastal human populations. The book, most of which is text and photographs, leads off with background chapters on the origin of and current environments present in the world's oceans. The atlas maps (constituting about 30 pages) show regional bodies of water such as the Caribbean, the Southern Ocean, the Southeast Pacific, and the Arabian Sea. Each map shows the localized areas of greatest pollution, the location of known radioactive waste ocean dump sites, tourist areas, fishing centers, sea beds, protected marine areas, reefs, and mangrove swamps. The work concludes with a list of threatened marine species, a list of map sources, and an index.

MATHEMATICS

930. Bendick, Jeanne. **Mathematics Illustrated Dictionary: Facts, Figures, and People.** Rev. ed. New York, Franklin Watts, 1989. 247p. illus. $14.90. ISBN 0-531-10664-0.

The 2,000 terms briefly defined here include mathematical terms, concepts, processes, and people. Coverage encompasses geometry, algebra, statistics, trigonometry, and business-related mathematics, as well as applications of mathematics within the fields of astronomy, physics, and computer science. Definitions are brief but clearly written, frequently include hand-drawn black-and-white illustrations, and often indicate pronunciation. Many entries are cross-referenced, and selected biographical entries are accompanied by small drawings or photographs. In addition to a periodic table, there are tables of formulas, mathematical symbols, logarithms, square roots, and the metric system. Although the ostensible audience for this resource is the young mathematician, it will be useful to anyone with an interest in mathematics.

931. Beyer, William. H., ed. **CRC Handbook of Mathematical Sciences.** 6th ed. Boca Raton, FL, CRC Press, 1987. 872p. illus. $89.95. ISBN 0-8493-0656-6.

Like its sibling, the *CRC Handbook of Chemistry and Physics* (entry 915), this handbook has long been a standard desk reference for those working in the mathematical disciplines. Formerly titled the *CRC Handbook of Tables for Mathematics*, it includes an extensive compilation of tables of values for mathematical functions and lists of formulas and constants in pure and applied mathematics. Although it is considered somewhat advanced for those unfamiliar with mathematical concepts, its wealth of information recommends it to all reference collections.

932. Borowski, E. J., and J. M. Borwein. **The HarperCollins Dictionary of Mathematics.** New York, HarperCollins, 1991. 659p. $25.00; $16.00pa. ISBN 0-06-271525-9; ISBN 0-06-461019-5pa.

Intended for students of mathematics at all levels (secondary school to master's degree) as well as interested lay persons, Borowski and Borwein's dictionary provides in-depth explanations and examples in more than 4,000 entries drawn from all major mathematics subjects. In addition, biographies of major mathematicians provide detailed descriptions of their contributions to mathematics. Some 400 diagrams further clarify the text.

There are several other reliable choices for mathematics dictionaries, depending on how much libraries wish to spend and how comprehensive coverage needs to be. Douglas Downing's *Dictionary of Mathematics Terms* (Barron's Educational Series, 1987, 241p., $10.95pa. ISBN 0-8120-2641-1) aims to "collect in one place reference information that is valuable for students of mathematics and for persons with careers in this field." In pursuit of this goal, it provides definitions for some 600 terms related to algebra, geometry, analytic geometry, trigonometry, probability, statistics, logic, computer math, and calculus. Formulas, theorems, and derivations that review material covered in high school and college courses are also included. Entries range in length from several lines to, occasionally, several pages. Separate sections are devoted to symbols, a list of selected entries arranged within 12 subject categories, and tables of such items as logarithms, trigonometric functions, and frequently used distributions. Another excellent work, especially for nonmathematicians, is Glenn James and Robert James's *Mathematics Dictionary* (5th ed., Van Nostrand Reinhold, 1992, 548p., $42.95; $29.95pa. ISBN 0-442-00741-8; 0-442-01241-1pa.). This well-known reference, first published in 1949, is composed of in-depth definitions for more than 8,000 terms encountered in mathematics and related disciplines. A multilingual (French, German, Russian, and Spanish) index of mathematical terms, an index, and appendixes that list symbols, differentiation formulas, and tables of integrals supplement the easily understood text. Although it is substantially more expensive than the HarperCollins work or Downing's reference, *Mathematics Dictionary* is well worth its purchase price for those who can afford it.

933. Burington, Richard S. **Handbook of Mathematical Tables and Formulas.** 5th ed. New York, McGraw-Hill, 1973. 500p. $61.19. ISBN 007-009-0157.

Burington's handbook, arranged in two parts, covers the main formulas and theorems of algebra, geometry, trigonometry, calculus, vector analysis, sets, logic, matrices, linear algebra, numerical analysis, differential equations, some special functions, Fourier and Laplace transforms, complex variables, and statistics (part 1); and tables of logarithms, trigonometry, exponential and hyperbolic functions, powers and roots, and probability distributions (among others) in part 2. Students and professionals in the fields of mathematics, engineering, physics, chemistry, and other technical disciplines will find the wealth of tabular information especially useful.

934. Hopkins, Nigel J., John W. Mayne, and John R. Hudson. **The Numbers You Need.** Detroit, Gale, 1992. 439p. illus. index. $29.95. ISBN 0-8103-8373-X.

The intent of *Numbers* is to provide answers to the types of numerical questions we all encounter in everyday life. It presents hundreds of formulas used at work, home, and play, with the tables, statistics, definitions, and examples necessary to understand the calculations involved. Materials are grouped topically to cover common consumer money matters; banking; health and fitness; weather and the environment; the numerical aspects of gambling, cards, and other such games; the statistics found in daily newspapers' sports pages; numbers for common home activities; and popular science calculations. The three accompanying appendixes include an overview of the basic mathematical tools needed for common numerical problems, an expansion on units of measure involved in many numerical problems, and mathematics for financial dealings.

PHYSICS

935. Daintith, John. **The Facts on File Dictionary of Physics.** Rev. ed. New York, Facts on File, 1988. 235p. $24.95. ISBN 0-8160-1868-5.

This dictionary is an especially good resource for less technically advanced patrons. The entries are short and written in a style easily understood by a physics novice, and the revised edition has been expanded to include terms in nuclear physics, particle physics, and superconductivity, thus bringing it current with state-of-the-art physics advances. Although it lacks the breadth and sophistication of more technical resources, the dictionary's strength is its accessibility for general readers.

936. Parker, Sybil P., ed. **McGraw-Hill Encyclopedia of Physics.** 2d ed. New York, McGraw-Hill, 1993. 1624p. illus. index. $95.50. ISBN 0-07-051400-3.

The 828 signed articles found in the second edition of the *McGraw-Hill Encyclopedia of Physics* encompass "all major branches of physics, including acoustics, atomic physics, particle physics, molecular physics, nuclear physics, classical mechanics, electricity, electromagnetism, fluid mechanics, heat and thermodynamics, low-temperature physics, optics, relativity, and solid-state physics." Article length runs from 6 lines to more than 25 pages; most entries include bibliographies as well as cross references to related topics. More than 1,000 illustrations—photographs, tables, charts, and drawings—enhance the text, and appendixes cover the International System of Units (SI); tables of conversion factors for SI, the metric system, and the U.S. customary system; chemical symbols; symbols and abbreviations used in scientific writing; mathematical signs and symbols; mathematical notations; a table of fundamental constants; and a periodic table of the elements. Drawn from the seventh edition (1992) of the *McGraw-Hill Encyclopedia of Science and Technology.*

Resource and Environmental Sciences

ATLASES

937. Mason, Robert J., and Mark T. Mattson. **Atlas of United States Environmental Issues.** New York, Macmillan, 1990. 252p. illus. maps. index. $80.00. ISBN 0-02-897261-9.

The full range of environmental issues—from agriculture to toxins—are explored here, with both their national and regional aspects examined. The more than 130 maps, photographs, charts, graphs, and diagrams enable readers to visualize problems as well as read about them. Not only are issues examined relative to economics, politics, and policy development, but their causes and effects are also explored. Supplementary materials include a bibliography organized by chapter, a chronology of major environmental legislation, and a small glossary.

938. Middleton, Nick. **Atlas of Environmental Issues.** New York, Facts on File, 1989. 63p. illus. maps. index. $16.95. ISBN 0-8160-2023-X.

Middleton's atlas aims to present an in-depth analysis of major global environmental issues. Topics addressed include acid rain, alternative energy, Antarctica, big dams, carbon dioxide, deforestation, drainage, irrigation, mining, modern agriculture, noise, nuclear power, oil pollution, overfishing, endangered species, transportation, urban environment, war, and wildlife tourism. Color illustrations further clarify concepts. This reference will be especially valuable for explaining these important issues to young readers.

ALMANACS

939. Golob, Richard, and Eric Brus. **The Almanac of Renewable Energy.** New York, Henry Holt, 1993. 348p. illus. index. ISBN 0-8050-1948-0.

The main part of this almanac consists of chapters covering hydroelectric; biomass; geothermal; solar thermal; photovoltaic conversion; wind; and tidal, ocean thermal, and wave energy. Each chapter describes the scope and distribution of each energy source, different approaches for using each source, environmental considerations, and future prospects for their contribution to the energy supply. In addition, the authors have included three other chapters to help place the role of renewable energy in the context of the overall energy picture. Two appendixes—statistical tables and information sources—and an index complete the almanac.

940. Hoyle, Russ. **Gale Environmental Almanac.** Detroit, Gale, 1993. 684p. illus. maps. index. $79.95. ISBN 0-8103-8877-4.

The goal of Hoyle's work is to encourage environmental literacy by providing a thoughtful range of impartial information that can serve as the basis for broader understanding and new perspectives. To this end, the work is arranged thematically: 12 essays by leading international environmental activists and writers treat such topics as the legal, political, and business history of the environmental movement; the Earth's changing climate; biodiversity; energy; and the impact of pollution on health. The first eight essays are accompanied by lists of useful resources, such as a directory of experts, a list of parks, a chronology of events, and a guide to environmental education. A 28-page index and an 11-page glossary conclude the almanac.

Where patron interest warrants and budgets allow, libraries may also wish to consider a related Gale title, *Environmental Encyclopedia* (William P. Cunningham and others, eds., 1994, 981p., $195.00, ISBN 0-8103-4986-8), which is made up of more than 1,000 alphabetically arranged articles that treat the wide range of topics encountered in environmental studies. Entries include scientific definitions, public policy issues and events, biographical sketches, organizations, and environmental movements, among other topics. The chronology of U.S. environmental legislation that follows the main body of text is especially useful.

941. **The Information Please Environmental Almanac, [yr.].** Compiled by World Resources Institute. Boston, Houghton Mifflin, 1992– . Annual. 1v. maps. index. $21.95; $10.95pa. (1994 ed.). ISSN 1057-8293.

The *Information Please Environmental Almanac* is intended as an environmentalist's handbook of statistics on a variety of topics of local, national, and global importance. The work is divided into four major sections: "State of the Planet," "Close to Home," (local issues and grassroots activities), "A National View," and "A Global View." Also included are tabular country comparisons including such concerns as population density, life expectancy, and commercial energy use. Finally, characteristics of environmental importance are discussed in 143 country profiles. Articles are well-written, appropriate to lay readers, and supplemented by numerous text boxes, graphs, and figures. A strong reference source for environmental data and analysis of all the current issues.

BIBLIOGRAPHIES

942. Jansma, Pamela E. **Reading about the Environment: An Introductory Guide.** Englewood, CO, Libraries Unlimited, 1993. 252p. index. $27.50. ISBN 0-87287-985-2.

The purpose of this annotated bibliography is to provide a layperson with quick access to relevant information from reliable sources. Especially helpful for the nonspecialist, the more than 750 entries included here are either in books or popular magazines found in most public libraries. The work is organized into 16 topical chapters, each of which begins with a summary essay describing important elements of the topic at hand. Within chapters, each reference lists the author, publisher, and date of publication, and discusses the scope, organization, bias, and overall scientific level of each entry. A thorough index rounds out the bibliography.

943. Meridith, Robert. **The Environmentalist's Bookshelf: A Guide to the Best Books.** New York, G. K. Hall, 1993. 272p. index. $40.00. ISBN 0-8161-7359-1.

Meridith has surveyed more than 200 prominent environmentalists and compiled a list of the 350 books considered by them to be most significant in terms of understanding environmental issues. The books represent a broad spectrum of opinions on environmental topics and were written from the mid-19th century to the present. Meridith's unique approach has resulted in an unusual and informative bibliography of use for collection development as well as general environmental studies.

DICTIONARIES AND ENCYCLOPEDIAS

944. Crump, Andy. **Dictionary of Environment and Development.** Cambridge, MA, MIT Press, 1993. 272p. $40.00; $16.95pa. ISBN 0-262-03207-4; 0-262-53117-8pa.

The alphabetically arranged articles in this dictionary emphasize the economic, political, and social aspects of environmental issues, with little coverage of strictly scientific or technological subjects; they include topics (mostly broad), organizations, people (mostly politicians, not environmentalists), and a few specific places and events. Clearly written and easily understood by nonspecialists, the entries vary in length from a paragraph to two pages. Although the work reflects a strong viewpoint on "the misuse of resources from the wealthy, industrialized, 'developed' nations," as well as British spellings and metric measurements, it can nevertheless be a useful resource for most libraries.

As an alternative or secondary purchase, somewhat similar coverage is afforded by Irene Franck and David Brownstone's *The Green Encyclopedia* (Prentice-Hall General Reference, 1992, 486p., $35.00; $20.00pa., ISBN 0-13-365685-3; 0-13-365677-2pa.). This work provides much more coverage of scientific concepts, environmentally significant locations, and individual species of plants and animals and is generally more balanced in presenting all sides of controversial issues. The works, however, are more complementary than competitive, so libraries that can afford to do so will want to acquire both books.

945. Parker, Sybil P., and Robert Corbitt, eds. **McGraw-Hill Encyclopedia of Environmental Science & Engineering.** 3d ed. New York, McGraw-Hill, 1993. 749p. illus. maps. index. $85.50. ISBN 0-07-051396-1.

Derived mostly from the seventh edition of the 20-volume *McGraw-Hill Encyclopedia of Science & Technology* (1992), the 217 alphabetically arranged articles found here range from acid rain to zooplankton. Articles generally run from one to several pages in length, depending on the complexity of the topic, and are written at a level appropriate to an educated lay reader. Well-rendered illustrations and maps further clarify concepts discussed in the main entries, and a detailed index facilitates access to the hundreds of subjects touched on throughout the work.

946. Slesser, Malcolm, ed. **Dictionary of Energy.** 2d ed. New York, Nichols, 1988. 300p. illus. $59.95. ISBN 0-89397-320-3.

The second edition of the interdisciplinary *Dictionary of Energy* is intended to cut across specialized fields and provide definitions intelligible to the lay reader interested in understanding the dynamic field of energy studies. Topics include fuel technology, science, economics, the built environment, the external environment, renewable and alternate energies, energy transformation, biology, fossil and nuclear fuels, and fuel treatment. Definitions are brief but clear, and are occasionally accompanied by diagrams and cross references. Lists of acronyms and symbols are appended.

947. Stevenson, L. Harold, and Bruce Wyman. **The Facts on File Dictionary of Environmental Science.** New York, Facts on File, 1991. 294p. $24.95. ISBN 0-8160-2317-4.

More than 3,000 terms are defined in Stevenson and Wyman's interdisciplinary dictionary. Definitions are clearly written and easily understood by the lay reader. An appendix provides a list of acronyms and other abbreviations; unit prefixes for the metric system; the unit equivalents for metric and U.S. units; the technical guidelines for measuring concentrations of contaminants; physical standards for humans; a list of chemical elements; and the Greek alphabet.

Where patron interest warrants, libraries may also wish to consider Michael Allaby's *Dictionary of the Environment* (3d ed., New York University Press, 1991, 423p., $18.50pa., ISBN 0-8147-0597-9). Although intended for readers familiar with basic science terminology, Allaby's dictionary is nevertheless a good starting point for students, professionals, and individuals trying to understand the complex interrelationships of environmental issues. The mainstream terms from such areas as biology, botany, zoology, geology, geology, chemistry, physics, and the social sciences are defined here; relevant government agencies, voluntary organizations, and significant environmental regulations are described as well. Entries are generally one or two sentences and include cross references as appropriate. No illustrations are included. For a much less expensive—and extensive—resource, there is *The HarperCollins Dictionary of Environmental Science* (Gareth Jones and others, HarperPerennial/HarperCollins, 1992, 453p., ISBN 0-06-461040-3). Geared toward college students, the dictionary covers four major areas of study: the physical world, the biological world, the built environment, and the agro-economic infrastructures. The 2,000 definitions are clearly written and provide complete explanations of the terms.

948. Winter, Ruth. **A Consumer's Dictionary of Household, Yard and Office Chemicals.** New York, Crown, 1992. 329p. $12.00pa. ISBN 0-517-58722-X.

This resource covers chemicals found in such everyday products as building materials, fabrics, paper, cleaning materials, paints and varnishes, fertilizers, pesticides, fuel, and lubricants. The alphabetically arranged entries include name, synonyms, a brief description of the chemical and its uses, information about possible harmful effects, and references to related entries. In addition, there are directories of organizations concerned with environmental health, regional EPA offices, and regional poison control centers. Brief bibliography, extensive cross references, no index.

DIRECTORIES

949. Hill, Karen, and Annette Piccirelli, eds. **Gale Environmental Sourcebook: A Guide to Organizations, Agencies, and Publications.** Detroit, Gale, 1992. 688p. index. $75.00. ISBN 0-8103-8403-5.

A mammoth undertaking, *Environmental Sourcebook* provides directory-type information for 8,634 international, federal, governmental, independent, commercial, nonprofit, published, and videotaped sources of environmental information. All aspects of the environmental arena are covered, including advocacy and education, policy and enforcement, research and development, and consumer issues/products. Entries note full names and addresses of organizations or agencies, telephone numbers, contact names, and a brief summary of essential activities. Appendixes list worldwide endangered or threatened species and rank Superfund sites. Also available on disk and magnetic tape.

950. Lilienthal, Nancy, Michele Ascione, and Adam Flint. **Tacking Toxics in Everyday Products: A Directory of Organizations.** New York, INFORM, 1992. 179p. $19.95pa. ISBN 0-918-780-56-X.

The first part of *Tackling Toxics* consists of seven brief chapters that survey the toxic chemical situation. The second part, the core of the directory, lists organizations involved in monitoring, controlling, or otherwise overseeing toxic chemicals and their risks. Standard contact information is provided for each organization, giving concerned individuals just the information they need to deal positively with the problem at hand. This is an especially good resource to have on hand in communities struggling with government agencies to resolve local toxic waste issues.

951. Seredich, John, ed. **Your Resource Guide to Environmental Organizations: Includes the Purposes, Programs, Accomplishments, Volunteer Opportunities, Publications, and Membership Benefits ... .** Irvine, CA, Smiling Dolphins Press, 1991. 514p. index. $15.95pa. ISBN 1-879072-00-9.

The 150 environmental groups identified here include specialty groups, such as the Mountain Lion Preservation Foundation and Bat Conservation International, as well as broader-based organizations such as Greenpeace and the Sierra Club. Each entry contains basic directory information for that organization: name, address, telephone number, head of the organization, membership fee, and major interests, plus a detailed description of each organization's purpose, programs, accomplishments, volunteer opportunities, publications, and membership benefits. Indexed by name of individual, by subject, by special program, and by alternative organization name.

An equally reliable title is *The Nature Directory: A Guide to Environmental Organizations* (Susan D. Lanier-Graham, New York, Walker, 1991, 190p., $22.95; $12.95pa. ISBN 0-8027-1151-0; 0-8027-7348-6pa.). It describes 120 American environmental groups, noting address and contact person, history and goals, past achievements, ongoing projects, future plans, and membership/volunteer information. Organizations identified range from conservative (National Wildlife Federation) to mainstream (National Audubon Society) to radical (Earth First!). A subject-arranged bibliography is an especially helpful feature of this directory, making it a good complement to *Your Resource Guide*. Libraries that can afford to do so will probably want to buy both of these resources.

HANDBOOKS AND YEARBOOKS

952. Altman, Roberta. **The Complete Book of Home Environmental Hazards.** New York, Facts on File, 1990. 290p. illus. index. $24.95. ISBN 0-8160-2095-7.

The facts about various indoor pollutants are presented here, as is directory-type information for all relevant agencies. The three-part arrangement covers hazards inside the home (radon, asbestos, lead, water, pesticides, formaldehyde, tobacco smoke, etc.); hazards outside the home (hazardous waste sites, nuclear power plants, weapons plants); and how to buy an environmentally sound house. An appendix lists helpful U.S. and Canadian organizations, such as the National Asbestos Council. The glossary includes acronyms and abbreviations. A well-conceived and executed handbook that will be useful for all public libraries.

953. Chichonski, Thomas J., and Karen Hill, eds. **Recycling Sourcebook: A Guide to Recyclable Materials.** Detroit, Gale, 1993. 563p. index. $75.00. ISBN 0-8103-8855-3.

Intended as a "comprehensive and convenient guide to the recycling of household, office, and other consumer-generated waste," *Recycling Sourcebook* consists of two major sections. The first comprises concise essays on materials currently being recycled, and covers, for example, such topics as the production of original materials, possible problems with isolating materials, current recycling technology, and potential markets for the recycled product. These essays are followed by reviews of specific projects that can serve as practical models for developing local recycling initiatives—rural and urban, industrial and home. The second part of the book consists of an extensive list of recycling organizations, agencies, and publications; an appendix; a glossary; and an excellent index.

Complementary coverage of this topic is provided by Debi Kimball's *Recycling in America: A Reference Handbook* (ABC-Clio, 1992, 254p., $39.50, ISBN 0-87436-663-1). It provides an excellent introduction to and overview of the recycling process, including two especially useful sections that discuss specific materials that are often recycled and summarize state laws and regulations. Other helpful material includes a brief history of the recycling movement; names and addresses of local, state, and national organizations concerned with recycling; a reference list; a glossary of terms; a list of acronyms; and a good index.

954. Darnay, Arsen J., comp. and ed. **Statistical Record of the Environment.** Detroit, Gale, 1992. 855p. index. $89.50. ISBN 0-8103-8374-8.

The environmental statistics presented here are organized into 10 chapters: the media (land, air, and water); pollutants and wastes; effects of pollution; costs, budgets, and expenditures; tools and solutions; the pollution control industry; general industry and government data; environmental facts at the community level; laws and regulations; and politics and opinions. Within these chapters, the work's 851 statistical tables, maps, graphs, and diagrams are organized under topical subdivisions. Each figure provides a complete citation to the original source (usually a national or state government report or article); 150 sources were used from more than 200 consulted. Appended materials include a complete listing of primary sources with contact information, a list of abbreviations and acronyms, and a cross-referenced keyword index that provides access by subject, company, institution, agency, and geographical entity.

955. Harte, John, and others. **Toxics A to Z: A Guide to Everyday Pollution Hazards.** Berkeley, CA, University of California Press, 1991. 479p. index. $75.00; $30.00pa. ISBN 0-520-07223-5; 0-520-07224-3pa.

The first half of Harte's guide surveys what is known (and what is still being debated) about toxic hazards, whereas the second half provides specific information about more than 100 commonly encountered toxicants. Geared toward a scientifically literate reader, the narrative is clear, accurate, and objective, and strives to help individuals understand that small changes in their everyday lives will decrease their risk of exposure. A thorough index, an extensive glossary, and a bibliography of suggested readings round out the work.

Transportation

AIR

Almanacs and Handbooks

956.   Curtis, Anthony. **Space Almanac: Facts, Figures, Names, Dates, Places ... .** 2d ed. Houston, TX, Gulf, 1992. 760p. illus. maps. index. $24.95pa. ISBN 0-88415-030-5.

Space Almanac is a compendium of facts, figures, names, dates, places, lists, tables, drawings, photographs, and charts covering space from Earth to the edge of the universe. Topics addressed include space stations, astronauts, cosmonauts, shuttles, rockets, satellites, planetary explorers, the moon, the sun, comets, asteroids, the solar system, the Milky Way Galaxy, neighboring galaxies, pulsars, quasars, and black holes. In addition, there is international coverage of space-related news and events and technology advances. A chronology identifies highlights of space history from 1903 to the early 1990s.

957.   Davies, J. K. **Space Exploration.** New York, Chambers Kingfisher Graham, 1992. 275p. illus. index. $9.95pa. ISBN 0-550-17013-8.

This handy work provides brief explanations of 100 topics in space exploration, providing for each a brief explanation of its origin, developments in its field, its potential for future research and use, and any troubles encountered. Written in a style that is intelligent, interesting, and readable, most entries also have one or more shaded sidebars giving information on people involved or specific examples of events or activities significant in the item's importance to the overall topic. A complete subject index provides access to specific items, names, and subjects within individual entries. Overall, Davies has put together a good overview of the essential facts of space exploration.

958.   **Jane's All the World's Aircraft, [yr.]** New York, New York, Jane's, 1909- . Annual. 1v. illus. index. $245.00 (1994 ed.). ISSN 0075-3017.

Although expensive, this Jane's annual has long been considered the standard reference on the world's aircraft. Encompassing the aircraft of roughly 50 countries, coverage includes commercial and military aircraft, aero engines, private aircraft, airships, microlights, sailplanes, hang gliders, and balloons. The material is arranged by country and manufacturer, for which is provided address, divisional organization, and senior executive names. Each entry gives program history, current versions, customers, costs, design features, flying controls, structure, landing gear, power plant, accommodations, systems, avionics, equipment, armament, dimensions, performance, and other significant details. The text is augmented by more than 1,500 pictures and 300 detailed drawings. A glossary of terms and acronyms, lists of first flights during the preceding year, and a schedule of events through the year 2000 round out the annual.

Biographies

959. Hawthorne, Douglas B. **Men and Women of Space.** San Diego, CA. Univelt, 1992. 904p. $90.00. ISBN 0-912183-08X.

Men and Women of Space is a comprehensive biographical dictionary that profiles 650 individuals who have traveled in space, including Russian cosmonauts, United States test pilots, and people from "all space-faring nations of the world." Biographical information is quite detailed, and covers current status in space program, nickname, date and place of birth, military and marital status, children, education, publications, memberships, decorations and awards, physical description, recreational interests, life experience, space experience, spaceflight assignments, and place and manner of death (if deceased). An extensive bibliography is appended to each individual's profile. Especially recommended for collections serving young adults.

Dictionaries

960. Gunston, Bill, ed. **Jane's Aerospace Dictionary.** 3d ed. New York, Jane's Information Group, 1988. 605p. $45.00. ISBN 0-7106-0580-3.

Jane's Aerospace Dictionary defines approximately 28,000 terms and phrases (8,000 new to this edition) drawn from the aviation, space, and defense disciplines. These include acronyms, aerodynamic equations, military terms, Soviet reporting names, electronics, meteorology, data processing terminology, and much more. Many proper names are included, but names of individual persons and business firms are excluded, as are most but not all trade names of products. Entries are arranged alphabetically, are usually a single sentence, and include cross references as appropriate.

A less technical resource in this subject area is Paul Garrison's *The Illustrated Encyclopedia of General Aviation* (2d ed., TAB Books, 1990, 462p. $34.95; $24.95pa., ISBN 0-8306-8316-X; 0-8306-3316-2pa.). Basically an update and revision of the original *Illustrated Encyclopedia of General Aviation* (TAB Books, 1979), it is an alphabetically arranged compendium of aviation topics, players, companies, products, acronyms, and abbreviations. Performance and specification data for popular aircraft, details of aircraft engines, avionics and aircraft accessories, manufacturers and their addresses, aviation associations, publications, and federal and state aviation agencies are all included here. If possible, both works should be purchased for their complementary coverage.

961. **The Visual Dictionary of Flight.** New York, Dorling Kindersley, 1992. 64p. illus. index. $14.95. ISBN 1-56458-101-2.

Part of the publisher's well-received Eyewitness Visual Dictionaries series, this resource ranges from 1783's Montgolfier balloon to today's SST and Airbus, identifying nearly 2,000 aeronautical terms to be found between them. Each double-page spread covers one major topic, providing for each a short summary text accompanied by fully labeled, richly detailed color paintings and photographs. A thorough, detailed index provides access. Although this work could certainly not function as the primary aeronautic dictionary for a library, it is certainly a wonderful complement to the more mainstream works.

Directories

962. Morlan, Michael. **Kitty Hawk to NASA: A Guide to U.S. Air & Space Museums and Exhibits.** Shawnee, KS, Bon A. Tirer, 1991. 304p. illus. index. $15.95pa. ISBN 1-878446-04-5.

Morlan identifies 136 museums that exhibit "historically significant" airplanes and prototype aircraft, including space vehicles. In addition to descriptions of the museums and their holdings, entries also include clear directions for locating the sites, admission rates, hours and days of operation, whether aircraft are displayed indoors or out, and the availability of food service, gift shops, and film. A list of specific aircraft on display for each museum includes the name of the manufacturer, the model number, and the popular name or nickname. This information is included in its own index, in addition to a regular index for museum names and text information.

963. Wilson, Andrew, ed. **Jane's Space Directory.** 5th ed. New York, Jane's Information Group, 1993- . Annual. 1v. illus. index. $245.00 (1994 ed.). No ISSN available.

Known previously as *Jane's Spaceflight Directory* and more recently as the *Interavia Space Directory*, this familiar work seemingly covers every aspect of the international space scene and those who are involved in it. Topically arranged chapters include directory information on national and international space programs, military space, launchers, communications, navigation, earth observation (ground and space), microgravity, world space centers, the solar system, and the space industry. Of special interest are the chronological "space log" tables that lay out the previous year's space activities. In addition to some 600 photographs and line drawings, the directory also provides roughly 1,400 names, addresses, and telephone and fax numbers. Also available on CD-ROM.

GROUND

Dictionaries and Encyclopedias

964. Edwards, John. **Auto Dictionary.** Los Angeles, HPBooks/Price Stern Sloan, 1993. 194p. illus. $24.95; $16.95pa. ISBN 1-55788-067-0; 1-55788-056-5pa.

In addition to providing brief histories of major automotive manufacturers, this practical dictionary covers engineering terms, automotive components, equipment, technology, racing jargon, and hot-rod slang. The definitions, written for the lay reader but equally valuable to the automotive professional, are further clarified by the frequent use of high-quality photographs, diagrams, and other illustrations. Useful, reliable, and a good value for the price.

A good complement to the Edwards title is *The Visual Dictionary of Cars* (Dorling Kindersley; distr., Houghton Mifflin, 1992. 64p., $14.95, ISBN 1-56458-007-5). Because, for the most part, its superb cutaway and exploded photographs and illustrations take the place of text, it is especially useful if one knows what a car part looks like and wants to know what it is called, or if one knows a part's name and wants to see what it looks like.

965. Tobolt, William K., Larry Johnson, and Steven W. Olive. **Goodheart-Wilcox Automotive Encyclopedia: Fundamental Principles, Operation, Construction, Service, Repair.** South Holland, IL, Goodheart-Wilcox, 1989. 815p. illus. index. $39.60. ISBN 0-87006-691-9.

A combination textbook and encyclopedia, the *Goodheart-Wilcox Automotive Encyclopedia* provides a wealth of easily understood definitions accompanied by illustrations on virtually every page. Arrangement is by 61 topical chapters on such automotive items as fasteners, gaskets and seals, emission controls, and speedometers. Review questions conclude each chapter. Handy for both circulating and reference collections.

Guides and Handbooks

966. Drury, George H., comp. **The Train-Watcher's Guide to North American Railroads.** 2d ed. Waukesha, WI, Kalmbach, 1993. 288p. illus. maps. index. $14.95. ISBN 0-89024-131-7.

Covering U.S., Canadian, and Mexican lines, this book includes all railroads more than 200 miles long or with more than 1,000 freight cars in interchange service, as well as all commuter operating authorities. The alphabetically arranged entries include a short description, a route map, address, mileage, reporting marks, number of locomotives and cars owned, principal freight commodities handled, location of repair shops, junctions with other lines, radio frequencies, and passenger routes if still operated. Of special interest is that many entries also include bibliographical references. In addition to the main entries, there are a list of rail transit systems, a key to reporting marks, a brief guide to the best train-watching spots, and a glossary.

For coverage of U.S. short-line railroads, there is Edward A. Lewis' *American Shortline Railway Guide* (4th ed., Kalmbach, 1991, 320p., $18.95pa., ISBN 0-89024-109-0), which describes about 725 short-lines and regional railroads, some of which date back to the earliest days of railroading. Entries provide a brief history, ownership, address, telephone and fax numbers, mileage, radio frequency, engine house location, locomotives owned, and number of cars. Supplementary sections include a list of railroads merged or abandoned since 1970, a glossary, a list of railroads grouped by state, and a list of last-minute changes.

967. Gillis, Jack. **The Car Book: The Definitive Buyer's Guide … [yr].** New York, HarperCollins, 1980- . Annual. 1v. illus. maps. index. $26.95pa. (1994 ed.). ISSN 0893-1208.

Gillis emphasizes safety, fuel economy, insurance, and the practical aspects of operating costs in his well-known *Car Book*. Although the chapter on safety is the longest and most prominent, there is also excellent coverage of maintenance, warranties, insurance, tires, complaints, and shopping, with prices and useful advice on negotiating the purchase. Two other annuals by the same author and publisher—*The Truck, Van and 4x4 Book* (1v., $12.95pa. [1994 ed.], ISSN 1050-9259) and *The Used*

Car Book (1v., $11.95pa. [1994 ed.], ISSN 0895-3899)—will be equally useful for individuals considering purchase of either of these vehicular alternatives.

There are a number of similar resources libraries may also wish to have on hand depending on patron interest. These include the annual guides put out by Consumer Guide Books, *Consumer Guide Automobile Book: The Complete New Car Buying Guide [yr.]* (1985- , $8.95pa. [1994 ed.], no ISSN available) and *Consumer Guide Used Car Book [yr.]* (1985- , $8.95pa. [1994 ed.], no ISSN available). The latter is especially noteworthy for its "inclusion of a "recall history" for each entry. The primary competitor to these books is Consumer Reports Books' *New Car Buying Guide [yr.]* (1989- , $8.95pa. [1994 ed.], no ISSN available) and *Used Car Buying Guide* (1989- , $8.95pa. [1994 ed.], no ISSN available). The latter is especially useful for its five-year "Frequency-of-Repair" data.

968. Gross, Steve, ed. **The Complete Car Cost Guide.** San Jose, CA, IntelliChoice, 1987- . Annual. 1v. (various paging). illus. index. $45.00pa. (1994 ed.). ISSN 1045-2206.

Based on the premise that a car's true cost encompasses much more than just its purchase price, this highly useful guide takes into account such financial considerations as depreciation, insurance, financing costs, fuel, repairs, and maintenance to arrive at the overall costs of purchasing and owning some 500 of today's automobiles. The information is consistently arranged, facilitating easy comparison among makes and models. A real eye-opener as to long-term ownership costs, this modestly priced work should be available to all potential car-buying patrons.

969. Hill, Karen, ed. **Gale's Auto Sourcebook. [yr.]: A Guide to Information on Cars and Light Trucks.** Detroit, Gale, 1991- . Annual. 1v. illus. index. $93.00 [1994 ed.]. ISSN 1056-4330.

The primary section of this work presents information on more than 300 automobiles and trucks sold in the preceding five-year period. Each entry notes model description, major features, dimensions, engines, tests, recalls, safety and repairs, pricing history, repair manuals, other information sources, and enthusiasts' associations. In addition to the vehicle listings, separate sections are devoted to general and other information sources, automotive industry directories, manufacturer profiles, and a variety of consumer and industry magazine rankings. Also available on disk and magnetic tape.

970. **Jane's World Railways.** New York, Jane's Information Group, 1958- . 1v. illus. index. $275.00 (1994 ed.). ISSN 0075-3084.

Jane's World Railways describes more than 500 railway systems from 113 countries in this authoritative reference. Arrangement is alphabetical by country. Each system is surveyed as to management, budget, operating expenditures, government oversight, passenger capacity, equipment, infrastructure, expansion plans, cooperative agreements with other nations, and contact information. In addition, more than 1,300 manufacturers are profiled by equipment type. Photographs and diagrams supplement the text; an extensive, well-executed index concludes it.

971. **Official Used Car Guide.** National Automobile Dealers Association, 1933- . Monthly in nine regional editions. 1v. $43.00/yr. (1994 ed.). ISSN 0027-5794.

When people refer to the "blue book" price of a used car, this is the book they mean. For six decades, this has been the price authority that car dealers, purchasers, and traders, as well as insurance claims adjusters, have relied on to come to agreement on a fair price (or its rough approximation). Coverage goes back through the seven previous years; coverage for cars older than the seven-year range can be found in the same publisher's *Official Older User Car Guide* ($40.00/yr. [1994 ed.], no ISSN available).

WATER

972. Delgado, James P., and J. Candace Clifford. **Great American Ships.** Washington, DC, Preservation Press, 1991. 311p. illus. index. $19.95pa. ISBN 0-89133-189-1.

Great American Ships catalogs more than 225 ships that have been preserved and are open to the public in the 50 states. Ships covered include Confederate gunboats, submarines, battleships of World War I and World War II, private yachts, Mississippi riverboats, tugs, lightships, 18th- and 19th-century sailing vessels, and small fishing craft. Arrangement is by state within broad geographic region, with ships listed alphabetically under the places where they are berthed. Entries for each ship include brief histories plus details on the current state of restoration. Separate sections chronicle America's lost maritime heritage, identify vessels in the National Register of Historic Places, provide a list of recommended titles for further reading, and list maritime organizations and agencies as sources for additional information.

973. Sharpe, Richard, ed. **Jane's Fighting Ships.** New York, Jane's Information Group, 1897- . Annual. 1v. illus. index. $245.00 (1994 ed.). ISSN 0075-3025.

The standard resource in this subject area, *Jane's Fighting Ships* provides clear, accurate data on more than 8,000 warships, auxiliaries, and armed vessels owned by some 150 nations. In addition to the main entries, the sourcebook surveys the operational strengths of each country's navy, new construction, modernization programs, new weapons systems, and new capabilities. The ship-reference section, which makes up the bulk of the book, is arranged alphabetically by country. Entries for each ship describe main machinery, speed, missiles, countermeasures, combat data systems, radars, programs, and modernization and sales. Detailed line drawings identify the position of major weapon systems; more than 3,000 photographs further aid identification and recognition. Also available on CD-ROM.

974. Smith, Robert H. **The Naval Institute Guide to Maritime Museums of North America: With Selected Lighthouse, Canal, and Canal Lock Museums.** Annapolis, MD, Naval Institute Press, 1990. 388p. illus. index. $19.95pa. ISBN 0-87021-640-6.

The 306 museums described here include both the well known (for example, the Mariners Museum) and the less familiar. The museums are grouped according to nine geographic regions: the Canadian maritime provinces and New England, the mid-Atlantic, the southeast, the Gulf Coast, the Great Lakes, the midwest, the central plains, the Pacific northwest, and the West Coast and Hawaii. Entries note in what town the museum is located, as well as the museum's name, address, telephone number, highlights, general background information, activities, admission, and days and hours of operation. In addition, each entry includes instructions on how to get to the museum.

975. **Visual Dictionary of Ships and Sailing.** New York, Dorling Kindersley; distr., Houghton Mifflin, 1991. 64p. illus. index. $14.95. ISBN 1-879431-20-3.

This graphic dictionary presents information on ships and sailing, both historical and contemporary. The materials fall into three groups: the history and development of ships and sailing, attributes of contemporary boats and ships, and special topics such as battleships and scuba and diving gear. Each two-page entry focuses on a single theme, within which are presented exquisitely detailed photographs of scale models (or, occasionally, beautifully rendered and detailed illustrations) of which nearly every visible part is identified. Each entry is accompanied by a brief narrative that describes the items presented and explains why those items are important and how they fit into the general context of the history and development of ships and sailing. An index of all identified terms concludes this engaging work.

Author/Title Index

Numbers cited in the index are entry numbers. This index lists titles of works that are given full annotations, as well as authors, editors, compilers, and corporate bodies. Numbers in italics are in-text citations.

Subject Index

This index covers entries for all books, periodicals, and annuals in this guide. Numbers cited are entry numbers.